James Sibree

Madagascar Before the Conquest

The Island, the Country, and the People

James Sibree

Madagascar Before the Conquest
The Island, the Country, and the People

ISBN/EAN: 9783743417090

Manufactured in Europe, USA, Canada, Australia, Japa

Cover: Foto ©Andreas Hilbeck / pixelio.de

Manufactured and distributed by brebook publishing software (www.brebook.com)

James Sibree

Madagascar Before the Conquest

MADAGASCAR BEFORE THE CONQUEST

THE ISLAND, THE COUNTRY, AND THE PEOPLE

WITH CHAPTERS ON TRAVEL AND TOPO-
GRAPHY, FOLK-LORE, STRANGE CUSTOMS
AND SUPERSTITIONS, THE ANIMAL LIFE
OF THE ISLAND, AND MISSION WORK
AND PROGRESS AMONG THE INHABITANTS

BY THE
REV. JAMES SIBREE, F.R.G.S.
Missionary of the L.M.S.
AUTHOR OF "THE GREAT AFRICAN ISLAND," "A MADAGASCAR BIBLIOGRAPHY,"
"THE BIRDS OF MADAGASCAR," ETC.

WITH MAPS AND NUMEROUS ILLUSTRATIONS
FROM PHOTOGRAPHS

NEW YORK
THE MACMILLAN CO.
LONDON
T. FISHER UNWIN
1896

PREFACE.

THIS is my third book on Madagascar, and probably some of my readers may be disposed to ask what more I can have to say about the country or the people. The following pages form a reply to such a question, and it may be further said in explanation that it is now twenty-six years since the publication of my first book [1] and sixteen since the second [2] was issued; and that since the latter of those dates much new information has been accumulating with regard to the physical geography, geology, fauna and flora, and ethnology of Madagascar.

During the thirty-two years that I have been connected with this great island, I have been continually collecting information and writing about it, chiefly in the *Antanànarìvo Annual*, a publication issued every year in the capital, as well as in the Proceedings of various English societies; but as these papers are only known to a limited class of readers, I have thought that at this time, when public attention is being again called to Madagascar, the information given in the following pages would be interesting to the public generally. They will, I trust, give to many a clearer notion of what kind of place this country is, and what sort of people they are who inhabit it.

I here express my obligations to my friend, M. Alfred Grandidier, for permission to translate and reproduce much that is valuable from his numerous publications referring to Madagascar in the French language.

[1] *Madagascar and its People* (R.T.S., 1870).
[2] *The Great African Island* (Trübner, 1880).

I have also to thank my friends, Mr. J. Parrett and Dr. S. B. Fenn, for being able to reproduce several photographs which adorn these pages.

And, lastly, my grateful thanks are due to the Rev. W. E. Cousins for his great kindness in correcting the proofs, so far at least as Malagasy words are employed. It has, of course, been a disadvantage that I could not personally revise the proofs when the work was passing through the press, and I must plead that in excuse for any faults that may be discovered by the critical reader. The publisher has done his best to minimise the difficulties necessarily involved in writing a book in Madagascar and publishing it in England.

J. S.

LONDON MISSIONARY SOCIETY'S COLLEGE,
    ANTANÀNARÌVO, MADAGASCAR.
    November 30, 1893.

NOTE.—All through this book Malagasy words are accented on the syllables which should be emphasised. And if it is borne in mind that the vowels have as nearly as possible the same sound as in Italian, and that the consonants do not differ much in sound from those in English, except that *g* is always hard, *s* always a sibilant and not like *z*, and *j* is like *dj*, there need be no difficulty in pronouncing Malagasy words with a fair amount of accuracy.

CONTENTS.

CHAPTER I.

FROM COAST TO CAPITAL : NOTES OF A JOURNEY FROM MÀ-
HANÒRO TO ANTANÀNARÌVO 1

Various routes to interior—Màhanòro—Madagascar travelling—
Filanjàna or palanquin—Native bearers—Native villages—Bètsimisàraka
Cemetery—Canoe travelling—Canoe songs—Tropical vegetation—
The Travellers'-tree—Scenery—Native houses and arrangements—A
tiring Sunday's journey—Butterflies and birds—A village congrega-
tion—Forest scenery and luxuriance—Romantic glens and glades—
Uplands and extensive prospects—In Imèrina at last—Over old
haunts in forest—Màntasòa and its workshops—Native bridges—
War preparations—A hearty welcome to the capital.

CHAPTER II.

IMÈRINA THE CENTRAL PROVINCE : ITS PHYSICAL FEATURES AND
VILLAGE LIFE 15

Recent advances in knowledge of Madagascar geography—Recent
journeys—Tamatave—Mode of travelling—Coast lagoons—Scenery—
Forest and climbing plants—Ankay Plain—Upper forest belt—Imèrina or Ankòva "Home of the Hova"—Mountains and prominent
peaks—Bare uplands—Geology and colour of soil—Extinct volcanoes
—Watershed of island—Lakes—Population—Sacred towns—Village
fortifications—Maps of Imèrina—An Imèrina village—Ancient villages
on high hills—Hova houses and arrangements—Ox-fattening pits—
Native tombs—Trees—Hova children and games—Village chapels
and schools.

CHAPTER III.

ANTANÀNARÌVO, THE CAPITAL : ITS PUBLIC BUILDINGS, MEMORIAL
AND OTHER CHURCHES, AND RELIGIOUS AND CHARITABLE
INSTITUTIONS 34

Scenery around the capital—Its picturesque situation—Rugged streets
and paths—Houses and other buildings—Recent introduction of

bricks—Royal palaces—Fàravòhitra—Ancient gateway—Sacred stones—Weekly market of Zomà—Amusements—L.M.S. churches and religious institutions—Ambàtonakànga Church—Other memorial churches—"Mother churches" and districts—Chapel Royal—Sunday observance—Colleges and school-buildings—Dispensaries and hospitals—Other missions—Extent of Christian work carried on—Civilising work of L.M.S. mission—Population—Plans of the capital—Antanànarìvo the heart of Madagascar.

CHAPTER IV.

THE CHANGING YEAR IN CENTRAL MADAGASCAR: NOTES ON THE CLIMATES, AGRICULTURE, SOCIAL CUSTOMS OF THE PEOPLE, AND VARIED ASPECTS OF THE MONTUS 52

The seasons in Madagascar—Their significant names—Prospect from summit of Antanànarivo—The great rice-plain—Springtime: September to October—Rice-planting and rice-fields—First crop—Trees and foliage—"Burning the Downs"—Birds—Summer: November to February—Thunderstorms and tropical rains—Effects on roads—Rainfall—Hail—Magnificent lightning effects—Malagasy New Year—Native calendar—Royal bathing—Conspicuous flowers—Aloes and agaves—Christmas Day observances—Uniformity in length of days—Native words and phrases for divisions of time—and for natural phenomena—Effects of heavy rains—Wild flowers of Imèrina—Autumn: March and April—Rice harvest—Harvest thanksgiving services—Mist effects on winter mornings—Spiders' webs—Winter: May to August—Winter the dry season—Ancient villages and fosses—Hova tombs—Great markets—Aspects of nightly sky—Epidemics in cold season—Vegetation.

CHAPTER V.

THE CRATER LAKE OF TRITRÌVA: ITS PHYSICAL FEATURES AND LEGENDARY HISTORY; AND THE VOLCANIC REGIONS OF THE INTERIOR 82

Ancient volcanoes of Central Madagascar—Hot springs—Fossil remains in limestone deposits—Crater lake of Andràikìba—Tritrìva Lake—Colour of water—Remarkable appearance of lake—View from crater walls—Mr. Baron on volcanic phenomena—Ankàratra Mountain—Ancient crater—Lava streams—Volcanic rocks—Recent character of volcanic action.

CHAPTER VI.

AMBÀTOVÒRY: ONE OF OUR HOLIDAY RESORTS IN MADAGASCAR; WITH NATURAL HISTORY AND OTHER NOTES 97

The rest-house—Ambònilòha Hill—A deserted village—Ambàtovòry rock—Woodland paths—Birds—Lizards and chameleons—Grass-

CONTENTS.   ix

PAGE

hoppers—Protective colouring—Warring colours—Beetles—Ants and ant-nests—Ball insects—Spiders—Butterflies—King butterfly—Solitary wasps—Wasp nests—Angàvokély Mountain—Extensive prospect.

CHAPTER VII.

MALAGASY PLACE-NAMES 109

Mixed nomenclature of coast and interior places—Early European influence—Arab and Portuguese names—Influence of *fàdy* or taboo —Name of Madagascar—Mountain names—The name-prefixes *An-* and *Am-*—Height and prominence—Mystery and dread—Size—Words meaning rock and stone—Animals and birds—Personal names for hills—Grandeur of mountain scenery—River names—Descriptive epithets—Lake names—Town and village names—Dual names— Names of capital and its divisions—Town names from natural features—forests — river banks — from animals — Personal — Tribal— Province names—Appendix on Bètsilèo place-names.

CHAPTER VIII.

CURIOUS WORDS AND CUSTOMS CONNECTED WITH CHIEFTAINSHIP AND ROYALTY AMONG THE MALAGASY; AND NOTES OF THE SIGN AND GESTURE LANGUAGE 149

The Bètsilèo—Special words, or "chief's language"—in Malayo-Polynesian languages—for Malagasy sovereigns—Illness and death —Burial— Mourning — Diseases — Royal servants — Royal houses— Chief's words among Bètsilèo—for family of chiefs—for elderly chiefs—for chiefs old and young—Extreme honour paid to chiefs —*Fàdy* or taboo in words—Tabooed animals—Royal names—Sacred character of—Veneration for royalty—Sàkalàva chiefs—Posthumous names—Relics of the sign and gesture language—Salutations—Symbolic acts—Royalty—" Licking the sole "—*Kabàrys*—The taboo.

CHAPTER IX.

ALAGASY FOLK-LORE AND POPULAR SUPERSTITIONS . . . 174

Animals—The ox—Birds—Insects—Fabulous animals—*Fanàny*, or seven-headed serpent—Footprints of giants—Trees and plants— Ordeals—Folk-lore of life—Lucky and unlucky actions—Sickness and death—Witchcraft and charms— Food and *fàdy* of the Sihànaka— Snakes and lemurs—Tabooed days—in clans—and villages—Good omens—for food—and wealth—Evil omens—as to famine—Trade —Poverty, and death—Weather prognostics—Various portents— dreams.

CHAPTER X.

MALAGASY ORATORY, ORNAMENTS OF SPEECH, SYMBOLIC ACTIONS, AND CONUNDRUMS 191

Introductory historical sketch—Folk-lore—Folk-tales—Proverbs—*Kabàry*—Oratory and figures of speech—The desolate one—Mutual love—The bird—A divorced wife—Transitoriness of life—Bereavement—Death—Imagination—Boasting—The crocodile—A place for everything—Filial love—Friendship—Thanksgiving—Evil speech—Symbolic acts—The two kings—The heir to the throne—Riddles and conundrums.

CHAPTER XI.

MALAGASY SONGS, POETRY, CHILDREN'S GAMES, AND MYTHICAL CREATURES 213

Songs to the sovereign—Dirges—Sihànaka laments—Ballad of Benàndro—Friendship—Children's games—*Rasarìndra*—*Soàmiditra*—*Sakàda*—"Leper" game—"Star killing"—New Year's games—Counting games—Marvellous creatures—*Songòmby*—*Fanàny*, or seven-headed serpent—*Tòkandia*, or "Singlefoot"—*Kinòly*—*Dòna*, or *Pily* (serpent)—*Làlomèna* (Hippopotamus ?)—*Angalàpona*—*Siona*.

CHAPTER XII.

MALAGASY FOLK-TALES AND FABLES 237

Bonia—Crocodile and dog—Three sisters and Itrimobé—The members of the body—The little bird—Rapèto—The lost Son of God—The five fingers—The earth and the skies—The birds choosing a king—The lizards—Hawk and hen—Vazìmba—Chameleon and lizard—Serpent and frog—The rice and sugar-cane—Two rogues—Wild hog and rat.

CHAPTER XIII.

DIVINATION AMONG THE MALAGASY, TOGETHER WITH NATIVE IDEAS AS TO FATE AND DESTINY 262

The *Sikìdy*—Subject investigated by Mr. Dahle—Little organised idolatry among the Malagasy—Diviners—Divination and fate—Invocation of the *Sikìdy*—Sixteen figures of the *Sikìdy*—Sixteen columns of the *Sikìdy*—Erecting the *Sikìdy*—Working of the *Sikìdy*—Identical figures—Unique figures—Combined figures—Miscellaneous *Sikìdy*—Gun charms—Trade charms—Medicinal charms—Fortunate places and days—*Ati-pàko*—Fate as told by zodiac and moon—Lucky and unlucky days—House divinations—Fate as told by the planets—Days of the week—Decreasing influence of the *Sikìdy*.

CHAPTER XIV.

FUNERAL CEREMONIES AMONG THE MALAGASY 286

Two great divisions of the people—Idea of impurity in connection with death—A revolting custom—Funeral feasts—Tankàrana—Their carved coffins—Analogies to those of Philippine Islanders—Bètsimisàraka—Rànomèna—Tàmbahòaka, Taimòro and Tanòsy—The Fanàno—Tandroy and Màhafàly—Sàkalàva—The Zòmba, or sacred house—The Vazìmba—Behìsotra and Tandròna—Sihànaka—Bezànozàno—Tanàla—Vorimo—Ikòngo—Hova—Bètsilèo—Bàra—Funeral of Radàma I.—Enormous wealth put in tomb—Silver coffin.

CHAPTER XV.

DECORATIVE CARVING ON WOOD, ESPECIALLY ON THE BURIAL MEMORIALS OF THE BÈTSILÈO MALAGASY ; TOGETHER WITH NOTES ON THE HANDICRAFTS OF THE MALAGASY AND NATIVE PRODUCTS 313

Absence of artistic feeling among the Hova—The Bètsilèo—Carved memorial posts—Various forms of tombs—Character of the carving *Vàto làhy*, or memorial stones—Graves of great depths—Carving in houses—Collection of rubbings—General style of ornamentation—Symbolic meaning ?—Malagasy handicrafts—Spinning and weaving—Different kinds of cloth—Straw-work—Bark-cloth—Metal-work—Pottery—Building—Canoes and boats—Cultivated products of country—Exports.

CHAPTER XVI.

ODD AND CURIOUS EXPERIENCES OF LIFE IN MADAGASCAR . . 335

The comic element everywhere present—First experiences—Native dress—Borrowed garments—Christmas Day exhibition—Interruptions to Divine service—A nation of bald-heads—Native houses and their inmates — Receptions by Hova governors — Native feasts — Queer articles of food—First attempts at speaking Malagasy—"Try a relative"—Transformations of English names—Biblical names—Odd names—English mistakes—The "southern" side of his moustache—Funeral presents—Church decoration—Offertory boxes—Deacon's duties.

CHAPTER XVII.

THE FAUNA AND FLORA OF MADAGASCAR IN CONNECTION WITH THE PHYSICAL GEOGRAPHY OF THE ISLAND ; WITH NOTICES OF THE EXTINCT FORMS OF ANIMAL LIFE OF THE COUNTRY . 353

General characteristics of mammalian fauna—Remarkable difference to that of Africa—An ancient island—Wallace's "Island Life"—Oriental and Australian affinities—Vegetable productions—Botanising in

Madagascar—Three-fourths of the flora endemic in the island—Three different regions described by Mr. Baron—Floral beauty—Orchids—The eastern region—The central region—The western region—Extinct forms of animal life—Grandidier's discoveries—Geology—Huge lemuroid—Link between apes and lemurs—Small hippopotamus—The Æpyornis—Crocodiles—Enormous terrestrial lizard—Primæval Madagascar.

LIST OF ILLUSTRATIONS.

1. CENTRAL PORTION OF ANTANÀNARÌVO . .	*Frontispiece*	
2. HOW WE TRAVEL IN MADAGASCAR	To face p.	1
3. CANOES ON RIVER NEAR COAST .	,,	4
4. VILLAGE ON COAST	,,	15
5. STONE GATEWAY OF ANCIENT TOWNS IN IMÈRINA	,,	26
6. NORTHERN PART OF ANTANÀNARÌVO .	,,	34
7. VIEW FROM ANDOHÀLO	,,	46
8. ANTANÀNARÌVO FROM THE WEST. SOUTH END OF CITY		
	To face p.	52
9. A SÀKALÀVA WARRIOR .	,,	149
10. BÈTSIMISÀRAKA WOMEN	,,	191
11. TAISAKA CHIEFS .	,,	286
12. BÈTSIMISÀRAKA CEMETERY .	,,	290
13. MALAGASY LOOM, AND WEAVING A LÀMBA .	,,	313
14. A HOVA OFFICER, MALAGASY ARMY	,,	336
15. TRAVELLERS' TREES, LOWER FOREST .	,,	353
16. RIVER SCENE IN FOREST	,,	368

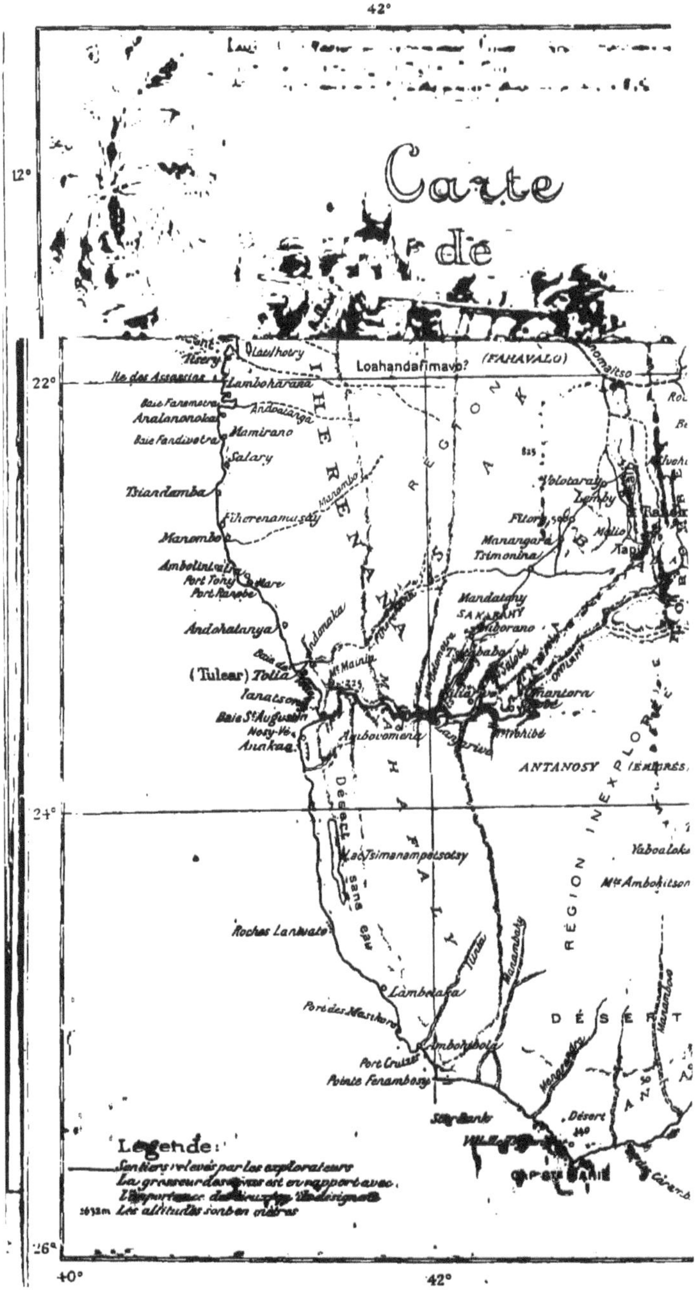
42°
Carte
de
12°
22°
24°
26°
+0°
42°
Tisery
Ile des Assassins
Lambohara
Baie Fanemotra
Analanonoka
Baie Fandivotra
Mamirano
Salary
Tsiandamba
Fiherenamasay
Manombo
Port Tony
Port Ranobe
Andohalanya
(Tulear) Tolia
Ianatsoa
Baie St Augustin
Nosy-Vé
Ankaa
Mt Mainty
Ambovomena
Loahandafimavo?
(FAHAVALO)
Volotaralo
Lemby
Manangara
Tsimonina
Mandatany
SAKARAHY
Mantora
ANTANOSY
Désert sans eau
Lac Tsimanampetsotsy
Roches Lanivato
Lambelaka
Port des Masikoro
Port Cruizer
Pointe Fenambosy
Ambohibola
Manambaly
Menarandra
Manambovo
RÉGION INEXPLORÉE
DÉSERT
Yaboaloka
Mt Ambohitsona
Désert
Cap Ste Marie
Legende:
Sentiers relevés par les explorateurs
La grosseur des rivières est en rapport avec l'importance des rivières désignées
Les altitudes sont en mètres

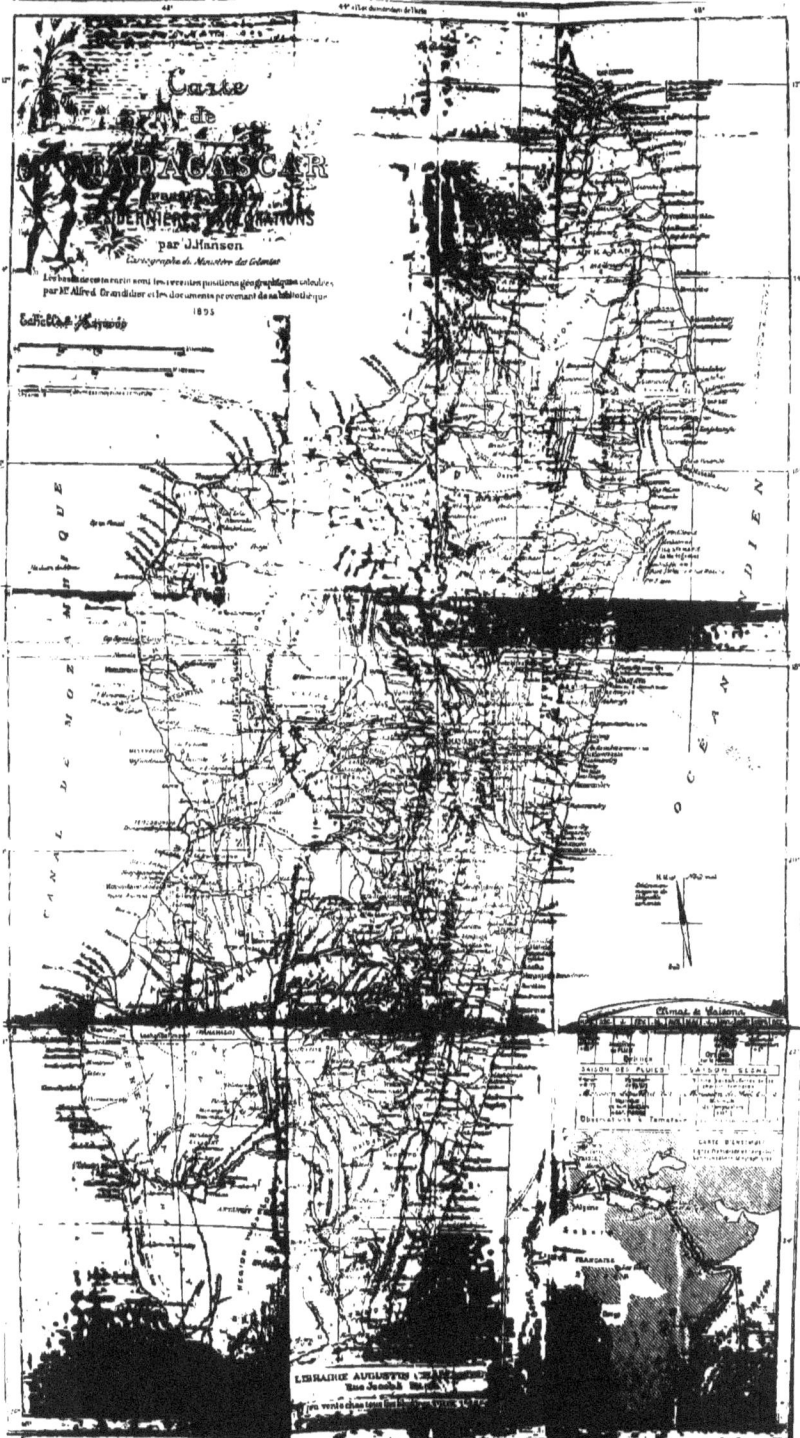

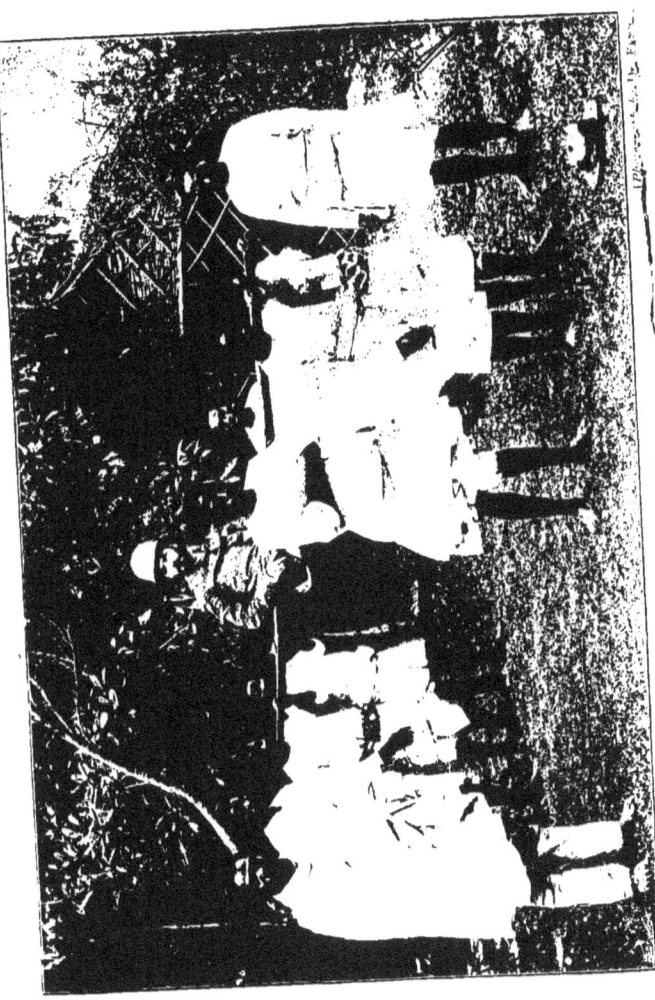

CHAPTER I.

COAST TO CAPITAL; NOTES OF A JOURNEY FROM MÀHANÒRO TO ANTANÀNARÌVO.

routes to interior—Màhanòro—Madagascar travelling—Filanjàna or
palanquin—Native bearers—Native villages—Bètsimisàraka cemetery—
Canoe travelling—Canoe songs—Tropical vegetation—The Traveller's-tree—
Scenery—Native houses and arrangements—A tiring Sunday's journey—
Butterflies and birds—A village congregation—Forest scenery and luxuriance—
Romantic glens and glades—Upland and extensive prospects—In Imèrina at
—Over old haunts in forest—Màntasòa and its workshops—Native
lodges—War preparations—A hearty welcome to the capital.

T the time of the Franco-Malagasy war of 1883-1885, the route to the capital from the East Coast, by way of Tamatave, was closed for many months, and the roads from Màhanòro and Mànanjàra became the usual route of foreigners going into the interior. It was my good fortune to be able to come up to Imèrina by the Màhanòro route in the month of November, 1883; and it may perhaps not be uninteresting to give here the substance of my daily notes describing our journey.

We found ourselves, early in the afternoon of Thursday, November 8th, fairly on our way towards the interior. Our carriages were the ordinary native *filanjàna*, or light, open palanquin; our motive power, strong Malagasy bearers, eight to each person, in two sets of four each; the roads we traversed, mere paths made simply by the bare feet of the natives, generation after generation, mounting hills, floundering through bogs, and fording through streams, just as they happened to come; our inns, the huts of rush or wood, innocent alike of doors or windows, table or chairs or beds, and boasting only a clean mat spread for us over many dirty ones; our cuisine, the rice and fowls always to be got on the way, supplemented by a few stores taken in tin boxes; and our accommodation for the night, light, portable "stretchers" carried by our men, with the bedding secured in similar watertight contrivances. Our party consisted of my wife and little girl, two years old, and myself, together with our friend Mr. Houlder.

I should perhaps add a few words here in answer to a possible question as to what kind of vehicle we travel in in Madagascar. This contrivance, generally called "palanquin" by Europeans, but *filanjàna* by the Malagasy (from the verb *milànja*, to carry on the shoulder), consists of a couple of two light, strong poles, about 10 feet long, kept together by red stout iron rods, and with a seat framed of iron and covered with leather, hung from the poles. Ladies' *filanjàna* are a kind of oblong basket, made of fine strips of sheepskin plaited together, and carried on two poles made of the strong but light midrib of the leaves of the *rofia* palm. When travelling long distances, a hood of *rofia* cloth is fixed over ladies' *filanjàna* as a protection from the sun and rain. The "bearers" are as a rule, strong, active, and cheerful fellows, generally very kind and helpful, and most careful of the safety of those whom they carry, hour after hour and day after day, on their shoulders.

The first stage of our journey was northwards, along a narrow breadth of land, between the belt of trees which line the coast and the lagoons. Beyond these trees, to the left, extends some wooded country, with a range of low hills west of it, gradually approaching the lagoons, and then showing line after line of higher hills towards the interior. The Traveller's-tree is very plentiful, as well as several species of Pandanus, and large Arums in the shallow waters. After four hours and a quarter at steady march we came to a village called Bèparàsy, where nearly one hundred houses. This afternoon we passed a small Bètsimisàraka cemetery, where we saw at a little distance the curious fashion they have of wrapping up the corpses in mats and enclosing them in planks, and then fixing them on a stage, 4 or 5 feet above the ground.[1] Near the village were tombs of a different description, resembling a house-roof, enclosed by a double line of pointed stakes. In the centre of the village is fixed a post, whose top is sharpened into two long "horns," and on this are the mouldering remains of an ox-skull. This, they told us, was a circumcision memorial.

Friday, Nov. 9th.—We were up soon after four o'clock, got our things packed, had a good breakfast, took our quinine, and were all clear away before six o'clock. Going down to the foot of the rising ground on which the village is built, we came to a narrow creek, where a canoe was awaiting us. Going along this creek we came to a broader reach of the lagoon, and were soon admiring the great *Vìha* arums, 9 or 10 feet high, just flowering, and one of the various species of Pandanus, which has an almost grotesque but withal a very graceful and slender outline. After passing through another short, narrow channel, we came out on a broad, widespreading lake.

Few experiences are more pleasant in Madagascar travelling to glide rapidly down or across one of the large rivers in arly morning—the time when the eastern rivers, at least, are moothest—and in a large canoe, with plenty of paddlers, :en to the rowers' songs, which are often both amusing and :al. They will frequently improvise a song, one of them ng up a recitative, in which circumstances which have red on the journey are introduced, while the others chime ith a chorus at regular intervals, a favourite one being *·isy và ?*"—"Oh! is there some?" This question refers is good things they hope to get at the end of the day's such as plenty of rice, beef, sweet-potatoes, &c., these

ıbsequent chapter on "Funeral Ceremonies," for fuller information on burial customs.

articles of food being mentioned one after another by the leader of the song. A little delicate flattery of their employer, the Englishman they are rowing, is often introduced, and praises of his hoped-for generosity in providing these luxuries for them; something in this style:—

E, misy và ?	Oh, is there any ?
E, misy ré !	O yes, there's some !
E, ny vorontsiloza, zalàhy é ?	Oh the turkeys, lads, O ?
E, misy ré !	O yes, there's some !
E, ny gisy matavy, zalàhy é ?	Oh the plump-looking geese, lads, O ?
E, misy ré !	O yes, there's some !
E, ny akoho manatody, zalàhy é ?	Oh the egg-laying fowls, lads, O ?
E, misy ré !	O yes, there's some !
E, ny Vazaha bé vola, zalàhy é ?	Oh the very rich foreigner, lads, O ?
E, misy ré !	O yes, here he is !

and so on, *ad libitum*.

In another song heard by the writer on the Màtitànana river (south-east coast), the chorus was *Mandàny vatsy, Toamàsina malàza é !*" *i.e.*, "Consumes provisions for the way, famous Tamatave O!" while the recitative brought in all the different villages on the journey from Tamatave to the capital, ending with Andohàlo (the central space), and Avàra-dròva (the northern and chief entrance to the palace).

The lagoons of the eastern coast form a very marked feature in the physical geography of the island. They extend for more than three hundred miles, that is, from north of Tamatave to south of Mànanjàra, forming an almost continuous line; at east the cutting of about thirty miles of canal would make them into an uninterrupted waterway between all the chief ports of the eastern coast. During the reign of the enlightened Radàma I. (1819–1828) the work of uniting these lagoons was commenced, but was soon stopped by his death. It may be hoped that it will not be long before this work will be again taken in hand. It would, doubtless, be of great value to the commercial inter-communication of the eastern coast.

These coast lagoons sometimes take the form of

CANOES ON RIVER, NEAR COAST.

an
ig
er

running for several miles in almost a straight line, while in many places they broaden out into extensive lakes.

After leaving the canoes we began to turn westward and then north-westward, over a wooded country. The most noticeable feature in the vegetation is the Traveller's-tree, which is very abundant, almost covering the hills wherever the virgin forest has been cut down. The Pandanus and the *rofia* palm are also very plentiful; and the dense secondary woods, through which the narrow path winds, were most beautiful, many trees and plants being just at the time of flowering.

On all parts of the East Coast, from the sea level up to 1,000 feet above the sea, the most prominent and interesting tree is this well-known Traveller's-tree. This tree, which seems to form a link between the bananas and the palms, gives a peculiar character to the vegetation, and at once marks the landscape as a Madagascar one. From a palm-like trunk, usually from 10 to 30 feet high, but in certain situations reaching from two to three times the latter height, springs a gigantic fan of long and broad leaves like those of a banana, often forming an almost complete circle of 20 to 30 feet in diameter. These have a peculiar effect, especially when a line of them crown the sides and summit of a hill. Mr. Ellis has compared them to the feathered crest in the head-dress of an Indian sachem, and there is much truth in the comparison.

Although it has been sometimes denied, it is perfectly true that a good supply of pure and cool water can always be obtained by piercing the base of the leaf stalks; and I have myself been thankful, when travelling along the coast, and could get no water except from the stagnant and brackish contents of the lagoons, to tap these living fountains and take a hearty draught from the Traveller's-tree.

The *Longòzy* (cardamom) is also very abundant, and the small curving Bamboo. We soon began to ascend hill after and presently caught sight of the sea, many miles behind The hills and forest appear to come here nearer to the coast than on the Tamatave route. On reaching the end of a ridge, we caught sight of a river roaring over rapids below us, a mile or two away, and flowing to the sea (at Màroslky). We had a long ride of (including stoppages for canoes) five hours and twenty minutes. Many of the ascents and descents were very steep, and the paths narrow. There appears to be a considerable number of small villages on the road. Our afternoon's ride was much shorter than that of the morning, two hours and a half only, but generally following the valley of the pretty river Mànampòtsy, which flows westwards and southward, frequently foaming over rocky bars and rapids. We passed large masses of pinkish quartz, and in some places the rocks in the bed of the river were tilted, with their strata almost perpendicular. All over this country the air was thick with the smoke from the burning of the trees and grass on the hillsides, in order to plant rice in the ashes—a most wasteful and barbarous custom, which causes a great destruction not only of the secondary woods and jungle, but also of the virgin forest. Before four o'clock we stopped at a village called Ambòdimànga, built on rising ground some 200 feet or so above the river, which here flows nearly north and south. On both sides of the river-valley rise high hills to a height of several hundred feet, and covered with patches of old forest on their summits.

Saturday, Nov. 10th.—We must now have ascended to between 1,000 and 2,000 feet above the sea, and a thick rug became a very comfortable covering towards the small hours of the morning. We were off before six o'clock, and immediately commenced a steep ascent of several hundred feet. Our road lay along a ridge, and then west and northwest, up and down, over some very rough paths. The river Mànampòtsy is still our companion to the right, flowing a[..]t due east. Here there is no continuous forest, but only pat[..] of it left on the summits and sides of the hills. We ma[..] short morning's ride of two and a half hours, and stoppe[..] a village called Antánambè. In the house where we rested [..]

a number of pretty little mats called *làkatra*, about 18 inches square, with a variety of patterns in brown straw. These, they told us, were for ornamenting the house, and were here fixed on the walls. We tried to buy some, but they had none new enough to sell us. In these Bètsimisàraka houses the arrangement of the single room is thus: door at the left-hand side; another facing it on the opposite side; on the right-hand nearest corner, as you enter, is the hearth, with four massive posts supporting two stages, and called *salàzana*. Near the door is fixed a large cylindrical box, hollowed out of a tree trunk, 3 feet high and 18 inches wide, and used for storing rice. As in Hova houses, the soot is allowed to accumulate, and to hang in long strings from the roof.

Our second stage, of between six and seven hours, was very hot and wearisome. We crossed a lovely glen, with rocks and stream overhung by forest, and here the men enjoyed a bathe. During the afternoon we crossed the higher waters of the Mànampòtsy, here flowing from the south. We stayed for nearly an hour, about half way, under some trees, to rest a little from the great heat. The hills around are very high, and are covered with virgin forest. The house in which we stayed for the night was the smallest in which we have yet put up; it was only about 12 feet by 10 feet, and had about as much room as we should have had in the cabin of a ship. This was the coldest night we have yet had. We fairly entered the great forest before getting to our halting-place.

Sunday, Nov. 11*th*.—This day's march, of more than six hours, was through a part of the old forest; some of the trees were of great height, but none were of considerable bulk. I was struck by the variety of lichens and mosses on the tree drauks; on some single trees there must have been dozens of different species, but not being on foot one could collect only by making a snatch at some of the aerial lichens, which were within reach of one's hand. I noticed that the forest was by no means so silent as I had remarked at other times. Former journeys were made, however, in the colder winter months of the year, but now that the warm weather is approaching, some bird or other was almost always heard. Every quarter of a mile or so we heard the noisy call of the *Kankàfotra* Cuckoo, *kow-kow, kow-kow*, repeated; then the flute-call of another cuckoo, the *Tolòho*, whose notes were heard all the way from Màhanòro; also the chirp and whistle of the *Railòvy* or King-crow, as well as the incessant twitter of many smaller birds. Then came, now and then, the melancholy cries of the Lemurs high up among the trees. Numerous butterflies crossed our path, seven or eight different species at least: the rather common green one with yellow spots, the blackish brown with two large blue spots, the widely distributed brown one with black-edged wings, the pure white one, the white with orange edges, white with black edges, white with crimped edges, the small yellow species, the small buff, the minute brown and blue, and many others. We have now lost the Traveller's-tree; the *rofia* palm, however, is seen in the damp hollows, but not so large as lower down the country. The Bamboo, a slender graceful species, growing singly and bending over in an arched form, is plentiful in some of the valleys and on the hillsides. Here and there, high up on the hills, I caught the blaze of colours of one of those called Flamboyant. But the most plentiful tree with bright-coloured flowers is one bearing pinkish-red flowers, on some of which there is a mass of yellow stamens.

At last we came up to a village, called Antènimbè, where we got a much larger house than on the previous evening. We were glad to throw ourselves on the mats and lie down until dinner was ready. The heat was very great and stifling in the houses with their single door. But by five o'clock I was ready to take part in our little service, which we held out of doors. Most of our bearers came, and some of the people the village. We sang three or four hymns; one of our bea prayed, and H. and I both read a portion of Scripture and a short exposition.

Monday, Nov. 12th.—We have to-day been travelling more than nine hours. Our road lay first to the south, so as to get round a towering height, and then turned westward through deep valleys, with a sparkling river, which we repeatedly crossed. Again we noticed the destruction of the forest and the wanton waste of the trees. We stopped at a small village of some sixteen houses, after nearly three and a half hours' ride.

We now ascended to the pass between the ridge of mountains which bounds the eastern side of the Mangòro valley, and must have risen 500 or 700 feet before gaining the summit. On our right a river, broken by many rocks and falls, poured eastward. In the small space allowed by the river-bed the trees rose to an unusual height, and on either side of the gorge forest-clothed mountains towered to elevations of at least 2,000 feet above us. The path was difficult, but the deep cuttings we continually passed through were fringed by ferns and other plants. I noticed, however, that all along the route we had come there were no orchids, at least none conspicuous by flowering, and hardly any palms. At one point I noticed a nest suspended from a twig over the water, in shape exactly resembling that of an inverted chemical retort, and made by the *Fòdifètsy*, or "Crafty Weaver" (*Ploceus pensilis*).

At last we reached the highest point of the pass, and began to descend by a path more steep and rugged than the one we had mounted by. Gradually we got clear of the forest, and the view would have been magnificent had it not been dimmed by the clouds of smoke rising in every direction from the burning forest. At one place we were almost suffocated by the blazing wood and jungle close to our path, and narrowly escaped being stopped by the flames. Presently we caught a glimpse of the Mangòro far below, and we could hardly have differed less than 1,000 feet from the summit of the pass to water level. Beyond the river the western range of mountains rose in great grandeur, line after line—all forest-clad; these form the eastern edge of the upper plateau; and I do not remember to have seen anywhere else in Madagascar such a magnificent mountain scene. At a little before two o'clock we got down to the Mangòro, here a smooth rapid stream from 200 to 300 feet wide, and in a few minutes were ferried across in a large new *làkana* (canoe). It was easy to see that at this point the physical geography of the country is very different from that of the same river valley on the Tamatave route. There—between Mòramànga and the Ifòdy hills—it widens out into an extensive plain, but here the river valley is very narrow, the mountains descending by steep slopes, and rising on the western side, as already remarked, into ridges of great height.

Our road lay along the valley, generally following the course of the stream. It can be traversed by canoes for no great distance, since it is broken up repeatedly by rocky bars and by falls over ledges of rock; at one point it is contracted to a narrow gorge, through which the water rushes with a tremendous swirl and roar.

We were glad, after our long ride of nine hours, to see a small village, Andrànotsàra, before us, on a rising ground 80 or 90 feet above the river. We found two sufficiently decent houses in the fifteen or sixteen composing the village. Hereabouts the *wet* culture of rice begins[1]; and here the people brought us small presents.

Tuesday, Nov. 12*th.*—We left Andrànotsàra at five o'clock, and for two hours went northward, following the course of the Mangòro, which is beset with rocks, and forms rapids and falls in several places. A bright, clear river, the Manàkona, falls into the larger one close to a village of the same name. After this we left the river, and began a long, stiff ascent up the hills on the west side of the river valley. Our road then turned west and north-west over rugged ground of hill and valley, through patches of old forest, with d[...]hes paths. Then the road cut diagonally across the spur[...] a

[1] For fuller information as to rice culture in Madagascar, see su[...] chapter on "The Changing Year."

rock-capped and forest-covered hill, called Marìvolànitra. Rounding one shoulder of this, we now saw part of the Ankay plain, the Mòramànga hills on the east, the great mass of Ifòdy standing out like an outwork of the walls of the central plateau, and then Angàvo and the line of hills which form the edge of the interior highland. The Ankay plain appears to end here, southwards, rather abruptly. The Angàvo chain of heights seems to curve round in crescent-shaped masses, and then joins the mountains which bound the Mangòro valley. Near Farìhimazàva we found a flourishing rice valley cultivated after the Hova fashion, and the appearance of the country and the methods of cultivation told us that we were getting near Imèrina.

After four and a half hours' ride we came to the village of Bèparàsy, quite a Hova-looking place, with the houses made of thick planking, "horns" to the gables, and a native chapel. Here the people brought us rice and eggs for our entertainment.

Leaving again after noon, we had a weary journey over another great mass of hill, and then over the plain, still going north-west, and approaching the blue, forest-covered slopes of the wall of the plateau. We were glad at a little before five o'clock to stop at a poor little hamlet, called Ambòdimivòngo, where, however, we both got tolerably good houses; but the bearers of our luggage only just managed to get in in time to escape a heavy thunderstorm. Our house began to leak a little; but happily it rained heavily only for a short time. This is the beginning of the rainy season in the interior, but thus far we have had no rain on our journey, and so our things have kept dry. We have also had no annoyance from rats, and hardly any from mosquitoes. The people of the houses here have been more intelligent and conversable than a glim,st of the places where we have stayed. They brought diffe·d raspberries and blackberries as soon as they found we maḱiated these fruits. The former we have had as dessert with¹ all the way up from the coast, and a very acceptable ·e ᶠn to our fare they have proved.

Wednesday, Nov. 13th.—There was a thick drizzly rain as we commenced our ascent up the hills into the regions of the interior. In a little time we got up to Andràngolòaka. A great many trees and plants were in flower, and the deep cuttings through which the path winds were lined with ferns and other plants. For nearly two and a half hours we made an uninterrupted ascent, very difficult in many places, and the rain was still falling.

Then we came to a part of the forest where we recognised some of our favourite haunts during our holidays at Andràngolòaka, but when we came up to the house we were grieved to see how it was falling into ruin through neglect. The old house-keeper and his wife immediately recognised us, and were the first to welcome us to Imèrina. Then we descended the hill, and after an hour or more we came to the single-plank bridges over deep water, which had always been a terror in the journey to or from Andràngolòaka, and now seemed more difficult than ever, but which we crossed in safety. After nearly five hours' ride we came to Màntasòa, and its ruined workshops and houses constructed by M. Laborde. We stayed for lunch at the large house, and here felt we were getting back to civilisation again, as we ate our meal off a table and sat to it on chairs!

Màntasòa was a remarkable place, for Madagascar, and when I first visited it, in 1872, was in a much more perfect state of preservation than it was at the time of this journey in 1883. It was a large collection of massively built workshops, made for the manufacture of cannon, pottery, glass, gunpowder, brass, steel, paints, soap, refined sugar, bricks and tiles, &c. These were erected during the reign of the Queen Rànavà Our (1828–1861), under the direction of M. Laborde, a Frenít of of great skill and inventive genius. To supply power the various workshops, a stream was diverted from the rive a by and brought by iron aqueducts into the buildings s turn a number of large water-wheels. At the time of visit to Màntasòa the largest workshop was still crowned by its high-pitched roof covered with tiles. The walls of this building are of dressed stonework, massive as that of a castle and about 6 feet in thickness. In this building the furnaces and cannon-casting apparatus were still existing, and in the four smaller workshops much of the water-wheel machinery still remained. The forge, of beautifully dressed stone, had then its roof nearly perfect, surrounding the openings to the furnaces; and there were two kilns, also of well-finished masonry, for firing the pottery manufactured there. Many of the buildings and workshops, however, were made of clay, and had become shapeless heaps of earth. All around the hillsides were covered with the ruins of villages which had been built for the accommodation of the various workpeople, about two thousand in number.

One other point may be mentioned in connection with this remarkable creation of M. Laborde's skill, but one of a less pleasing character, viz., that during the long persecution between the years 1836–1861, many of the Malagasy Christians had to work as a punishment at these great buildings. For several years some of them had to labour in quarrying the stone and in building these massive workshops. I have been told by the pastor of one of the country churches formerly under my charge, that he and others had no rest either on Sundays or on other days, and that their bondage was very severe, many of them dying under its pressure. So that the accession of Radàma II. was welcomed by them especially as a time of "liberty to the captives and the opening of the prison to those that were bound."

A leisurely ride of about two hours brought us early in the afternoon to Ambàtomànga; and here we stayed at the big houses of the *Andrìana*, the feudal lord of the place, where we had a glimpse of the comfort of a good house, and had a good deal of different experiences with the native evangelist stationed here. For the first time we came upon signs of war preparation: all the lads were armed with shield and spear, and are being constantly exercised in their use. Going to the tomb on the rock above the town, just before sunset, the great, bare hills, with their bones of rock showing through the skin of turf; the bright, fresh green of the newly planted rice-fields; the red clay roads on the brownish-green hills, all told us we were again in the heart of Madagascar.

It is needless to describe our five hours' ride into Antanànarìvo on the following day, or the hearty welcome from our friends, both English and Malagasy, on our arrival. This was all the more hearty, as we had come up when war was going on, and when some had feared to come at all at such a time. But we never doubted then or afterwards that we did the right thing, for our work suffered little interruption during the war, and our help was needed after six years' absence from the country and the people whom we wished to serve.

VILLAGE ON THE COAST.

CHAPTER II.

IMÈRINA, THE CENTRAL PROVINCE; ITS PHYSICAL FEATURES AND VILLAGE LIFE.

Recent advances in knowledge of Madagascar geography—Recent journeys—Tamatave—Mode of travelling—Coast lagoons—Scenery—Forest and climbing plants—Ankay Plain—Upper forest belt—Imèrina or Ankòva, "Home of the Hova"—Mountains and prominent peaks—Bare uplands—Geology and colour of soil—Extinct volcanoes—Watershed of island—Lakes—Population—Sacred towns—Village fortifications—Maps of Imèrina—An Imèrina village—Ancient villages on high hills—Hova houses and arrangements—Ox-fattening pits—Native tombs—Trees—Hova children and games—Village chapels and schools.

SINCE 1861, when the reign of terror under the Queen Rànavàlona I. came to an end, great advances have been made in our knowledge of the topography and physical geography of the island, and of its geology, botany, and natural history; much has also been ascertained as to its people, their divisions, language, customs, traditions, and folk-lore; and every year sees additions made to a fuller understanding both of Madagascar and of the Malagasy. Papers on the geography of the island, and describing various exploratory journeys, have appeared in the *Proceedings* of the Royal Geographical Society and in those of the Scottish Geographical Society; and we owe much to the late Rev. Dr. Mullens, the Rev. W. Deans Cowan, Mr. William Johnson, Captain S. P. Oliver, and others, for thus giving the results either of their own researches, or for summarising the journeys of other travellers.[1] Comparatively little, however, has been made known as to the central province of Imèrina, the heart of Madagascar, the home of the dominant tribe, the Hova, and the centre of government; or about the capital city, Antanànarìvo, where civilisation, education, and Christianity have made the greatest progress.

Before, however, describing Imèrina, I will give a very brief summary of what has been done during the last few years to fill up the blanks on the map of the great island. In 1879 I contributed a paper to the *Proc. Roy. Geogr. Soc.*, entitled, " The History and Present Condition of our Geographical Knowledge of Madagascar," in which I pointed out what had been done up to that date[2]; and since then several journeys have been made in various directions into regions either previously altogether unknown or only very superficially explored.

In the years 1877 and 1878 journeys were made in the northern and north-western parts of the island, as well as from thence to the capital, by a German naturalist, Dr. Chr. Rutenberg. His researches added a good deal to botany and natural history, but not much to geography, although probably we should have learnt more on this point but for his murder by his treacherous native followers. It was not until 1880 that detailed accounts were published of his collections and discoveries.

A valuable addition was made in 1882 to our knowledge of the southern central provinces of Bètsilèo, Bàra, and Tanàla, by a paper contributed to the *Proc. Roy. Geogr. Soc.* by the Rev. W. D. Cowan, giving a very full map of those portions of Madagascar from personal survey. Mr. Cowan was a missionary of the London Missionary Society in the Bètsilèo for several years, and utilised his numerous journeys for teaching

---

[1] I would remark here that I must not be understood as ignoring the valuable work of several French cartographers, as MM. Laillet and Suberbie, Père Roblet, and especially M. Alfred Grandidier. In the above paragraph I am specially noticing the work of *English* labourers in the field of Madagascar geography.

[2] This paper forms the first chapter of *The Great African Island.*

IMÈRINA, THE CENTRAL PROVINCE. 17

and evangelising by doing useful geographical work, as well as by contributing to fuller knowledge of the natural history of the island.

During the progress of the Franco-Malagasy war in 1884, an American naval officer, Lieut. Mason Shufeldt, made a journey from Mòrondàva, on the west coast, to Antanànarivo. I have, however, been unable to obtain any account of Lieut. Shufeldt's travels, although, no doubt, full reports have been presented to the United States Government.

In 1886 my friend, the Rev. R. Baron, F.L.S., made a long journey through the Antsihànaka province northwards, and crossing to the north-west coast, by the districts called Andròna and Béfandrìana, to the Hova garrison town of Anòrontsànga. The most interesting discovery was the former existence of a large lake, running north and south for more than two hundred miles, with a breadth of from fifteen to twenty miles. Of this lake, the present lake of Alaotra, in Antsihànaka, about twenty-five miles long, is the small and still slowly diminishing remnant. Mr. Baron traced indubitable proofs of the former height of the waters of this ancient lake at no less than 1,140 feet above the present level of the Alaotra, and he was enabled to make important additions to our knowledge of the geology of Madagascar, which he communicated in a paper to the Geological Society in 1889.

During 1887 Mr. Neilsen-Lund visited a part of the Bàra province, and also the district inhabited by the "emigrant Tanòsy," being for some time in no little peril from the unfriendly Bàra people. He then turned to the south-east, over mountainous and desert country, eventually reaching the Hova military post of Fort Dauphin, at the south-eastern corner of the island. Unfortunately his journey, although very interesting, added little to the map of Madagascar.

The same must be also said about two journeys made in 1888 by the Rev. E. O. MacMahon, of the Anglican mission, to the west of the island into the Sàkalàva country, to the district occupied by the Bètsirlry tribe. In 1888 also the Antànambàlana river, flowing into Antongil Bay, was surveyed by Mr. L. H. Ransome, and a detailed map of its course, with descriptive paper, appeared in the *Proc. Roy. Geogr. Soc.* for May of the following year.

A fully equipped expedition, under MM. Catat and Maistre, arrived in Madagascar in 1889, and explored portions of the eastern side of the island, and crossed the previously unmapped region of the extreme south. Excursions were made in various directions from the capital, and then the old route from Imèrina to Tamatave was explored; this proved to be difficult to traverse, taking about three times as many days as the usual route. The principal journey was through the Bètsilèo province into the Bàra country, and then into that of the "emigrant Tanòsy." The sources of the river Onilàhy were discovered, and important corrections made in the mapping of its course. The region to Fort Dauphin was crossed, and the fertile valley of Ambòlo visited; and the expedition returned to Bètsilèo through the Antaisàka country. The botanical and natural history collections made by MM. Catat and Maistre are extensive and valuable, as well as those relative to anthropology and ethnology; and these have now been described in French, English, and German geographical and other scientific journals.

In 1891 another long journey, covering more than a thousand miles of country, was made by Mr. Baron along the north-east and north-west coasts of Madagascar, as far as the extreme northerly point of the island. Detailed accounts of this journey have been published: two, giving information as to topography, ethnology, and philology, in the *Antanànarìvo Annual* for 1892 and 1893, under the title of "Twelve Hundred Miles in a Palanquin"; and another, with maps, in *Quart. Journ. Geol. Soc.* 1895, giving the geological results of the journey. (This is reproduced in the last number of the *Annual*, xix., 1895.)

In concluding this brief sketch of the most important journeys made in Madagascar during the last few years, I may also mention the issue by the eminent French traveller and scientist, M. Alfred Grandidier (Member of the Institute), of the geographical section of his great work on Madagascar, in from twenty to thirty quarto volumes, still in progress. In 1879 he published the first part of an atlas of ancient and early maps of the island, including that of the Arabic geographer Edrisi (1153), the curious wall-map at Hereford Cathedral (*circa* 1300), and other quaint and interesting mediæval maps, down to those—often very erroneous ones, mere fancy sketches—put forth as "maps of Madagascar," up to as recent a date as thirty years ago. In 1885 M. Grandidier issued a volume of text, giving a detailed historical account of Madagascar map-making, as well as a minute list of the geographical features, place-names, &c., of the entire coast-line of the island. In 1894 a much enlarged edition of this work was published, together with the second part of the atlas of maps, giving fac-similes of other ancient and curious maps of the island, as well as of various portions of the coast, harbours, islands, &c. In 1880 he published a map of the Imèrina province to a scale of $\frac{1}{200.000}$; and in 1886 a map of the remarkable chain of lagoons on the east coast, extending for about three hundred miles. M. Grandidier is now putting the finishing touches to his atlas of Madagascar maps, in which he will give, to a large scale, the results of all his own explorations, and include all geographical data of any value supplied by other travellers up to the present time.

The eastern port of Tamatave, not far from the centre of that side of the island, is still, as it has been for more than three hundred years, the usual place of landing for all those who are going to the central province of Imèrina and to the capital of the country. Travelling is still in a rather primitive stage in Madagascar. There are no roads practicable for wheeled vehicles, and except a few bullock carts on the level grassy plains of the east coast, there is nothing in the way of carriage or waggon for the use of travellers. Europeans, therefore, as well as all well-to-do Malagasy, make use of the light palanquin or *filanjàna*, carried on the shoulders of four stout bearers, who mostly belong to the tribes formerly conquered by the Hova. On long journeys a double set of men is usually taken with each palanquin, while bed and bedding, stores and clothing, and all other necessaries, must also be carried by other bearers. Travelling is tedious as well as expensive.

The road from Tamatave to Antanànarivo passes first for about sixty miles, or two days' journey, southward, along the coast, generally between the line of lagoons and the sea. The path is perfectly level, along greensward, dotted with clumps of trees and patches of forest, with the lagoons on one side, often expanding into broad lakes of calm water, while on the other we have the Indian Ocean, with the never-ceasing surf, driven by the south-east trade winds.

At Andòvorànto, canoes are hired for a half-day's voyage up the river Ihàroka and one of its tributaries. The palanquin has, however, soon to be resumed, and we begin to traverse hilly country. Here, for about a day's journey, we are in the region of the Traveller's-tree, the Bamboo, and the *rofia* palm, which fill every hollow, and give a special character to the scenery. We gradually get higher until, as we approach the outskirts of the forest-belt, we are about 1,300 feet above sea-level.

The comparatively easy travelling is now succeeded by three days' very hard work for our bearers, as we cross the forest which extends round so large a portion of the coast regions of Madagascar. The path goes up and down the hills at very steep gradients; and these ascents and descents are, after two or three days' rain, just slopes of adhesive slippery clay, up and down which our men toil heavily with their loads. The path, although apparently descending as often as it ascends, is really rising to a higher level, and by the time we get clear of forest, we have ascended the first great step upwards to the interior highland.

Half a day's journey over the Ankay plain, and then across the Mangòro river, brings us to the foot of the second step of our road. Then comes the narrow belt of upper forest, very beautiful, but with as difficult a path through it as on any part of the route; and then we emerge on the bare hills of the upper region, and are in the province of Imèrina.

This central region of Madagascar is sometimes termed by the people themselves Ankòva, that is, "The place of the Hova," the dominant tribe of the island, who, advancing from the East Coast, drove out the aboriginal inhabitants, the Vazĭmba, and made it their home, probably many hundred years ago. It is, however, usually called Imèrina, a name as to whose origin there have been many conjectures; the most likely one of these appears to be that it is from a Malagasy root, *èrina*, meaning "elevated," "prominent," "conspicuous." It is difficult to give the exact boundaries or extent of Imèrina, as Malagasy provinces are not defined as minutely as English counties. On the east it is marked by the line of upper forest; on the north and west it shades off into the uninhabited region which there divides the Hova from other tribes; while on the south it ends at the southern slopes of the Ankàratra mountains, and the thinly peopled region which separates the Hova territory from that of the northern Bètsilèo. Roughly speaking, Imèrina forms an irregular parallelogram, extending about one hundred miles north and south, and about seventy miles from east to west, with an area of about 7,000 square miles—in other words, it is considerably larger than the county of York.

Imèrina is a mountainous country, with but little level ground except on the western side of Antanànarìvo, where the dried-up bed of an extensive ancient lake forms the great rice-plain known as Bètsimitàtatra. This is the granary of the capital, and doubtless accounts for its position, and for the comparatively dense population around it to the north, west, and south. But there are innumerable valleys where the slopes are terraced with rice-plots, like great green staircases, where the grain is first sown broadcast, and from which the young plants are taken up and transplanted in the larger fields along the banks of the rivers, and in the beds of small dried-up lakes of ancient date. There are numerous lofty hills, of which Angàvokèly to the east, Ambòhimiangàra in the extreme west, Ihàranandrìana to the south, Milangàna, Ambòhimanòa, and Andrìngitra more central, and Ambòhipanìry and Vòhilèna to the north, are the most prominent, all forming capital landmarks and points from which angles can be taken in filling up details of the map. Then on the south-west the whole province is dominated by the central mass of Ankàratra, the peaks of which form the highest points in the island, although they are a little under 9,000 feet above the sea. Mr. Baron calls it "the wreck of a huge but ancient sub-aerial volcano." It covers an area of from fifty to sixty square miles, and its highest peaks, called Tsiàfakàfo, Tsiàfajàvona, and Ambòhimiràndrina, are visible for an immense distance, especially to the west. Imèrina is from 4,000 to 4,500 feet above the sea level, so that, although well within the tropics, it enjoys a temperate climate, made cool and bracing in the cooler season by the south-east trade winds which come fresh and moist over the forest belt and the wooded eastern plains. The atmosphere is wonderfully clear, so that hills many miles away stand out with a distinct outline that is very deceptive to those newly come from our more misty air and our grey English skies. The aspect of this region is bare, as it is destitute of wood, except in the hollows, although there are patches of forest still left in the northern parts of the province. There is a great extent of moor-like hills, so that but for the brilliant sunshine and the generally clear skies, Ìmèrina would, like much of the other central portions of Madagascar, be somewhat dreary, especially as the grass gets brown and parched towards the middle of the dry season.

The geological nature of the central region is shown by the numerous masses of granite or gneiss rock which form the summits of all the hills. In many cases these take the form of enormous "bosses," or rounded hills of rock; in others they have the appearance of Titanic castles; while others, again, might be taken, in certain aspects, to be stupendous cathedrals. Overlying the primary rocks there is an immense extent of what I must call clay, although it is not true clay, but appears to be decomposed granite. This is usually deep red in colour, from the large amount of iron oxide, although it is occasionally brown, and sometimes white, like China clay. Iron is abundant, and gold has recently been discovered in many places. Quartz in many varieties, quartzite, graphite, galena, copper, saltpetre, tourmaline, and some other minerals, are also found in Imèrina.

Two groups of ancient and extinct volcanoes which were described by the late Rev. Dr. Mullens hardly come into any description of Imèrina proper, as one of them is just outside its western boundary and the other group is beyond the Ankàratra mountains, to the south-west. There are, however, within the district some detached hills which appear to be old volcanic vents; and these, with occasional lava flows, as well as basaltic dykes in several places, give evidence of ancient subterranean forces, now shown only by slight earthquake shocks, and by hot springs in certain localities.

The water-parting of the whole island lies much nearer its eastern than its western side, so that all the largest rivers flow across Madagascar and fall into the Mozambique Channel. The head-waters of the two chief rivers of Imèrina, the Ikòpa, and the Bètsibòka, and of their numerous affluents, are therefore on the eastern side of the province. The Ikòpa, fed by the Sisaony, the Andròmba, the Màmba, and other streams, flow through the fertile plain of Bètsimitàtatra, going north-west, and is joined by the Bètsibòka further north; the united streams, now known by the latter name, falling into the head of the Bay of Bembatòka. The province is thus well watered by numerous rivers, although the annual rainfall only averages about 53 inches at Antanànarìvo.

The only lake of any size in Imèrina is that of Itàsy, on its extreme western limits; close to it, on the west, are numerous extinct craters; indeed, the lake itself has probably been formed by the sinking of the ground, consequent on the discharge of so much matter from these old volcanoes.

The name Imèrina is used by the Malagasy in two senses: one, with a wider meaning, including the districts of Imàmo to the west, and Valàlafòtsy to the north-west, and including all the Hova people; and then it is also used more restrictedly for the part which is exclusive of these two divisions of the country. This narrower Imèrina is divided into six sections, known as "*Imèrina-ènin-tòko*," and comprising Avàradràno, which includes the capital (to the north-east), Vàkintsisaony (south-east), Màrovàtana (north-west), Ambòdiràno (south-west), Vònizòngo (further north-west), and Vàkinankàratra (further south-west), which last division is named from the mountain mass which it includes, and which cuts it off from the others.

These divisions are largely tribal, and are used by the native government in arranging the different shares of military levies, taxation, and all the various unpaid and forced service due by the people to their sovereign.

There are no means of ascertaining with certainty the population of Imèrina, as no census has ever been taken. But from calculations which have been made as to the number of villages and houses, and the average occupants of a house, it is believed that the population of the province is about 1,100,000.[1] Antanànarìvo is by far the largest town in Imèrina or in Madagascar. There is hardly any other town of great size, although there is a considerable number of large villages, and these are rather closely crowded together in some parts, especially to the north and north-west of the capital. Several of these places were formerly of greater relative importance, as they were the capitals of the many small states, or "kingdoms," into which Imèrina

[1] The recent census—March, 1896—gives only 600,000 souls as the population of the province Imèrina.—ED.

was anciently divided, before the supreme authority became centred in the chief of Antanànarìvo. Of these former chief towns the following are the most noteworthy: Ambòhimànga, a place which still retains a nominal equality in royal speeches with Antanànarìvo a picturesque old town built on a lofty hill surrounded with woods, about eleven miles north of the modern capital; also Ambòhidratrìmo, Ambòhidrabìby, Ilàfy, Alasòra, and some others. In former times, every royal speech mentioned *twelve* old towns or hills ("*Ny Tèndrombòhitra ròa àmbin' ny fòlo*"), each of which had a semi-sacred character as being the seat of ancient chiefs; the places just mentioned were included in these twelve, but others are now mere hamlets, if not as much deserted villages as Old Sarum was in pre-Reform days in England.

All the ancient towns and villages in the interior of Madagascar were built on the top of hills, sometimes of considerable height. This was of course for security against enemies in the former warlike times, when every petty state was frequently fighting with its neighbours, like the barons of European castles in the mediæval period. Protection was further given by deep fosses dug out of the hard red clay, and surrounding the towns. These are frequently double, or even treble, one outside the other, and must have formed a very effectual defence in the days when firearms were unknown, and especially when helped by the earthen ramparts often added inside the ditches from the material dug out. Some of these fosses look like a railway cutting through red sandstone, and although they are in many cases probably two or three hundred years old, the sides are generally as perpendicular and unbroken as when first excavated. A narrow bridge of the red earth leads to the gateway, which is formed of massive blocks of rock. Two different forms of gateway are found in these old towns: one kind is defended by a great circular slab of stone 10 or 12 feet in diameter, which, in time of war, was rolled between upright stones, so as to effectually block up the entrance. Another kind of gateway was formed by massive upright monoliths, between which heavy wooden gates were fixed. In many cases there is a treble gateway of this kind, with a narrow passage between each gate, so that the enemy could be speared from above, if the first or even the second line of defence had been broken through. Many of these old towns are now deserted, but their ancient defences form the chief antiquities of Madagascar, and are interesting memorials of a state of society now passed away in the central provinces.

The ancient graves of the Vazìmba, the aboriginal inhabitants of the interior, are found scattered over the central province. These are shapeless heaps of stone, generally overshadowed by a *fàno* tree, a species of acacia, which has a semi-sacred character, its seeds being used in divination. Could these graves, like our ancient English barrows, be opened, doubtless much light would be thrown on the rather difficult question of the affinities of these Vazìmba; but to meddle with any tomb, much more one of these ancient ones, is one of the most heinous offences among the Malagasy.[1] A considerable number of upright stones, termed *vàtolàhy* (lit. "male stones"), huge undressed blocks of granite, are also found on the hills and downs. These are memorials of former chieftains, or of battles of the old times.

As regards maps of Imèrina, I believe that I was the first (in 1867) to make a sketch-map of the country round Antanànarìvo. This was, however, made chiefly to show the mission stations of the London Missionary Society. Parts of the province to the south-west were subsequently given much more fully by Mr. J. S. Sewell and Mr. W. Johnson; but the first detailed map of Imèrina and the surrounding regions was published by the Rev. Dr. Mullens in 1875, as the result of a large number of observations taken by himself, and founded on positions fixed by Mr. James Cameron. A map to a much larger scale (1 : 200,000) was published by M. Grandidier in 1880; and he issued more recently (1883) a beautiful hypsometrical map of the province, showing by graduated tints the heights of every

[1] For fuller information as to the Vazìmba, see subsequent chapter.

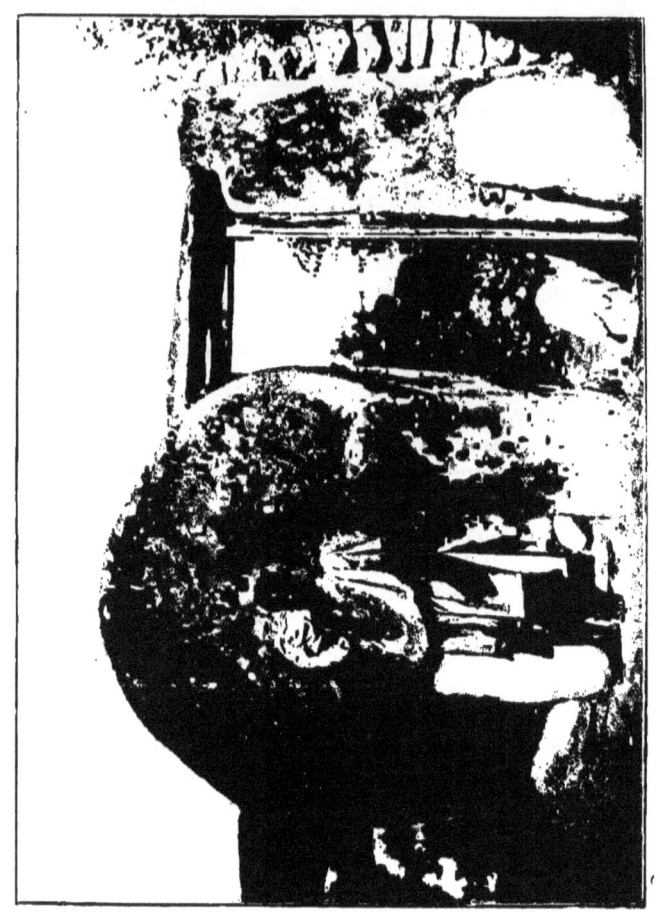

STONE GATEWAY OF ANCIENT TOWNS IN IMÉRINA

part of the country from the river-beds to the summits of Ankàratra. "This," says M. Grandidier, "is, I believe, the first and only contour map which has been made of an uncivilised country on such a large scale. This map enables one to see at a glance the zones of altitude characteristic of this province, which is so mountainous and desolate beyond the great plain west of Antanànarìvo; and it shows clearly the manner in which the waters part themselves."

A few words may be here added as to the external aspects of an Imèrina village. As already mentioned, all the ancient villages and towns were built on the tops of high hills, and are consequently rather difficult to approach; and although a great many of them are now deserted, and the more modern villages are built either on the plains or on the lower rising grounds, numbers of the old places still remain inhabited; and the people who live in them must have a weary climb every evening as they go home from their work in the rice-fields, or return from a neighbouring village or market. Even the capital city, Antanànarìvo, is built on the top and the sides of a long, narrow ridge rising about 600 feet above the plain below. The old capital, Ambòhimànga, is on an equally high hill, and so are most of the ancient and famous towns and villages. Some of these hills rise to 700 or 800 feet in height; and a few years ago I had to climb up to a village called Vòhilèna, which is built on a tremendous hill no less than 1,500 feet above the valley at its foot. Never shall I forget my ascent up its steep side in the darkness, without a guide, and unable to find any path in the woods that cover its slopes!

The deep fosses which surround these old villages have already been alluded to. Most of them are from 20 to 30 feet wide and as many feet deep, although sometimes they are much deeper. But although so deep, these trenches are not full of water, for this is always drawn off by another trench leading down the hillside. They are, however, of course damp, and good soil gradually increases there, so that ferns and wild plants grow luxuriantly; and the bottom of the fosse therefore forms a plantation, in which peach, banana, guava, and other fruit-trees are cultivated, as well as coffee, arums, and a variety of vegetables. Tall trees of other kinds also grow there, so that these *hàdy*, as they are called, are often by far the prettiest feature of the village. On many hill-tops in Imèrina, where no villages now exist, the *hàdy* may be seen from a great distance, scoring the hillsides, and showing that in former times a village crowned the summit.

In some parts of the central provinces of Madagascar there is no deep fosse, such as those just described, but the village is protected by a dense and wide plantation of prickly-pear.[1] This shrub is armed all over with spines and prickles 2 inches long, sharp as a needle and somewhat poisonous. The thick, fleshy, twisted stems, the gaily-tinted flowers, and even the pear-shaped fruits, are all armed with spines and stinging hairs; and it is no easy matter to get rid of the minute little needles if they once get into one's skin. So it is easy to see that a hedge of this prickly-pear, several feet wide and 8 or 10 feet high, is a very effectual defence against enemies or robbers, especially when it is remembered that the majority of people wear no shoes and so have no protection for their bare legs and feet. In many places, instead of prickly-pear, the fence round the village is made of *tsiàfakòmby* ("impassable by cattle"), a shrub with bright yellow flowers and full of hook-like prickles.[2]

Now let us get up into the village and see what it looks like. Crossing the deep *hàdy* by a kind of bridge of earth, we come to the entrance or *vàvahàdy* ("mouth of the fosse"). This is generally a narrow gateway formed of roughly-built stonework; and on its inner side, in a groove, is a great circular slab of granite, for rolling across the opening, so as to quite close it up. But for many years past, in most villages, these great slabs of stone have been unused, and the grooves are filled up with dust

[1] *Opuntia Dillenii*, Haw.
[2] The Mysore thorn, *Cæsalpinia scpiaria*, Roxb.

and dirt, so that it is not very easy to move the stone out of its place. In many villages the great stone lies on the ground, and the children play games upon it, showing that for a long time there has been no war in the interior of the island, but people have been able to live in security and peace, "none daring to make them afraid." In some cases, instead of a door at the gateway, a number of short poles are hung from a cross-piece at the top, which passes through a hole in each of them ; and one has to hold up two or three of them in order to pass through. This kind of gate is chiefly for the purpose of preventing the pigs and sheep from getting in and out of the village. In some parts of Imèrina, to the west and north, where there is frequent danger from roving parties of robbers, the villages are still carefully guarded, and many of them have a treble gateway, with three pairs of thick wooden doors, and connected by a kind of tunnel.

Here, however, we are at last inside the village, and we see at once that there are no streets intersecting it. The houses are built without any order or regularity, except in one point, namely, that all the old-fashioned houses are built north and south, and that they have their single door and window always on the west side, so as to be protected from the cold and keen south-east trade-winds, which blow over Imèrina during the greater part of the year. The houses are mostly made of the hard red earth, laid in courses of a foot or so high. They are chiefly of one storey and of one room, but they generally have a floor in the roof, which is used for cooking, and are sometimes divided into two or three rooms by rush and mat partitions. On the east of Imèrina, near the forest, the houses are made of rough wooden framing, filled up with bamboo or rush, and often plastered with cow-dung ; and in the neighbourhood of the capital a great many houses are now built of sun-dried bricks in two storeys, with several rooms and often with tiled roofs. These, however, belong to the richer people.

Ambòhitritankàdy, one of the villages in my mission district, is on a high hill, and in the centre of the village are ten large houses of massive timber framing and with very high-pitched roofs, with long "horns" at the gables, arranged five on each side of a long oblong space sunk a couple of feet below the ground. Here, in former times, bull-fights took place, and various games and amusements were carried on. One of the houses, where the chief himself resided, is much larger than the rest, and the corner posts, as well as the three great central posts supporting the ridge, are very large, massive pieces of timber. It was all in one great room without any partitions, the whole being well floored with wood, and the walls covered with neat mats. Such fine old houses are now, however, becoming very rare, and are being fast superseded by much less picturesque, but perhaps more comfortable, as well as cheaper, houses of sun-dried or burnt brick.

The houses of most villages are scattered about the place in a very irregular fashion. There is no privacy or retirement about them, no backyard or outbuildings, although occasionally low walls do make a kind of enclosure round some of them. Here and there among the houses are square pits, 5 or 6 feet deep and 8 or 10 feet square, called *fàhitra*. These are pens for the oxen, often very fine animals, with enormous horns and humps, which are kept in them to be fattened, mostly for the national feast of the Fandròana ("the bathing") at the New Year. All sorts of rubbish and filth accumulate; there are no sanitary arrangements; frequently the cattle are penned for the night in a part of the enclosure, and the cow-dung makes it very muddy in wet weather, and raises clouds of dust when it is dry. Frequently the cow-dung is carefully collected and made into circular cakes of 6 or 8 inches diameter, which are then stuck on the walls of the houses to dry. It is afterwards used as fuel for burning off large slabs of the hard gneiss rock, which are employed by the people in making their tombs.

The pits in which the people store their rice are bottle-shaped holes, from 8 to 10 feet deep, dug out of the hard red earth, and will contain a large quantity of grain. They are closed up by a flat stone and covered with earth, so it is not easy for a stranger to know where the rice-store is. In former times these pits were now and then used as places of refuge, and even of worship, by Christian people in the time of persecution; and occasionally those who had offended the sovereign were placed in the pits, which were partly filled up with earth, boiling water being then poured over them until they were killed.

In the centre of the village may often be seen the large family tomb of the chief man of the place, the owner of the land and the rice-fields in the neighbourhood. This is a structure of dressed or of rough stonework, from 12 to 20 feet square, and about 6 to 8 feet high. Generally it has two or more stages diminishing in area, and frequently at the east end is a kind of headstone, in modern tombs sometimes with a name and date cut upon it. These tombs are vaults made of great undressed slabs of blue rock, partly sunk under ground, and with stone shelves on which the corpses, wrapped in silk cloths, are laid. The steps down to the vault are always on the west side, and the door is a massive stone slab turning on pivots at the top and bottom. In the case of people who are *Andrìana*, or of noble birth, the stonework is surmounted by a small wooden house, with thatched or shingled roof and a door, but no window. This is called *tràno màsina* ("sacred house") or *tràno manàra* ("cold house"), because it has no hearth or fire. In some villages, where the people are almost all of high rank, a line of these tombs, with their little wooden houses, may be observed.

Seen from a distance, these Malagasy villages often look very pretty and picturesque, for "distance lends enchantment to the view." Round some of them tall trees, called *Aviàvy*,[1] a species of fig-tree, grow, which are something like an English elm in appearance. In others one or two great *Amòntana*[2] trees may be seen; these are also a species of fig-tree, and have large and glossy leaves. A beautiful tree called *Zàhana*[3] is also

[1] *Ficus megapoda*, Baker. [2] *F. Baroni*, Baker. [3] *Phyllarthron Bojerianum*, D.C.

common, with hundreds of large pink flowers; and in the fosses the *Amìana*,[1] a tall tree nettle with large, deeply-cut, and velvety leaves, with stinging hairs, frequently grows. Many kinds of shrubs often make the place gay with flowers; but these all grow wild, and the people have not yet learned to plant flowers in beds and gardens for their own pleasure.

The Hova children are brown-skinned, some very light olive in colour, and some very dark. As a rule, they have little clothing, and no caps, shoes, or stockings, and are usually very dirty and uncared for. On Sundays and on special occasions the girls are often dressed in print frocks, and the boys in jackets of similar material, and with clean white calico *làmba* over all; but on week-days a small *làmba*, of soiled and coarse hemp cloth, often forms almost their only clothing. Of course the children of well-to-do people are sometimes very nicely dressed, although they too often go about in a rather dirty fashion. I am here, however, speaking of the majority of the children one sees, those of the poorer people of the village. One day some of us went for a ride to a village about two miles away from Ambòhimànga. A number of children followed us about as we collected ferns in the *hády*, and as a group of seven or eight of them sat near us, we calculated that the value of all they had on would not amount to one shilling!

Poor children! they have few amusements. They sometimes play at a game which is very like our "fox and geese"; the boys spin peg-tops; the little children make figures of oxen and birds, &c., out of clay; and the big boys have a rough and violent game called *mamèly dìamànga*, in which they kick backward at each other, with their feet lifted almost as high as their heads. Perhaps the most favourite amusement of Malagasy children is to sit in parties out of doors on fine moonlight nights, and sing away for hours some of the monotonous native chants, accompanying them with regular clapping of hands.

One thing more may be noticed about our Malagasy village,

[1] *Urera* sp. and *Obetia* sp.

and that is, that in almost all the larger villages of Imèrina there is now to be seen a building for Christian worship. In many places this is a rough and plain structure, made of clay or of sun-dried brick, often with no glass in the windows, and no pews or benches on the floor. Still, in these rude country churches, God's Word is read and preached, the love of Christ is made known, and some light is being shed upon the minds of the people, who are most of them still very ignorant and superstitious. In the neighbourhood of the capital, however, as well as in some other districts, many very neat and pretty village churches are now to be seen. These are plastered and coloured, and often have tiled roofs and glass windows; there are low benches and clean mats on the floor, and some few have well-carved stone and wood pulpits, showing that the people have worked hard and done their best to make a building that shall be suitable for the worship of God.

Besides being used for Divine service on Sundays, the village church is also the school-house on week-days. Here may be seen bright children repeating their *a, b, d* (not *c*), reading and writing, doing sums, learning a little grammar and geography, and being taught their catechism and something about the chief facts and truths of the Bible. And perhaps there is no more pleasant sight to be seen in Madagascar than one of the larger chapels filled to the doors on the annual examination day with children from the neighbouring villages, all dressed in their best eager to show their knowledge, and pleased to get the Testament or hymn-book or other prize given to those who have answered well.

Thank God there are now hundreds of such village churches and schools in Central Madagascar. May they soon be seen all over the provinces of the great island!

CHAPTER III.

ANTANÀNARÌVO, THE CAPITAL: ITS PUBLIC BUILDINGS, MEMORIAL AND OTHER CHURCHES, AND RELIGIOUS AND CHARITABLE INSTITUTIONS.

Scenery around the capital—Its picturesque situation—Rugged streets and paths—Houses and other buildings—Recent introduction of bricks—Royal palaces—Fàravòhitra—Ancient gateway—Sacred stones—Absence of wheeled vehicles and of gas and water supply—Street scenes—Weekly market of Zomà—Amusements—L.M.S. churches and religious institutions—Ambàtonakànga Church—Other memorial churches—"Mother churches" and districts—Chapel Royal—Sunday observance—Colleges and school buildings—Dispensaries and hospitals—Other missions—Extent of Christian work carried on—Civilising work of L.M.S. Mission—Population—Plans of the capital—Antanànarìvo, the heart of Madagascar.

THE chief city of Madagascar is situated nearly in the centre of the island, as regards its length from north to south, but is much nearer the eastern than the western side of the country. It is about one hundred miles from the Indian Ocean to the east, while the Mozambique Channel is nearly twice that distance from it to the west.[1]

Let us suppose that we have just come up from Tamatave, and, by the route described in the first chapter, have passed through the two belts of forest, and are now on the open, breezy moorland of eastern Imèrina. Antanànarìvo is still about thirty miles distant, a good day's journey from the upper line of forest. We see signs of a denser population as we advance: well-

[1] By the latest and most reliable observations, the following has been settled as the position of Antanànarìvo: Lat., 18° 55′ 2·10″–2·18″ S.; long., 47° 31′

NORTHERN PART OF ANTÁNANARÍVO.

cultivated rice-fields in every valley, plantations on the hillsides, numerous villages, and scattered homesteads, the houses being built of the hard red clay or decomposed granite, while the walls enclosing the compounds are also of this material. We pass the long mountain of Angàvokèly, with its double summit, one peak having a remarkable resemblance to a mediæval castle ; and then the rounded, dome-like mass of Ambàtovòry, with its woods—a remnant of the primeval forest—nestling in the valley at its base; and then a long, gradual ascent brings us to a high moor, from which a very extensive prospect is unfolded ; the greater part of Imèrina lies before us, and most of its prominent hills and its chief towns can be clearly seen. Before us, at nine or ten miles' distance, is a long and lofty ridge, stretching north and south, on which buildings can be plainly discerned, cutting the sky-line; in the centre are the lofty white roofs of the group of royal palaces; to the north are the towers of the Prime Minister's house, its glass dome shining in the sunlight ; while the spires and towers of churches can also be distinguished, especially at each extremity of the long line of hill. From this lofty point we descend into deep river valleys, and ascend again several times before the two hours' ride still to be accomplished is completed ; we lose sight of the city again and again, until another long ascent brings us up to the last hill before we descend into the valley which surrounds Antanànarìvo ; and at last the capital of the island stands before us, at a distance of three-quarters of a mile or so across the rice-fields.

It is certainly a very picturesquely situated town ; the rocky ridge, on the summit and slopes of which the houses are built, rises at its highest point, near the centre, to from 500 to 600 feet above the surrounding valleys and the western plain, and its length, north and south, is not far short of two miles. At the southern extremity it slopes down abruptly to the valley, but at the northern end the descent is more gradual. At about two-thirds of its length from the south, a large branch or spur of the hill separates from the main ridge and curves round to the north-west with a tolerably easy gradient; so that the actual extent of the city is not realised from the eastern side, and one must ride round to the west to see how large a place it really is. The ridge, though long, is narrow, so that there is little level ground on the summit; and the majority of the houses are built on terraces, cut away on one side and built up with retaining walls on the other. At the junction of the two northern branches of the hill there is a large triangular open space called Andohàlo, where a market is held, and where great public assemblies are convened, as at the promulgation of any new law, or the reception of the sovereign on her return to the capital, &c.

East and west, the sides of the hill are very steep; indeed, on the western side they are precipitous. On this side is the precipice of Ampàmarìnana (" the place of hurling "), the Tarpeian of Antanànarìvo, where those accused of sorcery were formerly killed by being hurled from the summit; and where also, in 1849, many Malagasy Christians suffered death, being supposed to have been enabled, by some powerful charm, to be disobedient to their heathen sovereign's will.

Antanànarìvo, or "City of a thousand," that is, probably, a thousand settlers or military colonists, is certainly "a city set on a hill which cannot be hid." As already remarked, it is by far the largest town in Madagascar, only two or three places reaching a tenth of its extent or population. Its ancient name was Iàlamànga, *i.e.*, "At the blue (or famous) wood," probably from the forest formerly covering its summit and slopes, as is still the case with Ambòhimànga, the ancient capital. Antanànarìvo has attained its present important position in the island only within the last hundred years, greatly increasing in size and population since it became no longer merely the chief town of one Malagasy tribe—the Hova—but also the capital of the country through the Hova making themselves the dominant tribe of Madagascar.

It need hardly be said that road-making is very difficult in a place like Antanànarìvo. The naked rock comes to the surface almost everywhere; and the gradients, east and west at least, would be almost impossible for a carriage, even could the path be paved smooth. There are, in fact, only about two main roads in the city, one going north and south, and the other east and west. These are roughly paved in some parts; but it requires care even to ride on horseback along Antanànarìvo streets. The houses are not built adjoining each other, as in European towns; each one stands in its own compound; although certainly in the centre of the city they are packed pretty closely together, and often the only path to large and respectable houses is by climbing low walls and struggling up and down narrow and steep rocky stairs.

Notwithstanding these drawbacks, Antanànarìvo now possesses a large number of substantial and often handsome houses, as well as many public buildings which would not disgrace a European town. A great change has come about since I first knew the place in 1863. Then it was a town built entirely, within the city proper, of wood or rush and bamboo. By an old law, or rather custom, no building of stone or clay was allowed to be erected within these limits; and there was a similar custom in many of the other ancient towns. The houses of the nobles and the wealthier people were all of massive timber framing, fitted in with thick upright planking, and the roof of extremely high pitch, with long crossed gable-timbers or "horns." These houses were sometimes roofed with wooden shingles, but more frequently with thatch of a species of sedge. It will be easily seen that with such combustible materials fires were of frequent occurrence, especially at the end of the dry season ; and twenty, thirty, or even a hundred houses were not unfrequently burnt down at one time. The acceptance of Christianity by the Queen and Government in 1868 put an end to this foolish custom, as well as to many other still more harmful things; and the old timber houses have now almost disappeared from the city. An interesting relic of the past is still preserved with religious care in the palace yard among more modern buildings. This is the ancient royal house called Bésákana, where the corpse of a deceased sovereign lies in state, the building being draped entirely in scarlet cloth.

The introduction of sun-dried brick and tiles by Mr. James Cameron and Mr. W. Pool, of the London Missionary Society, as well as the erection of the stone Martyr Memorial Churches, of which I was the architect, has completely revolutionised the building art in Imèrina and in Bètsilèo. And Antanànarìvo, instead of being a town of wooden and rush houses, as I knew it thirty-two years ago, has become a city containing hundreds of good two- and three-storied brick houses, with many public buildings of stone. Within the last ten or twelve years burnt brick has come into much more general use; and many substantial houses and some churches are now to be seen erected of this more durable material. Scores of houses have their verandah pillars of moulded brick, or of stone with carved capitals. There are, it must be confessed, some drawbacks to the otherwise pleasant picture. There are too many houses unfinished, and a general aspect of disrepair visible, and a want of neatness and tidiness.

Among the most prominent buildings of the capital are the group of royal palaces, the largest of which, an immense three-storied timber structure, has been surrounded with triple stone verandah and arches, and strengthened with corner towers. This largest of the royal buildings is known by the name of *Manjàkamiàdana, i.e.*, "Reigning peacefully"; it is about 120 feet in height to the ridge of the high-pitched roof, which is surmounted at each end by tall lightning-conductors, and in the centre by an enormous gilt copper figure of an eagle—a bird which is used as a kind of national emblem, much as is the case with the eagles of America and several European states. Close to this largest palace stands the *Trànovòla* or "Silver house," about two-thirds the size of its larger neighbour, but entirely of timber. There are several other palaces, each having its proper name, as *Manàmpisòa* ("Adding good"), *Bésàkana* ("Great breadth"), &c. This last-named building is the most ancient and venerated of all; it is a simple oblong structure of framed timber, with upright planking, and a roof of enormously high pitch, covered with wooden shingles, and crossed "horns," 10 or 12 feet long, at each gable.[1]

In the palace courtyard the spire and tower of the Chapel Royal is a conspicuous feature. The building is constructed of stone and roofed with slates from the Bètsilèo province. It boasts of a pipe organ, tinted glass windows, and a good deal of elaborate carving both in wood and stone. Further south is the great square stone and brick house of the Prime Minister, and other handsome residences of nobles and high officers, and the High Court of Justice, with its Ionic columns. Very prominent in Antanànarìvo also are buildings for religious and educational purposes; the four Memorial Churches of the London Missionary Society, each with spire or tower, together with about a score more (belonging to the same mission), less ornate in style, in the city and its suburbs; the Anglican Cathedral, although still wanting its spires; the Roman Catholic Cathedral, with its elegant lantern-crowned towers; the Norwegian Lutheran Church; the College of the London Missionary Society and the High Schools of the same society, as well as those of the Friends, the Anglican, and the Jesuit missions; the Mission presses; the London Missionary Society's and Norwegian Hospitals and Dispensaries; while about two miles to the east is a French Observatory, superintended by a Jesuit priest.

As one's eye passes along the long wavy ridge of the city hill, from south to north, it is seen to slope gradually to the plain at the northern extremity. This portion of the capital is called Fàravòhitra, *i.e.*, "Last village," its former extremity northward,

---

[1] It is the custom for Malagasy sovereigns to build a new house for themselves soon after their accession.

although the city has now extended far beyond this spot. Thirty years ago this part of the ridge was a desolate-looking place, with hardly a house upon it; a number of ancient tombs stretched along the rough footpath; it was one of the places of execution, and no one would walk along it after nightfall. Now, however, and for many years past, it is a favourite part of the city, the majority of the English mission families residing there; while amongst them is seen the square tower of the Fàravòhitra Memorial Church, and many of the educational establishments of the L.M.S. and Friends' Missions.

The most ancient structure in Antanànarìvo is the old gateway to the east of the city, the only one now remaining of several gates formerly guarding the chief approaches to the capital. This interesting relic of the olden time is a mass of rude masonry of thin, flat stones laid without mortar, with large upright slabs of blue gneiss at the angles. The opening is a square doorway several feet deep, and in time of war was closed by a huge flat circular stone which was rolled out of a groove inside the gateway. The name of this ancient gate is Ankàdibèvàva, *i.e.*, "At the Fosse with the great Mouth," or opening; but it is also as often called Ambàvahàdimitàfo, *i.e.*, "At the Roofed Gateway," because it is covered with a rush roof.

The "sacred stones" of Antanànarìvo are objects which are onnected with royalty among the Hova and mark it—amongst many other things—as a different place from European cities. One of these is situated in Andohàlo, a spacious triangular open space in the centre of the capital, where a large daily market is held, where public assemblies take place, and where some of the sovereigns have been crowned. The sacred stone here is nothing but the underlying gneiss rock, which in one spot comes to the surface; but upon it the sovereign must always stand on special occasions, as when returning from a visit to Ambòhimànga or more distant places, and is there saluted by the army and by the people generally. The other sacred stone is a much more prominent object, and appears to be a boulder-like mass of gneiss which has at some remote time tumbled down from the precipitous western side of the city hill, and stands nearly in the centre of a large square plain on that side of Antanànarìvo. This open space is called Imàhamàsina, *i.e.*, " Place of making sacred " (or establishing or confirming). Some Hova sovereigns have been crowned here (or rather, first appeared in state for the homage of their subjects), and the throne is always placed on the sacred stone. One is here reminded of the sacred stones on which the kings of other nations have been enthroned in ancient times, and especially of our own " Stone of Destiny " from Scone now and for so many centuries past placed under the chair of Edward the Confessor in Westminster Abbey.

From whatever side one goes up into Antanànarìvo, the ascent is steep, in most places exceedingly so, and most rugged and uneven. It is immediately evident that no carriage could traverse these roughly-paved roads; such things are in fact unknown in this large city, and so the streets are singularly quiet, with no rush of wheels or tramp of horses, while the great majority of human feet are shoeless and so almost noiseless in their tread. There are only two or three streets, in our sense of the term, in this capital of Madagascar, that is where a tolerably good pavement has been laid down with side gutters, &c. The greater part of the houses are reached by narrow paths winding in and out among the compounds, and sometimes there is no access to a house but by crossing the yards of others, and often only by climbing over the low clay walls which surround them. As we pass along we see how difficult and costly it would be to make roads and streets in Antanànarìvo, for each compound is a terrace cut out of the steep hillside, built up on one side by the soil and rock removed from the other. Of course drainage is all surface, and in the heavy rains of the wet season each street and path is swept by a furious torrent, often forming a series of rapids and waterfalls, and constantly cutting deep trenches in the red soil, so that every path not protected by some kind of rough paving is being constantly lowered, some streets being many feet below the compounds on either hand.

It need hardly be said that there are no water-pipes or gas mains in the streets of Antanànarìvo. The want of the former is supplied by the primitive plan of all water being fetched from springs at the foot of the city hill by the women and girls—slave or free—of every household. Long lines of these may be seen in the evenings going up and down the rough paths with their water-pots on their heads. At nights the streets are dark and almost deserted, but for the lantern carried by an occasional passenger. Few Europeans or respectable natives care to risk their limbs by going without a light over these breakneck paths.

A prominent feature in the life of Antanànarìvo is the great weekly market held every Friday on a place in the north-west side of the city. This is called Zomà (Friday), from the day on which it is held, and although a large daily market is also held there, on Fridays an immense concourse of people from the surrounding country, as well as from the city itself, is gathered together. All the chief roads are thronged with people bringing in their goods for sale, and by an early hour in the forenoon probably 10,000 or 12,000 persons are assembled, and the hum of voices can be heard from a considerable distance. Here everything that is grown or manufactured in the interior province can be procured, and in no place can a better idea of the productions of the country or of the handicraft skill of the Malagasy be obtained than in this great Zomà market. There is, of course, a rough division of the various objects for sale in different sections of the market-ground. Here is a forest of timber, rafters, joists, and boards; here are doors, bedsteads, and chairs; here are enormous piles of *hèrana* rush for roofing and long dry grass for fuel; here is the grain, fruit, and vegetable division of the market, with heaps of salt and chillies for condiments; here is the cattle market, and not far off the beef and mutton, and the poultry section, with hundreds of fowls, ducks, turkeys, and geese; here is the "dry goods" division, with English calicoes, American sheeting, gay prints, and native cloths of hemp, cotton, and *rofia* fibre; here are piles of snowy cocoons of raw silk for weaving into fine *làmba;* here is ironwork of all kinds, nails and hinges, bolts and screws; and here is native pottery, water-jars, and cooking-pots, and so on. The Zomà market is certainly one of the most interesting sights of Antanànarìvo, and is without doubt one of the chief delights of life to the native residents in the capital.

To Europeans there is a great absence in Antanànarìvo of anything like entertainments or amusements. A French gentleman, newly arrived in the city, truly observed: "*Il n'y a pas des distractions ici!*" And doubtless he felt the want of the *café* and theatre and boulevarde of his beloved Paris. Probably the Malagasy themselves do not feel this need, and are sufficiently amused and entertained by the mild excitement of their New Year's festival, by an occasional *kabàry* or public assembly, by the return of the queen from a visit to some other part of the country, with the state and ceremony attending it, by a review of troops, and perhaps still more by the frequent markets and their gossip, together with the delights of bargaining and seeing others buy and sell. Of late years these purely native amusements have been added to by the introduction of occasional lectures, concerts, and other entertainments, chiefly held in the educational buildings or the different missions; the school children also often have their "treats," when they sport their gayest dresses and are feasted in some garden or mango orchard in the suburbs of the city; and it may be added that the *Lòhavòlana*, or service held at one of the larger Antanànarìvo churches in rotation on the first Monday morning of every month, is also a time of great enjoyment to the younger people from the new sacred music introduced on many of these occasions.

On referring to the map it will be seen that there are in Antanànarìvo and its suburbs, no fewer than thirty-five churches, twenty-seven of which are connected with the London Missionary Society. And when the population[1] of the capital is remembered—probably from 80,000 to 100,000—it will be evident that these thirty-five churches provide by no means too large an accommodation for those who should attend public worship, indeed it is still greatly inadequate to the needs of the city.

It will be noticed that little attempt has been made in the map to show the remarkably irregular and very picturesque site of Antanànarìvo, as this would have interfered with its main purpose. This has been already sufficiently described in the earlier portion of the chapter.

The first building erected for Christian worship in Antanànarìvo was at Ambòdin' Andohàlo, on the spot where the London Missionary Society Girls' Central School stood until very lately (see map). For some time the school-house adjoining Mr. Griffiths' residence on this site appears to have been used for worship, and this continued for several years to be the sole place of meeting. In 1831, however, as the number of worshippers increased, a second building was erected at Ambàtonakànga (1)[2]; and, as the first site at Andohàlo was not, in this later period of the Mission, used again for worship, the congregation meeting in the Memorial Church there may be justly regarded as the "mother church" of Madagascar. Ambàtonakànga is certainly the most interesting spot in the island as regards its religious history. It is a commanding position at the junction of the two chief roads in the city—it might almost be said in the island—and the site was originally granted for a workshop to the L.M.S. On this spot the first printing-press was erected and set to work; subsequently the second place in the country ever erected for Christian worship was built here; on the outbreak of persecution this building was turned into a stable and afterwards into a

[1] The population of Antanànarìvo has recently been ascertained—March, 1896—not to exceed 43,000 souls.—ED.

[2] The numbers following the names of churches are those by which they are marked on the map and in the list at the end of this chapter.

prison for the punishment of the "praying people"; and finally, the first of the four Martyr Memorial Churches was commenced here in 1864 and opened in 1867. This is a substantial stone structure with tower and spire, built in a simple Norman style, the first stone building ever erected in the country.

When Mr. Ellis arrived in Antanànarìvo in June, 1862, soon after the country was re-opened to Christian effort, he found three large congregations already gathered together, and all meeting in the same quarter of the city, the north-west—one at Ambàtonakànga; another at Anàlakèly (2); and the third at Ampàribè (3). These congregations met in very rough and unattractive buildings—one being an old stable; another several native houses patched together; and the other an old workshop. For many years past, however, these congregations have been housed in large buildings; and these three still continue in the front rank as regards numbers and influence, Ampàribè probably containing the largest congregation to be seen in any part of the island. During the twelve years or so following the year 1862 numerous offshoots sprang from the three just named, until the city churches reached the number shown on the map. Ten of these are *rèni-fiangònana* ("mother churches"), having large districts connected with each, which stretch for many miles in all directions, and contain in all no fewer than *six hundred congregations*. The largest of these districts includes 120 churches and is worked most efficiently by the Friends' Mission, in complete harmony with the London Missionary Society, and has its mother church at Ambòhitantèly (8).

Of these ten, four are the Memorial Churches at Ambàtonakànga (1), Ambòhipòtsy (2), Ampàmarìnana (6), and Fàravòhitra (9). The first of these has already been described. The second occupies a most commanding position at the southern extremity of the city ridge, and is visible for many miles in every direction. It is built in a simple Early English style of Gothic, and has a tower and spire. Ambòhipòtsy is the St. Albans of Madagascar, for it is the spot where the heroic

Rasalàma, the first Christian martyr, was speared in the year 1837. The third church is built on the edge of the "precipice of hurling," as its name signifies, and commemorates thirteen brave confessors who were, in 1849, dashed down the steep cliffs for refusing to deny their Saviour. The building is designed in a simple Romanesque style, and has a lofty campanile; the interior, with its galleries all round, looking very much like an English Nonconformist chapel. The fourth of these Martyr Memorial buildings occupies a very prominent position at the northern end of the city ridge. Fàravòhitra Church is a very plain stone structure, with low square tower, and marks the exact spot where, in 1849, four Christian Malagasy were burnt to death, together with the mangled remains of those thirteen who had been hurled over the precipices at Ampàmarìnana on the same day.

The Queen's Church in the palace courtyard is attended by Her Majesty and her Court, as well as by many of the chief people of the city. The congregation here gives liberally towards the support of native evangelists and teachers in the different districts, and it is distinctly a Congregational church. The other churches in the city and suburbs are mostly of sun-dried brick and stone, but some of the more recently-erected ones are of burnt brick, and are handsome buildings. On Sunday mornings they are all well filled, especially on the first Sunday in the month, the congregations numbering in several instances over a thousand people. The afternoon congregations are not quite so large. Some of the surburban churches are just as largely attended as those in the city proper.

The observance of Sunday is a marked feature in the life of Antanànarivo. No markets are held, all Government business is stopped, and large numbers of people in clean white dresses and *lamba* crowd the roads going to and from the various places of worship. The sound of bells is heard from many towers, and as one passes by the churches, the familiar strains of many well-known English tunes may be heard sung accompanied by the

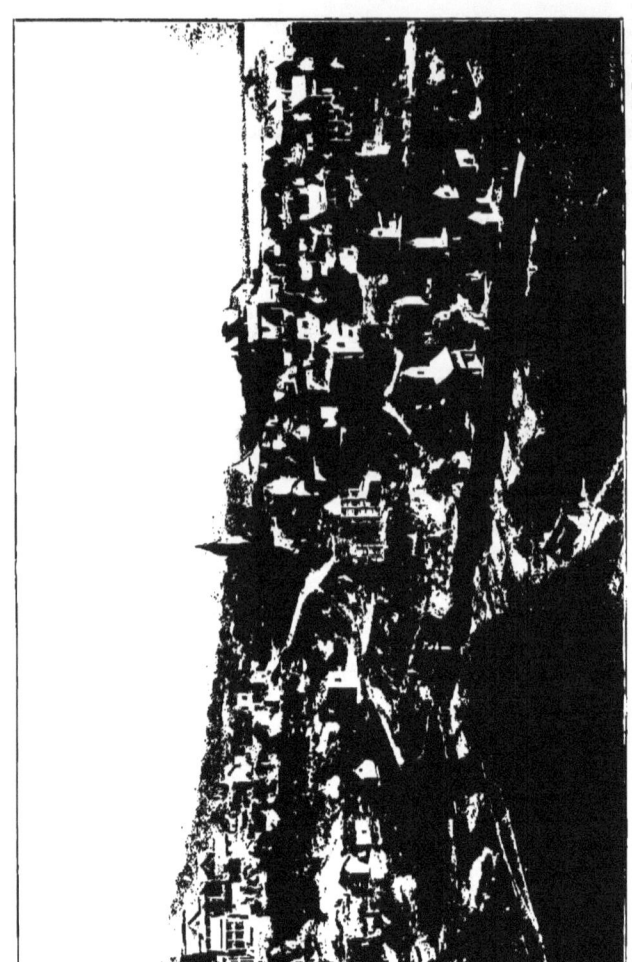

VIEW FROM ANDOHALO, ANTÁNANARIVO.   [*Photograph by* Dr. FENN.

notes of American organs or harmoniums. A Sabbath quiet and calm is over the whole city; not only is divine worship attended by thousands, but hundreds of children are learning in Sunday schools; and it may be said that in Antanànarìvo, as well as in many other Madagascar towns and villages, the Day of Rest is as well observed as in most parts of England, or even of Scotland.

In addition to the churches of Antanànarìvo, other institutions connected with the London Missionary Society and the Friends' and other Missions are also shown on the map. Of these, the largest building, and one seen most prominently on approaching the capital from Tamatave, is the L.M.S. College, a massive and substantial structure of brick and stone. The College teaching was commenced in 1869, and the present building was opened in 1881. The accommodation includes, besides spacious class-rooms and tutors' residences, a lecture hall, arranged in theatre fashion, where lectures are delivered and meetings of all kinds are constantly held, there being room for about five hundred auditors. About seventy to eighty students of different grades are usually under training, the majority of these being educated for the Christian ministry, while some are secular students.

A little below the College, to the north, is the L.M.S. Normal School, also housed in a substantial stone and brick building; and here teachers for the town and country schools receive a thorough course of instruction for their work. The Girls' Central School is in Ambòdin' Andohàlo, nearer the centre of the city. Not far from this is the L.M.S. Press, from which a large number of books and other publications are constantly being issued.[1]

Lower down, to the north-west, at Anàlakèly is the Dispensary, under the management of a joint committee of the London Missionary Society and Friends' Missions. Within the last four or five years a new, larger, and very complete Hospital has been

[1] About 150,000 books of various kinds yearly.

erected at Isoàvinandrìana, a place about a mile from the northern extremity of the capital. This is also under the joint control of the two societies, although the Friends take the larger share of the expenses of all medical work. Here the sick are nursed and attended to; and young men are trained as doctors and surgeons, and women for the work of nursing and midwifery. A Medical Mission Board gives diplomas of efficiency in surgery and medicine, and a considerable number of young Malagasy are now qualified medical practitioners.

The Friends' Mission Central Girls' School and their press are on the Fàravòhitra hill close to the College; and their excellent upper Boys' School is at Ambòhijatòvo, nearer the centre of the city. So close is the connection between the two Missions, that for all practical purposes they may be regarded as one; all plans of work, church government, and worship being the same in almost every respect in the churches of the London Missionary Society and those in charge of the Friends.

A word or two must also be said about the other churches of Antanànarìvo.

Those of the "Society for the Propagation of the Gospel" Episcopal Mission are four in number, the chief being the stately stone Cathedral, which occupies a most commanding position on the north side of Andohàlo in the centre of the city. This is a cruciform structure with three towers, which will eventually be crowned with spires. This Mission has also good High Schools for boys and girls in the city, while their college, with some elegant stone buildings, is situated about twelve miles to the north.

The Norwegian Lutheran Mission has a representative church in Antanànarìvo, as well as a training institution, orphanage, schools, and hospital. Its chief work is south of Imèrina and in the Bètsilèo province, where there are a large number of stations.

The Roman Catholic Jesuit Mission has four churches in the capital. Of these, the largest one, or cathedral, close to Andohàlo, is a handsome stone structure with towers crowned by octagonal lanterns. There are also large buildings as residences for priests, lay brothers, and sisters of mercy, and for schools and press.[1]

It will be seen from the above sketch that Antanànarìvo is the centre of a large amount of Christian work and activity. Its twenty-seven L.M.S. town and suburban churches and schools, although they all have their own native pastors and preachers, still, however, need the help and guidance and teaching of English missionaries; and for a long time to come its college, schools, presses, hospitals, &c., will require the same oversight. And when it is remembered that, in addition to the above churches and their large districts, there are also five out-stations of the L.M.S. at a few miles' distance from the capital, with about three hundred more congregations, it is evident that English missionaries in the central province of Madagascar have unusual opportunities of service for Christ. The greater part of all these nine hundred congregations have only come out of heathenism within the last twenty-five years, and numbers of the people are still (can we wonder at it?) very ignorant and superstitious. The claims of the still completely heathen districts of Madagascar are, it is true, very urgent; but while more ought to be done for these, we cannot afford at present a single man from the wide field close to our hands and open to our teaching with hardly any external hindrance. It may safely be said that in no other part of the world are there such favourable opportunities of service for our Master. In almost every other mission-field the people have with difficulty to be drawn out of heathenism to hear the sound of the Gospel; *here* they are already gathered into hundreds of congregations, their idols destroyed, and are willing to listen to the Word of Life.

[1] A new French Protestant Church has been established (1896), under the auspices of the French Resident-General, M. Hippolyte Laroche, at Ambàtonakànga, where services are conducted by the Pasteurs, MM. Logat and Kruger. —ED.

In concluding this description of Antanànarìvo it will be evident from what has been said that this capital of the Hova Malagasy is no mere collection of huts, nor is it like a Kaffir kraal, but is gradually becoming a respectable city; and it is only fair to add that the advances in civilisation, enlightenment, and intelligence, which are so manifest in the capital, and also, in fair proportion, in other towns throughout the central provinces, are the direct results of the labour of Christian missionaries, chiefly those of the London Missionary Society. This society, more than sixty years ago, sent to Madagascar artisan missionaries, as well as those whose work was more directly educational and religious; and to their united efforts the Malagasy chiefly owe the material progress they have already made, as well as the Christian teaching which has broken down the old idolatry of the people, which has covered the central provinces with hundreds of churches, which is teaching a hundred thousand children in its schools, and is gradually raising up a formerly ignorant and semi-barbarous tribe to the position of an enlightened and Christian people.

The population of Antanànarìvo is difficult to estimate exactly. No census appears to have been taken by the native Government, but the houses have been counted by some of my friends, and careful inquiries made as to the average number of occupants, and from these it is believed by some that the population of the city is much over 100,000. I should be inclined to put it at from 60,000 to 70,000.[1] There is frequently a large number of strangers in the capital, as people come constantly from all parts of the island on Government business, bringing tribute, and receiving orders from the Sovereign; and on special occasions, as when levies of troops are being made, &c., the ordinary population of the city must be swelled by many thousands.

Many years ago, during the time of the early mission of the London Missionary Society, a plan of Antanànarìvo was made

[1] *Vide ante*, p. 44. Population is only 43,000.—ED.

by Mr. Cameron (whose name has already been mentioned in this chapter), and was published in Ellis's *History of Madagascar* (1838). The city has of course greatly increased since then; and within the last six or seven years a new detailed plan to a large scale has been made from surveys by French officers.

Antanànarìvo may justly be considered the heart of Madagascar. There is the seat of government and of the most advanced civilisation of the country; from it go out the Hova officers and soldiers who garrison every port on the coast and every important town in the interior; from it go out weekly thousands of books and copies of the Sacred Scriptures; and there are trained the native doctors and surgeons and nurses, the schoolmasters and evangelists and teachers, who are sent to distant places to labour together with their European teachers in various ways to benefit their fellow-countrymen, and to hasten that day when, as we hope, the whole of Madagascar shall share in the advance and enlightenment which is already so marked in the central province of Imèrina and in the capital city, Antanànarìvo.

INDEX TO NUMBERS ON MAP.

	Commenced.		Commenced.
Palace Church	1869	13. Ambàtomitsàngana	1863
1. Ambàtonakànga	{1831 / 1861}	14. Fiadànana, E.	1867
		15. Fiadànana, W.	1872
2. Anàlakèly	1861	16. Isòanieràna	1867
3. Ampàribè	1861	17. Ankàdimbahòaka	1865
4. Ambòhipòtsy	1863	18. Andròndra	1867
5. Ankàdibèvàva	1863	19. Mahàzoarivo	1863
6. Ampàmarinana	1864	20. Ambòhimiàndra	1863
7. Andohàlo	1864	21. Andraisòro	1866
8. Ambòhitantèly	1864	22. Ambàtoròka	1869
9. Fàravòhitra	1868	23. Ankàdifòtsy	1868
10. Imàhamàsina	1867	24. Tànimèna	1869
11. Isòtry	1867	25. Anjànahàry	1869
12. Ambànidìa	1868	26. Manjàkaray	1861

CHAPTER IV.

THE CHANGING YEAR IN CENTRAL MADAGASCAR: NOTES ON THE CLIMATE, AGRICULTURE, SOCIAL CUSTOMS OF THE PEOPLE, AND VARIED ASPECTS OF THE MONTHS.

The seasons in Madagascar—Their significant names—Prospect from summit of Antanànarivo—The great rice-plain—Springtime : September and October—Rice-planting and rice-fields—First crop—Trees and foliage—"Burning the Downs"—Birds—Summer : November to February—Thunderstorms and tropical rains—Effects on roads—Rainfall—Hail—Magnificent lightning effects—Malagasy New Year—Native calendar—Royal bathing—Conspicuous flowers—Aloes and agaves—Christmas Day observances—Uniformity in length of days—Native words and phrases for divisions of time—And for natural phenomena—Effects of heavy rains—Wild flowers of Imèrina—Autumn : March and April—Rice harvest—Harvest Thanksgiving Services—Mist effects on winter mornings—Spiders' webs—Winter : May to August—Winter the dry season—Great markets—Aspects of nightly sky—Epidemics in cold season—Vegetation.

MY object in this chapter is to describe the varied aspects of the different months throughout the year in this central province of Imèrina, as they present themselves to any one who lives in the capital city of Antanànarìvo, and is frequently travelling in the country around it. I want to show the variety of Nature during the changing seasons, as the result of the heat or cold, and of the moisture or drought of the climate, and to point out the changes resulting from the different processes of agriculture carried on by the Malagasy. And it must be remembered that although this central province of Madagascar is by several degrees well within the tropics, our climate for some months of the year is by no means the

ANTÀNANARÌVO FROM THE WEST, SOUTH END OF THE CITY.

"tropical" one supposed in our ordinary English use of that word. On these interior highlands, from 3,000 to 5,000 feet above the sea level, the south-easterly winds blow from June to August with a keenness and force which it needs thick clothing to withstand, and makes a wood fire during the long evenings a very pleasant addition to the comforts of home life.

The seasons in the central regions of the island are practically only two : the hot and rainy period, from the beginning of November to the end of April; and the cool and dry period, during the other months, from May to October. The Malagasy are, however, accustomed to speak of four seasons of their year, viz., the *Lóhataona*, *i.e.*, "head of the year," during September and October, when the planting of rice is going on everywhere, and a few showers give promise of the coming rains; the *Fàhavàratra*, *i.e.*, "thunder-time," when severe storms of thunder and lightning are frequent, with heavy downpours of rain, from the early part of November to the end of February or into March; the *Fàraràno*, *i.e.*, "last rains," from the beginning of March and through April; and lastly, the *Rirínina*, *i.e.*, "time of bareness," when the grass becomes dry and withered, from June to August.

Taking, therefore, the seasons in order, from the beginning, not of January, which gives no natural division of the year, but from the early part of September, when the blossoms on the trees speak of the "good time coming" of renewed verdure, I shall note down, in their succession, the varying aspects of the country, in climate, vegetation, and culture of the soil, throughout "the changing year."

Before, however, proceeding to do this, it may give greater distinctness to the mental picture I want to draw for those who have never been in Madagascar, if I try to describe in a few words the appearance of this central province of the island, especially of that portion of it which is in the neighbourhood of the capital. Let us go up to the highest point of the long rocky ridge on and around which Antanànarlvo is built, from which we can "view the landscape o'er," and try and gain a clear notion of this "heart of Imèrina," as it is often called by the Malagasy. The city hill reaches its greatest elevation at a point called Ambòhimitsímbina, *i.e.*, "Hill of regarding," which is 700 feet above the general level of the rice-plains around it. From this "coign of vantage" there is of course a very extensive view in every direction, and we see at once that the surrounding country is very mountainous. East and south there is little but hills of all shapes and sizes to be seen, except along the valleys of the river Ikòpa and its tributaries, which come from the edge of the upper forest, thirty miles or so away to the east. To the north the country is more undulating, but at ten or twelve miles away high hills and moors close in the view. Some of the hills rise into mountains, as in the case of Angàvokèly to the east, Milangàna, Andríngitra, and Lòhavòhitra to the north and north-west, and Ihàranàndriana to the south. The country is everywhere in these directions, except in the river valleys, covered with red soil, through which the granite and gneiss foundations protrude at almost every elevated point in huge boulder-like rocks.

There is little foliage to be seen, except on the top of some of the hills, where the ancient towns and villages were built, and in such places a circle of old *Aviàvy* trees, with an occasional *Amòntana*[1] tree, gives a pleasant relief to the prevailing red and ochre tints of the bare hills. The largest mass of green is at the old capital, Ambòhimànga, eleven miles away to the north, where the steep sides of the hill are still covered with a remnant of the original forest, which formerly was doubtless much more extensive in this part of Imèrina.

To the west, from north to south, the prospect differs considerably from that to the east. To the south-west there rises by very gradual slopes, at some thirty-five miles' distance, the mass of Ankàratra, the highest point in the island, its three or four crowning peaks reaching an elevation of nearly 9,000 feet

[1] *Ficus Baroni*, Baker, and *Ficus trichosphæra*, Baker.

above the sea, and something more than half that height above the general level of the country. Due west and north-west is a considerable extent of level country, beyond which the mountain of Ambòhimiangàra, sixty miles away, is seen on the horizon, as well as many other hills. In the foreground, stretching away many miles, is the great rice-plain of Bètsimitàtatra, from which numbers of low red hills, most of them with villages, rise like islands out of a green sea when the rice is growing; along the plain the river Ikòpa can be seen, winding its way north-westwards to join the Bètsibòka; the united streams, with many tributaries, flowing into the sea at the Bay of Bèmbatòka. This great plain, "the granary of Antanànarìvo," was formerly an immense marsh, and earlier still a lake; but since the embanking of the river by some of the early kings of Imèrina, it has become the finest rice-plain in the island, and, with its connected valleys, furnishes the bulk of the food of the people of the central province.

From this elevated point at least a hundred small towns and villages can be recognised, many of them marked by the tiled roof of the village church, which shines out distinctly in the sunshine amid the brown thatched roofs of most of the houses, and can be easily distinguished at distances of ten or twelve miles away. This view from the summit of the capital is certainly in its way unrivalled for variety and extent, as well as for the human interest of its different parts, as shown by the large population, the great area of cultivated land, the embanked rivers, and the streams and water-channels for irrigation seen in every direction.

SPRINGTIME: SEPTEMBER AND OCTOBER.—With the early days of September we may usually say that springtime in Imèrina fairly sets in, and that the year in its natural aspects properly commences. By a true instinct, arising doubtless from long observation of the change of the seasons, the Malagasy call this time *Lòhataona*, i.e., "the head, or beginning, of the year," when nature seems to awake from the comparative deadness of the cold and dry winter months, during which the country has looked bare and uninviting, but now begins again to give promise of fertility and verdure. The keen cold winds and drizzly showers of the past few weeks give place to warmer air and clearer skies, and although usually there is but little rain during September, the deciduous trees begin to put forth their leaves, and flower-buds appear as heralds of the fuller display of vegetable life which will be seen after the rains have fallen.

The great rice-plain to the west looks, during the early days of the *Lòhataona*, bare and brown; but we shall see that in various places, where the plain borders the low rising grounds on which the villages are built, there are bright patches of vivid green. These are the *kètsa* grounds, or smaller rice-fields, where the rice is first sown thick and broadcast, and where it grows for a month or two before being planted out in the larger fields. These *kètsa* patches begin to be very numerous also in the smaller valleys which are found in every part of the province; and as soon as the young plants are 4 or 5 inches high they are frequently strewn over with long dry grass to protect them from the hot sun by day as well as from the cold winds by night. In other rice-patches large fronds of bracken fern are used for the same purpose, and small branches of trees are also stuck along the edges of the enclosures, which are divided from each other by a low bank of earth, a few inches broad and only a foot or two in height.

As the season advances the people begin to be busy digging up their rice-fields, the clods being piled up in heaps and rows in order to give the soil the benefit of exposure to the sun and air. All this work is done by the native long-handled and long- and narrow-bladed spade, driven into the ground by the weight of the handle, as the Malagasy wear no shoes, and so could not drive down the spade by the foot in European fashion, while the plough is still an unknown implement to them. The watercourses, by which water is brought to every rice-plot, are now being repaired in all directions. The chief supply of water is from the springs found at the head of almost every valley, which is carefully led by channels cut and embanked round the curves of the hillsides, being often taken thus for a considerable distance from its source. Eventually this little canal resolves itself into a small stream traversing the valley, from which smaller channels convey the water to every field, so as to moisten the clods after they have been dug over.

The water-supply for the great Bètsimitàtatra plain is derived from the Ikòpa river and its tributaries the Andròmba, the Sisaony, the Màmba, and other streams. Canals tap these rivers at various points, in order to irrigate the fields at lower levels further down their course. A large quantity of water is thus diverted from the rivers during September and October, so that the smaller streams are almost dry, and even the Ikòpa and its affluents, good-sized rivers at other times of the year, then become shallow and easily fordable.

Before the end of October a large extent of the great plain, especially to the north and north-west, is completely planted with rice; and a green level, looking like one vast lawn, stretches away for many miles in this direction, without any break or visible divisions. This green is the *vàry alòha*, or "former rice," the first crop, which will become ripe in the month of January, or early in February. Smaller expanses of bright green appear in other directions also, especially along the courses of the rivers, but a considerable extent of the plain directly to the west of the capital is still russet brown in colour, and will not be planted until a month or two later. From this will come the later rice crop, or, as it is called, the (*vàry*) *vàky ambiàty*, which is planted in November or December, and becomes fit for cutting about April. This latter crop is so called because the flowering of the *Ambiàty* shrub,[1] about November, gives notice to the people that planting-time has come. This shrub is very conspicuous about this time of the year from its masses of white flowers.

[1] *Vernonia appendiculata*, Less.

The *kètsa* grounds are covered before sowing with a layer of wood and straw ashes, so that they have quite a black appearance. Before this, however, the clods have been broken up and worked by the spade into a soft mud, with an inch or two of water over all, and on this the grain is sown broadcast, springing up in two or three weeks' time and looking like a brilliant emerald carpet.

There are usually a few heavy showers about the end of September or the early part of October, which are called *ránonòrana mámpisàra-taona*, *i.e.*, "rain dividing the year"; but occasionally no rain falls until the rainy season regularly commences, so it is dry and dusty everywhere, the ground cracks, and everything seems thirsting for moisture. The heat increases as the sun gets more nearly vertical with the advancing season, although the nights are pleasantly cool. Yet notwithstanding the dry soil, the trees are beginning to blossom. Most conspicuous among them is the Cape-lilac,[1] a tree introduced from South Africa about seventy years ago by the first L.M.S. missionaries, and now thoroughly naturalised. It grows to be a good-sized tree, and many hundreds of them are to be seen in all the suburbs of Antanànarìvo, making them gay with the profusion of lilac flowers which cover the trees, and fragrant with their strong perfume.

There are many large orchards in Imèrina, thickly planted with mango-trees, and about this time the green of the leaves is largely mingled with a tinting of reddish brown, which is caused by the masses of flowers in the upper part of the trees. The low banks of earth which form the boundary walls of plantations are largely planted with a species of *Euphorbia*,[2] of which there are two varieties—one with brilliant scarlet bracts, and the other of pale yellow tint, the leaves appearing on the prickly stems later on.

As the season advances, the people burn the grass over the hillsides and the open moor country, so as to get rid of the

---

[1] *Melia Azederach*, L.   [2] *Euphorbia splendens*, Bojer.

long dry grass and to obtain a crop of green herbage as soon as the rains have fallen plentifully. This has an unpleasant appearance by day, from the immense black patches of charred vegetation to be seen in every direction; and frequently the hedges and smaller trees are destroyed as well. There can be no doubt that to this practice of *mandóro tanèty* ("burning the down"), as it is called, is largely attributable the bare and treeless appearance of the central provinces. The young trees which would spring up, especially in the hollows and sheltered places, have no chance against the yearly fires which sweep over the country, and the little vegetation which has held its own is constantly liable to be lessened as time goes on. Sometimes a dozen fires, long curving lines of flame, may be seen at night in different directions; and a ruddy glow in the sky often shows the places where the actual fire is hidden from view by intervening hills. *Mandòro tanèty* thus gives a strangely picturesque appearance to the nights of springtime in Imèrina.

The weather often gets very hot and sultry before the rains come on, indeed the heat is greater and more trying at this time than in the summer itself, when the frequent storms freshen the air, and the rain cools the earth. The clear skies and pure atmosphere of other months are exchanged for thick, oppressive days, when the distant hills disappear altogether, and the nearer ones seem quite distant in the dense haze. These atmospheric conditions are probably due to the grass-burning just described, and also to the frequent burning of the forest away to the east. As the weather gets warmer, a few birds come up from the wooded regions of the island, and wherever there is a small patch of wood, the oft-repeated cry of the *Kankàfotra*, the Madagascar Cuckoo, may be heard, much resembling the syllables "*kow-kow, kow-kow-koo.*" The querulous cry of the noisy little *Hìtsikìtsika*, or Kestrel, is heard continually, for he and his mate are now bringing up their young brood and busily seeking food for them. As we walk over the downs, the *Soròhitra*, the native Lark, darts up from her nest on the bare ground, with a note somewhat like that of her European cousin's, but not so full and sweet.

As the end of October draws near, the people are busily at work, not only in the rice-fields, but also repairing their houses, mending their grass or rush roofs, and hurrying on their sun-dried brick or clay building before the heavy rains fall. Although a large number of burnt-brick houses, with tiled roofs, have now been erected, the majority of native dwellings are still of the cheaper materials; and everything of the kind must be finished, or at least well protected from the weather, before the rainy season comes on. The watercourses, too, need attention, and the river banks must be repaired, lest a succession of heavy rains should swell the streams, break through the embankments, and flood the rice-plains.

SUMMER: NOVEMBER, DECEMBER, JANUARY, AND FEBRUARY.—Summer is not only the hot season, but it is also the rainy season, very little rain falling at any other time of the year. It is accordingly called by the Malagasy *Fàhavàratra*, *i.e.*, "thunder-time," since almost all heavy rain is accompanied by a thunderstorm; and taking the average of a good many years, this season may be said to commence at the beginning of November.

As the sun gets every day more nearly vertical at noon, on his passage towards the southern tropic, the heat increases, and the electric tension of the air becomes more oppressive. For a week or more previous to the actual commencement of the rains, the clouds gather towards evening, and the heavens are lighted up at night by constant flashes of lightning. But at length, after a few days of this sultry weather, towards mid-day the huge cumuli gather thickly over the sky and gradually unite into a dense mass, purple black in colour, and soon the thunder is heard. It rapidly approaches nearer and nearer, the clouds touching the lower hills, then down darts the forked lightning, followed by the roar of the thunder, and presently a wild rush of wind, as if it came from all quarters at once, tells us that the storm is upon us, and then comes the rain in big, heavy drops for a few seconds and soon in torrents, as if the sluice-gates of the clouds were opened. The lightning is almost incessant, and for half an hour or so there is often hardly any interval between the crashing and reverberations of the thunder peals, the hills around the capital echoing back the roar from the clouds. Certainly a heavy thunderstorm in Madagascar is not without a considerable element of danger, especially for any one caught in a storm in the open, or in a house unprotected by a lightning-conductor. Every house of any pretensions in the central provinces has this safeguard, for every year many people are killed by lightning—some while walking in the road, and others in houses unprotected by a conductor; for instance, one of our college students, travelling with wife and children to the Bètsilèo, was killed instantaneously, as well as a slave near him, when sitting in a native house, while a child he was nursing at the time escaped with a few burns only.

A large quantity of rain sometimes falls during such storms in a very short time. On the 19th of January, 1892, $3\frac{1}{4}$ inches fell in less than half an hour; and as the streets and paths through the capital are all very steep, and from the rocky nature of the whole hill there can be no underground drainage, it may be imagined what a roar of water there is all over the city after such a storm. The three or four chief thoroughfares are transformed into the beds of rushing torrents and series of cascades, and it is no wonder that most of the highways of the capital get deeper and deeper every year. Even where there is an attempt at a rough paving, a single storm will often tear it up and pile the stones together in a big hole, with no more order than obtains in the bed of a cataract. After the rains are over, the red soil is dug away from the sides to fill up the channel cut by the torrent, and so the road gradually sinks below the walls of the compounds on either side of it.

Taking the average of eleven years (1881-1890), the annual rainfall of Antanànarìvo was 52 inches; and of this, omitting decimals, $5\frac{1}{2}$ inches fell in October, $5\frac{3}{4}$ inches in November, $10\frac{1}{3}$ inches in December, 11 inches in January, 9 inches in February, 8 inches in March, and 2 inches in April; so that December and January are the wettest months, during which rain falls usually on two days out of every three.

It is very unusual for thunderstorms to occur in the morning, they mostly come on in the afternoon; and after the first heavy downpour, a steady rain will often continue for three or four hours, and occasionally far into the night. It is generally bright and fine in the early morning; all vegetation is refreshed by the plentiful moisture; and the people are busy in their plantations on the sloping hillsides, digging up the softened earth for planting manioc, sweet potatoes, the edible arum, and many other vegetables.

Hail also very frequently falls during these thunderstorms, and should it be late in the season, when the rice is in ear, great damage is often done to the growing crop. A large extent of rice-field will sometimes be stripped of every grain, the stalks standing up like bare sticks. Charms against hail had therefore in the old heathen times a prominent place in the popular beliefs and, there can be little doubt, are still trusted in and used by many of the more ignorant people. Occasionally the hailstones are of very large size and kill sheep and small animals, if they are left unsheltered. I remember a storm of this kind (Oct. 22, 1887), when the hailstones were as large as good-sized nuts, while some were cushion-shaped and hexagonal with a hollow in the centre, and nearly $1\frac{1}{2}$ inches in diameter. In other cases they have been seen as jagged lumps of ice; and it may be easily imagined that it is very unpleasant and somewhat dangerous to be exposed to such a fusilade.

Besides the thunderstorms like those just described, which come so close and are often so awful in their results, there is another kind of storm we frequently see in the rainy season which is an unmixed source of delight. This is when, for two or three hours together in the evening, a large portion of the sky is lighted up by an almost incessant shimmer of lightning. All the time no thunder is heard from this celestial display, but it is most fascinating to watch the infinitely varied effects of light and darkness.

As the Malagasy New Year's Day now comes in the month of November, it may be fitting to say something here about the native division of time. The Malagasy months are lunar ones and therefore their year, reckoning by the months, is eleven days shorter than our own, the first day of their year coming consequently at different times, from the first to the twelfth month, until the cycle is complete. When I first came to Madagascar (in 1863), the Malagasy New Year's Day, that is, the first of Alàhamàdy, was in the month of March, and in this year, 1894, the first of that Malagasy month fell on the 6th of April, the cycle of thirty-three years being thus nearly finished. But since the accession of the present Sovereign, Queen Rànavàlona III., in 1883, the 22nd of November, which is her Majesty's birthday, has been fixed as the invariable New Year's Day; and most of the old ceremonies always observed previous to the year 1883 on the first day of the first month (Alàhamàdy) are now kept up on the eve of November 22nd. The old New Year's Day, the birthday of the father of Radàma I., is still, however, held in remembrance by the firing of cannon on the first of Alàhamàdy. The Malagasy appear never to have made any attempt, by the insertion of intercalary days or any other contrivance, to fill up their shorter year to the true time occupied in the earth's annual revolution round the sun; for of course they must have noticed that their months came at quite different periods after a very few years. The names of the Malagasy months in use in the central province and in most other parts of the island are all Arabic in origin, as indeed are the names of the days of the week. In some districts, however, other names are employed, which mostly appear to be purely Malagasy words. It may be noticed here that the Malagasy month-names are not the Arabic names for the months, but are the Arabic words for the twelve constellations of the Zodiac. Thus, Alàhamàdy is the Ram, Adaoro is the Bull (*daoro=taurus*), Adizaoza is the Twins, and so on. This appears to have arisen from the connection between astrology and the divination (*sikìdy*) introduced by the Arabs several centuries ago.

A full account of the *Fandròana* or "Bathing," as the New Year's festival is called, cannot be given here, as a complete description would form a separate chapter of some length. It must suffice to say that although some of the ancient customs have fallen and are still falling into disuse, most of them are still kept up. The most prominent of these are the following:— (1) The lighting of little bundles of dried grass at dusk on the evenings of the 20th and the 21st of November, the latter, the eve of the 22nd, being considered as the commencement of the New Year's Day itself, for the Malagasy, like other Orientals, reckon "the evening and the morning" as the proper order of the day. These fires, possibly a relic of the old fire-worship, are called *harèndrina*, and form one of the most pleasing features of the festival in the gathering darkness of the evening. (2) The ceremonial Royal Bathing at the great Palace, when all the principal people of the kingdom are present, as well as representative foreigners, is perhaps the most prominent of all the ceremonies, giving, as it does, the name to the whole festival. This is followed by a ceremonial bathing, or at least sprinkling of water, by all households. (3) On the following day comes the killing of oxen, doubtless the most important of all Fandròana observances in the estimation of the people generally, at any rate of the poorer classes, who then get, for once a year at least, a plentiful supply of beef. Presents of the newly-killed meat are sent about in all directions to relatives and friends, and feasting and merrymaking prevail for several days among all classes. (4) For some time previous to the actual festival, it is customary for the Malagasy to visit their elders and superiors in rank, bringing presents of money, fowls, fruit, &c., using certain complimentary formulæ and expressions of good wishes.

The abundant rains which usually fall in November soon make the hills and downs, which have got so brown and dry during the cold season, to become green again, and although wild flowers are certainly not plentiful, there are several kinds which now make their appearance. Among these are the *Vonènina*,[1] with large pink flowers; the *Avòko*,[2] bright crimson; the *Nìfinakànga*,[3] deep blue; several small vetch-like plants with yellow flowers; many others with minute yellow compound flowers, and some few other kinds.

Besides flowers growing on the ground, there are many shrubs and small trees now in blossom, although some are by no means confined in floral display to the warm and rainy season. Along the hedges in one or two localities is a small bush, with clusters of purple flowers, called *Famàmo*;[4] branches of these shrubs are sometimes placed in a pool or stream, so as to stupefy, and thus easily obtain, any fish present in the water. Very conspicuous are the bright yellow flowers of the *Tainakòho*[5] and the *Tsiàfakòmby*,[6] and the orange yellow spikes of the *Seva*.[7] More showy and handsome still perhaps are the abundant large yellow flowers of the prickly-pear, which is so largely used for hedges and for the defences of the old towns and villages. A species of *Hibiscus*,[8] is not uncommon, with yellow flowers, which have deep red in the centre; yellow seems indeed the most common colour in the flora of Imèrina. At this time of the year also three or four species of aloe come into flower. The larger of these, called *Vàhona*[9] by the Malagasy, is much used for planting as a hedge, from its fleshy leaves being armed with sharp prickles; its tall flower-spike shoots up very rapidly to a height of 4 or 6 feet. Another and smaller one, called *Sahòndra*,[10] has its flowers branching at the top of the stalk something like a candelabrum. The numerous flowers attract, as they expand,

[1] *Vinca rosea*, L.
[2] *Vigna angivensis*, Baker.
[3] *Commelyna madagascarica*, C. B. Clarke.
[4] *Mundulea suberosa*, Benth.
[5] *Cassia lævigata*, Willd.
[6] *Cæsalpinia scpiaria*, Roxb.
[7] *Buddleia madagascariensis*, Lam.
[8] *Hibiscus diversifolius*, Jacq.
[9] *Aloe macroclada*, Baker.
[10] *Aloe capitata*, Baker.

swarms of bees. Another plant, like an aloe in appearance, called *Tarétra*[1] by the natives, has long leaves, with a sharp spine at the ends only; and its flower-stalk shoots up like a small mast to a height of 20 feet, with widely-spreading branchlets and an immense number of light-coloured flowers. Strong fibre used as thread is obtained from the leaves, the name of the plant being indeed that used for "thread." The tall flower-stalks of these aloes and agaves form quite a noticeable feature in the Imèrina landscape in the early summer. In the orchards, soon after the mango has finished flowering, we may see the curious whitish flowers of the Rose-apple,[2] a sort of ball of long stamens, showing conspicuously among the foliage.

Towards the beginning of December the earlier crop of rice comes into ear; and should the rains fall as usual during November, the remaining portions of the great rice-plain will be all planted out with the later crop, the whole of the level and its branching valleys presenting an unbroken expanse of green. Of this, the early rice shows distinctly as a darker shade of colour, although it will soon begin to turn yellow, as the grain ripens under the steady heat and the plentiful rainfall. Perhaps this is the time when Bètsimitàtatra is seen in its most attractive and beautiful aspect, for every part of it is covered with rice in some stage or other of growth and cultivation.

Since the reception of Christianity by the people of the central provinces of Madagascar, Christmas Day has become a very generally observed festival. As far as can be ascertained, the first Protestant missionaries (1820-1836) do not appear to have enjoined its observance upon their converts; it seems to have become customary to keep it as a festival at some time during the suppression of open Christian worship, probably during the latter years of Rànavàlona I., when severe measures against the "praying people" became less common. However this may be, on the re-establishment of the L.M.S. Mission in 1862, the observance of Christmas became very general with the

[1] *Agave Ixtli*, Karw. [2] *Eugenia malaccensis*, L.

Christians, and it has kept its hold upon them ever since. Every congregation meets in the morning of the day, either in its own church, or, more frequently, in the case of the country people, in large united gatherings of half a dozen to a dozen neighbouring congregations in the open air. Looking round on the country from any good position in the capital during the forenoon of Christmas Day and following days, one may see at many miles' distance, on various elevated points, a great mass of white, showing where one of these large assemblies is gathered together for worship. To such services people who are seldom seen at church on other occasions make a point of coming; although one can hardly believe that their motives for attendance even then are of a very high order. It is a great day for showing off the best dresses the people possess, or can borrow or hire for the occasion; the men often look very uncomfortable and awkward in suits of European cloth clothing, instead of their far more becoming and graceful native *làmba*, over white shirt and trousers. And the women, although they wisely retain the *làmba*, often have these of brightly coloured silk, and they also consider it a point of good breeding to sport the smartest of shoes and boots they can procure, although they seldom cramp their feet in such uncomfortable contrivances on other occasions. Jewellery, coral beads, and other ornaments are brought out, their hair is elaborately plaited, handsome embroidered dresses are worn, smart parasols and sun-shades are carried, and every one tries to get something extra to show himself, and especially herself, to the best advantage.

Great pains and trouble are often taken to get up special hymns, or at least musical compositions with some Scripture or religious allusions in them, for the Christmas services; these are often elaborate and wonderful performances, and sometimes the teacher is paid a considerable sum for his trouble in training his choir. Several sermons or addresses are delivered at these outdoor gatherings, and the services of popular and eloquent preachers are often secured, so as to give greater interest to the occasion.

About Christmas-time also many congregations have a feast together, generally in some mango orchard, for the sake of the shade. Here the people are arranged in rows on either side of primitive tablecloths consisting of fresh banana-leaves. Great piles of boiled rice are brought in huge wooden platters, generally the *sahàfa* or rice-winnowing dish ; while the *laoka* or accompaniments, consisting of stewed beef or geese or fowls, with gravy and green vegetables, is brought in any and every kind of crockery that can be borrowed for the feast. The repast is concluded by a dessert of sliced pineapple, peaches, and bananas, all of which fruits are cheap and plentiful ; and it is a pleasant sight to see the people enjoy themselves in this innocent fashion.

In Imèrina there is only about two hours' difference in the length of the longest day, about Christmas, and the shortest day, early in July. It is dark at about seven o'clock on the 1st of January, and at about six o'clock on the 1st of July. Thus we have no long evenings ; but, on the other hand, we escape the long nights and the short days of the English winter. We lose also the long twilights of the temperate zone, although I have never seen the almost instantaneous darkness one sometimes reads about in books as following the sunset. There is a twilight of from fifteen to twenty minutes' duration in this part of Madagascar. Very seldom have we a wet morning in any part of the year, and the heat is not more oppressive than it often is in hot summers in England.

It may be interesting to notice at this point the numerous words used by the Malagasy to indicate the different times of the day, from morning to evening. Clocks and watches are comparatively a recent introduction into Madagascar, nor do the people ever seem to have contrived any kind of sun-dial, although, as will be seen, they did use something else as a kind of substitute for such a timekeeper. It should be remembered that the hours given (counting in European fashion) as equivalents for these native divisions of the night and the day are only approximations, and must be taken as the *mean* of the year, or, in other words, at about the time of equal day and night, towards the end of March or of September. They are as follows:—

Malagasy	English	Time
Mamàtou' àlina, or *Misàsaka àlina,*	Centre of night, or Halving of night,	about 12.0 midnight
Manéno sàhona,	Frog-croaking,	„ 2.0 a.m.
Manéno akòho,	Cock-crowing,	„ 3.0 „
Maraina àlina kòa,	Morning also night,	„ 4.0 „
Manéno goaika,	Crow croaking,	„ 5.0 „
Mànga vòdilànitra, *Mangòan' atsinànana,* *Mangìrau-dràtsy,*	Bright horizon, Reddish east Glimmer of day,	„ 5.15 „
Ahitàn-tsòratr' òmby,	Colours of cattle can be seen,	„ 5.30 „
Mazàva ràtsy	Dusk,	„ „ „ „
Mifòha òlo-mazòto,	Diligent people awake,	„ „ „ „
Maraina kòa,	Early morning,	„ „ „ „
Vàky màsoàndro, *Vàky àndro,* *Pìakàudro,*	Sunrise, Daybreak, „ „	„ 6.0 „
Autoàudro be nànahàry, *Efa bàna ny àndro,*	Broad daylight, „ „	„ „ „ „
Mihíntsana dudo,	Dew-falls,	„ 6.15 „
Mivòaka òmby,	Cattle go out (to pasture),	„ „ „ „
Maim-bòhou-dràvina,	Leaves are dry (from dew),	„ 6.30 „
Afa-dràuom-panàla, *Manàra vàva ny àndro,*	Hoar-frost disappears, The day chills the mouth, [1]	„ 6.45 „
Misàudratra àndro,	Advance of the day,	„ 8.0 „
Mitatao hàratra,	Over (at a right angle with) the purlin,	„ 9.0 „
Mitatao vovóuana,	Over the ridge of the roof,	„ 12.0 noon
Maudray tokónana ny àndro,	Day taking hold of the threshold,	„ 12.30 p.m.
Mitsídika àudro, *Làtsaka iray dìa ny àndro,* *Solàfak' àndro,*	Peeping-in of the day, Day less one step (=hour ?), Slipping of the day,	„ 1.0 „ „ 1.3 „
Tàfalàtsaka ny àndro, *Mihílana ny àudro,*	Decline of the day = afternoon,	to „ 2.0 „
Am-pitotòam-bàry,	At the rice-pounding place,	„ „ „ „
Mby amin' ny àudry ny àndro,	At the house-post,	„ „ „ „
Am-pamatòrau-jànak' òmby,	At the place of tying the calf,	„ 3.0 „
Mby am-pisòko ny àudro,	At the sheep or poultry pen,	„ 4.0 „
Mòdy òmby téra-bao,	The cow newly calved comes home,	„ 4.30 „

[1] These only refer to the two or three winter months.

Tàfapàka ny àndro,	Sun touching (i.e., the eastern wall),	about	5.0 p.m.
Mody òmby,	Cattle come home,	„	5.30 „
Ména màsoàndro,	Sunset flush,	„	5.45 „
Màty màsoàndro,	Sunset (lit. "Sun dead"),	„	6.0 „
Miditra akòho,	Fowls come in,	„	6.15 „
Somàmbisàmby,	Dusk, twilight,	„	6.30 „
Maizim-bàva-vilàny,	Edge of rice-cooking pan obscure,	„	6.45 „
Manókom-bàry òlona,	People begin to cook rice,	„	7.0 „
Hómam-bàry òlona,	People eat rice,	„	8.0 „
Tàpi-mihìnana,	Finished eating,	„	8.30 „
Màndry òlona,	People go to sleep,	„	9.0 „
Tapi-mandry òlona,	Every one in bed,	„	9.30 „
Mipòa-tafòndro,	Gun-fire,	„	10.0 „
Mamàton' alina,	Midnight,	„	12.0 „

This list is, I think, a very interesting one and shows the primitive pastoral and agricultural habits of the Hova Malagasy before they were influenced by European civilisation. Previous to their knowledge of clocks and watches (which are still unknown to the majority of people away from the capital), the native houses thus served as a rude kind of dial. As, until recent times, these were always built with their length running north and south, and with the single door and window facing the west, the sunlight coming in after mid-day at the open door gave, by its gradual progress along the floor, a fairly accurate measure of time to people amongst whom time was not of very much account. In the forenoon, the position of the sun, nearly square with the eastern purlin of the roof, marked about 9 o'clock; and as noon approached its vertical position, about the ridge-pole, or at least its reaching the meridian, clearly showed 12 o'clock. Then, as the sunlight gradually passed westward and began to peer in at the door, at about 1 o'clock, it announced "the peeping-in of the day" (*mitsídika àndro*); and then, as successive points on the floor were reached by the advancing rays, several of the hours of the afternoon were sufficiently clearly marked off:—"the place of rice-pounding" (*am-pitotòam-bàry*), as the light fell on the rice-mortar, further into the house; "the calf-fastening place" (*am-pamatòran-jànak'* òmby), as the rays reached one of the three central posts supporting the ridge, and where the calf was fastened for the night; and then, "touching" (tàfapàka), when the declining sunshine reached the eastern wall, at about half-past four in the afternoon. Other words and notes of time, it will be seen, are derived from various natural phenomena. There is a phrase, ñnja àndry, meaning "house-post notching," to denote notches or marks cut in the southern ridge-post to mark the gradual advance of the sun's rays, and from them the hours of the afternoon. Some other words for the divisions of time used by the Malagasy may be here noted. Thus "a rice-cooking" (indray màhamàsa-bàry) is frequently used to denote about half an hour; while "the frying of a locust" (indray mitòno valàla) is a phrase employed to describe a moment.

Many words exist in the Malagasy language to denote different appearances of Nature which are somewhat poetical and seem to show some imaginative power. Thus the light fleecy clouds in the upper regions of the atmosphere are called "sky gossamer" (faròra-dànitra); the sun is the "day's-eye" (màsoàndro); the galaxy is the "dividing of the year" (éfitaona); the rainbow is "God's large knife" (àntsibén' Andrìamànitra); and a waterspout is the "tail of the sky" (ràmbon-dànitra).

January is usually the wettest month in the year in Imèrina; and in some years there occurs what the Hova call the hafitóana or "seven days," that is seven days of almost continuous rain, although it more often lasts only three or four days. Such a time is not only a most uncomfortable one for all who have to go about, especially for the Malagasy, with their thin cotton clothing; but it is also most disastrous for the houses, compounds, and boundary walls. The continuous rain soaks into these and brings them down in every direction. From the steep situation of the capital, almost every house compound is built up on one side with a retaining-wall, and on the other is cut away so as to form a level space. These walls or "batteries," as they are termed, are often badly constructed and of very insufficient strength and thickness; the constant moisture soaks in, and down come hundreds of stones and tons of earth, blocking up the narrow paths and making locomotion more difficult than ever. The enclosing walls of compounds and gardens, made of several layers of the hard red soil, are also apt to be brought down in ruin at such times, although it is wonderful to see for how many years such structures will endure the storms and heavy rains of successive seasons.

The prolonged moisture combined with the heat of this time of the year naturally makes everything grow luxuriantly. Our gardens are gay with flowers; and in many places the open downs display a considerable amount of floral beauty. I have never seen elsewhere so beautiful a display of wild flowers as that which met our view when travelling from Antsìrabè in Vàkinankàratra to Antanànarìvo in the middle of December, 1887. Leaving Antsìrabè and proceeding for several miles towards the north-east, the level country up to the foot of the long ridge running north and south, which is ascended about four hours after leaving Antsìrabè, was gay with flowers, which covered the downs, and in places gave a bright colour to the surface of the ground. Among these the most prominent was a pale pink flower on stems from a foot to eighteen inches high (called by the people *Kòtosay*),[1] and also the lovely deep-blue flower called *Nìfinakànga* (lit. "guinea-fowl's tooth," see p. 65 *ante*), which latter occurred abundantly among the grass.

In many places, especially near villages, a plant with small pale-blue flowers,[2] almost exactly like our English "forget-me-not," grew in dense masses, but on stems a foot or two feet high, showing a blue-tinted surface even at a considerable distance. The *Vonènina* (see p. 65), with a pale-pink flower, was very frequent, as well as several species of bright yellow flowers.

[1] *Sopubia triphylla*, Baker.   [2] Various species of *Cynoglossum*.

Three or four species of white-flowered plants, one of which was a clematis,[1] were very frequent; and here a few late examples of terrestrial orchids were seen.

We reckoned that there were from twenty to thirty different species of wild flowers then in bloom on these downs of Vàkinankàratra, gladdening our eyes by their varied beauty and abundance as we travelled northwards on that glorious morning. As we got to the higher ground, however, I noticed that the blue *Nìfinakànga* became very scarce. The pale-pink *Kòtosay* was also much less abundant on the heights, but the white orchids were still in flower in many places. Seven weeks previously these upper downs had been also gay with great masses of a brilliant crimson flower, a leguminous plant, probably an *Indigofera*, which grew in clusters of many scores of spikes growing close together. But in December only here and there was there a flower left, and hardly a seed-pod, the great majority having been scattered by the winds.

Not only do flowers and verdure delight our eyes at this time of the year, but this is the season when the greatest variety of fruit comes in. Bananas, pine-apples, and two or three other fruits may be had all the year round, but in the rainy season we also get grapes, peaches, mangoes, plums, quinces, and oranges, and latterly apples are also becoming plentiful.

AUTUMN: MARCH AND APRIL.—Generally, both crops of rice—the earlier and the later—are all cut by the end of April, although in the northern parts of the province harvest is usually five or six weeks after that date. But if the rains are late and should happen to be scanty in February and March, as was the case this year (1894), harvest work is still going on at the end of May. In fact, owing to there being these two crops of rice, with no very exactly marked division between the two, autumn, in the sense of rice-harvest, is going on for about four months, and sometimes longer, as just mentioned, and extends over the later months of summer as well as the two months of autumn

[1] *Clematis Bojeri*, Hook.

or *Fàraràno* (March and April). In January those portions of the great rice-plain which lie north-west of the capital become golden yellow in hue, and after a few days, patches of water-covered field may be noticed in different places, showing where the crop has been cut, and the few inches of water in which it was growing show conspicuously in the prospect. As the weeks advance, this water-covered area extends over larger portions of the rice plain, until the whole of the early crop has been gathered in, so that in many directions there appear to be extensive sheets of water. I well remember, when once at Ambòhimanàrina, a large village to the north-west of Antanànarìvo, how strange it appeared to see people setting out to cross what seemed a considerable lake. But of course there was no danger, as the water was only a few inches deep.

As there are channels to conduct water to every rice-field, small canoes are largely used to bring the rice, both before and after it has been threshed, to the margin of the higher grounds and nearer to the roads. At the village just mentioned, which is like a large island surrounded by a sea of rice-plain, there is one point where a number of these channels meet and form quite a port ; and a very animated scene it presents at harvest-time, as canoe after canoe, piled up with heaps of rice in the husk, or with sheaves of it still unthreshed, comes up to the landing-place to discharge its cargo.

In a few weeks' time the watery covering of the plain is hidden by another green crop, but not of so bright and vivid a tint as the fresh-planted and growing rice. This is the *kòlikòly* or after-crop, which sprouts from the roots of the old plants. This is much shorter in stalk and smaller in ear than the first crop, and is often worth very little ; but if the rains are late, so that there is plenty of moisture, it sometimes yields a fair quantity, but it is said to be rather bitter in taste.

In cutting the rice the Malagasy use a straight-bladed knife ; and as the work proceeds, the stalks are laid in long curving narrow lines along the field, the heads of one sheaf being covered over by the cut ends of the stalks of the next sheaf. This is done to prevent the ears drying too quickly and the grain falling out before it reaches the threshing-floor. This last-named accessory to rice-culture is simply a square or circle of the hard red earth, kept clear from grass and weeds, and plastered with mud, and generally on the sloping side of a hill or rising ground close to the rice-field. Here the sheaves are piled round the threshing-floor like a low breastwork. No flail is used, but handfuls of rice are beaten on an upright stone fixed in the ground, until all the grain is separated from the straw. The unhusked rice is then carried in baskets to the owner's compound, and is usually stored in large round holes with a small circular opening dug in the hard red soil. These are lined with straw, and the mouth is covered with a flat stone, which is again covered over with earth; and in these receptacles it is generally kept dry and uninjured for a considerable time. In most years the end of April and the beginning of May are very busy times with the Malagasy; almost all other work must give way to the getting in of the harvest; the fields are everywhere dotted over with people reaping; almost all slaves, as well as the poorer people we meet along the roads, carrying a considerable load of freshly-cut grain on their heads, or a basket filled with *akòtry* or unhusked rice, and large quantities are spilt all along the roads and paths. Hence some of the most frequented thoroughfares, like the chief embankment leading out from the city westwards, swarm with rats and mice, which must pick up a very good living at this time of the year. Other animals also take toll from the harvest, especially the *Fòdy*, or Madagascar cardinal-bird, which may be seen sometimes in large flocks, the bright scarlet plumage of the cockbird making him a very conspicuous feature of the avifauna during the warmer months. These birds sometimes do considerable damage to the rice-crop. Large quantities of rice-stalks are now to be seen in all directions, spread out to dry in the sun, and they are also placed for the same purpose on the top of the clay boundary walls of the compounds.

Of late years it has become rather common for the Christian congregations to have a Harvest Thanksgiving service in their churches. The church is often elaborately decorated with rice and fruits of all descriptions, sometimes in fact to an absurd extent, so that the building looks like a greengrocer's store, as indeed may be occasionally seen even in churches in England. A much more commendable feature of these thanksgiving services is the bringing of offerings of rice and various kinds of produce for the support of the evangelists and school teachers.

As the colder weather advances, the mornings are often foggy, at least a thick white mist covers the plains and valleys soon after the sun rises, and remains for an hour or two until his increasing power disperses it. Seen from the higher grounds, and from the most elevated parts of the capital, this mist often presents a very beautiful appearance: a billowy white sea of vapour is brilliantly lit up by the sunlight, and out of this sea the hill-tops rise up like islands. But these misty mornings also reveal many things which can only be seen by very close observation, in clear sunshine, especially the webs of various species of spider. Many kinds of bush are seen to be almost covered by geometrical webs: one species seems to choose the extremities of the branches of the *Sòngosòngo*,[1] but the most common is a web averaging five or six inches in diameter, vhich is spread horizontally on tufts of grass, and may be seen by thousands, half a dozen or so in a square yard.

The aspect of vegetation, except in the rice-fields, can hardly be said to change much during the autumn months. A plant with pale yellow flowers[2] may be noticed by thousands in marshy grounds, giving quite a mass of colour in many places. A significant name given to autumn is *Ménàhitra*, *i.e.*, "the grass is red," that is, turning brown.

[1] *Euphorbia splendens*, Bojer.   [2] *Grangea madcraspatana*, Poir.

WINTER: MAY, JUNE, JULY, AND AUGUST.—We have no snow, nor is there any native word for it, for even the highest peaks of Ankàratra are too low for snow to fall on them; we never see ice (although adventurous foreigners have once or twice seen a thin film of it on pools on the highest hillsides); hoar-frost, however, is not uncommon, and occasionally the leaves of some species of vegetables, as well as those of the banana, turn black with the keen night air. And since there is no rain during our Imèrina winter, the paths are dry, and it is the best time for making long journeys, especially as there is little to be feared from fever. Winter is therefore a pleasant time; the skies are generally clear, the air is fresh and invigorating, and to the cool and bracing temperature of the winter months is doubtless largely due the health and strength which many Europeans enjoy for years together in the central provinces of Madagascar.

The long period without rain at this season naturally dries up the grass, and the hills and downs become parched and brown. *Maintàny, i.e.*, "the earth is dry," is one of the native names for this season, and it is very appropriate to the condition of things in general.[1] The rice-fields lie fallow, affording a scanty supply of grass for the cattle; and many short cuts can be made across them in various directions, for the beaten track over embankments, great and small, may be safely left for the dry and level plain.

The winter months are a favourite time for the native custom of *famadíhana*, that is, of wrapping the corpses of their deceased relatives in fresh silk cloths, as well as removing some of them to a new tomb as soon as this is finished. These are quite holiday occasions and times of feasting, and, not unfrequently, of much that is evil in the way of drinking and licentiousness.

Another very prominent feature of the social life of the Hova Malagasy is the system of holding large open-air markets

[1] Another curious native name for the end of the dry season is *Màharòra vàvy àntitra, i.e.*, "making the old women spit"!

all over the central province on the various days of the week. The largest of these is that held in the capital every Friday (Zomà), at which probably 10,000 people are densely crowded together, and where almost everything that is grown or manufactured in the province can be purchased. But two or three of the other markets held within four or five miles of Antanànarìvo do not fall far short of the Zomà market in size, especially those at Asabótsy (Saturday) to the north, and at Alàtsinainy (Monday) to the north-east. To a stranger these great markets present a very novel and interesting scene, and a good idea may be obtained as to what can be purchased here by taking a stroll through their crowded alleys and noticing what is offered for sale. The market is roughly divided into sections, according to the kind of goods sold. In one part are oxen and sheep, many of which are killed in the morning, while the meat is cut up and sold during the day. Here are turkeys, geese, ducks, and fowls by the hundred; here are great heaps of rice, both in the husk and either partially cleaned, as "red rice," or perfectly so, as "white rice"; here are piles of grey locusts, heaps of minute red shrimps, and baskets of snails, all used as "relishes" for the rice; here is *mángahàzo* or manioc root, both cooked and raw, as well as sweet-potatoes, earth-nuts, arum roots (*saonjo*), and other vegetables. In another quarter are the stalls for cottons and prints. American sheetings and Lancashire calicoes, as well as native-made cloths of hemp, *rofia* palm fibre, cotton, and silk; and not far away are basketfuls and piles of snowy cocoons of native silk for weaving. Here is the ironmongery section, where good native-made nails, rough hinges, and locks and bolts can be bought; and near them are the sellers of the neat little scales of brass or iron, with their weights for weighing the "cut money" which forms the small change of the Malagasy. There we come to the vendors of the strong and cheap native mats and baskets, made from the tough peel of the *Zozóro* papyrus,[1] and from

[1] *Cyperus imerinensis*, Boeckl.

various kinds of grass, often with graceful interwoven patterns. Yonder a small forest of upright pieces of wood points out the timber market, where beams and rafters, joists and flooring boards can be purchased, as well as strong bedsteads and doors. Not far distant from this is the place where large bundles of *Hérana* sedge,[1] arranged in sheets or "leaves," as the Malagasy call them, for roofing, can be bought; and near these again are the globular water-pots, or *sìny*, for fetching and for storing water. But it would occupy too much time and space to enumerate all the articles for sale in an Imèrina market. It is greatly to be lamented that native rum is now largely sold at many markets, in bottles, gourds, and in big earthen pots; and it must be added that at the Antanànarìvo market slaves are also exposed for sale. This is done in rather a quiet corner of the market, as if the people were a little ashamed of it.

Perhaps the star-lit skies of the evenings of the summer months are the most beautiful of all the year. At this season some of the finest of the northern constellations are seen at the same time as several of the southerly ones. The Great Bear stretches over the northern sky; higher up is the Northern Crown; the Pleiades,[2] and Orion[2] with his many brilliant neighbours, are overhead; the Southern Cross, with its conspicuous "pointers" in the Centaur, is high in the southern heavens; and the Magellan Clouds are clearly seen nearer the horizon; and all across the firmament is the Galaxy, or, as the Malagasy call it, the *efi-taona*, "the division," or "separation of the year." And then, as the circling year revolves, the great serpentine curve of Scorpio appears, and Sirius, Capella, Canopus, and many another glorious lamp of heaven light up the midnight sky. Imèrina is certainly a very favourable

[1] *Cyperus latifolius*, Poir.
[2] Curiously enough, the Malagasy appear to have given names only to these two prominent clusters of stars. The Pleiades they call *Kòtokèli-miàdi-laona*, i.e., "Little boys fighting over the rice mortar"; while the three stars of Orion's belt they call *Tèlo-no-ho-réfy*, i.e., "Three make a fathom." They have no name for the first-magnitude stars, or for the planets, except for Venus, as a morning star, viz., *Fitàrikàndro*, i.e., "Leader of the day."

country for astronomical observation, and good work may be expected from the Observatory established five years ago by the Jesuit Mission.

The month of August, the closing one in this review of the year, is often the coldest month of all, cold, that is, for a country within the tropics. All through August the keen south-eastern trades generally blow strong, and although in sheltered places the afternoon sun may be quite warm, the mornings and evenings are very cold, and during the night the mercury will often descend to very near the freezing point. The mornings are frequently misty; on some days there are constant showers of *èrika* or drizzly rain, alternating with bright sunny days and clear skies; these latter seem the very perfection of weather, bracing and health-giving. But this cold weather often brings malarial fever, which attacks great numbers of Malagasy, and also brings affections of the throat and chest, to which many fall victims. At such times their thin cotton clothing seems ill adapted for protection against the climate. This circumstance has often struck me as showing how difficult it is to change the habits of a people; for centuries past the Hova have lived in this cool highland region, yet, until very lately, few of them have made any change in their dress, which was well enough adapted for the purely tropical region from which they originally came, but quite unfitted for the keen cool air of the winter months in a country nearly 5,000 feet above the level of the sea.

The great rice-plain to the west of the capital and all the broader valleys still lie fallow, although in various places extensive sheets of water show that irrigation is commencing. Many of the fields are now being dug up, and water is allowed to flow over them to prepare the soil for planting. In the lesser valleys and at the edges of the larger rice-plains the landscape is enlivened by the bright green of the *kètsa* grounds, the smaller rice-fields or nurseries, where, as already described, the rice is sown broadcast before transplanting into the larger fields.

There are not many deciduous trees in Imèrina, so the

numerous orchards, chiefly of mangoes, look green throughout the year. Several prominent trees, however, do cast their leaves, notably the *Aviàvy*,[1] the Cape-lilac,[1] and the *Vòanónoka*,[2] a large tree very like an oak. But the Cape-lilac is beginning to put out its green buds; the peach-trees are a mass of blossom, and the *Sòngosòngo* [3] in the hedges is beginning to show its brilliant scarlet or pale yellow bracts. Wild flowers are still scarce, but the lilac flowers of the *Sèvabè* [4] bloom all through the year. The golden-orange panicles of the *Sèva* [5] now come into bloom. Nature is arousing from the inaction of the cold season, and the few trees now flowering give promise of the coming spring and summer.

Towards the end of this month the people begin to burn the dry and withered grass on the hillsides, as previously described. This time of the year is that during which, as well as in the earlier months of the cold season, the Malagasy are busy with house building and house repairing. Many of their houses are still built of the hard red clay which covers most of the country, although sun-dried brick is rapidly superseding this; and now is the time when both clay and bricks can be made as well as built into houses. There being no heavy rain, there is no risk of the work being injured if finished before the rainy season comes on.

But it is time that I conclude these sketches of Imèrina, and of the varied aspects of Nature, as well as of some of the social aspects of the people, which may be observed throughout the year. Much more might be recorded, but what has been now noted down must suffice. My principal object in writing this chapter has been to endeavour to give, if possible, to people in England some clear notion of that part of the country where we live, and of the climate and conditions surrounding us here as well as some aspects of the social life of the people amongst whom we work day by day.

[1] See pp. 54, 58, *ante*.   [2] *Ficus Melleri*, Baker.   [3] See p. 76.
[4] *Solanum auriculatum*, Ait.   [5] *Buddleia madagascariensis*. Lam.

CHAPTER V.

*THE CRATER LAKE OF TRITRÌVA : ITS PHYSICAL FEA-
TURES AND LEGENDARY HISTORY ; AND THE VOL-
CANIC REGIONS OF THE INTERIOR.*

Ancient volcanoes of Central Madagascar—Hot springs—Fossil remains in limestone deposits—Crater-lake of Andràikiba—Tritrìva Lake—Colour of water
—Remarkable appearance of lake—Legends—Mythical monsters—Depth of
lake—View from crater walls—Mr. Baron on volcanic phenomena—Ankàratra Mountain—Ancient craters—Lava streams—Volcanic rocks—Recent
character of volcanic action.

MADAGASCAR is not at present one of those regions of the earth where volcanic disturbances occur; but there is ample evidence, from the numerous extinct craters found in various parts of the island, that at a very recent period, geologically considered—possibly even within the occupation of the country by its present inhabitants—it was the theatre of very extensive outbursts of subterranean energy. The whole island has not yet been examined with sufficient minuteness to determine the exact extent of these old volcanoes, but they have been observed from near the south-east coast in S. Lat. 23°, and in various parts of the centre of the island up to the north-west and extreme north, a distance of 680 miles; and probably a more careful survey would reveal other links connecting more closely what is at present known as only a series of isolated groups of extinct craters. In the central provinces of Mada-gascar there are two large clusters of old volcanic cones and vents; one of them in and about the same latitude as the capital (19° S.), but from fifty to seventy miles away to the west of it, in the neighbourhood of Lake Itàsy; the other in the district called Vàkinankàratra, situated about eighty miles to the S.S.W. of Antanànarìvo, and south-west of the great central mountain mass of Ankàratra.

This second volcanic region stretches from twenty to thirty miles from Antsìrabè away west to Bètàfo and beyond it, and contains numerous and prominent extinct craters, such as Ivòko, Iatsìfitra, Vòhitra, Tritrìva, and many others, some of which have been described by the graphic pen of the late Dr. Mullens, in his *Twelve Months in Madagascar* (pp. 214–219). The doctor says that he counted in this southern group about sixty cones and craters.

There are also many hot springs in this Vàkinankàratra region, the most noted of which are those at Antsìrabé. At this place one of the chief springs is largely charged with lime, which has formed an extensive deposit all over a small level valley sunk some 20 feet below the general level of the plain around the village. For a long time past this place has furnished almost all the lime used for building in the capital, and the central province of Imèrina. Besides the deposit over the floor of the valley, there is also a compact ridge-shaped mass of lime accretion, 70 feet long by 18 to 20 feet wide, and about 15 to 16 feet high. This has all been deposited by the spring which kept open a passage through the lime to the top. Within the last ten or twelve years, however, the spring has been tapped by a shaft, of no great depth, a few yards to the north, over which a large and commodious bath-house has been erected by the Norwegian Lutheran Mission; and here many visitors come to bathe in the hot mineral water, which has been found very beneficial in rheumatic and other complaints. A little distance to the south-west is another spring, not, however, hot, but only milk-warm, the water of which is drunk by those who bathe in the other spring. This water has been shown to be, in chemical constituents, almost identical with the famous Vichy water of France. All over the valley the water oozes up in various places; and about half a mile farther north are several other springs, somewhat hotter than that just described, to which the natives largely resort for curative bathing.

During the excavations for the foundations of the bathhouse, the skeletons of several examples of an extinct species of hippopotamus were discovered, the crania and tusks being in very perfect preservation. Some of these are now in the Museum at Berlin; the finest specimen was sent to the Museum of the University of Christiania in Norway. This Madagascar hippopotamus was a smaller species than that now living in Africa, and is probably nearly allied to, if not identical with, another hippopotamus (*H. Lemerleï*), of which remains were found in 1868 by M. Grandidier, in the plains of the south-west coast. I was informed by the people that, wherever in these valleys the black mud is dug into for a depth of three or four feet, bones are sure to be met with. Probably a series of excavations would reveal the remains of animals, birds, and reptiles formerly inhabiting Madagascar. From the internal structure of the teeth and bones of the hippopotami discovered at Antsìrabè, traces of the gelatine being still visible, it is evident that the animals had been living at a comparatively recent period. There have been occasional vague reports of the existence of some large animal in the southern parts of the island; possibly the hippopotamus is not yet absolutely extinct there; and perhaps the half-mythical stories of the *Songòmby, Tòkandìa, Làlomèna*, and other strange creatures current among the Malagasy are traditions of the period when these huge pachyderms were still to be seen in the lakes and streams and marshes of Madagascar.

Within a few miles of Antsìrabè are two crater lakes. The nearer and larger of these is called Andràikìba, which lies distant about four miles due west. This is a beautiful sheet of water, blue as the heavens in colour, in shape an irregular square, but curving round to the north-west, where it shallows into a marsh, which is finally absorbed in rice-fields. The lake is said to be of profound depth, but the hills surrounding it are not very lofty, rising only about 200 feet above the surface of the water, from which they rise steeply. Fish and water-fowl and crocodiles also are said to be very abundant in and on its waters.

But the most interesting natural curiosity to be seen in the neighbourhood of Antsìrabè is the crater-lake of Tritrìva. This is situated about ten miles to the south-west, and is a pleasant ride of two hours by palanquin. Travelling at first in a westerly direction, the road then turns more to the south-west, and skirts the southern foot of the old volcano of Vòhitra (already mentioned). Passing some mile or two south of the high ground round the southern shores of the Andràikìba lake, the road gradually ascends to a higher level of country, so that in about an hour and a half's time we are about as high as the top of Vòhitra—probably about 500 feet. Reaching a ridge between two prominent hills, we catch our first sight of Tritrìva, now about two or three miles distant in front of us. From this point it shows very distinctly as an oval-shaped hill, its longest axis lying north and south, and with a great depression in its centre; the north-eastern edge of the crater wall being the lowest part of it, from which point it rises gradually southwards and westwards, the western edge being, at the centre, from two to three times the height of the eastern side. To the north are two much smaller cup-like hills, looking as if the volcanic forces, after the main crater had been formed, had become weaker and so been unable to discharge any longer by the old vent, and had therefore formed two newer outlets at a lower level.

Descending a little from the ridge just mentioned, we cross a valley with a good many scattered hamlets, and in less than half an hour reach the foot of the hill. A few minutes' pull up a tolerably easy slope, perhaps 200 feet in height, brings us to the top, at the lowest part of the crater edge; and on reaching the ridge the crater of the old volcano and its lake is before us, or, rather, below us. It is certainly an extraordinary scene, and unique of its kind. The inner sides of the crater dip down very steeply on all sides to a deep gulf, and here, sharply defined by perpendicular cliffs all round it, except just at the southern point, is a rather weird-looking dark green lake far below us, the water surface being probably from 200 to 300 feet lower than the point we are standing upon, and consequently below the level of the surrounding country. The lake, exactly shut in by the cliffs of the crater surrounding it, is not blue in colour, like Andràikìba, although under a bright and cloudless sky, but a deep and somewhat blackish green. It is undoubtedly an old volcano we are now looking down into; the spot on which we rest is only a few feet in breadth, and we can see that this narrow knife-edge is the same all round the crater. Outside of it the slope is pretty easy, but inside it descends steeply, here and there precipitously, to the edge of the cliffs which so sharply define the actual vent and, as distinctly, the lake which they enclose. Looking southwards, the crater edge gradually ascends, winding round the southern side, and still ascending as the eye follows it to the western, the opposite side, where the crater wall towers steeply up from 200 to 300 feet higher than it does on the east, where we are standing. The lake we judge to be about 800 to 900 feet long and 200 to 250 feet wide, forming a long oval, with pointed ends. The cliffs which enclose it appear to be from 40 to 50 feet in height, whitish in colour, but with black streaks where the rain, charged with carbonic acid, has poured more plentifully down their faces. These cliffs are vertical and in some places overhang the water, and from their apparently horizontal stratification are no doubt of gneiss rock. In coming up the hill I noticed a few small lumps of gneiss among the basaltic lava pebbles. The strongest feature of this Tritrìva is the sharply defined vertical opening of the vent, looking as if the rocks had been cut *clean through* with an enormous chisel, and as if they must dip down—as is doubtless the case—to unknown depths below the dusky-green waters. At the northern end of the lake is a deep gorge or cleft, partly filled with bushes and other vegetation. Southward of this, on the eastern side, the cliffs are still lofty and overhang the water, but at about a third of the lake's length they gradually decrease in height, and at the southern point they dip down to the level of the lake, so that at that part only can the water be approached. On the western side the cliffs keep a pretty uniform height all along the whole length.

So steep is the inward slope of the crater walls, that we all experienced a somewhat "eerie" feeling in walking along the footpath at its edge; for at a very few feet from this a false step would set one rolling downwards, with nothing to break the descent to the edge of the cliffs, and then to the dark waters below. We proceeded southwards along the crater edge to the higher part at the south-east, where the view is equally striking, and the depth of the great chasm seems still more profound. Here we waited some time, while most of our men went down to one of the hamlets in the plain to the east to get their meal, in which quest, however, they had only poor success. On expressing a wish to taste the Tritrìva water, one of our bearers took a glass, and descending by a breakneck path, went to fetch some water from the lake. He was so long away that we were beginning to feel uneasy, but after a quarter of an hour he reappeared with the water, which tasted perfectly sweet and good. He also entertained us with some of the legends which were certain to have grown up about so weird-looking a place as Tritrìva. Pointing to two or three small trees or bushes growing on the face of the cliffs near the northern point of the lake, he told us these were really a young lad and lass who had become attached to each other; but the hard-hearted parents of the girl disapproving of the match, the youth took his loin-cloth, and binding it round his sweetheart and his own body, precipitated her with himself into the dark waters. They became, so it is said, two trees growing side by side, and they now have offspring, for a young tree is growing near them;

and in proof of the truth of this story, he said that if you pinch or break the branches of these trees, it is not sap which exudes, but blood. He appeared to believe firmly in the truth of this story.

He also told us that the people of a clan called Zànatsàra, who live in the neighbourhood, claim some special rights in the Tritrìva lake; and when any one of their number is ill, they send to see if the usually clear dark green of the water is becoming brown and turbid. If this is the case they believe it to be a presage of death to the sick person.

Another legend makes the lake the former home of one of the mythical monsters of Malagasy folk-lore, the *Fanànim-pìtolòha*, or "seven-headed serpent." But for some reason or other he grew tired of his residence, and shifted his quarters to the more spacious and brighter lodgings for seven-headed creatures afforded by the other volcanic lake of Andràikìba.

This same bearer assured us that in the rainy season—contrary to what one would have supposed—the water of the lake diminishes, but increases again in the dry season. He told us that there is an outlet to the water, which forms a spring to the north of the mountain. I noticed a white line a foot or two above the surface of the water all round the foot of the cliffs, showing a probably higher level than at the time of our visit.

Walking round to the southern end of the crater edge, I proceeded up the far higher saddle-back ridge on the western side. Here the lake seems much diminished in size, and lying far down at an awful depth. But a magnificent and extensive view is gained of the surrounding country; the long flat-topped lines of hill to the east running many miles north and south, and surrounded directly east by two perfect cones (old volcanoes, Vòtovòrona and Ihankìana); the peaked and jagged range of Vòambòrona to the south-east; the enormous mass of Ibìty to the south; and then west, a flat region broken by abrupt hills; to the north-west are the thickly populated valleys towards Bètàfo, with many a cup-shaped hill and mountain marking old volcanic vents; and beyond this a high mass of country, with serrated outline against the sky, showing the district of Vàvavàto and the peaks of Iàvohàika; and finally, coming to due north is the varied grouping of the hills which form the northern termination of the central mountain mass of Ankàratra. Between us and these again is the extensive plain of Antsìrabè, with the white walls and gables of the church and the mission buildings plainly visible in the bright sunshine, although ten or eleven miles distant—altogether a panorama long to be remembered. From this point also the significance and appropriateness of the name given to the old volcano is clearly seen: Tritrìva is a combination of the words *trìtry*, a word used to describe the ridge on the back of a chameleon or a fish, and *ìva*, low, deep; so that the name very happily describes the long steep western ridge or crater wall, and the deep chasm sweeping down from it.

It may be added in conclusion, that the slopes of the crater both inside and out are covered over with turf, which grows on a dark brown volcanic soil, mingled with rounded pebbles of greenish or purple lava, very compact and close in structure, and containing minute crystals scattered sparingly through it. Occasional blocks of this are found round the edge of the crater wall, and the same rock crops out at many places on the steep inner slopes. I did not notice any vesicular lava or scoria; and at a little homestead not far from the north-eastern foot of Tritrìva, I was surprised to find the *hàdy* or fosse dug to 12 or 14 feet deep almost entirely through the red clay found all through the central regions of the island. The dark brown volcanic soil, here seen in section, appeared to be only 18 inches deep, with layers of small pebbles. So that the discharge of the volcanic dust and ash appears to have extended only a short distance from the mountain, at least it does not appear to have been very deep, unless, indeed, there has been much denudation. It must be remembered, however, that this point is to the windward side of the hill; probably the volcanic soil is deeper to the west of it. The much greater height of the western wall of the crater is no doubt due to the prevailing easterly winds carrying the bulk of the ejected matter to the west, and piling it up to two or three times the height of the eastern side. After seeing the amount of gneiss rock which must have been blown out of the vent, I expected to have found much greater quantities of it, and in larger blocks, than the very few and small fragments actually seen on the outer slopes. The greater portion, however, is probably covered up under the quantities of volcanic dust and *lapilli* which were subsequently ejected.

The Rev. Johannes Johnson, of the Norwegian Missionary Society, says: "It will interest you to hear that the depth of the Volcanic Lake of Tritrìva has been measured. Here is a rough diagram showing the places where soundings were made, S <̄ 1 2 3 >̄ N. At 1 it was found to be 328 feet deep, at 2 it was 443 feet, and at 3 it was 474 feet in depth. The natives expected it would prove to be much deeper than this." Thus it appears that although not, as popularly supposed, unfathomable, the depth of this remarkable sheet of water is still very considerable for its small area, and is quite sufficiently profound to have given rise to the many weird legends connected with it in the popular imagination.

The two best known volcanic regions of Central Madagascar have already been referred to in this chapter, and as some of the readers of these pages may like to have fuller information as to these interesting parts of the country, I will not attempt to describe them myself, but will quote half a dozen paragraphs from a paper by my friend and brother missionary, the Rev. R. Baron, F.L.S., F.G.S., contributed to the *Quarterly Journal of the Geological Society*, for May, 1889, and entitled "Notes on the Geology of Madagascar." Mr. Baron is the chief authority on the geology of the island and has made a special study of the petrology; and all that he describes is from personal observation and microscopic examination of all the known rocks of the country.

"VOLCANIC PHENOMENA.—The scene of the greatest display of former volcanic activity in Central Madagascar has undoubtedly been Ankàratra. This mountain, situated some twenty to thirty miles to the south-west of Antanànarìvo, is the highest in the island, attaining an altitude of nearly 9,000 feet above the sea. It is a broad and elevated mass of land, with no very sharp peaks or ridges, and having, for the most part, a gentle slope of 4°–8° on all sides, so that it is not easy to define its exact limits. Roughly speaking, however, it may be said to cover an area of perhaps fifty square miles. It is the wreck of a huge, but ancient, subaerial volcano. There are at present, so far at least as my observations go, no traces of cones or craters, but there are volcanic ejectamenta scattered about which bear witness to their former existence. From this volcano vast floods of liquid lava have issued and overflowed the surrounding country to the extent, probably, of from 1,500 to 2,000 square miles. In fact, almost the whole of Vàkinankàratra province has been covered by a sheet of lava. This lava has been poured out at various times, several beds being superimposed on one another. Some of the lava-streams are probably no less than twenty or twenty-five miles in length, and, before they thin out, from 300 to 500 feet in thickness. They are mostly of a basaltic character.

" The lava which has issued from the north, north-east, and north-west of the mountain seems to be almost entirely olivine-basalt; whilst that which has issued from the south, south-east, and south-west seems to be mainly nepheline-basalt. Trachyte also exists in sheets, apparently below the basalt, on the south-east and south-west side of the mountain. The three highest points of Ankàratra are Tsiàfajàvona, 8,494 feet above the sea; Tsiàfakàfo, 8,330 feet; and Ambòhitrakòholàhy, 7,730 feet. Tsiàfajàvona, the highest peak, and Tsiàfakàfo consist of olivine-basalt, Ambòhitrakòholàhy of trachyte.

"It would be interesting to know at what period Ankàratra was in a state of eruption; but our knowledge of the mountain and the surrounding district is, as yet, too scanty to help us to any conclusion on the matter. There is evidence sufficient, however, to show that the volcano is of comparatively ancient date; for, in the first place, all signs of craters or cones seem to have been effaced through denudation, though the presence of fragmentary materials (which, however, have largely disappeared) manifest their former existence. Then, again, numerous deep valleys have been excavated out of the hard basaltic covering by the many streams that come down from the mountain, leaving long tongues of lava diverging from the central mass. Many of these streams have cut clean through the beds of lava, bringing into view the gneiss upon which they are superimposed.

"Some thirty or forty miles to the south of Ankàratra there are to be seen about a dozen remarkably conical hills without craters. Whether they are the cores of former volcanoes or eruptive bosses or remnants of a former lava sheet, it would be difficult to say, though I am inclined to regard them as the last. Vòtovòrona and Iakìana (or Ihankìana?) are probably the highest of these cones, though even these are of no great height. Vòtovòrona is 350 feet high, and has been protruded through granite. The angle of its slope is over 50°. The rock is nepheline-hornblende-phonolite. A few similar cones exist on the south-east of Vàvavàto mountain. About twenty or twenty-five miles N.N.E. of Ankàratra, and some seven or eight miles W.S.W. of Antanànarìvo, there is another of these probably eruptive bosses. It is a low conical knob of perhaps 150 or 200 feet high, and is also known by the name of Vòtovòrona. It consists of olivine-basalt. There seem to have been a few small outflows of lava from the hill, and it not improbably forms the core of an old volcano.

"In Mandrìdràno district, on the western side of Lake Itàsy, and in the neighbourhood of Bètàfo, in Vàkinankàratra (the former being fifty-five miles west, and the latter seventy-five miles S.S.W., of the capital), there are numerous volcanic cones, which are undoubtedly much more recent than the volcanic pile of Ankàratra. Both localities are about 130 miles from the east coast of the island, and 170 from the west coast. It is hardly necessary to say that all these volcanoes are extinct, and that there are none in activity at the present time in any part of Madagascar. On the west side of Lake Itàsy the volcanic cones exist in great numbers, and these therefore shall be first described.

"The extinct volcanoes of the district of Mandrìdràno extend for a distance of about twenty miles north and south, and perhaps three or four east and west. The cones are thickly studded over the district, in some parts clustering together more thickly than in others. Occasionally there is a series of cones which have evidently been heaped up by the simultaneous ejection of scoriæ from different vents situated on the same line of fissure, but so that the cones have run one into the other, leaving a ridge, generally curvilinear, at the summit. None of these extinct volcanoes reach the height of 1,000 feet. Kàsigè, which is probably the highest, I found by aneroid to be 863 feet above the plain. This is a remarkably perfect and fresh-looking volcano, whose sides slope at an angle of 32° or 33°. The scoriæ on the sides have become sufficiently disintegrated to form a soil, on which is found a by no means scanty flora. On its top is an unbreached funnel-shaped crater, which measures, from the highest point of its rim, 243 feet in depth. Contiguous with Kàsigè, and adjoining its south side, though not so high, there is another volcano, Ambòhimalàla, and many others are to be seen near by.

"One thing with regard to these volcanic piles soon strikes the observer; this is, that in the majority of the cones one side of the crater is higher than the other. Not only so, but the higher side is situated in most instances on the north, north-west, or west of the crater. This is accounted for by the direction of the wind during the eruption, causing the ejected fragments to accumulate on the leeward side of the vent. Now we know that the south-east trades blow during the greater part of the year in Madagascar, hence the unequal development of the sides of the cones. The same thing may also be observed in the volcanic piles in the neighbourhood of Bètàfo.

"A very large number of the cones have breached craters, whence lava has flowed in numerous streams and flooded the plains around. These streams and floods consist, in most instances, of black basaltic lava; a sheet of this lava, the mingled streams of which have flowed from Ambòhimalàla and some other vents, has covered the plain at the foot of Kàsigè to such an extent as almost to surround the mountain. Similar sheets are to be seen in other parts of the district, but they are so much alike, that a description of one will suffice for all. Ambòditai-màmo is a small volcanic cone at the south-west end of Ifànja marsh, and at the northern confines of the volcanic district. It possesses a breached crater turned towards the east. From this has issued a stream of lava which, following the direction of the lowest level of the ground, has swept through a small valley round the northern end of the cone, and spread out at its western foot. This sheet of lava, which is extremely rough on the surface, occupies but a small area of some two or three square miles. It has been arrested in its flow in front by the form of the ground. It is cut through in one part by a stream (Ikòtombòlo) which, in some places, has worn a channel to the depth of eighty or ninety feet. Its surface, which is slightly cellular, is covered by hundreds of mammiform hillocks, which must have been formed during the cooling of the liquid mass. The hillocks are mostly from twenty to thirty feet high, and apparently are heaped-up masses of lava, and not hollow blisters. The lava itself is black, heavy, and compact, being porphyritic with somewhat large crystals of augite. As yet it is scarcely decomposed sufficiently to form much of a soil, though grass and a few other plants grow on it abundantly.

"As to the nature of the volcanic rocks of the district, it may be said that these comprise basalt, andesite, trachyte, trachytic tuff, palagonite tuff, and limburgite. Some of the trachytic rocks contain large porphyritic crystals of glassy felspar (sanidine). Pumice, obsidian, and pitchstone do not seem anywhere to be found.

"In addition to the numerous scoria-cones, there may be seen scattered here and there in the district some dozen or more other volcanoes, differing entirely in character from those which have been spoken of above. These are large bell-shaped hummocks of trachyte or andesite. They are without definite craters, though one or two of them have more or less conspicuous depressions on their summits, showing that eruptive action has not been altogether wanting. These hummocks are chiefly composed of a light-coloured compact rock. This rock, having originally had a highly viscid or pasty consistency, has accumulated and set immediately over the orifice through which it was extruded.

"It is hardly necessary to say that these extinct volcanoes of Mandrìdràno must have been in activity in comparatively recent times. Possibly they belong to the historic period, though, so far as I am aware, no tradition lingers with regard to their being in a state of eruption. That they are, at any rate, of recent date is shown by the good state of preservation in which most of the cones are still found and by the undecomposed (or slightly decomposed) character of the lava-streams that have issued from them. There have been no terrestrial disturbances or modifications of any magnitude since the days of their fiery energy; the conformation of hill and dale was the same then as now, for in every instance the lava-streams have adapted themselves to the form of the existing valleys."

CHAPTER VI.

AMBÀTOVÒRY, ONE OF OUR HOLIDAY RESORTS IN MADAGASCAR; WITH NATURAL HISTORY AND OTHER NOTES.

The Rest-house—Ambòniloha Hill—A deserted village—Ambàtovòry rock—Woodland paths—Birds—Lizards and chameleons—Grasshoppers—Protective colouring—Waning colours—Beetles—Ants and ant-nests—Ball-insects—Spiders—Butterflies—King Butterfly—Solitary wasps—Wasp-nests—Angàvokély Mountain—Extensive prospect.

BY the kind consideration of the Directors of the London Missionary Society for the comfort and health of their missionaries in the central province of Imèrina, we have had for some years past a pleasant Country-house or Sanatorium, to which, after a year or so of steady labour in college, or school, or hospital, or church and district, we can go for a fortnight or a month's quiet holiday. This peaceful resting-place is situated about twelve miles east of Antanànarìvo, on the Tamatave road, a mile and a half beyond the mission station of Isoàvina, and a mile or less west of a great rounded mass of granite rising about 400 feet above the rice-valleys, and known as Ambàtovòry, *i.e.*, " Round rock." On the summit and eastern and western slopes of this huge boss of rock are numerous trees, much more plentiful on the western side, where they stretch down into a deep valley and form an amphitheatre of wood and bush. This vegetation is probably a remnant of the original forest, which once covered a much larger area of this mostly bare and treeless Imèrina, and it forms a refreshing contrast to the moory hills and rocky mountains which are seen in every direction. The Mission Rest-house is a good six-roomed dwelling on the slope of the hill facing the south, and from it the ground falls rapidly down to the rice-valleys a couple of hundred feet below, the large piece of ground belonging to the house joining on to the bush and scattered trees of the Ambàtovòry forest, so that in two minutes' time one can stroll into the woods, through which a number of paths have recently been cut, or, turning in the opposite direction, can walk over the breezy downs towards Isoàvina. Here is the pleasant mission-house of Mr. Peake, with its long row of cottages for the workmen in the industrial school which he has carried on for several years, its school- and class-rooms and its pretty church and school-house, forming altogether a model mission station.

Behind the Rest-house rises for several hundred feet above it a rounded hill called Ambònilóha, *i.e.*, "Over-head," a not inappropriate name. Like scores of hills throughout Imèrina, a number of deeply-cut lines round the summit show that this place was formerly the site of a well-fortified town. These lines, which can be seen for miles away, prove on closer inspection to be deep fosses cut in the hard red earth, a treble line of defence one within the other, the innermost rampart being strengthened by a low wall of massive stones. No building now remains in this "deserted village," but many squares of grass-grown stones can be traced, showing the former outline of the wooden framework of the houses; and on the highest spot there is an ancient tomb, where doubtless some of "the rude forefathers of the hamlet" sleep their last sleep.

In front of the house, looking south-west, the view is partly shut in, at a mile or two's distance, by lofty rocky hills rising high above the rice-valleys far below ; but to the south-east one gets a peep into a distant prospect of lines of hills, some of the nearer ones being enormous masses of bare rock ; while to the east the view is closed by the smooth, rounded slopes of Ambàtovòry itself, with the woods around it and stretching down into the deep valley at its base.

There are many pleasant walks in the neighbourhood of the Sanatorium. One of these is to the top of the Ambàtovòry rock, from which there is an extensive view, and around which, to east and south, are fine trees and pleasant shady spots, where a picnic party can be improvised, and where ferns and other plants can be gathered. A few years ago there was a small village on the spot; four or five years ago there were about that number of houses; while now there is not one left, the people, as is usual throughout Imèrina, deserting these inconvenient heights for the plains. But a row of half-a-dozen old tombs, with small timber houses on their tops, shows that this was a village of one of the noble clans or *Andrìana*, who alone are allowed to make such wooden houses, *Tràno màsina* or *Tràno manàra*, as they are called (*i.e.*, "Sacred houses," or "Cold houses"[1]). These are, however, now tumbling to pieces, and after two or three more rainy seasons heaps of rotting wood will be all that is left over the tombs of these departed great ones of the district.

Another easily reached spot is a detached rock, something like a miniature Ambàtovòry, but a short distance to the south of it. Here a scramble over a great sloping surface of gneiss brings us to a rough ascent leading to an ancient gateway. The top of this rock was evidently a fort of the old times, for, except where we climb up, there is no approaching the summit and no need of fosses or ramparts, as the smooth rock slopes away perpendicularly all around, and in the days before guns and gunpowder a dozen resolute men could have barred the narrow approach against a hundred assailants.

The paths through the woods are, however, among the most pleasant places for a walk in the neighbourhood of Ambàtovòry; and although the small remnant of old forest is too

[1] "Cold," because they are houses having no hearth or fire to warm them.

limited in extent to furnish much variety in animal life, there is still a great deal to interest those who have a taste for natural history, especially if they will only use their eyes.

Of four-footed creatures in the shape of mammalia there are none, except possibly some of the small hedgehog-like creatures (the Centetidæ), as the woods are far too restricted in range for any species of the lemurs to find a home there, and there is no great variety even of birds. There is a space of fifteen or sixteen miles of bare moors between this place and the upper forest, so that few of the numerous feathered tribes of the wooded regions come over the intervening country. In the warm season the *kow-kow kow-koo* of the *Kankàfotra*, the Madagascar cuckoo, is continually heard among the trees and bushes, as well as the chirping and whistling cries of a few of the smaller and less conspicuous birds, and the cooing note of one of the wood-pigeons. About the rocks one may constantly hear the querulous cry of the little *Hítsikìtsika*, or kestrel, and see them hovering in the air or darting about; and now and then we come across a flock of the *Papàngo*, or Egyptian kite, perched on the trees, or swooping down near the native houses to carry off an unwary chicken or mouse. Of course the ubiquitous *Goaika*, or native crow, is never far away. With his fine white collar and square white patch on his breast, he has a very clerical appearance; he haunts the neighbourhood of the great open-air markets, where he apparently picks up a good living from the scattered rice and refuse of various kinds. In the warm season flocks of the little weaver-birds may be seen, both the *Fódy*, the male of which is mostly of a brilliant scarlet at the hot season of the year, and the smaller *Tsikirìty*, in sober brown livery, which darts down like an arrow on the rice-fields in companies of thirty or forty together. In the rice-fields the *Tàkatra*, a brown stork, may be sometimes seen stepping solemnly about. He builds an enormous nest, which looks as large as a truss of hay and is fixed on the fork of a tree or on the edge of a large rock, and there are many superstitions and fables connected with him. In the old times of idolatry, if one of these storks crossed the path along which any of the chief idols was being carried, it was immediately taken back, and it was thought equally unlucky if it crossed the road in front of the sovereign.

The reptiles to be found near Ambàtovòry are small and inconspicuous. Two or three species of lizard are frequently seen : the pretty little *Antsiàntsy*, with brown coat and white lines and dark spots along its sides, eight or ten inches long, darts about like an arrow on rocks and sunny banks, while a smaller species, about four inches long, is of an exquisite green colour above, with black and white lines along its sides, and pale grey underneath. It is often seen running around the fleshy leaves of the aloes, its tinting forming a protective resemblance among its surroundings. Equally beautiful are the bright tints of some of the small chameleons—black and yellow, and red and green—and equally protective also, in case of need, is their power of changing into dull grey or brown when alarmed. Small pretty brown snakes may be often seen, from eighteen inches to two feet long, and happily they are perfectly harmless, as, indeed, are all the serpents of this great island—at least, there are none whose bite is dangerous. And yet it is amusing to see how the Malagasy leap out of their way with the greatest alarm. We found on one occasion a very large earthworm, three times as long and bulky as any we had ever seen in England.

But perhaps it is the insects which attract one's attention most constantly. On the open downs, and when the sun is shining, the air is filled with the hum of chirping insect life from the many species of grasshoppers, crickets, and small locusts which cover the ground. Every step among the long dry grass disturbs a score of these insects, which leap in all directions from one's path as we proceed, sometimes dashing on one's face with a smart blow. The majority of these are of various shades of brown and green, and some of the larger species of grasshopper are remarkable for their protective colouring. Here is one whose legs and wings are exactly like dry grass; the body is like a broad blade of some green plant, the antennæ are two little tufts like yellow grass, and the eyes are just like two small brown seeds. But, curiously enough, when it flies a pair of bright scarlet wings make its flight very conspicuous. You pursue it, to catch such a brightly coloured insect, when it settles, and lo! it has vanished; only something resembling green or dry grass remains, which it requires sharp eyes to distinguish from the surrounding herbage. Other grasshoppers are entirely like green grass blades and stalks, and others, again, resemble equally closely dried grass, and unless the insects move under one's eyes it is almost impossible to detect them. One is puzzled to guess where the vital organs can be placed in such dry-looking little sticks. There is one species of mantis also, which, in the shape and colour of its wings, legs, antennæ, and body, presents as close a resemblance to its environment as do the grasshoppers. Their curious heads, however, which turn round and look at one in quite an uncanny manner, and their formidably serrated fore-legs or arms, put up in mock pious fashion, give them a distinctly different appearance from the other insects. In the dry and cooler season, on almost every square foot of ground is a large brown caterpillar, often many of them close together, feeding on the young blades of grass.

But the most handsome insect one sees on the downs is the *Valàlanambóa*, or dog-locust. This is large and is gorgeously coloured, the body being barred with stripes of yellow and black, while the head and thorax are green and blue and gold, with shades of crimson, and the wings are bright scarlet. It seems a most desirable insect for a cabinet, but it is impossible to keep one, for it has a most abominable smell, and this, as well as its probable possession of a nauseous taste, appears to be its protection, so that no bird or other creature feeds upon it. This insect seems, therefore, a good example of "warning colours"; it has no need of "protective resemblance" lest it should be devoured by enemies; it can flaunt its gay livery without fear, indeed this seems exaggerated in order to say to outsiders: "Hands off!" "*Nemo me impune lacessit.*" The Malagasy have a proverb which runs thus: "*Valàlanambóa : ny tompony aza tsy tia ;*" *i.e.*, "The dog-locust, even its owner dislikes it."

There are many species of beetles to be seen, although none of them are very handsome or conspicuous. The most common kind is a broad flat insect, about an inch long, and dull dark-brown in colour, which crosses one's path at every step. Another is seen chiefly on the bushes, a smaller insect, but bright shining jet-black. Another, which appears as if it mimicked a wasp in its habit of flight, is shot with brown and green, with very long legs, and is constantly taking short flights or running rapidly. Another one, but much more rare, has golden green and metallic tints on its wing-cases. But the insect which has puzzled us most is one that I have never seen but on one spot, viz., on a large bush of *Róimémy*, a plant with acacia-like leaves, with prickles along the leaf-stalks, and on only one bush of this, which is within a few yards of the Rest-house at Ambàtovòry. It is like a beetle about five-eighths of an inch long, and almost hemispherical in shape. It is warm reddish-brown in colour, with a line of black and then of yellow next the head, and is perfectly flat below. These insects cluster closely, as thick as they can lie, in groups of from a dozen to more than a hundred together, all round the thicker stems, so that they look at a little distance like strings of large brown beads; and in some of the topmost branches they form a continuous mass for two or three feet. Amongst these shining brown insects are a few others of quite a different colour and shape, perfectly flat, like a minute tortoise, and of a uniform grey, exactly resembling the lichen on the bark of the tree, and the edges of the carapace scolloped.[1] These grey insects are in

---

[1] Mr. Baron tells me that both kinds are certainly species of bug, and that they are common on other kinds of trees. They have a very bad smell. Nearer the forest are other kinds of bugs, but of the most brilliant colours, and also evil smelling.

the proportion of about one to forty or fifty of the darker-coloured ones. There are also a few individuals of the same shape as the brown one, but yellowish-green in colour. What these grey insects can be, and what relation they bear to the much more numerous brown one, I cannot make out. Nor can I ascertain why they all remain motionless and in the same position for weeks together. During the three weeks of our stay here, at any rate, they seem not to have altered in position, although I think the lower clusters are slightly diminished in number. I thought at first that they must be feeding in some way on the tree, as their heads seem closely fixed to the bark, as indeed is the whole body; but on minute examination I can find no trace of any puncture or sign of their gnawing or eating the bark, although the branches on which they are most thickly clustered seem more dry and withered than the others. Their torpid condition certainly does not arise from inability to move, for, on being disturbed or shaken off, they will fly a considerable distance, and will creep along the branches. I have noticed these insects on the same bush, and nowhere else, during previous visits to Ambàtovòry at this time of the year (December), but not during the cold season.[1]

[Since writing the above, I have had another inspection, in the cold season, of the tree with these curious insects. There are now (June) to be seen not a single one of the brown bugs, but the branches are thickly covered with hundreds of young ones, about one-fourth to one-third of an inch long, but these are all flat, and grey in colour, with the edge of the body serrated. The difference in shape and colour in insects so closely associated together certainly seems remarkable.]

The ants are, as in all tropical countries, very numerous and of many species. All of them, from minute kinds not an eighth of an inch long to others half an inch to five-eighths of an inch in length, appear to make nests in the ground, with circular shafts leading down to them from the surface. It is amusing to

[1] I have subsequently seen it in other places.

watch the busy industry of these little creatures, the sides of the shafts being covered with their shining black bodies, those coming up being laden with a little pellet of earth, which they deposit outside the slope, and then hurry back down below. All round the mouth of the entrance is a considerable mound of earth, all brought up grain by grain by the busy workers. The ants are the scavengers of the country. No beetle, or worm, or grub, or animal matter of any kind, can be many minutes on the ground before it is detected by some ant, who communicates the fact forthwith to its fellows, and they immediately fall on the spoil, cut it in pieces, and convey it to their stronghold. It is astonishing to see the heavy loads—pieces of sugar-cane, or yam, or other food—that two or three ants will stagger along with for the common weal. Truly, although they are small folk, they are "exceeding wise." The thinking power in that minute point, an ant's head, is certainly one of the most marvellous things in animated nature.

While speaking of wingless insects, I may notice here a very different kind of one from the ants, viz., the ball-insect (*Spherotherium* sp.), of which there are several species in Madagascar. These insects, called not very elegantly by the Malagasy *Tainkìntana*, or "star-droppings," have the power of instantaneously rolling themselves into an almost perfect sphere, which form they retain as long as any danger threatens them, and no force short of pulling them to pieces can make them unroll. The animal is formed of nine or ten segments, each with a pair of legs, and covered with a plate of armour; while the head and tail are defended by large plates, each of which fits into the other and makes a more perfectly fitting suit of armour than was ever worn by medieval knight. There are several species of these pretty and curious creatures. The most common kind here is one which forms a ball barely an inch in diameter, and shining black in colour. Another, more rarely seen here, but common enough in the upper belt of forest, is of a beautiful brown colour like Russia leather, and is quite double the size of the first-mentioned one. In passing through the main forest in 1892, we came suddenly one day to a part of the road which was so thickly covered by such a great number of these creatures that our bearers could not avoid trampling on them. These were of a bronze-green tint and are probably a third species.

In all parts of Madagascar the spiders are very conspicuous members of the insect-world. The most common kind is a species of *Epeira*, which spins large webs and may be seen by scores between the branches of trees and the angles of buildings. These are large insects, their legs stretching over four or five inches, and their bodies being handsomely coloured with red and gold and silver markings. From the way in which these spiders cross with their great webs the fosses round the old villages they are called by the Malagasy *Mampìtahàdy*, i.e., "fosse-crossers." The main "guys" or stays of their webs are strong and thick yellow silk cords, which require an effort to break. Another species, also common, is somewhat crab-like in shape, with curious spiny processes on the abdomen and thorax. Other smaller species of spider, found on leaves and in flowers, are coloured exactly like their surroundings, some being of various shades of green, and others pure white, apparently that, with these protective resemblances, they may more easily pounce upon the smaller flies and other insects attracted to the flowers.

In these bare upper highlands of Madagascar butterflies are not found in as great variety as in the warmer regions of the island. Still there are a few species which are common enough, the most plentiful being one which is satiny-blue above, and spotted with brown and grey underneath. This is to be seen all the year round, especially hovering over the Euphorbia hedges which divide plantations from the roads. Another, also tolerably common, is a large reddish-brown butterfly, the wings edged with black and white. Much more rare is an insect with four large round white spots on dark chocolate-brown wings; and another, dark-brown in colour, with eye-like spots of blue and red. Several small species, yellow, white, or brown, or silvery-grey and blue, are found hovering over, or settling on, damp places; and there are two or three white species, with black spots or lines on the edges of the wings. In the warmer season a handsome large *Papilio* is rather common in our gardens, with dark-green and sulphur-yellow spots and markings. And lastly, but rather scarce, is one of the handsomest butterflies in the world (more strictly speaking, it is a diurnal moth), the *Urania riphœa*. This insect, with its colouring of green and gold, and scarlet and black, and its delicate fringing of pure white on the edges of the wings, is indeed one of the most lovely productions of Nature. The Malagasy call it *Andrìandòlo, i.e.*, "king butterfly" (or moth).

We do not see many bees in this Ambàtovòry wood, but there are several species of solitary wasps, whose habits are very interesting. One species excavates a hole in the ground or on the side of a bank, and then, capturing some unfortunate spider or caterpillar, which she benumbs with her sting, carries it into the hole and lays an egg in its body, so that the little grub, when hatched, finds itself surrounded by food, and then eats its way out into the daylight. The hole is, after being filled up, so carefully concealed that it is quite impossible to discover it. Another species of wasp builds a series of cells of clay, which the busy worker brings in pellets and builds up layer by layer, fixing them to the sides of houses and rocks, and storing each cell with living food for its progeny in the same fashion as its mining cousin.[1]

Our longest excursion was one to the grand mountain of Angàvokély, which is two or three hours' ride to the east, to the south of the Tamatave road. Angàvokély is one of the highest and most conspicuous mountains in Imèrina, rising 1,300 or 1,400 feet above the general level of the province; and it

---

[1] For a very full and illustrated account of these insects, see a paper by the Rev. C. P. Cory, "Notes on the Habits of the Solitary Wasps of Madagascar," *Annual* xiv., 1890, pp. 163-170.

extends for two or three miles east and west, with two summits nearly equal in height, and quite a mile apart. The easternmost of these rises steeply from the surrounding valleys, and is crowned by enormous piles of rock, while the western summit rises with much gentler slopes covered with bush, except on the south side, where great masses of granite appear, looking like the towers of some Titanic castle. A couple of hours' ride brought us to the rice-valley immediately under the eastern peak, and from which we commenced the ascent, a pretty steep one. At about a third of the way up is a large bare sloping surface of rock, on which we were glad to rest and take breath. Again we climb up, the grass being very slippery, and foothold very difficult. As we get higher we come into a dense shrubbery of bush and small trees; and all around are hundreds of the large showy white flower called *Tsingàtsa* (a species of *Crinum*), with its long ribbon-like petals and powerful scent. One more halt at the base of the immense bare rocks which form the summit, and which tower grandly for 300 or 400 feet above us, and make us all look like pigmies in contrast, and then we make a final effort, scrambling up among the huge stones, until at length we come to a rough staircase between two walls of granite, with beautiful embroideries of moss and lichen and fern. Up, up we go, and at last come upon a level platform several hundred square yards in extent, and are glad to throw ourselves down on the grass and recover breath after our climb.

From this "coign of vantage," many hundred feet above the valley, we have of course a very extensive and varied prospect. To the north-west is the round mass of Lòhavòhitra in Vònizòngo, and the long serrated ridge of Andrìngitra, with its cave (the Malagasy Delphi); away north is the line of Ambòhimiàkatra, and the point of Ambàravàrambato ("Stone-gateway"), on the way to Antsihànaka; from north-east to south-east is the long dark line of the upper forest, with Angàvo and Ifòdy mountains, over which we cross on our way to and from the coast; beyond this again is the treeless plain of Ankày; and still beyond and bounding the view, 50, 60, or 70 miles in the blue distance, is the larger and lower forest, and ridges and peaks which we can see clearly from Tamatave. Only due west is the view interrupted, for we are not yet on the topmost pinnacle, there being still a mass of rock 100 feet higher still, up to which our bearers scramble, but which we are quite content to leave them the honour of scaling, as the ascent appears somewhat difficult. Still, by going round the edges of the platform, we can catch all the more prominent points to the south and south-west: Ihàranandrìana, on the road to Bètsilèo; many familiar-looking hills west of the capital; Antanànarìvo on its long rocky ridge, crowned by the group of royal palaces and two of the memorial churches; and, rising gradually but unmistakably far above all, the mass of Ankàratra, the highest point of the island, 40 miles away, and its three or four central peaks nearly 9,000 feet above the sea, and about half as much as that from the general level of Imèrina. Truly a grand prospect, for, except from Ankàratra itself, there is hardly any point where we could command such an extensive view as this. Steep down below us to the east is a pretty rice-valley stretching in a remarkably straight line for several miles both to north-east and south-west. The houses and hamlets below look as if a stone could be thrown upon them from this 1,000 or 1,200 feet of elevation; and as our eyes follow the green rice-fields, village after village appears on the promontory-like *tanéty* or gentle rising grounds, so that we think what a fine field of work there would be in this valley alone for a resident missionary.

CHAPTER VII.

MALAGASY PLACE-NAMES.

Mixed nomenclature of coast and interior places—Early European influence—Arab and Portuguese names—Influence of *Fàdy* or Taboo—Name of Madagascar—Mountain names—The name-prefixes *An-* and *Am-*—Height and prominence—Mystery and dread—Size—Words meaning rock and stone—Animals and birds—Personal names for hills—Grandeur of mountain scenery—River names—Descriptive epithets—Lake names—Town and village names—Dual names—Names of capital and its divisions—Town names from natural features—Forests—River banks from animals—Personal—Tribal—Province names—Appendix on Bètsilèo place-names.

PLACE-NAMES, it is now acknowledged, form one of the most reliable sources of information as to ancient and prehistoric times, and are among the most enduring and unaltering records of the past. In all the older countries of the world the names of the mountains and rivers, of the fields and the valleys, of the farms and villages and towns, as well as of all other geographical features, reveal the existence and successive occupation of the soil from remote epochs by many different races of mankind. And in the newer countries the names given to places tell in the plainest terms of their discoverers, and often fix the date of their becoming known to the civilised world.

An inspection of a map of the island of Madagascar shows a curious difference between the nomenclature of the coast and that of the interior. In the latter the names are entirely native, for no European power has ever succeeded in establishing itself in the country for any lengthened period; but the coast is fringed with a variety of European words—English, French, and Portuguese—as well as with Malagasy names. Thus we find "William Pitt" Bay, "Chatham" Island, and Port "Liverpool," commemorating the leading English statesmen of the time when the first complete survey was made of the coast by Capt. W. F. W. Owen, R.N., whose ships' names are also perpetuated in "Leven" Port and "Barracouta" Island. The treachery of the native population is remembered in "Murder" and "Grave" Islands, where some of Owen's crews were killed by the people; English Admiralty and other officials' names were given to Port "Croker," Point "Barrow," "Dartmouth" River, Point "McClure," "Dalrymple" Bay, and "Barlow" Island; and British surveys of the western coast have also left their mark in "Barren" Isles, and in "Crab," "Coffin," and "Sandy" Islands, in the Mozambique Channel; and at the northern extremity of Madagascar we find "British" Sound (more properly Diego Suarez Bay), with four deep inlets called respectively by the names of "English," "Welsh," "Scotch," and "Irish" Bays.

The earlier French intercourse is marked by the names of Fort Dauphin, Port Choiseul, Foule Pointe, and Louisbourg, a record of the monarchical times, nearly two centuries ago, when so many disastrous attempts were made by the French to establish themselves on the eastern side of the island.[1] And going back further, to the discovery of Madagascar by Europeans, the maritime enterprise of the Portuguese three hundred and seventy or eighty years ago is marked indelibly on the map, together with their religious fervour, by the names of various saints which they gave to the chief capes all round its shores—St. Mary, St. Andrew, St. Vincent, and St. Sebastian[2]—as well as the Isle of St. Mary, the Bay and River of St. Augustine, the Bay of St. Luce, the Shoal of St. Bonaventura, the town of St.

---

[1] In certain old French maps Madagascar was called "Ile Dauphine," but this name did not obtain any permanence.

[2] The most northerly cape of Madagascar, now known as Cape Ambro or Amber, was formerly called Cape Natal, from its being discovered on Christmas Day (*dies Natalis Domini*).

Thomas (now called Tamatave [1]), and the name of San Lorenzo, by which the island was known for long after its discovery.[2] Two or three of their famous captains are also kept in remembrance in "Antongil" (Antonio Gil) Bay, "Diego Suarez" Sound, and "Juan de Nova" Island.

Going back earlier still, to the Arab settlements both on the south-east and north-west coasts of Madagascar, although these have left enduring traces of their presence in the language of the Malagasy, they do not seem, as far at least as our information at present extends, to have affected the place-nomenclature of the country. The Arabs have given the names used by many tribes to the days of the week and of the months, the terms connected with superstition, witchcraft, divination, &c., and words employed in the arts of civilised life—dress, money, bedding, music, &c.; but their influence does not appear to have extended to the names of towns or geographical features, with two or three possible exceptions.[3] Thus the name of the extensive lake of Alaotra, in the Antsihànaka province, which, according to the Rev. L. Dahle, is probably the Arabic *Al-lutat*, "the dashing of the waves," is the same word which is given as a name to the Arabs from beyond the Mozambique Channel, who are called by the Malagasy the "Talaotra."[4]

The object of this paper is, however, to call attention to the *Malagasy* place-names in Madagascar; to show how they illustrate the mental habits of the people and their powers of

---

[1] "Tamatave" is called by the Malagasy "Toamàsina," probably a corruption of "San Tomaso."

[2] Mr. A. Tacchi suggests that "Antongil" is rather a corruption of "Santa Angelo," as nothing seems to be certainly known of any "Antonio Gil." Ngontsy, the name of a place on the north-west coast, is thought by Mr. Tacchi to be a corruption of "Saint Gontran" and another word of Portuguese origin.

[3] M. Grandidier has, however, pointed out several other names of places on the western coast which he believes are of Arab origin, although he does not give their meanings; these are Kisimany, Kongony, Sada, Mibany, Kivinja, Sangoa, and Boinaomary. I should doubt some of these, which seem Malagasy words in whole or in part.

[4] In Dumont D'Urville's *Vocabulaire Madekass-Française*, *alaotr* is translated "au large."

observation; to point out some few historical facts which are probably preserved in certain names; and to note a number of words of obscure or doubtful meaning which are embodied in many of the names of places, and which are possibly relics of an occupation of the island anterior to the arrival of the present prominent Malayo-Polynesian element in the population. Our knowledge of the various dialects of the Malagasy language is still too fragmentary and imperfect to allow of much being done at present in the direction indicated in this last point; but one chief result aimed at in noting down here some of these particulars is to provoke inquiry and research on the subject. Madagascar will prove an exception to almost every other country if a careful analysis of the names of its mountains and rivers, valleys and plains, towns and villages, and other geographical features, does not throw some light upon the earliest occupation of the island, and the successive waves of population which have passed over its surface. There are several reasons for believing that an earlier and less civilised race than the present inhabitants once occupied the interior of Madagascar, and it is possible that some of the obscurer words embodied in certain place-names are relics of this aboriginal people.

There is, unfortunately, a peculiarity in the habits of the Malagasy, in common with all the Polynesian races, with regard to names, which introduces an element of uncertainty into geographical nomenclature, viz., the practice of tabooing words or particles which enter into the composition of the names of their chiefs. As all personal names have some distinct meaning, and are largely composed of commonly-used nouns, verbs, and adjectives, as well as the names of animals, plants, &c., it constantly occurs that the names of most familiar objects and actions have to be changed through forming part of their sovereign's or chief's names. From this cause, writes Mr. Hastie, British Agent at the Court of Radàma I. (1817–1826), "the names of rivers, places, and things have suffered so many changes on the western coast that frequent confusion occurs; for, after being prohibited by their chieftains from applying any particular terms to the accustomed signification, the natives will not acknowledge to have ever known them in their former sense" (*Tyerman and Bennet's Voyages*, p. 276, 2nd ed.). There is reason to believe, however, that this cause of change and uncertainty applies much less to the place-names of the central and eastern districts of the country, and that the *taboo* (Malag. *fàdy*) there more affects the names of objects and actions than those of places.

Before considering the names of places *in* Madagascar, a word or two may be said about the name of the country itself. There seems much reason to believe that the word "Madagascar" is not a native name, but is one that has been given it by foreigners. There appears to be no Malagasy root in the word, and the combination of the consonants *sc*, or *sk*, is one not allowed by the genius of the language. The island used to be termed by the people *Izao rehètra izao*, "This whole," in accordance with the belief of many insular nations that their own island is the principal part of the world; and in the time of Radàma I., and subsequently, it was also described as *Ny anìvon' ny rìaka*, "The [land] in the midst of the flood." According to some accounts, an old designation of the country was *Nòsin-dàmbo*, "Island of wild-boars," these animals being the largest wild creatures of the forests. The only attempt at explaining the derivation of the word "Madagascar" which I have seen is that given in one of the earliest books upon the island, a German work published at Altenbourg, in Meissen, in 1609, and entitled *Beschreibung der Mechtigen und Weitberhumbten Insul Madagascar*, by Jerome Megiser, in which it is affirmed that the African kings of Madagascar and Adel conquered the coast region of the island; that "the inhabitants have also been forced to swear to recognise no other for their king, and the island also is to be called nothing else but Magadaxo. This word was afterwards corrupted into Magadascar, and at last became Madagascar, which name it kept until the Portuguese afterwards gave it another name, as has been mentioned before." Whether or not this contains any historical fact it is now difficult to decide.[1] Besides the names for the island already mentioned, this German work also gives many others, most of them applied by the Arabic geographers, one being "The Island of the Moon"; they wrote the name either Kamar or Komr, the same word which enters into the name of the "Comoro" Group, to the north-west of Madagascar. These islands are called by the Arabs Komair, or the Lesser Komr. The name as applied to the whole island survived until the arrival of the Portuguese, for on one of the oldest maps, the *Charta Marina Portugalensium*, of the first decade of the sixteenth century, the name Komortina occurs for the island in addition to those of Madagascar and San Lourenço.

Coming now to the place-names *in* Madagascar, we may first look at those of *Mountains*, the most prominent and awe-inspiring of all natural features, and to which the imagination of simple peoples soon affixes descriptive epithets. The interior provinces of the island (from which regions almost all these illustrations are taken) constitute an extensive elevated mountainous region, occupying rather more than a third of the total area of the

---

[1] The Rev. Canon Isaac Taylor (author of *Words and Places*) offers the following suggestion as to the meaning of the word:—

"My guess is that the name Madagascar, which we got from Marco Polo, did not apply to the island, but to the Somali coast. He got the name from Malay sources. The question is whether *Mala-gosse* or *Mada-gosse* is its earlier form; *gosse* meant 'men' (='Bantu') in the *old* Swahili. $Ma(\frac{i}{a})$ *a gosse* would be $Ma(\frac{i}{a})a\text{-}men$, the *-ar* being the Malay suffix in Zanzib-*ar*, Nicoba-*ar*, Malab-*ar*, &c., and meaning 'land' or 'island.'

"The Hova language is a Malay dialect; 'Malay' means 'mountains.' Hence *Mala-gosc-ar* might be 'The land of the $(\frac{Malay}{hill})$ men,' while *Mada-gasc-ar* would be 'The island of the Mada or Madai men,' either the present Madai tribe southeast of the Victoria Nyanza, or else the land of the coast people in the present Somali Land, formerly called *Madun* or *Mädäin*. On this hypothesis, Polo's name would apply to the Somali Land. He describes Madagascar as Mohammedan and full of elephants, plainly *not* the island.

"We have another old form in one of the Polo MSS., *Magaster*, where the *Ma-* would be the Bantu plural prefix."

country, and raised from 3,000 to 5,000 feet above the sea. This hilly region is composed of primary rocks, and the loftiest summits are of granite, gneiss, and basalt. It will be seen, however, that one prominent descriptive class of names for mountains in most countries is wanting in these Malagasy names; there are none denoting the *whiteness* given by snow. Although the highest points are only a little under 9,000 feet above the sea level, this is yet, in that part of the tropics, too low for snow to lie; snow is indeed unknown in Madagascar, and so there are no equivalents in its mountain-names for the Snowdon, Ben Nevis, Snafells, or Sierra Nevada of Europe, or for the Hormus, Lebanon, or Himālayah ("Abode of Snow") of Asiatic countries.

It will also be noticed that almost all these mountain-names commence with the letters *I* or *A*. The former is merely a particle (it might almost be termed an article) which is prefixed to denote place-names, as well as tribal and personal names. The other letter is part of the preposition and demonstrative adverb *Any*, contracted to *An-* (changed for euphony to *Am-* before certain consonants), "at," giving a localising sense to the word it precedes. Further, it will be also remarked that the syllables following *An-* or *Am-* are, in a great number of cases, *bòhi-*, contracted from *vòhitra*, a word now usually taken as meaning a "town," and indeed forming the first part of a vast number of Malagasy town-names.[1] But as there are quite as many mountains as towns having *Ambòhi-* as the first part of their names, it is probable that *vòhitra* originally meant a "hill," especially when it is remembered that the root of this word is the same as that from which a number of words, such as *bòhy*, *bòhibòhy bòhitra*, &c., are derived, all of which have the idea of "swelling," "puffing," "convexity," and "protuberance."[2] One of the grandest mountains in Madagascar, situated near the

[1] Ambòhimànga, "At the blue town"; Ambòhidàva, "At the long town"; Ambòhitrandrìana, "At the prince's town;" Ambòhimanjàka, "At the king's town," &c., &c.

[2] I am confirmed in this opinion by seeing that the word used in the Malay Peninsula for "hill" is *bukit*, no doubt the same word as *vòhitra*.

northern extremity of the island, is called Ambòhitra and is said to be more than 6,000 feet high. The usual word for mountain, *tèndrombòhitra, i.e.,* " point of the town " or " hill," also confirms this ; the old towns in the centre of the island were always built for security on the tops of hills, so that the names of hill and town seem quite interchangeable.[1]

Before proceeding to point out some of the most interesting characteristics of Malagasy place-names, I will venture to translate a rather long extract from an essay by M. Alfred Grandidier on this subject, which forms an appendix to the volume treating of the Historical Geography of the island (vol. i.), forming part of his monumental work *Histoire Physique, Naturelle et Politique de Madagascar* (Paris: 1892). M. Grandidier says:

" At a first glance at a list of Malagasy place-names, one is struck by the fact that a larger number, more than half of them, commence with the syllable AM or AN, which is combined with one, two, and sometimes even three words, the sum of which very often describes, as we are about to show, some peculiarity characteristic of the place. This syllable AM or AN is a contraction of the demonstrative adverb ANY, which signifies *where there is, where one is found, near to, upon.* The first word which comes after this adverb is usually one of the following: *bòhi, bàto, bòdi, àla, kàzo, tanà, tsàha, dràno, pàsi, bàla, kàdi, kàra,* or *dàka,* but the most frequent of all these is the first ; about a quarter of these place-names in fact begin with AMBOHI, which is a contraction of *Any vòhitra,* lit., 'Where there is the mountain which ' . . ., ' Where there is the village which ' . . . Then come, approximately in the order of frequency: AMBATO (from *Any vàto,* lit., 'Where there is a rock which' . . .); AMBODI (from *Any vòdy,* lit., 'At the foot of' . . .) ; ANALA (from *Any àla,* lit., 'Where there is the forest which ' . . .); ANKAZO (from *Any hàzo,* lit., 'Where the trees are' . . .) ; ANTANA (from *Any tanàna,* lit., 'Where there is the village which' . . .); ANTSAHA

[1] A hill is *havòana,* lit a " height.

(from *Any sàha*, lit., 'Where there is the valley, the water-course, which' . . .) ; ANDRANO (from *Any ràno*, lit., 'Where the water is' , . .); AMPASI (from *Any fàsika* [Hova], *fàsy* or *fàsina* [prov.], lit., 'Where the sand is' . . .); AMBALA (from *Any vàla*, lit., 'Where there is an enclosure, a compound' . . .) ; ANKADI (from *Any hàdy*, lit., 'Where there is a fosse, a trench which' . . .); ANKARA (from *Any hàrana*, lit., 'Where there is a rock which' . . .); &c.

"This first syllable *Am, An, And, Ant* often disappears, and in this case the meaning of the name slightly changes; one may, in fact, say indifferently AMBOHIBE and VOHIBE (which signify respectively: *At the great mountain*, and *The great mountain*); ANALASORA (*Where there is the wood of hedgehogs*) and ALASORA (*The wood of hedgehogs*); ANDRANOMAMY (*Near the sweet water*) and RANOMAMY (*The sweet water*); ANTSAHAONDRY (*In the valley of sheep*); AMPASIMENA (*On the red sand*) and FASIMENA (*The red sand*); AMBALANOSY (*Where there is an enclosure for goats*) and VALANOSY (*The enclosure for goats*); ANKADIVORY (*Where there is a circular fosse*) and HADIVORY (*The circular fosse*); ANKARANANDRIANA (*Near the rock of the noble*) and HARANANDRIANA (*The rock of the noble*), &c. But in the second form of these names, the Malagasy often prefix to the word the article denoting a proper name, which is a simple I, and they say; IVOHIBE, IALASORA, IFASIMENA, IVALANOSY, IHARANANDRIANA, &c.

"Leaving out of consideration, amongst the words which commence with any other letter than A, those whose initial root is VOHI, VATO, VODI, HAZO, ALA, TANA, SAHA, RANO, FASI, VALA, HARA, or IHARA, and which, as we have said, are to some extent identical with those which have the prefix, we find that the greater number commence with BE- (large, numerous), FARA- (the last), MAHA- (that which is able to . . ., which is proper to . . ., which becomes . . .), MAN- (a verbal prefix which, joined to the root, forms the verbs), MANJAKA- (he who reigns, who governs), MARO- (much of . . .), NOSI- (island),

SARA- (?), SARO- (by contraction from SAROTRA, difficult, dangerous, dear), SOA- or TSARA- (beautiful, good, pleasant), TSI (that which is not, or which has not . . .), TSIAFAK- (that which cannot be attained by . . .), VINAN- (the mouth of a river), &c. All these words are often preceded by an I, which is, as we have observed, the article denoting a proper name; thus, Imanàkana, Inòsifìto, Ivinànimalàza, are the same names as Manàkona, Nòsifìto, Vinànimalàza."

As might be supposed, the idea of *height* and *prominence* is one of the most frequently occurring in mountain-names in Madagascar. Thus we find several called Angàvo, "The lofty," and one of the grandest mountains in eastern Imèrina is Angàvokély, "*Little*-lofty," to distinguish it from the Angàvo which forms a magnificent tower or outwork, so to speak, of the mountain wall on the eastern side of the upper plateau. There is also Avomàsina, the "Sacred-high" (place); and one of the loftiest peaks in the Vàvavàto district in southern Imèrina is Iàvohàika, "The-lofty-defying-one," a mountain nearly 7,000 feet high. The word *ambòny*, "above," also occurs in several names, as Ambònilòha, "Overhead," Ambònivòhitra, "Above-the-town" (or hill); as well as *lòha*, "head," in Iàvolòha, "Lofty-headed," Lòhavòhitra, "Head-of-the-hill" (or town), one of the highest mountains in Vònizòngo. *Asàndratra*, "raised," "exalted," forms part of several names, as Nasàndràtany; as also does *àrina* "set up," "lifted up," in such words as Ambòhimiàrina. There are numerous mountain-names in which the root *rìngy*, meaning "loftiness," "conspicuousness," comes in; thus we find Andringiringy, Màhakiringy, and Andrìngitra, a very prominent ridge fourteen miles north of the capital, and closely connected with the old idolatry; a cave in its steep southern slopes being a Malagasy Delphi, the former abode of the god Rànakandrìana. The same meaning of height and eminence is found in Milangàna (from the root *lànga*, "tall, lofty"), a lofty point north of the old capital Ambòhimànga. Much the same idea is implied in the root *rànga* "having, the ears erect," a word applied to animals, and found in the name 'Andràngarànga.'" The commanding position of some eight or ten Imèrina hills is implied in their name Màhatsìnjo, "Able-to-gaze" (from), *tsìnjo* being a word meaning to look at distant objects.[1] From an almost exactly synonymous root, *tàzana*, comes the name of another mountain, Fitazànana, "The Outlook." The sharply-pointed peaks of some hills, again, have suggested the idea of a "spur"[2] (Mal. *fàntsy*), which is accordingly given to some of them; while another is called Ambòhimarànitra, "Sharp-hill"; another is Antèndro, "At-the-point"; and others are Itsìloàbo, "Lofty-thorn," and Ivàtotsìlo, "Thorn-rock." One mountain name, Madìotàndroka, "Clean-horn," reminds one of the Matterhorn and Schreckhorn, &c., of the Alps.

Height of course involves some degree of *mystery* and *dread*, which ideas are accordingly embodied in several mountain-names. Thus we find Ambòhijànahàry, "God's-hill," in several districts; the word Zànahàry (Creator) being vaguely applied by the Malagasy to many things which they cannot understand; as is also the other word for God, Andriamànitra, as in Andriamànitravàto, "God's-rock," and Ambòhitràndriamànitra, "God's-hill" (or town). Of names of this class are Imanòndrolànitra "Sky-pointing," and Itsìandànitra, "Not-in-the-sky." A mountain in the Tanàla (forest) region is the Malagasy Hades, the caves in it being supposed to be the dwellings of departed spirits, and is called Iràtsy (or Iràty), "The-evil-place." The few Europeans who have ascended the peaks of Ankàratra, the highest mountain-mass in the island, have described the great reluctance of the natives to accompany them, and their terror of some supposed malignant influence on those lofty summits. *Zàvona*, "mist," enters into the composition of several mountain-names, as Ibézàvona, "Much-mist," Ifòtsizàvona, "Mist-whitened,"

---

[1] A hill from which the Imàmo district can be surveyed is called Màhatsìnjo-imàmo, *i.e.*, "Able-to-look-over-Imamo."

[2] Also found in reduplicate form, as Ampàntsifàntsy.

and Manélozàvona, " Mist-shaded " (?), and Tsiàfajàvona, " Not-free-from-mist," the name of one of the highest peaks of Ankàratra. *Inaccessibility* is involved in several other names; as Tsiàfabalàla, Tsiàfakalìka, and Tsiàfakàfo (another Ankàratra peak), which three names mean respectively " Impassable by a locust," " by a dog," and "by fire." Almost exactly the same meaning is giving in the names Tsiàzombòrona, Tsiàzonambòa, and Tsiàzompapàngo, which mean "Unattainable by a bird," " by a dog," and " by a hawk." The sharp cutting wind of these elevated points gives a name to one hill, Sàrodrìvotra, " Difficult (through) wind "; while the variety of blasts has probably suggested another name, Imàrorìvotra, " Many-winds." Possibly the howling of the wind round the top gives the name of another hill, Ambòhimitréna, " Bellowing-hill."

Somewhat poetical names occur in Ambòhijànamàsoàndro, " Hill-of-children-of-the-Sun," in Fònovàratra, " Thunderbolt-covering," in Tòmpombòhitra, " Lord-of-the-hills," in Andrìanàmbo, " King-of-the-heights " (or " Kingly-height"), and in Malàkiàlina, " Quickly-night," the name of a hill north of Ambòhimànga, whose height causes a deep gorge to the east of it to be soon in darkness after sundown.

As height also involves *size*, the word *bé*, "big," is found in many names, as Ambòhibé and Ivòhibé, " Big-mountain," Antànambé, " Big-town," Màngabé, " Big-blue " (probably referring to the colour of the basalt rock), Ivàtobé, " Big-rock," and Bòngabé, " Big-hill." The first part of the last-named word also enters into several hill-names; it means a clod, a turf, and also a round hill, so we find Bònga, Bòngabé, and Bòngakély, *i.e.*, hills, big and little.[1]

It has already been noticed that the primary rocks form most of the highest points of Madagascar, and the word *vàto* (euphoniously changed after *am-* to *bato*), " stone," is therefore a very fre-

[1] Probably the same idea of rounded convexity comes in, somewhat indelicately to our English notions, in Bévòhoka, " Pregnant " (lit., " Large-wombed "), and Kitròka, " Belly," both names of hills in Imèrina.

quently occurring one in these mountain-names, and in one connection or another forms part of about a fourth of all the names of hills in which natural features are referred to. Thus we find it in its simplest forms of Ambàto and Ivàto, and then in combination with the words for the colours blue, black, white, red, and speckled, as Ambàtomànga, Ambàtomàinty, Ambàtofòtsy, Ambàtoména, and Ambàtovàndana ; with those for size— little, big, and immense, as Ambàtokély, Ambàtobé, and Ambàtovavènty ; and with those for height, length, roundness, steepness, bareness (lit., "baldness"), and wooded outline (lit., "hairiness"), as Ambàtoàvo, Ambàtolàva, Ambàtovòry, Ambàtomihàntona, Ambàtosòla,[1] and Ambàtovalòina. Besides these are King's-stones, Prince's-stones, many Famous-stones, as well as some Level-topped-stones, Sharply-pointed stones, and Double-peaked-stones.[2] Some hills which terminate in a solitary column of rock, have the same name as that given to the memorial erected stones, so common in Central Madagascar, Vàtolàhy (lit., "Male-stone") ; one with a double-head is called Bàka, that is, V-shaped, a term applied to the horns of cattle ; others, with three points, are the "Three-sisters'-rock"—Ambàtotèlomiràhavàvy (a hill with a grand mass of rock of this name is conspicuous near the eastern edge of Imèrina, and looks from some points like a Titanic cathedral) ; while others again are the "Three-men-rock" (Ambàtotèlolàhy); and one is called Ambàtomandrìndry, probably from a root meaning "thickly studded," here, of course, with boulder rocks. Others, solitarily conspicuous, are called Ambàtotòkana, "Separated-stone" ; and the idea of an upright column gives another name, Maḥìtsy, "Straight" or "Upright" ; and we also find Antànjombàto, "Rocky promontory." A very remarkable rocky region southwest of Ankàratra is termed Vàvavàto, "Stone-mouth" ; another hill is Ambàtofidìrana, "Entrance-stone," while both in Northern

[1] Also simply as Antsòla, "Bald-one."
[2] Ambàtomanjàka, Ambàtonandrìana, Ambàtomalàza, Ambàtomàrina, Ambàtofìsaka, Ambàtosàmpana.

Imèrina and in Southern Bètsilèo are Vàravàrambàto, "Stone-gateway," names given to mountain-passes in those provinces. But it would be tedious to particularise all the varied combinations into which *vàto* enters in Malagasy mountain-names, the more so as many are now obscure in meaning.[1]

Another word for rock, *hàrana*, is also found in many names for hills. Ankàrana is the name of the most northerly province in the island, and is so called on account of its famous rocky fastness (see *Antan. Annual*, No. III. p. 27); and this word is probably the root of the word Ankàratra, the name, as already mentioned, of the loftiest mountain-mass in Madagascar. We also find Haràmbé, "Big-rock," Ankàrankély, "Little-rock," Ihàrana, Ihàranarìvo, "Thousand-rocks," Ankàraména, "Red-rock," Ihàranandrìana, "Prince's-rock," Ankàramaina and Ihàrandàva, "Dry-rock" and "Long-rock," and several names include both the words for stone and rock, as Ambàtoharànana.

While mountain summits in Central Madagascar are usually of bare rock, here and there their names show that wood, more or less extensive, once covered their heights, and in many names *àla*, "forest," comes into combination. Thus we find Iàlaròa, "Two-woods," Anàlabé, "Great-wood," Ivòhiàlabé, "Hill-of-much-wood," Anàlamanàntona, "Hanging-wood," Anàlamirà-viràvy, "Overhanging-wood," Anàlamanàra, "Cold-wood," Anà-lamahìtsy, "Upright-wood," Anàlambàno, "Heron's-wood," Anàlambàto, and also Isòmotra, "Beard," probably a fanciful allusion to woods; and several others, including words of obscure meaning. *Hazo*, "tree," also occurs in several hill-names, as Ankàzotòkana, "Solitary-tree," Ankàzobé, "Big-tree," and Ankàzomiròhitra (perhaps mirohotra, which would mean "a company of trees"). The names of separate trees or grasses distinguish other hills, as Ambérobé (*vero* is a long grass), Inàtobé, "Much-nàto," the name of a tree whose bark yields a red dye, Ambòlobé, "Much-bamboo," Ivoàra, "Fig-tree," and

---

[1] One of the tribal divisions of the Hova Malagasy bears the name of Mandia-vàto, "Treaders-of-the-rock."

Ambiàty, the name of a shrub. *Vàry*, "rice," and *fàry*, "sugar-cane," also occur in the names of three or four hills; Ambòhibàry is a very lofty mountain in S. Bètsilèo; and we also find Tàmponkétsa, "Summit-of-rice-ground," and Antsàhafàry, "Sugar-cane-field." The fragrant grasses found in many places have suggested names for several hills, the word *mànitra*, "fragrant," forming parts of the following: Isàhamànitra, Ivòhimànitra, and Avomànitra. A beautifully wooded mountain in the Anàtivòlo[1] district is called Vòhiléna, "Wet-hill" (?), probably from the moisture attracted by its numerous trees.

The generally waterless character of the hills is, however, indicated in several of their names, as Andrànorìtra, "Dried-up-water," Fàsina, "Sand," Ampàsimàvo, "Brown-sand," Vòvotàny, "Earth-dust"; while some others, which have lakes and springs as the source of rivers, are called Andrànofìto, "Seven-streams," Imàroràno, "Many-waters," Màsinòny, "Sacred (or salt) river," Farìhilàva, "Long-lake," and Mànjaràno, perhaps, "Dun-(coloured-)water" (this is also the word for plumbago). One hill is called Anìvoniràno, "In-the-midst-of-waters."

The pleasant situation and pure air of many hills is recognized in their names, as Ambòhitsàra, "Good-" and Ambòhitsàrabé, "Exceedingly-good-hill," Ambòhitsòa, "Pleasant-hill" (a frequent name), Nòsifàly, "Joyful-island," Nòsisòa, "Pleasant-island," Bémàsoàndro, "Much-sun," and Tòkotànitsàra, "Good-settlement"; while the steep ascents and difficulty of climbing to their tops are shown in the names of others, as Màhakétraka, "Disheartening," and Màharéraka, "Exhausting." The deep *hàdy* or fosses with which many hills are scored, and dug as defences for the town on the summit, give in various combinations several names, as Ankàdivòry, "Circular-fosse," Ankàdibé, "Big-fosse," Ankàdifòtsy, "White-fosse," Ihàdimànga, "Blue-fosse," &c. So also the word *vàla*, an inclosure, is a part of a few hill-names, as Ambàlahìrana and Ambàlafàsana, although it

[1] *I.e.*, "Amongst-the-bamboos."

is more strictly and frequently, as might be supposed, a town-name.

From a large number of extinct volcanic cones in the interior provinces of Madagascar, extending probably almost in an unbroken line from the south to the north and north-west, one might suppose that in the names of some of them at least we should find some reference to fire or heat. I can, however, find only two or three instances where possibly some remembrance of igneous forces is preserved, viz., in Ambàtomày, "Burnt-rock," and Iàmboàfo, "Lofty-fire," the names of two mountains in the Tanàla province, and in another named Kitròka, a word which means "lava."

A considerable number of mountains are designated after the names of *Animals* and *Birds*. Most numerous are those called after the guinea-fowl, *akànga*, there being probably at least a dozen named Ambàtonakànga, "Stone-of-the-guinea-fowl." Then come several called after the cock, Ambòhitrakòholàhy ; the large hawk, Ambàtombòromahèry; the kestrel, Ikìtsikìtsika; the kite, Masìapapàngo, *i.e.*, "Fierce-with-kites"; the dove, Ambòhibòromailàla ; the cardinal-bird, Ifòdy ; the peacock, Vòrombòla ; and there is one called "Feather," Vòlombòrona. (As already mentioned also in speaking of names denoting height, there are numerous hills called "Impassable" by birds hawks, kites, &c.) The largest and most valuable animal of the country, the humped ox, *òmby*, gives names to a good many hills ; in its simplest form, Ambòhitròmby, "Ox-hill," and Ambòhitròmbalàhy, "Bull-hill," and in Andràokòmby, "Licked-up-by-oxen," Antàndrokòmby, "Ox-horn," Antràfonòmby, "Ox-hump," and in Ambòhimanòto, "Butting-hill." The words for sheep (*òndry*), goat (*òsy*), and wild-hog (*làmbo*), are found in several hill-names ; as Ambàtonòndrilàhy, Antsàhanòndry, Ambòhitròndry, Ambàtonòsy, and Lòhalàmbo, "Hog's-head." Even the crocodile also appears in these mountain-names, as in Màmba, although, as might be supposed, it is more frequently found in river-names ; and also the hedgehog, in Ambòhitsòkina.

We also find "Many-rats," Màrovòalàvo; "Many-fleas," Màroparàsy (a rather frequent and uncomfortably appropriate name for many villages); "Many-ants," Màrovìtsika; and two or three "Honey-hills," Ambòhitantély.

A smaller number of mountains have received names which may almost be termed *Personal*, and are derived either from some renowned king or chief, or have some obscure reference to people, their numbers, relationships, &c. Thus we find the "mountains" of Ratrìmo, Rasòmotra, Razàka and Rafìlo; the "cattle-fold" *(fàhitra)* of Andriamandròso; and the "hill" of the renowned chief who founded the Hova monarchy and supremacy, in the unconscionably long name of Bòngan*àndrianimpòinimèrina!* The name of the supposed aboriginal tribe of the interior is contained in Soa*vazìmba*, and that of the Hovas in Famohìlan*kòva*. An Oriental exaggeration of numbers comes in in Ambòhitrarìvobé, "Hill-of-many-thousands," and in Ambòhipòloàlina, "Hill-of-ten-ten-thousands"; we find also "People's-hill," "Son-of-men's-hill," "Hill-of-the-old," "Slave's-hill," "Prince's-hill," "King's-hill" (in Manjàkabé, "Great-king," simply); and the hills of the "Good-father," the "Grandchild," and of "Sacred-chanting" (Ambòhimiràry). Two or three Imèrina hills have a strictly personal name, as Ramànarìvo and Ràntoàndro.

A very numerous class of mountain-names I have grouped as of *doubtful* signification, meaning thereby not that the words themselves are obscure in meaning, but that the reason for giving such names is doubtful. They comprise verbs, adjectives, and nouns, and while in some cases an examination of the particular hill, or inquiry among the nearest inhabitants, might very likely afford some clue to the origin of the name given, in many cases the reason is probably hopelessly lost. A few examples may now be given; and of *nouns* used as names we find the following: Anjòmba, "Conch-shell," Ambòhibòla, "Money-hill," Ampériféry, "Pepper-place," Bétòngotra, "Big-footed," Antémitra, "Matted," Sòmpitra, "Rice-basket," Vinàny

"A Guess," Ambilàny, "At-the-pot," Ambòhimizàna, "Money-scales-hill," Ankàfotra, "At-the-hàfotra" (tree), Laona, "Rice-mortar," &c.

Of *adjectives* employed as hill-names there are only a few, as Mangìdy, "Bitter," Mòra, "Easy," and Manéva, "Beautiful"; but a large number of verbs are used as hill-names; *e.g.*, Ambòhitsimiòza, "Not-bathing-hill," Mànana, "Having," Ambòhimanàhy, "Disquieting-hill," Ambòhimanòa, "Tribute-paying-hill," Ambòhimàhalàla, "Knowing-hill," Màhasàrotra, "Making-difficult," Ambòhimandràly, "Receiving-hill," Ambòhitsiléo, "Unconquered hill," Manadàla, "Making-foolish," Manàlalòndo, (perhaps) "Throwing-off-drowsiness," and Mahasòa, "Benefiting." A curious name occurs in Màntsihoàiza, which is, literally, "Say, where to?"

It will be thus seen from these examples, from a few groups of Madagascar mountain-names, chiefly taken in the centre of the island, that there is much variety in them; and that some of them give evidence of considerable imaginative power on the part of the early inhabitants of the country. I do not here attempt to speculate on the facts possibly embodied (fossilised, so to speak) in another large group of names whose meanings are obscure, and which may probably in some cases prove to be archaic words, and may in others preserve obsolete forms of the verbs and other parts of speech.

The *River*-names in Madagascar next claim a little notice, although they are less striking in their descriptive character than we have seen the hill-names to be. A glance at a map of the island shows that the largest rivers flow to the west, the water-shed being comparatively near the eastern coast, so that, except the Mangòro, few very large rivers flow into the Indian Ocean; but there are a great number of small streams, many of which have cut deep gorges in the chains of hills, and are broken by numerous cataracts and falls. Two words are used for "river" in Malagasy: *rénirâno*, which is literally "mother of waters," and *òny*, a word which, it will be seen, is frequently combined with others in forming river-names. (This latter word is Malayan in origin, and is the same as the Malayan *sugnie*, a river; *s* being in both languages a very loose noun prefix; *u* is the Malagasy *o*; and the coast *n* is nasal and equal to *gn*.)

Descriptive epithets of natural features are of course found in a good many river-names, as in Onibé and Onivé, "Big-river," Andrànobé, "Much-water," Lémpona, "Concave" or "Hollow," Ampòntàny, "In-the-heart-of-the-land," Ampivalànana, "At-the-descending" (water), and Andrànomàvo, "Brown-water." We also find Onimàinty and Onifòtsy, "Black-river" and "White-river," Onilàhy, "Male-river," and Imàintinàndro, "Black-by-the-day" (?). The power of some small streams when swelled by sudden and heavy rain is noticed in such names as Kélimahéry, "Little-(but) strong," Kélilàlina, "Little-(but) deep"; the difficulty of fording them in Fìtamalàina, "Unwilling-ford"; the noisy character of some, in Andriamamòvoka, "Dust-raising-prince" (probably alluding to the spray or mist caused by the rapids or falls); the broken channels of others in Imànandrìana, "Having-cataracts," while another bears the ominous name of Màtiandràno, *i.e.* "Drowned." The largest river in Madagascar is the Manìa, a word meaning "To go astray," and called in the lower portion of its course Tsiribìhina, *i.e.* "The unfordable," so it is said, but probably meaning "The impassable." Of this river Capt. Larsen, of the Norwegian mission-ship, says he believes that it brings down more fresh water than the Ganges; at its mouth the sea is fresh three miles from land. The meaning of Bètsibòka, the large river flowing from Imèrina to the north-west, is "Much-fresh-water," as its waters are still potable at a mile's distance from its outlet.

The names of *Animals* are applied to a few Madagascar rivers, as in Màmba, "Crocodile" (almost every river swarms with these reptiles), Ombifòtsy, "White-ox," Ambòrompòtsy, "At-the-White-bird" (an egret), Antànandàmbo, "Wild-hog's-foot" (lit., "hand"), Sàhalàmbo, "Wild-hog's-field," and Sàhanamàlona, "Eel's-field." This word *sàha*, "field," is found in some other river-names, as Sàhasàrotra, "Difficult-field," Sàhaòmby, "Spacious-(?) field," or perhaps "Ox-field," and Isàhanònja, "The-field- (or place) of-waves"; also Sàhafilo, *filo*="needle," or possibly *filao*, name of a fish.

Ambàto, "At-the-stone," is found in several river-names, as well as in those (as already seen) of mountains and towns; in these cases it probably refers to some hill or rock where the stream takes its rise or near which it flows, or possibly from its rock-impeded channel. Thus we find, Ambàtolàmpy, "At-the-rock," Ambàtomiàdy, "At-the-fighting-stone," Ambàtomàinty, "At-the-black-stone," and Ambàtotsipàhina, "At-the-kicked-stone" (probably with some reference to giant legends). One river is called Ankàzotsipìhina, "At-the-ruled-(or straightened) tree," another is called Fantàra, a name also given to meteoric stones, and another is Varàhina, "Copper."

As with mountains, so also a few rivers have names referring to persons; two or three have the personal prefix Andrian-, as Andriambilàny, and Andriaménakély, "Prince-of-the-estate." One is curiously called Ikòtoràtsy, "Bad-boy," another, Zànakòlona, "Son-of-men," and another, Andrànonandrìana, "At-the-prince's-stream."

It must be said, however, that the above examples include (excepting the Manìa and the Onilàhy) few of the largest streams of the island, such as the Bètsibòka,[1] with the Ikiòpa, the Mangòro, the Matsìatra, the Sofia, the Mànanàra, and Mànanjàra[2] (there are several examples of these two names), the Màhajìlo,[3] the Sisàony, and many others, the meaning of whose names is obscure. We probably need a fuller acquaintance with dialects other than the Hova to understand many of the names applied to rivers. In the name of the Màtitànana, *i.e.* "Dead-handed," a S.E. coast river, a piece of legendary

[1] Lit., "Many-not-lepers."   [2] Lit., "Having-a-share."
[3] *Jilo* is "sharp-pointed."

history of a giant having thrown his hand across the stream at an enemy, is said to be preserved; but it is probable that the story has been invented to account for the name. In some portions of the east coast of Madagascar the names of tribes and of the rivers flowing through the territory are identical, and it is often difficult to say whether the people took their name from the river, or *vice versâ*. Curious superstitions cling to some of the rivers, *e.g.*, of the Matsìatra in Bètsilèo, Mr. Shaw says, it is "a splendid river, though on account of the superstition of the people deterring them from putting a canoe upon it, it is one of the greatest obstacles in travelling to and from the capital in the wet season. In one itinerating journey, the only way of getting the writer's goods across was by balancing them upon the native water-pitchers, a man swimming on each side propelling the cranky vessel forward."

The *Lake*-names in Madagascar will not detain us long, as they are very few in number for so large an island. The largest one, of Alaotra, in the Antsihànaka province, has already been mentioned as probably embodying one of the few Arabic words in Malagasy place-names. (It will be remembered that the allied word "Laut" is largely used for "island," *i.e.*, "sea-surrounded," in the Malayan archipelago; as Timor Laut, &c.) The next in size is Itàsy, whose name at first sight would mean "shallow," the word *tàsy* being applied chiefly to plates and dishes. It is said that this lake is of recent formation, at least tradition goes back to a time when it is said to have been formed by the breaking down of some embankment by a Vazìmba chieftain. As, however, a considerable stream, which in the rainy season forms a grand waterfall, always issues from Itàsy and forms the river Lilia (a word of unknown meaning, to myself, at least), this seems a little mythical. In a map of the lake made by Mr. W. Johnson (see *Antanànarìvo Annual*, No. I., 1875), every bay and division of it has a separate name applied to it, a proof of the minute distinction by the Malagasy of places by giving appropriate names.[1] The full name of the lake is Itàsi-hànaka, the latter word being a root signifying "to run out as a liquid," as ink on blotting-paper, for example ; the word is also used as a synonym for others meaning lake, pool, &c., but is not much employed. This word is also found in the name of a northern central tribe, the Sihànaka, probably from the character of the country they inhabit, with extensive marshes, and the lake Alaotra, just mentioned, in its north-east corner. It is worth notice that the word *tàsy* is found in several of the Malayan island dialects, and there means "sea." A lake in the province of Pahang in the Malay peninsula is called *Tassek* Bera, evidently the same word as in the Malagasy. A small lake south-west of Ankàratra is called Vinàniòny ; *vinàny* is a word frequently used on the east coast for a river-opening through the bars of sand which partly block up the mouths of most of them, and means "breach," "irruption." On the south-west coast are two lakes called Heòtry (or Hoétry) and Tsimànampétsòtse, but the meaning of neither of them is clear.

On the eastern coast of Madagascar is a remarkable chain of coast lakes or lagoons, into which the rivers fall. These have doubtless been formed by the incessant strife between the rivers and the ocean, for there is a constant heavy surf raised by the south-east trade-wind. So nearly continuous are these lagoons that by cutting about thirty miles of canal to connect them, an unbroken water-way of two hundred and sixty miles in length could be formed along the eastern coast. These lagoons are distinguished by separate names, as Nòsibé, Iràngy, Rasòabé, &c.

There are two or three examples of small but profoundly deep lakes formed in the extinct craters of some of the old

[1] These are : (1) Taràzo, "Hereditary" (?) ; (2) Ampéfy, "At-the-embankment " ; (3) Kavànta, possibly "Opening," as this is the point where the river issues from the lake ; (4) Ambàvanandrìana, "At-the-prince's-mouth, or opening," a strait between broad reaches ; (5) Lohòloka, meaning doubtful ; (6) Anjìva, ditto ; (7) Fitandàmbo, "Wild-hog's-ford."

volcanoes. One of these, Tritrìva, is said to be unfathomable, and is the traditional abode of the *Fanàny*, a seven-headed dragon or monster, about which marvellous stories are told (*see* Chapter V.).

We now turn to the last division of the subject, that of the names applied to *Towns and Villages* in Madagascar.

Before giving a few examples of these under the different classes into which the mountain-names have been divided, there are two or three points which should be kept in mind in considering town and village names found among the Malagasy. The first of these is the fact already mentioned in speaking of the hill-names, viz., that on account of the ancient practice of the interior tribes of building their villages on the summits of hills and mountains, in very many cases it is impossible to distinguish exactly between what are strictly the names of hills and what are those of the villages. It is possible, therefore, that some of the examples already given of mountain-names may be names really applied to the settlements formed on their slopes or loftiest points; while, on the other hand, it may be the case that some of the town or village names to be presently mentioned are really those of the hills on which they are built.

Another point which should be borne in mind is, that while in the central and eastern provinces the population has a stable, settled character, having remained probably for centuries in many of the towns or villages originally founded by their ancestors on their first occupation of the country; those on the western side, on the contrary, the Sàkalàva tribes, are much more nomadic in their habits. They do not practise agriculture so much as the other peoples; rice, which in the wet method of culture, as followed by the Hova and Bètsilèo and east-coast tribes, requires a good deal of earth-work, embankments, aqueducts, &c., is little used by them; and they are more exclusively pastoral, keeping large herds of cattle. Besides this, their superstitious fear of death, or rather of some malign influence exerted by the spirits of the departed, leads them, it is said, to break up their villages when a death occurs, so that their settlements must be more like camps than villages, properly so called. The Sihànaka have the same superstition, but they avoid most of the inconvenience by removing any one who appears dangerously ill out of the village and placing him in a hastily-constructed hut, which is afterwards pulled down and left to decay. We shall therefore probably find little of interest in the village-names of the Sàkalàva. There is, however, this noticeable point in the principal names, whether of towns or geographical features, all round the island, that the majority of them are distinctly recognisable as containing roots which are Malagasy as spoken by the Hova, and thus they confirm the fact, supported also on other grounds, of the essential unity of the Malagasy language, notwithstanding various dialectic differences.

One more point may be here mentioned, viz., that in many places there occurs a rather perplexing duality of names, arising from the fact that the Hova, when forming military posts for the maintenance of their supremacy over various parts of the island which they have conquered, have generally given them a name differing from that of the native village on the same site or close to it. These latter usually retain the original appellation, so that sometimes a stranger is puzzled to understand where he his going, or what place the people are speaking about.

A word or two may be said first about the capital and chief towns of Madagascar, before proceeding to classify the smaller towns and villages according to the divisions already observed in other place-names. The name of Antanànarìvo, the capital city, signifies, somewhat in an Oriental vein of exaggeration, "City of a Thousand," that is, probably, settlers or military colonists, who were placed there after its conquest by the Hova chieftains. Some have considered the name as referring rather to the homesteads or compounds, which clustered probably for a long time as detached settlements round the slopes of the long steep ridge on which the city is built. There are no street-names in the city, indeed there are only three or four streets or principal roads through the dense mass of houses, but the position of most houses is ascertained tolerably exactly by the numerous names which are given to different portions of the varied and broken ground over which the capital extends, every prominent hollow or slope or level portion having some special and often very appropriate name. Thus we find Fàravòhitra, "Last-village" (or hill), at the northern extremity, and Ambòhipòtsy, "White-hill," from the white soil of that part, at the southern end of the ridge; while Ambòhimitsìmbina, "Hill-of-observation" (or attention), is the highest point. Then there is Antsàhatsiròa, "Not-two-fields" or valleys, a steep descent near the centre; the precipices of Ampàmarìnana, "Hurling-place," the Tarpeian Rock of the capital, on the west side of the hill; the open triangular space of Andohàlo, the coronation ground and place of public assemblies, on the upper part of the city; and the level square plain of Imàhamàsina, "Place-of-consecration," at the foot of the hill to the west, where military reviews take place and where some of the sovereigns were publicly recognised by their subjects. Near this is Anòsy, "At-the-island," an artificial lake with a small island in the centre. (Each royal house has its proper name, as Manjàkamiàdana, "Reigning-peacefully," Tràno-vòla, "Silver-house," Màsoàndro, "Sun," Manàmpisòa, "Adding-good," &c.) In other parts of the city are Ambòhitantély, "Hill-of-honey," Ambàtonakànga, "Guinea-fowl-stone," Ampàribé, "Much-sugar-cane," Anàlakély, "Little-wood," Zomà, "Friday," the great market-place, so called because the market is held on that day, &c., &c. South-west of the city is a large timber palace which was built by Radàma I. on the site of a hill which he partly levelled, and called Isoànieràna, "Good-for-inquiry," or consultation, *i.e.*, a convenient place where he might hear complaints and dispense justice. To the east of the capital is Ambàtoròka, "Craggy-rocks," a rough piece of ground covered with boulders, and a former place of execution; further south is Mahàzoarìvo, "Having-a-thousand"; while to the west is a rounded hill called Amhò-hijànahàry, "God's-hill"; and stretching for many miles west, north, and south is the immense rice-plain of Bètsimitàtatra, "Great-undivided," a name evidently given before its enclosure and cultivation, for it is now *much* divided by *tàtatra* or water-channels.

Ambòhimànga, "Blue-hill" or "Famous-hill" (or town), is the ancient capital, eleven miles north of Antanànarìvo, and possibly so called from the mass of bluish gneiss rock which forms the highest point of the triangular hill on which the town is built. The slopes are entirely covered with woods, which form a refreshing contrast to the generally bare and treeless character of the greater portion of Imèrina. As at Antanànarìvo, various parts of the more ancient capital are distinguished by special names, as Amboàra, "The fig-tree" (*voàra*), Ambàtomitsàngana, "The standing-stone," Antsàhamànitra, "The fragrant-field," Andàkana, "At-the-canoe," &c. Ambòhimànga is also the name of the chief town of the northern Tanàla, or forest people, and is given to some other towns as well, both in this form and in that of Ambòhimàngakély (*kély* = little). The capital of the Bètsilèo province has a name probably given by the Hova on their conquest of the country—Fianàrantsòa, "Good-learning"; it is a town with about 6,000 or 7,000 inhabitants.

The chief port of the N.W. coast of Madagascar, the town of Mojangà (incorrectly called by Europeans and on charts Majunga), derives its name from "a colony of Swahili-speaking Arabs, who were the first occupants of the site. They found, so say their descendants, the shore lined with flowering shrubs, which, as the most remarkable thing about the place, led them to call their village *mji-angaia*, 'the town of flowers.'" This was subsequently corrupted to Mojangà. The Bay of Bemba-tooka takes its name from a small village formerly existing on its shores, and called Fòmbitòka = *fòmby tòkana*, "One-rofia-palm," and corrupted by foreigners into Bembatooka.[1]

Turning now to the names of *Towns and Villages* generally, we find, as with those of the mountains, that natural features have frequently suggested their appellations. As already noticed, the building of all ancient towns of the interior on the summit of hills has made it difficult, if not impossible in many cases, to be sure whether the name given to a town on a hill is not more strictly that of the hill itself. So that, as with mountain-names, we also find the ideas of "height" in a few town-names; as Avomalàza and Avomànitra (*àvo*, "high"), Ambòdinàmbo, "At-the-foot-of-height," Ambònilòha, "Upon-the-head"; that of "ascending" in Fiakàrana and Iakàranòsy, "Goat's-ascent"; and that of "lifting up" in Ambòhimiàrina, Manàrinàrina, &c. The two words for rock, *vàto* and *hàrana*, form frequent combinations in village-names from the presence of bold rocks and precipices near many of the places thus named; as Ivàto, Ivàtovàvy, "Women's-stone" (probably from there being near to it one of the stones resorted to and anointed by women, from a belief in its virtue to give them children), Ambàtosòa, Ambòdivàto, "At-the-bottom-of-the-rock," Antòngombàto, "At-the-foot-of-the-rock," Ivàtofòtsy and Ambàtofòtsy, "At-the-white-rock," Ivàtolàvo, Ambàtofīsaka, Ambàtotòkana, "At-the-solitary-rock," Ampàrafàravàto, "At-the-stone-bed-stead"; this is one of the three Malagasy towns to which entrance is forbidden to Europeans by an article in the 1865 treaty, since they were then the seats of the chief idols. In the Sihànaka province is a town called Ampàrafàravòla, "At-the-silver-bedstead," and there are several Ambàtomalàza, "Famous-stones." Then there are found Ihàrana, Ankàranīla, Ankàramalàza, and Ankàratsinànana. The colour of the soil also gives frequent names, as Antànifòtsy, "White-earth," Ambòhipòtsy, "At-the-white-hill," Ankàdifòtsy, "At-the-white-fosse," Ampàsi-

[1] See paper by W. C. Pickersgill, Esq., in *L.M.S. Missionary Chronicle*, Oct. 1882, p. 323; and *Antanànarìvo Annual*, No. XII., 1888.

ména, "At-the-red-sand," Ivòhiména, "Red-hill," &c. We also find Ambòhidròa, "Two-towns," and Ifitobòhitra, "Seven-towns."

Trees and woods give many town-names, as Ambòlobé, "Much-bamboo," Anakakòndro, "At-the-plantain-shoots," Ambòdirofia, "At-the-foot-of-the-rofia" (palm), Antapiabé, "Much-*tapia*" (a tree with edible fruit, and used for silkworm culture), Ampàngabé, "Much-fern," Ivòhidròy, "Bramble-town," Ambòatàvo, "At-the-gourds," Ankàzomàsina, "At-the-sacred-tree," Iàlamalàza, "Famous-wood," Anàlamàizina, "At-the-dark-wood," Ambàniàla, "Below-the-wood," Béràvina, "Much-foliage," Tàmponàla, "Top-of-the-wood," &c. The pleasant situation of many villages gives appropriate names to not a few of them, which contain the words *tsàra* (good) and *sòa* (pleasant), the latter of which is especially frequent, as Antànantsàra, Ambòhitsàra, Itsàrafidy, "Well-chosen," Itsàrahonénana, "Good-for-dwelling-in," Ambòhitsòa, Ambàtosòa, Ambàlasòa, Antsàhasòa, Ikìanjasòa, Isòaririnina, "Pleasant-in-winter," and Sòamònina, "Pleasant-to-dwell-in." The latter word also comes in frequently in villages called Soàvina and Soàmànana; one is termed Sòatsimànampiovàna, "Unchangeably-pleasant," and the same idea of security is expressed in Fiadànana, "Peace," and Màhavélona, "Causing-to-live."[1] The open position of many villages, exposed to sunlight, gives a name to several; as, Màsoàndro, Bémàsoàndro, "Much-sun," and Ambòhibemàsoàndro; and the extensive prospect from others gives their names of Màhatsìnjo, "Able-to-overlook," and Tsìnjoarìvo, "Overlooking-a-thousand."

New settlements, now probably very ancient (like our own Newports and Newcastles), have left their traces in Ambòhibào, "Newtown," a very common village name in Imèrina; in Antòby, "At-the-camp," and Andrànovào, "At-the-new-house" (?); while the advance of settlers upon ground previously unoccupied seems to have given a name to the many places called Ambòhimandròso, "Progressing-town," and Mandrosòa, "Advance"

[1] I remember this name, a rather common one, is that of one of the filthiest villages I ever stayed a night in; the whole place being a foot deep in cowdung.

(verb imp.). Many village-names include the Malagasy equivalents for our Anglo-Saxon words *ton, ham, burgh, bury*, &c., and the Danish *by* and *thorpe*, in the words *vàla*, "a homestead," as Ambàlavòtaka, Ambàlatàny, Ambàlavòla, Ambàlasakày, and Ambàla, &c.; in *hàdy*, "a fosse," one at least of which surrounds every old village (and homestead), and very frequently several deep trenches are found one within the other; as Ankàdibé, Ankàdisàrotra, Ankàdimàinty, Ankàdifòtsy, Ambòdihàdy, and Ankàdivòribé, "Big-round-fosse" (the ordinary name for a country house is *hàdivòry*); and in *sàha*, "field," as Antsàhapétraka, Antsahafìlo, Antsàharòalòha, "Two-headed-field," Isàhafàry, "Sugar-cane-field," and Isàhabàto, "Stony-field," &c. There are a very few village-names referring to roads, or rather paths, as Antsàmpanimahàzo, freely translated, "You may choose your path," applied to two or three places at the junction of cross-roads; another bears the (probably often too appropriate) name of Ampòtaka, "In-the-mud."

From the situation of many Malagasy villages on the banks of rivers are derived several descriptive names, as Antsàmpandràno, "At-the-branching-of-the-waters," Ambòdirìana and Ambòniriana, "At-the-foot-of-" and "Upon-the-cataract," Ifàrahàntsana, "Last-rapids" (on the river Ikiòpa), Isaràhanòny, (perhaps) "At-the-separating-of-the-streams," Andrànomàndry, "By-still-waters," Amparìhy, "At-the-lake," Andòhatànjona, "At-the-head-of-the-promontory," and Imàvoràno, "Brown-water"; while we find an exact equivalent of "Oxford" in Ampìtanòmby, and an approach to "Cambridge" in Tetézambàto, "Stone-bridge." One name seems to complain of a lack of moisture, Itsimìsiràno, "There's-no-water!" On the sea-coast several village-names include the word *vinàny*, "river-mouth," as Ivinàny, Vinàniòny, &c., and also Màsondràno, a word of similar meaning, found both in this form and in that of Màsondrànokély.

A considerable number of village-names include the word *nòsy*, which is generally translated "island"; it appears, however, in many cases to mean, more exactly, a rising ground standing up from marshes and rice-fields, and more or less surrounded by them, a very near parallel to our Anglo-Saxon *ea* or *ey*, "an island," as in the names Chelsea, Thorney, Putney, Chertsey, &c.[1] Thus we find Nòsivàto, "Rocky-island," Nòsimanjàka, "King's-island," Nòsisòa, Nòsivòla, Nòsipàtrana, Nòsikély, Anòsivàrika, Nòsizàto, "Hundred-isles," Nòsiarìvo, "Thousand-isles," and, simply, Nòsy or Anòsy.

In the central district of Imèrina a number of village-names include that of the province, with some additional descriptive word; these are probably, in some cases at least, memorials of certain additions of territory or change of boundary; thus we find Imèrimandròso, Imèrinavàratra, Imèrintsiadìno, Soàvinimérina, and Imèrinarìvo. The western division of Imèrina, the Imàmo district, also gives a name to a few villages, as Arìvonimàmo and Tsinjòvinimàmo. The habit of the central Malagasy of assembling at large open-air markets for the sale and purchase of every kind of native product gives a name to many villages near such markets, according to the days of the week on which they are held. So we find numerous places called Alahàdy (although markets are no longer held on Sunday in the central provinces), Alatsinaìny, Talàta, Alarobìa, Alakamìsy, Zomà, and Asabòtsy.

As with mountain-names, so also in those of some towns and villages, the words for various animals enter into their formation; the words *màmba* and *voày*, "crocodile," *dìnta*, "leech," *ambòa*, "dog," *òsy*, "goat," *fòza*, "crab," *hàla*, "spider," and many others, all occurring; thus, Màmbazàto, "Hundred-crocodiles" (no exaggeration this in numberless places); less definite, but very suggestive, is Màrovoày, "Many-crocodiles," a Hova post and Arab settlement near the mouth of the Bètsibòka river; Màsomboày, Antsàhadìnta, Ambòatàny, Ambòhitròsy, Antsàhamàrofòza, and Antòhokàla. Most frequent are those compounded with *òmby*, "ox," as Màmiòmby, "Sweet-to-oxen," probably referring to good pastures (Sòaronòno, "Good-(for) milk," is

[1] Cf. *Words and Places*, p. 367 *et seq.*

probably of similar meaning to the foregoing), Antàndrokòmby, "Ox-horn," Lòhaòmby, "Ox-head," Ambòhitròmby, "Ox-town," and Ambòsitra,[1] "At-the-ox" (or oxen). *Fàhitra*, the word for the sunken pen or fold in which cattle are kept and fattened, enters into many village-names, especially places where these *fàhitra* were numerous or of great size, or made by some famous chief of former times; thus, Ampàhitra, Ampàhitrìzana, Ambòdifàhitra, Ampàhimànga, &c. Here we have a similar use of the word to that in our English place-ending *by* or *byr* (cf. Scot. *byre*, "a cow-stall"). A few villages take their name from some prominent or numerous tree or plant growing plentifully near it, as Ambòatàvo, "At-the-gourds," Ambòasàry, "At-the-lemons," &c.

The most common village-names of the class already grouped as *personal* are those derived from chieftainship, frequently including the words *manjàka*, sovereign, and *andrìana*, prince, noble; and our English Kingstowns, Kingstons, and Princetons find a Malagasy parallel in numerous places called Ambòhimanjàka, Ambòhitrinimanjàka, Ambàtomanjàka, Manjàkanandrìana, Miàdamanjàka, "Reigning-peacefully," Ambòhitrandrìana, Ambàtonandrìana, and Ihàranandrìana; some of these being probably the chief's village in earlier times. Of somewhat similar meaning is Ikiànjamalàza, "Famous-courtyard," and Ikiànjasòa; while the principal village of a former petty state, often a very little place, is remembered in many an Ambòhibé and Ivòhibé, "Big-village," and in frequent Antànamalàza and Ambòhimalàza, "Famous-towns" and "villages." We also find Ambòhitòmpo, "Lord's-town," and Ambàlampitsàra, "Judge's-homestead." Other villages preserve the name of a former famous king or chieftain, as Ambòhidrabìby,[2]

---

[1] *Vòsitra* is the ox, strictly so called; *òmby* being a wider word for cattle generally; hence *òmbilàhy*, "a bull," *zànakòmby*, "a calf," &c.

[2] Rabìby was an early king in Imèrina, who is said to have slain an enormous wild-boar; and he is also remembered as the first who discovered that beef was good to eat. This tradition is probably true so far as it recalls an early period when the ox was considered a sacred animal, and its flesh was only eaten as part of a religious service.

Ambòhidratrìmo, Ambòhidrapéto,[1] Ambòhidratàmo, Ambòhidramijày, and Ambàtondrazàka.[2]

Some tribal divisions or boundaries are probably preserved in the many village-names which include the word *arìvo*, "thousand," *zàto*, "hundred," and *fòlo*, "ten," as, Ivòhitrarìvo, Ambòhipòloarìvo (10,000), Soàvinarìvo, Ihàrinarìvo, Ambòhijàto and Ambijàto, and Ampòlo. Tribal names are given to some villages, which were formerly perhaps their chief settlement; as, Anjànadralàmbo (the Zànadralàmbo are the sixth and lowest rank of *andrìana*, the noble or royal clans; Ralàmbo, their ancestor, was the same as the Rabìby just mentioned, and was so called from his slaying the wild-boar or *làmbo*); and Ampàhidralàmbo, "Ralàmbo's-ox-fattening pit"; and Ambòdilàlangìna (the Làlangìna are the easternmost division of the Bètsilèo people). Bits of local and tribal or family history are probably fossilised in such names as Itélolàhy, "Three-men," Ivòhidràivo, "Ràivo's-town," Imàrovàvy, "Many-women," "Imàrozàza, "Many-children," Fierénana, "Dividing-place," Fierèna, "Refuge," Isòanieràna, "Good-for-inquiry" (an open-air court), Ampihàonana, "Meeting-place," Ambóhidrày, "Father's-village," Ambòhijàtòvo, "Youth's-village," Ambòhijànaka, "Children's-village," Ifénovahòaka, "Full-of-people,·' Tsàrahàvana, "Good-(by) relations," Itsiàzombazàha, "Not-taken-by-foreigners," &c., &c. Old sacred places and shrines are indicated by many an Ambòhimàsina and Ambàtomàsina, (*màsina*, sacred), and perhaps in Ambòhijànahàry and Ambòhitràndriamànitra, "Creator's-" and "God's-town." Sacred and venerated trees (*hàzo*) also give a few village names, as Ankàzomàsina and Ankàzobé.

About the other two divisions in which Malagasy town and village names may be classed, viz., those of "doubtful" or "obscure" meaning, it is unnecessary to speak here, for the reasons given in speaking of the names of mountains and rivers.

[1] Rapéto is said to have been a giant, and to have performed marvellous feats of strength. [2] The chief town of the Sihànaka province.

Some local allusions, obvious enough on the spot, would probably explain many of the first class of names; while fuller knowledge of old and obsolete or provincial Malagasy, and careful inquiry among the natives, will be required to elucidate the meaning of many of the second of these classes.

Before concluding, a few words must be added upon one other class of Malagasy place-names yet unnoticed, viz., those of *Provinces and Districts*. Here, however, a difficulty occurs in distinguishing many of them from those of the tribes who inhabit these various regions; since in many cases it is difficult to say whether the people take their name from the country they live in, or whether the country is called after the people. So that here the study of place-names is almost inseparable from that of personal, or rather, tribal, names. In other cases, as on the coast plains, river-names and tribal-names are equally difficult of exact discrimination, that is, as regards the priority of the two. These points cannot be now fully discussed, but a few examples may be given.

The meaning of the name of the central and leading province of Imèrina is obscure (to myself at least); the district is also occasionally termed Ankòva, from its Hova inhabitants. Among the subdivisions of Imèrina are Vàkinankàratra, the district "Cut-off-(lit. " broken-") by-Ankàratra" (mountains), Vàkintsisàony, "Cut-off-by-(the river) Sisàony," Imàmo, Vònizòngo, Valàlafòtsy, "White-locusts' a (tribal name), and to the north, Avàradràno, "North-of-the-water," Anàtivòlo, "Among-the-bamboos," &c. But the smaller district names are very numerous, and would require a separate article for their full treatment.

South of Vàkinankàratra is the Mànandrìana district, the northernmost division of the populous Bètsilèo province, home of the "Unconquered" tribe (so named, although they have been overcome by the dominant Hova); with the other subdivisions of Isàndra, so called from the river flowing through its centre, and this, again, traditionally said to be named after a

Hova, one Andriantsàndra; Ilàlangìna (literally, "Quiet-road," but there is probably some other meaning); and Iàrindràno "There-is-water,"[1] probably from the numerous streams. Further south still is the Bàra country. In this province, with its widely scattered population, there appears to be necessarily a good deal of change in its place-names, since the numerous petty kingdoms or chieftaincies are, like many African kingdoms,[2] called after the names of the reigning chief.

On the eastern side of the island, beginning at the northern point, is the Ankàrana, "the Rocky" province, possibly taking its name from a remarkable rock fortress where the inhabitants have often held their own against an invading force.[3] Coming south, are the districts of Vòhimàrina, " Level-hill," the promontory sheltering Antongil Bay and called Maròa (in Hova this word is an imperative form meaning "Be many," it is said to be so called from a small river of the same name, possibly thus named from its sudden increase in the heavy rains of the wet season); and south of this, again, are a number of districts, some called after the principal town in them, some after the chief river, and inhabited by numerous tribes generally termed "Bètsimisàraka, the "Many-unseparated." Inland from these is the Bétàniména country, "Much-red-earth," while the great marsh district—the Malagasy fen-country—around, but chiefly south of the chief lake, Alaotra, is called Antsihànaka, the "Lake-people's-district." South of this is the long open plain between the two eastern lines of forest, and called Ankày, the "Clearing," from its comparative absence of wood. Its inhabitants are called the Antankày, and also the Bézànozàno, "Bush people." The south-eastern forest region is called the Tanàla country, "home of the Foresters." East of this again, on the coast plains south of the Bètsimisàraka district, are the regions occupied by the Taimòro

---

[1] See Rev. G. A. Shaw's paper, "The Bètsilèo Country and People," *Antanànarìvo Annual*, No. III. pp. 74, 76.

[2] *E.g.*, Urambo, after Mirambo.   [3] See *Antanànarìvo Annual*, No. III. p. 27.

tribe, a word of probably similar origin to an identical one used in the Melanesian islands, and there meaning "the live sea," because of the active surf. The Taimòro occupy a coast exposed to the full force of the S.E. trade winds.[1] Then come the Taisàka, the Taifàsy, and other districts. At the extreme south-east corner of Madagascar is the fertile vale of Ambòlo, "At-the-Bamboos," and the region occupied by the Tanòsy, or "Islanders" (?); and proceeding round the southern point, and turning northward along the western side of the island, are the territories of the Tandròy, the Màsikòro, the Vézo, the emigrant Tanòsy, and the Antifiherénana; and north of these is the extensive region, extending nearly to the north of the island, inhabited by the various tribes loosely called Sàkalàva, because conquered by a warlike people of that name. This conquering race formed two kingdoms, that of Ibòina to the north, and Ménabé south of it. The latter of these two words is probably the same as that used by the Hova to denote an estate held direct from the sovereign.

It will be evident, therefore, that to treat this division of Malagasy place-names completely, it would be necessary to combine with it an examination of tribal names; and perhaps this may be attempted at some future time, when our information on these becomes more full and accurate than it now is. Enough has probably now been said to show how full of interest the inquiry is, and how much light is thrown upon the mental character of the Malagasy, as well as on some other subjects, by the names they give to the natural features of the country, as well as to the settlements and towns they have formed over its surface.

[1] See *Antanànarìvo Annual*, No. VI. p. 25.

APPENDIX.

BÈTSILÈO PLACE-NAMES.[1]

Among the most common and characteristic place-names amongst the Bètsilèo are the following :—

Towns.—Ivòhibé, Ambòhibé, Ambòhimandròso, Mahàzoarìvo, Vòhitrarìvo, really Vòhitsarìvo, Ivòhitròmby, really Ivòhitsaömbe, Ambòhitròmby, really Ambòhitsaömbe. The compounds with *-arìvo* ("thousand") are very frequent as names of towns; *e.g.*, Ivòhitsarìvo, Mahàzoarìvo (the ancient capital of the Isàndra province, where Andriamanàlina lived at the time of his famous negotiations with Andrianampòinimèrina), Akàrinarìvo, Ambòhimànarìvo, Andràinarìvo, Ilanjàinarìvo, Tòmboraìvo. As far as my own experience goes, towns with this noun of number (indicating great quantity of wealth of cattle, slaves, subjects, &c.) are or were invariably the seat of rather superior *tèmpo-mènakèly* (*i.e.*, feudal land proprietors), never, so far as I have seen, mere villages included in but not the capital of the *mènakèly* (estate). Fènoarìvo appears to be an Ambàniàndro (a name given to the Hova by the Bètsilèo and southern tribes) name. There is one Fénoarìvo in the Mànandrìana province, but not in the Bètsilèo proper, *i.e.*, south of the Matsìatra river; and that one Fènoarìvo is a Government town, probably named, as undoubtedly many Government towns in the south were named (*e.g.*, Fanjakàna and Fianàrantsòa), not by the aborigines, but by the colonists from the capital. There is another between Ikàlamavòny and Modòngy; but there are too many runaway slaves and Hova there to make it a real Bètsilèo village. The compounds with *-òny* are also characteristic. *Òny* in these words is not used as the equivalent for river; and, indeed, it is doubtful whether *ràno* (water) is not a more correct translation for that word at all times, the *òny* being simply the confluence

---

[1] This paper on the place-names of the southern-central province of Madagascar, the Bètsilèo, is from the pen of my friend and brother missionary, the Rev. Charles T. Price, formerly for several years resident in that part of the island, and which he kindly allows me to add to my own paper.

This chapter was written thirteen years ago, and first published in the *Journal of the Royal Asiatic Society*, April, 1873. Since that time M. Grandidier has published the volume on the Historical Geography of Madagascar, in his great work on this country; and in his very elaborate tables of all the known place-names both on the coast and the interior he has given the meanings of many hundreds of these. He has also added an essay on the place-names, from which I have extracted paragraphs as to the prefixes *An-* and *Am-* in the early part of this chapter. The only other paper I know of on the subject is an amusing one by Vice-Consul W. C. Pickersgill, in *Antanànarìvo Annual*, No. XII., 1888, entitled, "Revision of North-West Place-Names; some Curiosities of Topographical Nomenclature." He shows how Europeans, ignorant of Malagasy, and Hovas, ignorant of provincial dialects, have alike corrupted the coast names.

of the *tano*. At any rate, in place-names *òny* means the confluence of the people, a large gathering, *profanum vulgus* of Rome, or οἱ πολλοί of Athens. Thus, Nasàndratsoñy (corrupted by Hova and Europeans into Nasàndratòny) is the place that was raised up, or built, by the multitude —a name easily understood by any one who has seen the large gatherings of people in this comparatively small village assembled by Ramàvo, a descendant of Andriamanàlina, and chieftainess there. Other instances are Ambòhitsoaŏny, Ambàlamisaŏny=the homestead where there is a gathering of people), and Tondròinòny. Either by the "-*òny*" or "-*arivo*," or some other such addition, important towns generally have names far removed from the mean or commonplace. One might be tolerably sure, for instance, that such a place as Ambòasàry or Itaòlana was not anciently of great importance.

Villages and homesteads.—Frequently such names begin with the contracted place-form of *vòhitra* or *vàla*, as Ambòhibàry, or Ambàlabé.[1] *Vòhitra* is a village or town, and although *vàla* is often used of a collection of houses numerous enough to be called a village, yet strictly speaking a *vàla* is a homestead, the equivalent in Imèrina being *tambòho*. Our place at Fanjakàna, with its house and outbuildings, including kitchen, school-room, scholars' dwellings, &c., standing in a large garden, was correctly named Ambàtolàhinandrìanisiàhana = "At - Andrìanisiàhana's-*vàtolàhy*," or monument (not grave), which stood at the very gateway of the premises. But the place was usually spoken of as a *vàla*, occasionally as a *vòhitra*, and once I heard a native speak of going outside the compound, as going outside the *tanàna*. This seems to indicate that there is no fixed law for the use of either word in forming place-names of villages or towns. Not so, however, with the prefixes I- and Am- or An-. I am not referring to the simple omission of the I-, as in Fianàrantsòa for Ifianàrantsòa, which is a mere matter of habit and fashion; but to the non-interchangeability of the simple form with or without the I-, and the form with the Am- or An-. Vòhibé or Ivòhibé, for instance, is not the same as Ambòhibé, nor Ivòhipòtsy as Ambòhipòtsy. Vòdisàndra is the mouth of the Sàndra river; Ambòdisàndra is the name of the adjacent village. Vàtolàhinandrìanisiàhana is the name of the deceased judge's monument; but it would have been incorrect to call our place Ivàtolahinandrìanisiàhana; it was *Am*bàtolàhinandrìanisiàhana. I have heard *lèndrombòhitra* used for *vòhitra*: is it not possible that the true *vohitra* was situated at the *lèndrombòhitra?* that Ivòhipòtsy, for instance, was the village at the top of the hill Ivòhipòtsy, and Ambòhipòtsy the village on the hillside?[2]

Physical features.—The compounds with *hàrana*, a precipice, are very common in the more precipitous parts of the Bètsilèo province. Names with this compound invariably represent faithfully the nature of the place. Instances are, Ankàramalàza (at least two in the Iàrindràno, and one in

---

[1] Ambàlavào is one of the most common, wearisomely so.
[2] On this point, *cf.* p. 133 *ante*.

the Ilàlangìna), Ankàranòsy (the ascent to which might well be termed a "goat-tract," *òsy* = goat) and Ankàratsinànana. More common still are names recording other physical features of the locality, as Ivàtoàvo, Ambàtorèny, Ambàtosòa, Vàtomitàtana, Ambàtoména,Andrànovòrivàto, Vàtofòtsy, Anjòlobàto, Ambàtomàinty, Ambàtofinandràhana ("the chiselled rock"), Ambòhimiàrina (which is "perched up" near the crest of a high hill), Midòngy (on a hill in the south), and Modòngy (in the west; a cloud seems to be always sullenly[1] frowning round its overhanging brow), Ilamòsina, Ampàsina (= Ampàsika), Vinàny and its numerous compounds. There are at least three places in the Bètsilèo named Andrainjàto, one in each of the three provinces, and each of them rocky hills. That in the Isàndra is a prominent rather than lofty ridge, on which are many rocks curiously piled together. It is, and I believe always has been, uninhabited; but there are many other named places quite desolate. In the Sàndra there is a current proverb, as follows: "*Andrainjàto ro avo-tany, nasandratsa ny bìtsika : ko ny bìtsika ro be-loha, sasatsa ny nitao-tane,*" i.e., "Andrainjàto is lofty ground because raised by the ants; and the ants have big heads because they are weary with carrying earth."

The *plants* most plentiful or peculiar to the neighbourhood appear frequently to give the name to a village or uninhabited hill, *e.g.* Ikàndo (where the wild plant *kàndo* freely grows), Ambòasàry, Ankàzosòaràvina, Sàkaviro (? a transposition of *Sàkarìvo* = ginger), Beànana, Andrànoròndrona, Ankàfotsa (*hàfotra*), Anàhimalémy, Vàhambé, Ankàfina, Sàha, Sàhamalàza, Bésàkòana. There are two towns, both in the heart of the sweet-scented forest, named Ivòhimànitra (*mànitra* = fragrant); but one at least of these must be in the Tanàla (forest region).

Animals are represented in such names as Alàmbomandrévo, Iàvonòmby Vòhitròmby, Màroparàsy, Bévoalàvo, Iàrinòmby, Itàolana, Kalalào, Ankàranòsy. Ambòhitsandràzanimàmba is not such an instance. The *màmba* or *voày*, with the Bètsilèo, is not only the crocodile, but the big, awe-inspiring man—king, chief, or governor—in any place; and Ambòhitsandràzanimàmba was so named when old Andriamanàlina, in dividing his inheritance among his sons, directed that one of them—probably the eldest—should leave the old Isàndra capital of Mahàzoarìvo and reside at Ambòhitsandràzana. The *màmba* was to *miàndry fanjakàna* (guard the kingdom) there, and hence the name. When any of the family die, the body, in the course of the funeral ceremonies, involving a pilgrimage round the province lasting some weeks or months, is sure to lie in state for a time at Ambòhitsandràzana. The family tomb and favourite residence of Rajòaka, the present prince and descendant of Andriamanàlina, is at Ivòhitsasàky (Ivòhitsasàky = the "timid village"), so named because it lies completely hidden in a small wood at the base of the range of hills at the end of which stands Ambòhitsandràzana.

Farther on, under the same range of hills, is Isòrana, a village most of whose houses are built each on a separate boulder of rock of immense

---

[1] *Dongy* = sulky, morose.

size, so that to get to a neighbour's house quite a perilous journey has to be made from one boulder to the other. In some cases, to get from one house to the next you have to descend from the boulder and pass through an immense cave under the cliff. There are two of these large caves ; one would hold a thousand people, and the other was used for storing rice in the old days of civil war. They had a spring of water there also, if I am not mistaken. Other of the houses are situated between the foot of the cliff and the boulders, almost if not quite concealed from view from the high road. The houses being almost the same colour as the rocks, and being either perched aloft in most unlikely situations, or else hidden by the huge boulders scattered about before them, the village was analogous to Ivòhitsasàky in respect of its modest and retiring situation. Even if the village were observed, the inhabitants, in case of alarm, would not have been found—they would have *removed* by secret paths into the cave behind. This power of removing themselves may have been the origin of the name Isòrana, or Isòrane, as the pure Bètsilèo would have it. There is a proverb which runs : " Ivòhitsasàky ny añaty àla : ko Isòrane ny añaty vàto," *i.e.*, " Ivòhitsashky is within the forest, and Isòrane is within the rock." The whole of the valley in which these two villages are situated, and at the southern end of which Ambòhitsandràzana looks down from its lofty crag, is typical of the condition of insecurity in which, in former times, the Bètsilèo lived. Between Ivòhitsasàky and Ambòhitsandràzana the wall of rock which shuts in the valley on the west is cleft by a winding gully at right angles to the valley itself. On one of the steep sides of this gully, perhaps 100 feet or more from the bottom, the rock forms a natural ledge 30 or 40 feet wide, on which stands a single row of houses forming the village of Ivòhibaslana (*i.e.*, " the village which can (*only*) be shot at "—not reached in any other way). As you pass along the road in the valley this village is only perceptible from one particular spot, where, standing at exactly the right angle, you get in a line with that part of the tortuous gully in which the ledge is. Even then the path up to the village is unseen ; for the ledge appears to terminate abruptly, high up above the valley, on that side from which you would approach it from the road.

It is worth while to remark that the word Bètsilèo would seem to be a Hova name applied loosely and ignorantly to any place or people south of the river Sisàony. Immediately south of Imèrina comes Vàkinankàratra, then Mànandrìana, and after that Bètsilèo proper—south of the Matsìatra river. But these Bètsilèo do not like to be so called ; they prefer their own name, judiciously confirmed to them by the Queen in a *kabàry* in 1873 —Ambòhitròmby, or, more exactly and fully, Andriambòhitsaòmbelàhy, which, if shortened, should be Andriambòhitsa. They have great wealth in cattle ; though superficial observers and new-comers have denied this. The fact is that the pasture-land is getting less extensive in the central parts of the Bètsilèo, and that the wealthiest landed proprietors now keep most of their cattle in the extreme west, bordering on the Bàra country, where in one small village it is not at all uncommon to see 500 to 1,000 head of cattle, all belonging to some rich man living far away to the east, who places his cattle in these roomy plains under tne charge of herdsmen.

The tendency of the foregoing rambling notes, as will be seen, is to show that the place-names have an intimate connection with the characteristics of the places themselves. Even now, with our comparatively slight knowledge of Bètsilèo history, the connection between the names and the peculiarities or distinctive features of the places named is traceable in most cases.

A SÀKALÀVA WARRIOR (HEATHEN). [Photograph by Dr. FENN.

CHAPTER VIII.

CURIOUS WORDS AND CUSTOMS CONNECTED WITH CHIEF-TAINSHIP AND ROYALTY AMONG THE MALAGASY; AND NOTES ON RELICS OF THE SIGN AND GESTURE LANGUAGE.

The Bètsilèo—Special words or "Chiefs' language"—In Malayo-Polynesian languages—For Malagasy sovereigns—Illness and death—Burial—Mourning—Diseases—Royal servants—Royal houses—Chiefs' words among Bètsilèo—For family of chiefs—For elderly chiefs—For chiefs old or young—Extreme honour paid to chiefs—*Fàdy* or Taboo in words—Tabooed animals—Royal names—Sacred character of—Veneration for royalty—Sàkalàva chiefs' posthumous names—Relics of the sign and gesture language—Salutations—Symbolic acts—Royalty—"Licking the sole "—*Kabàrys*—The Taboo.

MY object in the present chapter is to call attention to and to describe some peculiar words and customs in use among the Hova, or people of the central province of Imèrina, and also among the Bètsilèo, the tribe inhabiting the district to the south of this first-named province. The Hova are probably the latest and purest Malayan or lighter Polynesian immigrants; they are also the most advanced, intelligent, and civilised of the various Malagasy tribes; among them education and Christianity have made the greatest progress; and, since the beginning of this century, they have become the dominant tribe of the country, and their queen is sovereign of the greater part of the island.

The Bètsilèo are a darker race than the Hova, being probably descended from Melanesian ancestors, or from a mixture of the dark and light Pacific islanders; they are also taller and perhaps stronger than their northern neighbours, although, owing to the superior discipline of the Hova soldiers, they were subdued by them about eighty years ago, and have ever since been obedient subjects to the sovereign at Antanànarìvo. They appear to me, as well as to others who have lived both in Imèrina and in the Bètsilèo province, to be less intelligent than the Hova, but possibly this may be because their advantages have been less. Among them, however, very satisfactory progress is being made, and both the London Missionary Society and the Norwegian Lutheran Mission have a large number of congregations and many thousands of children in their schools.

It is a fact well known to all philologists that in several groups of language there are found classes of words which are only used by the people when speaking of their sovereigns or chiefs, with regard to their persons, their actions, and their surroundings, as well as to the honours paid to them both when they are living and after death. And for a long time past it has been known that in the central province of Imèrina there are a number of such specialised words which are employed with regard to the sovereign, and these have probably been in use for centuries as applied to the chiefs of the central province. It will be seen that these are not words which are not also employed with regard to ordinary persons or things or actions, but are almost all of them commonly used words which have gained a special and different meaning when applied to the sovereign.

The more noticeable of these words are connected with the illness, decease, and burial ceremonies of a Malagasy sovereign, although there are also two or three which are applied to the living king or queen. (Perhaps, however, these are more of the nature of honorific titles than strictly coming within the class of words we are here discussing.) Thus, an old word for a sovereign is *Ampingàra-bólamèna*, literally "golden gun," the first part of the phrase being taken from the Portuguese *espingarda*, so that this term is not of more ancient origin than about three centuries ago, or, at most, three centuries and a half. Another term applied to the sovereign is *Fáhiray*, "first," a word which is not used with regard to things generally, although it is formed strictly according to the rule for making ordinal from cardinal numbers (*e.g., fáharòa*, second, from *ròa*, two ; *fàhatélo*, third, from *télo*, three), the word *vóalòhany* (*vóa*, fruit, *lóha*, head) being always used for "first."[1] A term sometimes applied to the queen by elderly officers in public speeches seems to our notions somewhat impertinently familiar, viz., *Ikàlatòkana ;* in ordinary talk by the people this means "our only lass," and the word *ikàla* is often applied also to hens. If one might venture on such a free translation, it seems to mean (*not* "cock of the walk," but) "*hen* of the roosting-place." It is, however, very like, in its free familiarity, the use of the word *Ialàhy* ("you fellow") to the former kings by some of their most privileged councillors. The members of the royal family are termed *Atinandrìana* (lit. "the liver," or "inside," of the sovereign or chief). And among some tribes the chiefs are termed *Màsondràno, i.e.,* "water channels," through whom all benefits are supposed to be derived, as the water flows along the bed of a river.

Returning, however, to the more exact illustrations of the subject, a Malagasy king or queen is not said to be "ill" (*maràry*), but "rather warm" (*mafànafàna*). And they do not "die" (*màty*), but are said to "retire," or "to turn the back" (*miambóho*). In parts of Madagascar distant from Imèrina, the word *fólaka* (bent, broken, weakened) is employed in speaking of a deceased chief. (With regard to people generally, among the Tanàla and other tribes, the phrase *fóla-mànta* [*manta*, raw]

[1] A curious word for chiefs and their wives is used by the Bàra, Sàkalàva and some other Malagasy tribes, viz., *bìby* which in Imèrina usually means "animal," "beast," or, as an adjective, "sensual," "brutal " ; although it is also used here of children as well, probably much in the same way as words of an unpleasant (and even nasty) meaning are often applied to children and infants from fear of some envious and malign influence, such as the "evil eye." Perhaps, however, it is really a word of entirely different origin, from the Swahili *bìby*, "my lady," "my mistress."

is used for sudden death; *fólaka an-dàntony* [*làntony*, the forearm?], for dying young; while *tràno fólaka* is the house [*tràno*] where a corpse lies in state.) Then the dead body of a sovereign is not termed "a corpse" (*fàty*), but "the sacred thing" (*ny màsina*). The late Queen Rànavàlona II., who died in 1883, is always spoken of as *Ny Màsina* in the government gazette and in proclamations, as well as by the people generally in ordinary conversation. There is among the Hova, as well as among the other Malagasy tribes, a deep sense of "the divinity that doth hedge a king"; and until the acceptance of Christianity by the late queen and her government, the Hova sovereigns were termed "the visible God" (*Andrìamànitra hìta màso*); other terms of similar import were also applied to them. In accordance also with this same belief, upon the stone structure covering the chamber formed of slabs of undressed rock, where the royal corpse is deposited, a small timber-framed building is erected, which is called the "sacred house" (*tràno màsina*). This is in appearance exactly like the old style of native house, made of timber framing, the walls of thick upright planking, and high-pitched roof covered with wooden shingles. This distinction of having a timber house built upon the stone tomb is also shared by the higher ranks of nobles, who, it should be remembered, are descended from ancient kings in Imèrina.

When the corpse of a sovereign is lying in state, the women in their various divisions or tribes are expected to come in relays to mourn; but this ceremonial mourning is not called by its usual name (*misaona*), but the people are said to "present" or "offer tears" (*miàti-drànomàso*). Then again, a sovereign is not said to be "buried" (*alévina*), but is "hidden" (*afénina*); and the massive silver coffin made of dollars hammered into plates, in which most of the Hova kings or queens in more recent times have been buried, is called the "silver canoe" (*làkam-bóla*), a word in which a little bit of history is doubtless preserved: a remembrance of a former period when the Hova were not, as they are now, an inland people, but a coast-dwelling or an island tribe, and buried their dead in an old canoe, as is still the custom with the Sàkalàva,[1] the Bètsimisàraka, and other Malagasy peoples living on the coast.

When the royal corpse has been deposited in its last resting-place, and the stonework at the entrance to the tomb is being closed up again, this act is called "stopping up the sun" (*tàmpimàsoàndro*); the sovereign being "the sun," the light and warmth of his people, and was formerly often so termed in public speeches.[2] Much the same idea appears in the phrase used by some of the coast tribes in speaking of the decease of their chiefs, viz., "the king is reclining," or "leaning on one side" (*mihìlana ny ampanjàka*). This same word is used in Imèrina to denote the afternoon, the "decline of the day" (*mihìlana ny àndro*). A very bold and poetical figure is also employed to express the general mourning at the decease of a sovereign, *Mihóhoka ny tány àman-dànitra*, i.e., "Heaven and earth are turned upside down"! This is not the place to describe in detail the many and curious ceremonies, as well as the numerous things prohibited to be done, at the decease of a Malagasy king or queen; suffice it to say that, with very few exceptions, every one's head had to be shaved; no hat could be worn or umbrella carried; the *làmba* only (no European dress) could be worn, and this had to be bound under the armpits, leaving the shoulders uncovered; all singing, dancing, or playing of musical instruments was prohibited, as well as the practice of many handicrafts, as spinning, weaving, making of pottery, gold and silver work, &c.[3] Of course some occupations could not be altogether

---

[1] A somewhat similar historical fragment lies under the word used for the water used in the circumcision ceremonies: it is termed *ràno màsina*, "salt water," and in the case of children who are heirs to the throne it must actually be fetched from the sea *(rànomàsina)*. Doubtless sea water was formerly used in all such cases while the Hova were still a shore-dwelling tribe.

[2] And so concealing property due to the sovereign, or peculation of government dues, is termed *manao màsoàndro an-kàrona*, i.e., "putting the sun into a basket."

[3] See account of the funeral ceremonies at the death of Radàma I., given in a subsequent chapter.

abandoned, such as the tilling of the soil, sowing and planting rice, &c. ; but such work was not called by the usual terms, but was mentioned as *milátsaka an-tsáha, i.e.*, " going into the country," or "settling down in the fields." So also, the usual word for "market" (*tsèna*) is not employed during the time of public mourning, but these great concourses of people are called simply "meetings," or " places of resort " (*fihàonana*). They are also called *tsèna màlahèlo*, "sorrowful markets." In speaking of the death of relatives of the sovereign, they are not said to be dead, but "absent," or "missing" (*dìso*). The same figurative phrase as is used by ourselves in speaking of friends or relatives who are dead as "departed," is also employed by the Malagasy, who say their friends are *làsa*, "gone"; they also speak of them as *rèraka, i.e.*, "faint," "exhausted," and as *làtsaka, i.e.*, "fallen," or "laid down"; while the surviving members of a family of which some are dead are spoken of as "not up to the right number" (*làtsak' ìsa*).[1] With regard to the ordinary people also, their dead relatives are said to be "lost" (*vèry*), and "finished," or "done" (*vìta*) ; and also *làsan-ko ràzana, i.e.*, "gone to become ancestors."

Although not strictly included in the present subject, it may be remarked that the same use of euphemistic expressions as those just mentioned with regard to death is also seen in those used by the Malagasy in speaking of things they have a great dread of, especially small-pox, which, before the introduction of vaccination, often made fearful ravages in Imèrina, as it still occasionally does among the coast tribes. This terrible disease is called *bélémby, i.e.*, "greatly deserted," no doubt from the condition of the villages where it had appeared. It is also called *lavìra*, an imperative or optative formed from the adjective *làvitra*, "far off," and thus meaning "be far away!" or "avaunt!" A feeling of delicacy causes other euphemisms, such as the

[1] A very poetical expression, in which the word *làtsaka* also occurs, is used in speaking of the dead, who are said to be as "Salt fallen into water which cannot be salt again" ("*Síra làtsaka an-dràno ka tsy himpódy intsóny*").

phrase *didíam-pòitra*, literally, "cutting the navel," instead of *fóra* and other terms denoting the circumcision ceremonies.

The use of some special words, as applied to certain classes of royal servants or attendants, may here be noticed; although possibly these also are not, speaking exactly, of the class of the euphemistic expressions like the majority of those described above. Thus the royal cooks are termed the "clean-handed ones" (*madìo tànana*); describing, no doubt, what they *should* be, even if they occasionally are not exactly what their name implies. Then some companies of royal guards a few years ago were termed the "sharp ones" (*maràntira ; cf.* Eng. "sharp-shooters"?). The government couriers in the provinces are called *kèli-lohàlika*, lit., "little-kneed"; while a class of palace servants in constant attendance on the sovereign, and from whom the queen's messengers are chosen, are the *tsimandó*, or *tsimandao, i.e.,* "never forsaking," because some of them are always in attendance, day and night, upon the sovereign. The queen's representatives at distant places are called *màsoivòho, i.e.,* "eyes behind"; but this word is also now used in the more general sense of an "agent" of other persons besides the sovereign.

It is an ancient custom that members of the royal family, and of the next highest class of *andrìana*, or nobles (the Zànak'-Andrìamàsinavàlona), who happen to have committed serious offences, are not put into *iron* fetters, but are bound with *cords*. And when any subject of high position is accused of crime, a spear with silver blade, engraved with the name of the sovereign, is carried by government officers and fixed in the ground opposite the door of the accused person's house. This spear is called *Tsitìalainga, i.e.,* "hater of lies"; and while it remains so fixed, no inmate of the house can leave it. Among the Taimòro chiefs, a house set apart for their wives who are of noble birth is called *Fènovòla, i.e.,* "full of money."

The rapacious character of the upper classes among the Malagasy is significantly shown by a provincial name given to the chief people, viz., *Aràralàhy*, *i.e.*, "gluttonous, eager to take one's share before others." The despotic nature of Malagasy sovereigns is clearly shown in many native proverbs ; *e.g.*, "*Ny manjàka toy ny lànitra, ka tsy azo refèsina; toy ny màsoàndro, ka tsy azo tohaina,*" *i.e.*, "The sovereign is like the sky, and cannot be measured ; like the sun, and cannot be contended with."

Another fact with regard to royalty may be recorded. During the reign of Queen Rasohèrina (1863-1868), a new royal house was erected in the palace yard at Antanànarìvo, as is customary when a new sovereign comes to the throne. But in this case the standard for all the chief dimensions of the building was the *réfy*, or fathom, as measured by the queen herself, between the tips of her fingers when the arms were stretched to their full extent—in her majesty's case, about five feet eight inches in length. And it was a matter of no small trouble and annoyance to Mr. J. Cameron, who designed and superintended the building, to make all his dimensions in accordance with the standard. He had, in fact, to make a new scale, for all the principal dimensions of the palace, and of its verandahs, doors, windows, &c., were multiples or fractions of the queen's personal *réfy*, as measured by herself.

One of the students in the London Missionary Society's College at Antanànarìvo, named Rajaonáry, from North Bètsilèo, told me that such special words, as applied to the chiefs, were a very marked feature in the speech of the Bètsilèo people, and that in fact there were a much larger number of these words employed in the southern province than were in use among the Hova. He gave me at the same time a number of examples ; and I then asked him to note down these words, which he accordingly did in a few days, writing quite a small essay on the subject. He entitles it—

"SPECIAL WORDS EMPLOYED AMONG THE BÈTSILÈO WITH REFERENCE TO THEIR CHIEFS.

"The Bètsilèo are a people who pay extraordinary respect to

their chiefs, and from this fact everything relating to them is a thing kept specially for them, and is not allowed to be mixed up with what belongs to the mass of the people. The chiefs houses, although there is very little difference between them and those of the people generally, are like something sacred or set apart in a special manner, so that no one can enter them at will, but only after having asked and obtained leave of the chief, or after being summoned by him. And again, after having entered, no one can push himself forward north of the hearth,[1] or stand idly about, but must sit quietly and respectfully south of the hearth. And in the same manner also the things in the house are set apart, for the drinking-tin, the spoons, the plates, &c., cannot be handled or put to the lips; for if any one drinks from them, the hand must be held to the mouth, and the water then poured into it from above. The chief's bedstead cannot be used by any person except one who is also a chief. The mat on which a chief sits in his house must not be trodden upon, but must be lifted up in passing, and cannot be sat upon by any one but himself. And all the furniture in the house is like something sacred, and must not be lightly touched when carried outside, for those who receive it are warned by the words '*andápa*' ('belonging to the palace'), that they may take care of it. And not only are the things in the chief's house thus set apart for his own use, but also even those in the people's houses, should the chief have chanced to use them; and even their own drinking-tins, ladles, &c., are often kept untouched by the lips, lest the chief should chance to pass by and require them, so that the Bètsilèo are accustomed to drink water out of their hands.

"But not only are *things* thus kept by the Bètsilèo for special use by their chiefs, but many *words* are also set apart for them, both the names for certain things and other names as well. These may be divided into three classes, as follows:—

"1. *Words specially applied to the Family of Chiefs*, from their

[1] The place of honour in a Malagasy house.

birth until maturity, but while their parents are still living. See the following :—

Ordinary Bètsilèo word.	English.	Word used for the Children of Chiefs.	Literal Meaning.
Kilònga	Children	Anakòva	Child of the Hova.[1]
Mihìnana	To eat	Misòa	Sòa, in Hova, good, pleasant.
Vilìa	Plate or dish	Fisoàvana	Verbal noun from above.
Velòma	Farewell	Mahazòa nòno màsina	Lit., 'May you get a sacred nipple.'[2]
Mitéraka	To bear offspring	Manìdina	To cause to descend.
Màty	Dead	Fòlaka	Bent, broken, weakened, see p. 151, ante.
Fàty	Corpse	Vòlafòlaka	Broken or bent money.

"2. *Words specially applied to Elderly Chiefs*—that is, those who are too old to have their father and mother still living. When that is the case, there is a considerable change made in the names given to the parts of the body, as well as in certain words describing their actions and their condition. This will be seen by the following list :—

Ordinary Bètsilèo word.	English.	Word used for Elderly Chiefs.	Literal Meaning.
Antitra	Old	Màsina	Sacred, established, &c., see p. 152.
Anakandrìana	An adult man (lit., 'child of the chief')[3]	Hòva, or ny an-drìandàhy	Hova (see ante), or the prince.
Andrànobé (wife of above)	An adult woman (lit., 'at the great house')	Hòva, or ny an-drìambàvy	Hova, or the princess.
Lòha	Head	Kabéso	Brains (?)
Màso	Eye	Fanìlo	Torch.[4]
Sòfina	Ear	Fihainòana	The listening (or listener).
Tànana	Hand	Faudray	The taker.

[1] The word *Hova* seems to convey the idea of "noble," "princely," in many of the non-Hova tribes. So when the Bètsilèo salute any of their own chiefs, they say, "*Manao akòry ny Hova é?*"—*i.e.*, "How is the Hova?"

[2] *Cf.* Isa. lx. 16 : "Thou shalt also suck the milk of the Gentiles, and shalt suck the breasts of kings."

[3] This phrase is customary in public speaking as a mark of respect to the chief's children, when deprecating blame (as is always done in the opening sentences of a *kabàry* or public speech).

[4] *Cf.* "The lamp of the body is the eye."

Ordinary Bètsilèo word.	English.	Word used for Elderly Chiefs.	Literal Meaning.
Tóngotra	Foot	Fandia	The treader.
Nify	Tooth	Fanéva	A flag (lit., the hoverer).
Tróka	Belly	Fisafòana	Safo is 'rubbing,' 'caressing.'
Mihìnana	To eat	Mifànjotra	(?)
Vilìa	Dish, plate	Fifanjòrona	(?) Verbal noun from preceding word.
Mitétraka	To sit	Midrina	To be erect (in Hova).
Mandéha	To go	Manindra	To remove (do.).
Màndry, or Matòry	To lie down, to sleep	Miròtra	(?)
Fàrafàra	Bedstead	Filànana	Place of desire (?)
Vàdy	Husband or wife	Fitdna	A ford (in Hova).
Màty	Dead	Vèry	Lost.
Fàty	Corpse	Haverézana	The losing, from vèry, lost, see p. 154.
Velòma	Farewell (lit., 'may you live')	Masìna	Be sacred, established, &c.
Akòry àngharèo?[1]	How are you?	Manao akòry ny ròtana?	How did you sleep? (see above, miròtra.)

[It will be seen from the above list that several of the words for the parts of the body—the eye, the ear, the hand, the foot—are simply words describing the actual office of those members, as light-giving, means of hearing, taking, treading, &c. Probably the very general practice of tabooing (making *fàdy*) words which form the names or parts of the names of chiefs (which we shall notice again further on) has had influence in producing some of these specialised words.]

"3. *Words specially applied to Chiefs, whether Old or Young.*

Ordinary Bètsilèo word.	English.	Word used for Chiefs.	Literal Meaning.
Tráno	House	Làpa	(?) Also used in Imèrina.
Maràry	Ill, unwell	Manélo	To shade, to shelter.
Mijàlo	To nurse (the sick)	Mitràmbo	(?)

[1] Sometimes this salutation of the common people is substituted by the phrase: "*Akòry ny nandriangharèo?*" a phrase of the same meaning as the one addressed to the chief, only that the ordinary word *màndry* is here kept instead of the special one *miròtra*.

Ordinary Bètsilèo word.	English.	Word used for Chiefs.	Literal Meaning.
Miandràvana	To sing at a funeral	Mampiòtraka	(?)[1]
Trànovórona	Bier (lit., 'bird house')	Trànovitana	The finished house (?).
Miàhy	To lie in state	Mampiàry	To cause to go round about.[2]
Fásana	Tomb	Trànoména	Red house.[3]
Mandévina	To bury	Manìritra	To plunge, to dive; in Imèrina the phrase *anìritra* is used to describe the temporary burial of a corpse until the proper tomb is completed.

"The poles on which a chief's corpse is carried to burial are termed *hàzomàsina*, 'sacred wood'; and the water into which they are cast away after the funeral is called *rànoàritra*, 'water of endurance'? (*àritra*, endurance, patience, &c.). When the dead from among the common people are spoken of, the words *Raivèlona* ('Living father') or *Rènivèlona* ('Living mother') are prefixed to their names; but in the case of deceased chiefs the word *Zànahàry* (God, lit. Creator) is prefixed to their names when they are spoken of; in the same way as the word *Rabevòina* ('The one overtaken by much calamity'?) is employed by the Hova in speaking of the departed, or simply, *Itòmpokolàhy* ('Sir,' or 'my lord'), or *Itòmpokovàvy* (Madam,' or 'my lady').

"The chiefs of the Bètsilèo are considered as far above the common people, and are looked upon almost as if they were gods. If anything angers a chief and he curses, the people consider the words he speaks as unalterable and must surely be fulfilled; so the persons whom he may chance to curse are

[1] In Hova *hòtraka* means "boiling," but perhaps there is no connection between the two words.

[2] Scarlet is the royal colour in Madagascar; at the funeral of Radàma I., one of the large palaces in which he lay in state was draped from the ridge of the roof to the ground with scarlet cloth; the sovereign alone has a large scarlet umbrella carried over her, and dresses in a scarlet *làmba* or robe.

[3] See Mr. Richardson's description of Bètsilèo funeral ceremonies, *Antananarìvo Annual*, I. p. 71, Reprint p. 74.

exceedingly afraid and in deep distress. And, on the other hand, if anything pleases him, and he thanks (lit., 'blesses') any one, then those who receive his blessing are exceedingly glad, because they suppose that that also must certainly be fulfilled. For the chiefs are supposed to have power as regards the words they utter, not, however, merely the power which a king possesses, but power like that of God ; a power which works of itself on account of its inherent virtue, and not power exerted through soldiers and strong servants. Besides which, when a person is accused by another of having done evil, and he denies it, he is bidden to lick (or kiss) the back of the hand of the chief, or to measure his house,[1] and to imprecate evil (on himself) while doing it. In this way, so they say, it is found out whether he really has committed the offence, or not ; if he did offend and yet still persists in denying it, then it is believed that the curse he invoked when licking the hand of the chief, or when measuring his house, will return upon him ; if, on the contrary, he is innocent, he will remain unharmed. In like manner also the chief is supposed to have power which works of itself, on account of his sacred character, to convict of any secret fault. And when the chiefs die they are supposed to really become God, and to be able to bless their subjects who are still living ; and the reverence in which they are held is extreme ; for when their name chances to be mentioned, the utmost respect is paid to it both before and after the utterance of it ; before it the words *Ny Zànahàry* (God) must be prefixed, and after it the following words are added : 'May the mouth strike on the rock, and the teeth flow with blood, for he has gone to be God'[2] (the speaker's mouth and teeth being meant). And when the chief's grave is cleared of weeds and rubbish the people dare not do that unless they have first killed

[1] Measuring the tomb of their master is, I am told, a practice followed by slaves in Imèrina as an invocation of evil on themselves if they have really done something of which they are accused.

[2] "*Mikapoha amy ny vato ny vava, ary mandehana ra ny nify, fa efa lasan-ko Andriamanitra izy.*"

oxen and made supplication with outstretched hands to the deceased."

A few remarks may be here made about the practice of tabooing—or making *fàdy*—the words or parts of words which happen to form the names of chiefs. This appears to be prevalent all over Madagascar, and is a custom the Malagasy have in common with many of the Oceanic races with which they are so closely connected. There are no family names in Madagascar (although there *are* tribal ones, and although also one name or part of a name is often seen in a variety of combination among members of the same family),[1] and almost every personal name has some distinct meaning, being part of the living and still spoken language, either as names of things—birds, beasts, plants, trees, inanimate objects, or names describing colour, quality, &c., or words which denote actions of various kinds. So that the names of the chiefs almost always contain some word which is in common use by the people. In such a case, however, the ordinary word by which such thing or action has hitherto been known must be changed for another, which henceforth takes its place in daily speech. Thus, when the Princess Rabòdo became queen in 1863, at the decease of Radàma II., she took a new name, Rasohérina (or, in fuller form, Rasohèri-manjàka). Now *sohérina* is the word for chrysalis, especially for that of the silkworm moth; but having been dignified by being chosen as the royal name, it became sacred (*fàdy*) and must no longer be employed for common use; and the chrysalis thenceforth was termed *zàna-dàndy*, "offspring of silk." So again, if a chief had or took the name of an animal, say of the dog (*ambóa*), and was known as Rambòa, the animal would be henceforth called by another name, probably a descriptive one, such as *fandròaka*, *i.e.*, "the driver away," or *famòvo*, "the barker," &c.

[1] Thus, a friend of mine at Ambòhimànga, who is called Rainizaivèlo, has four daughters named respectively Razaivèlo, Raovèlo, Ravèlonòro, and Ranòrovèlo.

Among certain Sàkalàva tribes certain birds and animals are *fàdy*, or sacred or tabooed by the chiefs and their families. Thus the grey or sooty Parrot [1] is *fàdy* to one of the Vèzo royal families,[2] and the *Tolòho* or lark-heeled Cuckoo [3] is sacred to one of the chief families of Mènabé, further north. Some have thought that we have here a relic of the system of totem, but the subject needs further investigation. A very curious superstition among the Bètsilèo and some other tribes is, that from the putrid liquid exuding from the corpses of their chiefs a serpent called *fanàny* is produced, and that this is an embodiment of the spirit of the departed. It is supposed to take up its abode near the tribe and to act as their protector.[4]

This tabooing of words in the names of chiefs seems hardly to have been carried out by the Hova to such an extent as it is, or has been, by the other Malagasy tribes. With one sovereign, instead of a number of petty chiefs or kings, the changes would be minute and would leave no great impression on the language. For we can easily conceive what an annoying uncertainty would be introduced into a language by a wide extension of such tabooed words, arising from a multiplicity of chiefs. It is as if we in England had had to avoid, and make substitutes for, all such words as "*geo*logy," "*geo*graphy," &c., because they formed part of the name of King George; and such words as "*will*," "*will*ing," "*wil*ful," &c., because they were part of the name of King William; or had now to taboo words like "*vict*ory," "*vict*im," "con*vict*," &c., because these syllables form part of the name of Queen Victoria. It can hardly be doubted that this fashion in language has done very much to differentiate the various dialects found in Madagascar; and it is a matter for some surprise that there is not a much greater diversity among them than we find to be actually the case.

Among the western tribes of the country, on account of the large number of petty but independent and absolute kings, a great deal of change in the spoken language does take place.

---

[1] *Coracopsis obscura.* [2] South-west coast.
[3] *Centropus toulou.* [4] *Vide infra*, Chapter IX., p. 176.

"The chieftains of the Sàkalàva are averse that any name or term should approach in sound either the name of themselves or any part of their family. Hence, when it was determined that the mother of Ratàratsa, who came unexpectedly into the world, should be named Ravahìny [*vahìny*, a stranger], it was forbidden that the term *vahìny* should be applied to any other person except herself, and the word *ampainsick*[1] was instituted to denominate 'stranger.'" (See also Chapter VII. pp. 112-113.)

It may be here noticed that it is considered highly improper to use the name of the sovereign frequently or lightly in ordinary conversation; and Europeans happening to do this, through ignorance of native customs, have been requested to desist by Malagasy officers who chanced to be present. The royal name has a kind of sanctity, and must not be taken in vain. This reverence for royalty extends also to royal property. For instance, it is a gross breach of propriety to sit or step upon a box or case containing anything belonging to or being sent to the sovereign. And when anything belonging to the queen is being carried or driven along the high road, whether cases, or water-pots, or bullocks, all passers-by must turn out of the road, or stop close to the side of the path, and remove their hats until the royal property has passed by. Further, it is improper to compare any other building to the royal palaces, or to use it as a standard of height and size; and it is little short of a crime to fire off a gun in the direction of the palace, as this would be a sort of threatening or defying its august owner. The sovereign must sit in the highest place in any public assembly, and accordingly the queen's pew in the Chapel Royal at Antanànarìvo, her majesty's seat is higher than the pulpit; while at the opening of one of our Memorial Churches at the capital a few years ago the late queen's seat was placed in the gallery of the transept, so that no subject might sit higher than their sovereign.

[1] In Dalmond's *Vocabulaire Malgache-Française pour les langues Sakalave et Betsimitsara*, p. 5, I find this word thus given : "Ampentzek, s. Neuf, nouveau, nouvel arrivé."

One more point as to Malagasy royal names may be mentioned. Among the Sàkalàva the chiefs' names are changed as well as among the Hova, not, however, at their accession to power, but after their death. A new name is then given to them, by which they are ever afterwards known, and it is a crime to utter the name by which they were called when still living. These posthumous names all begin with *Andrìan* (prince), and end with *arìvo* (a thousand), signifying that such a chief was a " prince ruling over," or " loved by," or " feared by," or " regretted by thousands," of his subjects. Thus a chief called Raimòsa while living was called Andrìamandìonarìvo after death ; another, called at first Mikàla, was after death known only as Andrìanitsòanarìvo. M. Guillain says : " This custom was not confined to the Sàkalàva ; it existed among the different populations of the south of the island, in Fiherènana, Màhafàly, and Andròy." Drury, who lived as a slave for fifteen years in Madagascar, from 1702 to 1717, also says of the south-western tribes : " They invoke the souls of their ancestors, and hold them in great veneration ; they call them by names which they give them after their death, and even regard it as a crime to mention them by that which they bore when living ; and these names are principally characterised by the word *arivou*, which terminates them."

The following particulars may be recorded as relics of the gesture and signs accompanying oral speech among the Hovas of Central Madagascar.

1. One of the native customs which will probably soon strike a foreigner coming into the country is that which is made use of in passing in front of a superior, or, indeed, any one to whom respect is due, or is desired to be paid. This is chiefly, though not exclusively, observed indoors, and consists in the person passing in front of another, who is usually sitting, bending the body low, and, with the right hand extended and nearly touching the ground, generally using at the same time the words *Mbay làlana, Tompoko é* (" Allow me to pass, sir "). These words are

also used, with or without the bending of the body, &c., when walking along a public path, and passing any one sitting at a door, or window, or on the *fijeréna*, or elevated seat above a boundary wall. I have not heard any explanation from a native of the meaning or origin of this particular gesture; possibly it may be now lost. But the Hovas look with scorn upon those who neglect such acts of politeness, saying of them, contemptuously, " He passes on like an ox, and does not say, ' Let me pass.' "

2. Another expressive gesture among the Hova Malagasy is that which is used in presenting *hàsina* (the dollar of allegiance), or any other present to the sovereign, or to the representative of royalty. At the close of the speech of formal complimentary phrases the speaker stretches out both outspread hands, with the palms outward, and, bending downward and forward, raises his hands towards the great person addressed until they are about level with his head. This appears a very natural and significant gesture when making an offering.

3. A sign of still more profound respect than is shown in the foregoing gestures is preserved in the phrase for abject submission still in common use, viz., *miléla-pàladìa*. The literal meaning of this is to "lick the sole" (of the foot). Among the Hovas this is now only a phrase, but up to a comparatively recent period the act it described was one in common use as a token of respect from slaves to masters, wives to husbands, and from inferiors generally to superiors. Robert Drury (referred to in the previous page) describes himself as frequently performing this act of homage, and seeing it constantly rendered by others. Scriptural parallels (*cf.* Isa. xlix. 23, lx. 14; Luke vii. 38) will occur to all readers of the Bible, as well as the homage paid by Roman Catholics to the Pope by kissing (not his toe, as commonly said, but) the cross on his slipper.

4. There are several Malagasy customs connected with royalty which are significant outward acts, although, perhaps, not strictly to be reckoned as portions of the gesture language.

Among these are the shaving of the head by the whole population at the death of the sovereign; the wearing at royal funerals of the *làmba*, or outer loose robe, below the armpits instead of over the shoulders, so as to leave the upper part of the body uncovered; and the turning out of the way and baring the head when any royal property is carried along. The bent of mind among the Malagasy leads them to use symbolic *acts*,[1] as well as to the profuse employment of figure and metaphor and parable in their public speeches and more formal addresses.

5. One can hardly be long in Madagascar without observing that the people use a different motion of the hand in beckoning another to come near from that which we employ in similar cases. They do this by stretching out the hand with the palm *downwards*, moving the fingers toward them, instead of turning the palm *upwards*, as we should do.

6. Again, in pointing out the position of anything near to them, the Hovas will not always trouble themselves to do so with the hand, as we usually do, but motion towards it with the *mouth*, stretching out the head, and protruding—in an ugly enough fashion certainly—the lower lip in the required direction.

7. Another point to be here noted is the act which takes the place which *kissing* occupies among Western peoples. The kiss seems almost unknown among the Malagasy, except as introduced by Arabs and Europeans, and its place is taken by nose-rubbing, or rather of nose-*pressing*, a custom, as is well known, widely used by uncivilised peoples, and apparently a relic of a very primitive habit of recognising another person by scent or smell. The native word for this is *manòroka*, a verb derived probably from the root *òrona*, nose (Javanese, *irong ;* Celebes, *urong*), the terminals *na* and *ka* being often interchangeable. The shaking of hands is not a native custom, but is being largely adopted where foreign influence prevails.

[1] See *Great African Island*, pp. 332–334.

8. In a recently published journal of a missionary tour along the east coast of Madagáscar, Mr. G. A. Shaw says: "Only a short time since, in a village in the south, pressure from the Hova being brought to bear on some Bètsimisàraka to send their children to a school which was in the same village, the women went about with their hands clasped on their heads (a Bètsimisàraka sign of grief), bewailing the loss of their children." In their ignorance of the milder Hova rule of recent times, they supposed that school training was only a preliminary to government service, as in the time of the first Radàma (1810–1828).

9. A piece of gesture language seems to be preserved in the Malagasy word for "blessing," or "benediction," which is *tsò-dràno*, literally, "blowing water." This act appears now to be almost, if not quite, obsolete among the Hova; but the word still commonly employed doubtless preserves the remembrance of an act formerly used by them in pronouncing a blessing. Some light seems to be thrown upon this custom by a very similar one described by the Rev. Dr. Turner, for more than forty-two years a missionary in the Samoan Islands, in his *Nineteen Years in Polynesia* (Snow, London, 1861, p. 224). In case of disease attacking a Samoan, the high priest of the village sometimes told the sick man's friends " to assemble the family, 'confess and throw out.' In this ceremony, each member of the family confessed his crimes, and any judgment which, in anger, he had invoked on the family, or on the particular member of it then ill; and, as a proof that he revoked all such imprecations, he took a little water in his mouth and spurted it out towards the person who was sick. The custom is still kept up by many." I am much indebted to several Madagascar missionaries for the following additional facts connected with sign and gesture language amongst the Malagasy.

In the ordinary salutation of the Hova, *Mandò akòry hiandò?* ("How dost thou do?") the head is usually thrown up instead of bending it down. In expressing astonishment, usually with the word *Odré!* ("Dear me!" or "Oh dear!") the fist is frequently held to the mouth. As Mr. Thorne remarks, the meaning of this gesture must have been originally to conceal a laugh, as it is also used when something funny has been said. In challenging, or expressing defiance, the *làmba*, or flowing outer garment, is waved about in the air. Although hardly gestures, strictly so called, there are sounds used by the Hova on certain occasions which are not speech. These are a kind of "click," made by the tongue, and employed to express admiration or approval of public speeches; and a deep humming sound, somewhat like "hoo, hoo," used when the sovereign is passing as a salutation to her. To spread a clean mat on the ground when the stranger enters the house is a usual sign of welcome.

Mr. Price remarks that among the Bètsilèo the gesture referred to in paragraph 1 (*ante*) is carefully observed along the roads with the shortened form of address, *Ombày*, or *Ombàko*. It implies respect, and especially *humility*, and is termed *manjòko*. Even in a church superiors expect an inferior or younger person to show this mark of respect when passing. (2) The second gesture noted above is used every Sunday in the Royal Chapel, after the prayer for the queen, or the playing of the National Anthem ; also by the troops in distant parts of the island, who turn towards the capital and thus salute their distant sovereign, when the national air (which is simply our "God save the Queen," curiously altered to *Tsidikinina!*) is played by the band. It is also used to other persons in giving thanks, as to a senior or superior when any special request is desired to be shown. (3) With regard to the third (*Miléla-pàladia*), Mr. Price says, "This may not now be literally performed, but that it is still more than a phrase I know from the fact that an old woman once, in begging me very earnestly to grant her some request, said *Miléla-pàladia*, &c., and at the same moment stooped down and stroked my boots with her hand, and very unpleasant it was.' Mr. Peill also says of this custom that "it is scarcely true that it is now merely a phrase among the Hova, as I have seen it actually done. Queen's messengers sent out to a certain village were not, as they thought, received with proper respect; they therefore left the village without having delivered the royal message. The chiefs of the village were dreadfully afraid, and followed after the queen's messengers with their hair all down (that is, with the numerous small plaits and knots unloosed) over their shoulders, dishevelled, and their *làmbas* down below their shoulders.[1] When they reached the royal messengers they at once fell at the feet of the principal one of them, a judge, and actually kissed or licked his feet, at the same time humbly begging his acceptance of their repentance. He yielded to their request, and returned with them. I have no doubt that while much less frequent than formerly was the case, the custom is still occasionally observed."

Mr. Price further remarks: "For what purpose do all the people, sometimes when there is a great *kabàry* (public assembly), and the queen appears, put down their umbrellas? It has been said that they do so whenever the queen spits, but whether that is a joke or not I cannot tell. More ridiculous customs are quite credible." "The use of the fingers in 'totting off' a number of heads or points in a discourse of private conversation is very remarkable. They do not merely touch the left-hand fingers on the *side* with the right forefinger, but holding the left hand out palm upwards, they pull up and lay over flat on the open palm the fingers one by one."[2] "In descriptions of persons, things, events, &c., they often take up little bits of stone or stick, or anything that is to hand, and lay them out in order to represent the different people, things, events, ideas, heads, &c., about which they are speaking. Frequently they

---

[1] These two acts are done not only at the death of a sovereign, but also at those of relatives and friends, and occasionally even the head is shaved. The hair is dishevelled for a long time, and children in the schools, and adults in the congregation, refuse to *sing* at all for a long time after the death of a relative.

[2] Malagasy children very frequently count on their toes, instead of their fingers.

make the talk much more emphatic by these means." "A loose woman may sometimes be known (*i.e.*, when she is plying her trade) by her going about the streets with her face covered with her *làmba*. I remember one case in which it was made a reproach to a woman that she, a stranger, walked through a certain town to the house at which she was to stay, 'with face covered like a harlot'" (*cf.* Gen. xxxviii. 15). The *làmba* is also used to denote other feelings: "Note the covering of the lower half or more of the face with the *làmba* when a person is sulky or sullen, squatting on the ground in silence. Here they may do this when they are simply lazy and not sulky, but they always do it when they *are* sulky." The covering of the mouth is also indicative of modesty or shame, often further shown by uncovering the feet and lower part of the legs. In giving assurances of loyalty and obedience at a public assembly the speaker often dances, flourishing his spear or sword, and throwing off the *làmba*. "This is intended to express rage at and defiance of an imaginary enemy." Mr. Peill adds: "At the end of a period (*i.e.*, of a public speech) they jump clean from the ground, and coming down stamp with both feet together on the ground, in order to emphasise what they are saying." "In walking together, friends do not go arm-in-arm, but hand-in-hand, or the hand of one may be thrown round the other's shoulder or round the waist." "The Bètsilèo in saluting a superior do not make the same gesture as the Hova. They bend forward and make a sort of scrape, at the same time laying hold of the forelock and tugging at it."

Mr. Peill remarks: "In pointing to an object some distance away, I have often noticed that the Malagasy point the finger far higher than Europeans under like circumstances would do. They point in the direction of the thing to which they wish to call attention, of course, but up to the heavens in that direction, not towards the earth." "Another custom illustrating this subject is the *màmpitàha*, one wife imitating another to show that she is equally clever, both with her hands and feet. I have watched young girls engaged in this game with great interest and amusement, and I imagine that apart from the general object of the elder wife showing that she is equally clever with the younger, each gesture conveys some definite idea to the natives, illustrating the things in which the one is supposed to equal or excel the other." " I have seen Malagasy women, on receiving news of the death of a near relative, throw themselves flat on their faces on the ground, and creep towards the bearer of the message, at the same time rolling in the dust, and tearing their hair in their grief."

Mr. Thorne points out that there are many symbolic acts used by the Malagasy, which are somewhat connected with signs and gestures. Among these are the *kiàdy*, or sign of ownership, or possession, or protection. This is, in fact, a mark of *tabu*, or *tapu*, and is usually a tall, upright stick, with a bunch of grass fastened at the top, and stuck into the ground; although how this came to signify possession needs further inquiry. Something similar to this is practised by bearers, who often come before a journey is made and tie a piece of grass round one end of the palanquin pole to signify that they are engaged for it and will claim to carry. A road or path is also *tabu*-ed by putting a stick or sticks across it to signify that those in the rear are to avoid it. Mr. Thorne further remarks : " Symbolic acts must at one time have been much more numerous among the Malagasy than at present. One naturally thinks of the piece of wood sent by Andrìamanàlina of Bètsilèo to Andrìanimpòina (King of Imèrina), as his *réfy* measure (about 5 feet 8 inches to 6 feet, a measure formed by stretching out the arms and hands as far as they will reach); and of the large *làmba* on which Andrìanimpòina killed the bullock, not one drop of whose blood fell outside it, and of the *làmba* afterwards sent by him with a hole cut out of the middle. Also of Andrìamampandry's symbolic teaching of Andrìamàsinavàlona.[1] Among symbolic acts still customary I have thought of the following :—Spitting

---

[1] See Chapter X. for fuller description of these symbolic acts.

on noticing a bad smell (perhaps rather a sensible sanitary precaution); *Ny mitsòngo dìa* (lit., pinching the sole), symbol of a desire to share in another's good fortune; *Ny miàla fàditra* [1] (throwing away some object which has a supposed connection, often merely verbal, with disease or calamity), symbol of a desire to be rid of some calamity; *Ny misòtro vòkaka* (drinking water mixed with dust from a royal tomb); and *Ny mivély ràno* (striking water with a spear, at the time of taking an oath to the sovereign), symbol of allegiance."

[1] See Chapter XIII. on "Divination," &c.

CHAPTER IX.

MALAGASY FOLK-LORE AND POPULAR SUPERSTITIONS.

Animals—The ox—Birds—Insects—Fabulous animals—*Fanàny* or Seven-headed Serpent—Footprints of giants—Trees and plants—Ordeals—Folk-lore of home-life—Lucky and unlucky actions—Sickness and death—Witchcraft and charms—Food and *Fàdy* of the Sihànaka—Snakes'and lemurs—Tabooed days, in clans, and villages—Good omens, for food, and wealth—Evil omens, as to famine, trade, poverty, and death—Weather prognostics—Various portents—Dreams.

IN one of the chapters of *The Great African Island* a number of particulars were given as to the popular superstitions of Madagascar. I shall not repeat these here, but give instead fresh facts of the same kind which have been collected since that paper was written. The first of these additional contributions to the subject is a reproduction of a short paper of my own contributed to the *Folk-lore Record*, 1881.[1] The second is a paper by Mrs. Mackay, of the L.M.S. Mission in Antsihànaka, on "The Food and *Fàdy* of the Sihànaka." And the third is a paper by the Rev. S. E. Jorgensen, of the Norwegian Lutheran Mission in Madagascar, on "Some Popular Malagasy Superstitions." These two latter papers were all contributed to the *Antanànarìvo Annual*, and by the kind permission of the authors I am allowed to reproduce them in this volume as a part of the present chapter.

SOME ADDITIONAL FOLK-LORE.

Animals.—Many curious customs and superstitions, it may be remembered by readers of the paper mentioned in the first paragraph, are connected with the largest animal found in

[1] "Some Additional Folk-lore from Madagascar."

Madagascar, the humped and long-horned ox. The Sàkalàva of Mènabé, on the west coast, not only seldom kill red oxen for food, but at their circumcision festivals, and then only, they kill a *bull*, instead of an ox ; and the child to be operated on is seated on the animal's back during the customary invocation. The royal tribes of Màroseránana and Andrévola, in the Fiherénana province (south-west coast), used sometimes to employ human sacrifices instead of those of oxen.

The tribe or clan of the south-eastern provinces, called Zàfy Raminìa, will not eat flesh unless the animal has been killed by the hand of one of their own tribe.

The Rev. C. F. Moss relates that "a place called Anàlavòry [between the capital and the north-west coast] was described to us as the burial-place of an extinct race of kings ; and it is said that every year, at the feast of the *Fandròana* [the New Year's festival, a very great occasion with the Malagasy], a herd of cattle gather of their own accord at the spot, whereupon the fat ones die of themselves without waiting for the butcher ; while the lean ones, led by an ancient cow, run away, to return to the same spot and go through the same course of procedure the following year. We were also assured that if we stood there and shouted, no matter how dry the day, rain would surely come."

Omby or *ombé*, the native word for ox, is an equivalent for "chief," "head," and the bull is held as sacred among the Sàkalàvas. In digging out the foundations for a new gateway to the royal courtyard at Antanànarìvo, a few years ago, the remains of one of the former queen's fighting bulls were discovered, carefully wrapped in a red *làmba*, the ample cloth forming the outer article of native dress.[1]

Among the Sihànaka tribe any one who sees a large black

---

[1] The close connection of the native name for the ox with many Malagasy words may be seen from the following examples :—
Ombalàhinìfy, eyetooth ; lit., "bull-tooth."
Ombalàhintòngotra, heel ; lit., "bull of foot."
Ombalàhi-fanòto, lit., "bull-pounder," a name given to the rice-pounder when used in the circumcision ceremonies.

moth called *kàkabémàso* (*i.e.*, "the enemy with many eyes," alluding to the eye-like spots on its wings) is believed to be liable to an attack of a disease called *sòratra* or *tròmba*. The same consequence also follows seeing the bird called *vòrondréo*.

A native evangelist living among the same people had a hare-lipped cow and two rabbits. These animals caused much anxiety to the superstitious folks, a number of whom waited upon him, and requested him either to remove or kill them, as such creatures were tabooed amongst them, and would bring sickness and other calamities if allowed to remain.

Among the Hovas a bit of folk-lore was connected with the whale. When an earthquake shock occurred they used to say, "*Mivàdika ny tròzona*" ("The whales are turning over") and "*Mampàndro ny zànany ny tròzona*" ("The whales are bathing their children").

Fabulous animals.—Some account was given in the chapter already referred to of a curious belief of the Bètsilèo (central southern Madagascar) in a kind of transmigration of souls; the spirits of those of noble blood being supposed to enter a creature called *fanàny*, variously described as a lizard, a worm, and a serpent, which is regarded with idolatrous reverence by the people.[1] My friend Mr. G. A. Shaw, who has resided for many years in the Bètsilèo province, has kindly given me some additional particulars as to this curious superstition. He says the *fanàny* is supposed to be the result of the *life* of the princes, and to come from below the left armpit; for the body, when dead, is bound tightly to one of the posts of the house, and the creature that appears in the liquid exuding from the body by the pressure applied is, they say, the life. This creature is carried to the nearest water, river or otherwise, which from that

---

Ombalàhi-vòla, "silver-bulls," are small ornaments of silver about an inch long, in the rude shape of an ox, worn about the wrist or chest as charms.
Ombalàhin' Andriamànitra, "God's bull," is the name of a bead.
Ombivòlavìta, "oxen finished (?) money," are speckled cattle, frequently used for sacrifices and as presents to the sovereign or chief.

[1] *Vide ante*, Chapter VIII., p. 163.

time becomes *fàdy* or tabooed. No more is seen of it (of course), but they think it is not killed, but changes into a snake or lizard, or some animal forming a connecting link between these two reptiles. Here native authorities differ, some asserting that it has legs, while some are uncertain whether the *dòna* (a species of serpent) is not it. When one of these is found the chief people from the district assemble round it, and alternately ask it if it be not the *fanàny* of such-an-one, until it moves its head, when they consider that it has answered in the affirmative. It is coaxed on to a clean cloth, an ox is killed, and the blood set before the *fanàny*, which is then carried to the chief village of the prince to whose name it is supposed to have answered. A great feast is made; oxen are killed; rum is drunk to excess; and at last the creature is carried to the same tabooed water into which the worm said to come from the body was originally placed. The *fanàny*, they say, can never die; if decapitated another head grows; if cut in halves the missing part is renewed; but any one injuring it will die. The belief is dying out, especially since such confusion of ideas exists as to what animal is really the *fanàny*.

While speaking of fabulous *animals* it may be here noted that there is, in Imèrina at least, some trace of that widespread belief in the footprints of supernatural beings, giants, mighty men, and gods.[1] Rapéto, traditionally known as a chief of the Vazimba, the aboriginal inhabitants of the interior provinces, has by the popular imagination been magnified into a giant, and some curious holes in rocks by the roadside, four or five miles north of Antanànarìvo, are supposed to be his footprints. A good deal of imaginative power is requisite, for they are shapeless cavities, probably produced by the action of rain-water. A village two or three miles west of the capital bears the name of this chief, Ambòhidrapéto, *i.e.*, the town of Rapéto.

Trees and plants.—In the times when bull-fighting was common, the owners of the bulls held a plant called *tsivà-*

[1] See Tylor's *Early Civilisation*, pp. 114–116.

londrìana in their hands to ensure victory. Concerning a hard-wooded tree called *hàzotòkana*, the Malagasy used to believe that if any part of it were brought into the house the rice-pans would be broken. And formerly, the root of a plant called *vàrikitìa* was brought by the father of a newly-born child (if the first-born), who held it over his head outside the house, then dashed it on the ground westwards, with the idea that the child was in some way or other benefited thereby.

In addition to what was said about Malagasy *Ordeals* it may be noted that in the *tangéna* ordeal the poison was occasionally given to dogs or fowls, instead of to the culprit personally, its effect upon these being the test of guilt or innocence. It was believed that certain charms could make the animals die; in the case of a dog these were called *tòlakambòandràno*.

Although the use of the *tangéna* ordeal was abolished in Madagascar by an article in the Anglo-Malagasy treaty of 1865, there can be no doubt that it is still believed in by numbers of the people. This was shown unmistakably in April, 1878; for the prevalence of a very fatal epidemic fever led many of the people in a village only a few miles distant from the capital to resort to the *tangéna*, several dying from the effects. The Government, however, promptly interfered and punished severely all the inhabitants of the place. Still more recently attempts have been made to revive the custom.

Folk-lore of home and family life.—Among the Bàra there are no midwives, or rather, the midwives are men, the husbands and elder sons doing all that is required at a birth. After giving birth to a child the mother remains in the house four days.

At the commencement of the new year red earth used to be taken from some specified spot and put at the foot of the middle post supporting the roof of the house; this was called *sàntatàona*, *i.e.*, "first fruits of the year."

On certain occasions a cord is directed by the diviners to be fastened from the south-west corner of the house to the north-east (the sacred) corner of it; this is done as a *sòrona* or means of obtaining blessing, and is called *tàdivìta*, *i.e.*, "finished" or "perfected cord."

The Tanàla (forest) people, as regards their way of eating, may be divided into two classes: from the boundaries of the river Rianàny, going southwards, they eat with wooden spoons; but going northwards, they eat with leaves. The Zàfimanélo tribe lock their doors when at their meals, and hardly any one ever sees them eating.

Lucky and unlucky actions, &c.—Of the river Fanìndrona, in Bètsilèo, Mr. Shaw says that, although it is a splendid river, "on account of the superstition of the people deterring them from putting a canoe on it, it is one of the greatest obstacles to travelling to and from the capital in the wet season. In one itinerating journey the only way of getting the writer's goods across was by balancing them upon the native water pitchers, and a man swimming on each side propelling the cranky vessel forward; and although scarcely a year passes without some being drowned, yet no inducement is sufficiently strong to overcome their superstitious dread of allowing a canoe to be used."

Sickness and death.—Among the Hovas the rough bier on which a corpse is carried is called *trànovòrona*, *i.e.*, "bird's house," possibly from the idea of the spirit of the departed having flown away, like a bird from its cage. A whirlwind (*tadiò*) is supposed to consist of the ghosts of the dead.

The sacredness attached to royal names among the Hovas is extended after the death of the sovereign to everything connected with their tombs and funeral ceremonies.[1] Thus, they do not say of a king that he has died, but has "retired," *miambòho*, lit., "turned his back" upon his subjects, or has "gone home to lie down," *mòdimàndry*. His corpse is not called *fàty*, the usual word for that of a subject, but *ny màsina*, "the sacred" (thing); and it is not buried (*alévina*), but "hidden" (*afénina*); and his tomb is not a *fàsana*, but *tràno màsina*, "the sacred

[1] *Vide ante*, Chap. VIII., pp. 151, 152.

house," in which is hidden the silver coffin, which is termed *làkambòla*, "the silver canoe." Everything, in short, is specialised by a name different from that applied to the same thing in connection with the people generally, whether nobles or otherwise.

The Rev. W. D. Cowan, in speaking of the epidemic of malarial fever in the Bètsilèo province in 1878-79, says: "One curious coincidence may be mentioned. The town and its suburbs were visited by an epidemic of catarrh. The natives at once said that locusts were near at hand. At this time we had heard of no locusts being in the neighbourhood, but, strange to say, they appeared in great numbers within the week."

Witchcraft and charms.—By mixing charms with the dust a person had trodden upon it was supposed that a disease called *raòdìa* (*rao* = *raoka*, gathered, collected, *dia*, footstep) would be caused to that person.

Of the Bètsilèo charms, Mr. Shaw says they consist "for the most part of pieces of wood about a span in length, cut from various trees, some growing only, it is said, in distant places, and hence costing considerable sums of money;" and that he had in his possession between twenty and thirty *òdy*, of each of which he had ascertained the use. Some are believed in simply as medicine, the sticks being rubbed on a stone, and the dust thus grated off eaten by the sick. One is used as an antidote to any poison an enemy may have placed in the food; while others are efficacious for curing cuts and open wounds, delirium, sudden illness, and as protection from thieves, lightning, crocodiles, &c.

Of the *Sihànaka*, the Rev. J. Pearse says: "In 1877 large numbers of the people wore a single grain of Indian corn around their neck as a talisman against a disease which, it was affirmed, a *Tenrec* (one of the *Centetidæ*, hedgehog-like animals) had announced would appear. During this year a similar story agitated the people. In the month of February a report was circulated that a dog had spoken, and announced that a hurricane causing grievous famine would devastate the district, that immense hailstones would descend, and that even the heavens would fall. To prevent this calamity the people were told to get six black and six white beads, and to wear them round the neck, as that would prevent any harm overtaking the wearer. The result was that men, women, and children were seen with these twelve beads hung round the neck as a charm." They also wear two white and two black beads to cause rain to fall, but if the string be broken the charm is useless.

THE FOOD AND "FÀDY" OF THE SIHÀNAKA.[1]

Of late years a good deal has been written in the *Antanànarìvo Annual* and elsewhere about the Antsihànaka province in N.E. Madagascar. But of the people, the Sihànaka, of their manners and customs, less has been written than of their country, and scope may still be found for a few remarks on their "Food and *Fàdy*."

The Sihànaka are no exception to the rule in Madagascar as to their staple diet, viz., rice, which is plentiful and very easily cultivated; but owing to the imprudence of the people, and probably also to their laziness, the supply sometimes runs short, when they are reduced to considerable straits. Those living on the eastern border of the province on the edge of the forest are in a less fortunate position than their neighbours with regard to their rice-fields, as very little suitable ground is available; and when, to make up the deficiency, they plant manioc and sweet potato, the wild boars chiefly reap the benefit.

But the food of the Sihànaka includes far more than rice and presents great variety and some considerable broadness of taste, as my readers will acknowledge when they hear that rats, snakes, and owls are included in the list of food-stuffs, not to mention crocodiles, and even cats! To be just, however, it is right to state, that of these only the cat is strictly a Sihànaka dish, its flesh being a delicacy which they compare to goose.

[1] Vide *Antanànarivo Annual*, Vol. IV. p. 301 *et seq*.

The crocodile was not originally used as food, as to eat its flesh seemed a too near approach to cannibalism ; but of later years some have come to consider it waste not to consume what is to hand in such abundance. With regard to snakes, their resemblance to eels is the attraction. Rats and owls are only very occasional dishes, and not by any means generally appreciated, but the Sihànaka seem to have something of Radàma II.'s turn of mind when he wished to know the distinctive merits of things of all sorts as food, and caused them to be tasted.

Besides these very striking articles of diet, there are others which, to most of us, would be little more inviting, but which are eaten by most Malagasy, viz., the various animals, &c., found in the forest, including the different kinds of lemur, the *fòsa*, the wild boar, and many other creatures. Finally, and in common with the Europeans in its neighbourhood, the Sihànaka find a never-failing source of appetising food in the fish and wild fowl of Lake Alaotra, and their free indulgence in the former may prove evidence for the fish theory in leprosy, as lepers are plentiful in the neighbourhood of the lake.

The first division of the title of this paper is a very familiar subject to us all, but as to the word *fàdy*, it may be necessary to explain that it signifies that which is tabooed. Malagasy *fàdy* is a large subject, as may be seen from Mr. Standing's interesting account of it in the *Antanànarìvo Annual* (Vol. II., No. vii., 1883).

It is a pleasing fact, however, that while writing on the *fàdy* of the Sihànaka one is treating of a subject which is certainly losing weight with those whom it most concerns, for superstition in Antsihànaka is being gradually cleared away by Christianity and civilisation.

As far as I can ascertain there are comparatively few things which are *fàdy* common to all the Sihànaka ; of these few, to work their rice-fields on a Thursday seems to be the most important as this may in no case be done. To build brick or mud houses is not permitted, death being the supposed penalty in case of transgression. To use hemp, either in the form of cloth or for smoking, is also universally tabooed. The last-named *fàdy* is remarkable from the fact that it is very unusual for the Malagasy to *mifàdy* (verb from *fàdy*) anything which is really injurious, and no doubt to smoke hemp is so; for instance, rum is never refrained from on the same grounds that other things are tabooed, that is by entire families and tribes. Many Sihànaka abstain most rigidly from pork, objecting to use ointment which they fear may be prepared with lard, and even refusing to carry a load which they suspect to contain it ; neither may their food be cooked in pots or pans previously used for cooking pork ; nevertheless they may eat the flesh of the wild boar, which seems rather inconsistent.

Besides the *fàdy* common to all Sihànaka, each family or clan has inherited a set of *fàdy* of its own ; so in addition to the universal *fàdy* for Thursday, there will be another day of the week on which nothing may be taken out of the house, the mats may not be swept, &c., &c. Some families may not sell eggs, and others may not sell anything which they have inherited, excepting cattle. Various foods too numerous to mention are included in this class of *fàdy*. Others, again, abstain from tobacco, and there are some insects and birds which may not be killed, and certain woods which may not be used for fuel. The foregoing are family *fàdy*, but there are some which pertain to individuals only ; and then again there are the *fàdy* of places or *fàdin-tàny*.

Separate villages, again, have their *fàdy*, and certain things may not be taken into them. At Imèrimandròso water-pots with broken rims, and rushes which have not lain overnight to dry after being cut down, are *fàdy*, and may not be taken into the town ; also the pad of grass which a woman wears on her head when carrying her water-pot must be perfect, *i.e.*, without a hole in it, or it comes under the same ban. At other places these things would be considered harmless, while other equally innocent practices would bring down all manner of evil on the heads of the inhabitants. Water also has its *fàdy*, and to carry lard across Lake Alaotra is to ensure rough weather, to pour *oil* on the troubled waters might then prove a curse, it being too near a relation of the lard.

Besides the universal *fàdy*, the *fàdy* of families, of individuals, and of places, we have *fàdy* for particular circumstances and for certain classes, and finally the *fàdin-òdy*, i.e., the *fàdy* of medicines. In sickness it is usual to abstain from eating chicken even before taking the medicine, which will require abstinence from a great variety of things. Nursing mothers must *mifàdy* the flesh of calves if they have not been separated from their mothers, lest they should have to mourn their children as the cows do their calves; moreover they may not eat a certain sort of banana until the baby can pronounce the name of it, neither may they look at a child's corpse. Young women must refrain from eating rice on a certain day every year.

Of all the *fàdy*, however, the *fàdin-òdy* seem to be the most onerous, not to mention the preparation of the medicine itself, which sometimes involves twelve or more pots containing many and various leaves, roots, &c., being kept boiling at the same time. The following are a few of the *fàdin-òdy*: the eating of anything in the form of herbs or vegetables, fresh beef, fresh fish, chicken, eggs and other wholesome foods; allowing any one to enter the house of the sick wearing a garment not made all in one piece, or with freshly plaited hair; or answering any one speaking outside the house. It is also *fàdy* for the sick to look at the sun rising or setting, or at anything red, or to lie down at sunset. The traders from Imèrina have introduced new *fàdy* in connection with foreign medicines, such as iodide of potassium; salt, rum, and cayenne pepper the people are told to refrain from. The traders do this, no doubt, to secure a better sale for their wares, for the Sihànaka have little faith in a medicine which has no *fàdy* in connection with it. The very latest *fàdy* which has come under my notice, and one I should think of recent invention, is very peculiar: a child is not allowed to accept a picture, lest it should be followed by European ghosts!

SOME POPULAR MALAGASY SUPERSTITIONS.[1]

Many of the Malagasy beliefs to be here described show great resemblance to those which are found both in Europe and elsewhere. They are of some value for the study of the daily life and habits of thought of the Malagasy, showing what occupies their thoughts, and how they think.

1. *Good Omens, or Tokens of Good Luck.*—The saying of Cæsar that people believe what they wish to believe is, to a large extent, true, and they usually look out for signs of good fortune and prosperity. This the Malagasy seem to have done with no small diligence, for among the signs of what may happen which I have gathered no small portion refers to the good they expect to obtain. Thorough materialists they seem to be, for of the various good omens in which they believe the great majority refer to obtaining *food and riches*. The following nine examples refer to food; and that the four of these have reference to *beef* will surprise no one who has seen Malagasy gather round a slaughtered ox. The nine examples are as follows:—

> When eating sweet-potatoes, if some portion falls out of the mouth, it is a sign that one will get potatoes to eat.
> When eating potatoes, if some portion falls down, one will get manioc to eat.
> When eating manioc, if some portion falls down, one will get maize to eat.
> When eating maize, if some portion falls down, one will get rice to eat.
> When eating rice, if some portion falls down, one will get beef to eat.
> When eating beef, if some portion falls down, one will get honey to eat.

The climax is of course clear; we are proceeding from the simpler to the better sorts of food. Of what, according to Malagasy notions, is one class of food, roots and grain, viz., rice is the highest ("Rice is *andrìamànitra*" [god], said an old man once to me); then comes the other class, what is eaten with the rice, &c. (*laoka*), and of this class, honey, remarkably enough, is reckoned higher than meat. As meat, however, is a

[1] *Vide Antanànarìvo Annual*, Vol. II., No. viii., 1884, p. 27.

very valued article of food, we find other tokens for obtaining it, for

> When one stumbles on going out, he will eat meat ; *and so also will he do*,
> When a fly comes into one's mouth, *and*
> When one treads on an animal going out.

The Malagasy are very fond of *money*, and it is quite in accordance with what we should expect to find that they have several signs betokening that they will become rich. Some such lucky omens with regard to getting wealth are the following :—

> When the rice, while being cooked, makes a border.
> When the rice, while being cooked, swells in the middle.
> When one has a boil on the shoulder.
> If any one finds fifteen maize stalks standing in a row.
> If any one has red hair on the top of the head or on the nape of the neck.
> If any one does not arrive in time for the meal.

Some omens refer to obtaining a *certain kind* of riches, as abundance of rice, as do the following :—

> When a hedgehog (*Tràndraka*) is not properly buried, the rice will grow well ; *and this will also be the case*
> When one gets sore eyes.

Other events, the occurrence of which must be considered as fortunate, and for which omens are found, are the following :—

> When one has white hairs appearing while still young, he will live to be old.
> If, when going on a journey, one is met by a crow (*Goaika*), the journey will be a lucky one ; *and so it will also be*
> If one is met by the kestrel-hawk (*Hìtsikìtsika* [1])

2. *Evil Omens, or Tokens of Calamity.*—Many of these are signs of calamity (*lòza*) in general, as are the following :—

> When a *Tàkatra* [2] (the tufted umber) crosses the village, some calamity will happen ; *as also*
> When the walls of a house crack in two places|opposite to each other ; *also*
> When a hen crows ; *and*
> When a hen lays small eggs ; *and*
> When a hen eats her own eggs ; *and*
> When one sees an *Andróngo* (a small lizard) with two tails.

---

[1] *Tinnunculus Newtonii*, Gurn. [2] *Scopus umbretta*, Gurn.

Some omens have relation to *famine*, as the following :—

When the dogs eat unboiled manioc.
When the dogs dig up earth-nuts (*voànjo*).[1]
When the opening in the *Tsikirìty's*[2] nest turns another way than is usually the case ; *and*
When the cry of the cuckoo (*Kankàfotra*[3]), is heard, the rice will not grow.

Some bad omens refer to *trade and travelling*, as do the following :—

When a trader on his way out is met by a certain hawk (*fihìaka*[4]) he will have no success ; *and*
When a traveller is met by a *Tàkatra* on the road, he will meet with something unfortunate during his journey.

Certain things are regarded as signs of *coming poverty*, as the following :—

When some one comes in unexpectedly to a meal ; *and*
When one has speckled finger nails.

Several are signs of *death*, as the following :—

When the eyelashes quiver, one will hear of death ; *as also*
When one's left ear tingles, one will hear about death being near ; *and*
When one's right ear tingles, one will hear about death being far off.
When the *antàmba's*[5] cry is heard near the house, somebody will die ; *and*
When one is met by a snake, one will hear about death.

The superstition about the cry of the *antàmba* reminds us of the evil significance of the cry of the owl, believed in in European countries.[6]

3. *Weather Prognostics.*—Of these there are probably many, but I have only collected a few, as follows :—

[1] *Voandzeia subterranea*, Thouars.
[2] A species of Weaver-finch, *Spermestes nana*, Pucher.
[3] *Cuculus Rochii*, Hartl.
[4] A species of Long-legged Hawk, *Polyboroides radiatus*, Scop.
[5] A mythical animal.
[6] The screech of some of the Madagascar owls at night has probably given rise to this superstition. It is certainly fearful enough to suggest evil.

> When the swallow (Sìdintsìdina [1]) flies low, there will be rain.
> When the screech of the owl (Katòroka [2]) is heard, drizzling rain (èrika) will fall.
> When the lark (Soròhitra [3]) makes a deep nest, heavy rain will fall.
> When the rain beats on the south-west corner of the house, there will be heavy rain ; *and*
> When it beats on the south-east corner, only a little rain will fall.

4. *Other Portents of Various Kinds.*—There are some portents where a remarkable likeness between the thing which is regarded as a sign and the thing or event signified seems to be the main idea. Thus we are told that

> When a hen crows, there will be a female sovereign ; *and*
> When any one having teeth set apart (*makàka nìfy*) plants maize, the plants will-grow far apart ; *while, on the other hand, if those* who plant maize carry a child on their back, they will have produce " with many children," *i.e.*, an abundant harvest.

No less strange than these is the notion that

> If a woman maintains a crooked or bending posture when arranging eggs in a nest to be hatched, the chickens will have crooked necks.

The Malagasy are a very hospitable people, and they have some signs which denote the arrival of strangers, for

> When the hens cackle at the door, strangers are coming ; *as also*
> When any one is digging manioc, and the root is struck by the spade ; *and*
> When people get sleepy in the middle of the day ; *and*
> When a spider falls down in the house.

Two very amusing ones relating to *household affairs* are as follows :—

> If the walls of the house (when not well built) incline towards the south, the wife will be the stronger one in the house ; *whereas*
> If the walls incline towards the north, the husband will have the best of it.

5. *Dreams.*—The Malagasy of course, as is the case with all other nations, notice their dreams and regard them as signs of what will happen to them. They are also troubled by their

---

[1] More exactly, the Edible-nest-building Swiftlet, *Collocalia francica*, Gon.

[2] A name given to two species of this bird : the Madagascar Scops Owl, *Scops rutilis*, Pucher ; and a Hairy-footed Owl, *Ninox superciliaris*, Vieill.

[3] *Alauda hova*, Hartl.

dreams, and consider what natural causes there might be for them, so as to counteract the evil forebodings which some of them suggest. They "console their hearts" when they have had an evil dream by saying: "Winter dream, it is unmeaning chatter; summer dream, it will be taken away by the streams (swollen to a larger degree than usual by the heavy rains); spring dream, the dry soil will absorb it; autumn dream, we are too satiated (by the recently harvested rice), and it chatters to no purpose."

In many cases there seems to be some connection between the dream and that which it is regarded as a sign of; sometimes this connection is shown by the similiarity of the two, but sometimes by the contradiction between them, the dream really denoting the very reverse of what one would have supposed it to signify. A few instances, in which a certain similarity is apparent, are as follows:—

> When one dreams that he is going to cross a river and does not get over, he will soon die; *as also*
> When one dreams that he is speaking with the dead,[1] and submits to their calling for him.
> When one is ill and dreams that the dead bring him medicine, he will recover.
> When one dreams about blood, he will have a fight with some one.
> If any one dreams that he meets the Sovereign, he will get a high position.
> If any one dreams that his spoon is lost, there will be famine; *but*
> If one dreams that he is buying a large spoon, the season will be fruitful.

More often, however, the very reverse of what is dreamt of is believed to be about to happen, as in the following:—

> When one dreams that he has made a lucky hit in trading, he will lose in his bargain.
> When one dreams that he is eating with the dead, he will live long; *as also*

---

[1] The Malagasy have a very strong belief in life after death. Very interesting are the words of Andrìanampòinimèrina shortly before his death: "My flesh will be buried, but my spirit and my mind will still be with you (*i.e.*, his subjects) and Radàma;" and, "I will not go away, but shall still whisper to him" (*i.e.*, to Radàma).—*Malagasy Kabáry;* collected by W. E. Cousins (p. 7).

When one dreams about a tomb.
When one has lost anything and dreams that it will be found, he will not find it ; *whereas*
If he dreams that he does not find it, he will find it very soon.
If one dreams about a green tree, some one will die.
If any one is ill, and some one else dreams that he is getting better, he will be ill for a long time.
If one dreams that he is crossing a river where there are many crocodiles, he will prosper in the business he is undertaking.
If any one who is far from home dreams that he has returned home, he will die on the road.

In the other dreams which I have noticed there seems to be nothing indicating any correspondence between the thing dreamt of and that which is supposed to be signified by it. Some examples are as follows :—

When one dreams that he is flying, he will die.
When one dreams that he is out catching fish, he will meet with some calamity.
When one dreams about a fight between red oxen, *or*
When one dreams about fire, he will be conquered by his enemies.
When one dreams about red soil (the soil here in the interior is mainly dark red in colour), he will come to poverty.
When one dreams that he is falling down from a precipice (the dream of young people everywhere), he will be taken ill ; *as also*
If one dreams that he is crossing dirty water.
When one dreams that he is drinking brandy, he will get well.
When one dreams about fog, he will lose his oxen.
When one dreams that mice are pursuing him, somebody will take away his wife.

BETSIMISÁRAKA WOMEN.

CHAPTER X.

MALAGASY ORATORY, ORNAMENTS OF SPEECH, SYMBOLIC ACTIONS, AND CONUNDRUMS.

Folk-lore—Folk-tales—Proverbs—*Kabàry*—Oratory and figures of speech—The desolate one—Mutual love—The bird—A divorced wife—Transitoriness of life—Bereavement—Death—Imagination—Boasting—The crocodile—A place for everything—Filial love—Friendship—Thanksgiving—Evil speech—Symbolic acts—The two kings—The heir to the throne—Riddles and conundrums.

THE most valuable contribution to our knowledge of Malagasy Folk-tales has been made by the Rev. Lars Dahle, of the Norwegian Lutheran Mission, who published at Antanànarìvo in the early part of 1877 a volume entitled *Specimens of Malagasy Folk-Lore*. Except the preface and title-page, this volume is entirely in Malagasy, and is therefore a sealed book to those who are unacquainted with the language in which it is written.

In 1877, several Europeans residing at Antanànarìvo formed a little society for the purpose of collecting and printing the Folk-lore of Madagascar, such as tales, fables and allegories, proverbs, public speeches, &c. Twelve numbers of the publications of this society were issued at somewhat irregular intervals, the whole forming a volume of 288 pages (1886).[1] In addition to the subjects already mentioned, this volume contains specimens of native riddles, and of rhymes which are a species of mnemonics, intended to aid in the learning of the numbers in arithmetic. Of these varied contents also I propose to give specimens and translations.

[1] *Folk-lore and Folk-tales of Madagascar.* L.M.S. Press.

In the year 1871 the Rev. W. E. Cousins and Mr. J. Parrett published a small volume of 76 pp., containing 1,477 Malagasy Proverbs, a branch of native traditional wisdom in which the language is very rich. A second and much enlarged edition of this work was published in 1885, containing 3,790 proverbs arranged in alphabetical order, so as to be easily found. And in the year 1882 the Rev. J. A. Houlder completed a work upon Malagasy proverbs, arranging them according to their subjects under a number of heads, giving also racy English translations and numerous illustrative notes. After a long delay this carefully arranged book is now in course of publication in the *Antanànarìvo Annual.*

In 1873, Mr. Cousins published another small volume containing twenty-six *Kabàry* or royal and other speeches and proclamations, dating from 1787 to 1872. These public addresses are not only of considerable interest as historical documents, but they have a great value as preserving archaic words and obsolete or obsolescent forms of conversation, and thus throwing important light upon the language.

Three years later still (in 1876), Mr. Cousins issued another small volume containing native accounts of Malagasy customs, including the circumcision observances, the administration of the Tangéna poison-ordeal, marriage and burial ceremonies, and those connected with the New Year's festival, &c. Use has been made of many of these in some of the chapters in the writer's book, *The Great African Island* (Trübner, 1880).

Mention must also be made of a work in Malagasy, which was printed at the Jesuit Mission Press in Antanànarivo at intervals between the years 1873 and 1881. This is a publication in three crown octavo volumes containing altogether about 2,059 pages, and is a *History of the Kings of Imèrina* (the central province), derived from native sources, that is, manuscripts written during the last few years, and traditions. This work gives, in addition to the political history, a considerable amount of information about the native customs, as they are supposed to have successively arisen from the earliest times, including not a little folk-lore, and native beliefs as to supposed supernatural beings, divination, witchcraft, the idols, &c.

Several articles containing information on folk-lore are also included in the contents of a Malagasy work entitled *Isan-kèrin-taona*, or "Annual," but of which only two volumes (for 1876 and 1877) were published at the press of the Friends' Mission in Antanànarìvo.

The substance of this chapter was given in various numbers of the *Folk-lore Journal* for 1883 and 1884, as well as a selection from Malagasy folk-tales. But as the proceedings of learned societies are but little known to the general reader, I have thought it well to produce in this volume most of the information there given.

Fuller particulars as to minor papers and articles referring to Malagasy folk-lore, folk-tales, songs, and popular superstitions may be found by those interested in the subject in an article in the *Antanànarìvo Annual* for 1889 (No. XIII. pp. 29-32), under the same title as this chapter.

SECTION I.: ORATORY AND FIGURES OF SPEECH.—The first of the nine sections into which Mr. Dahle's book is divided treats of *Hain-tény làvalàva*, lit., "Somewhat lengthy clever speeches," *i.e.*, Oratorical Flourishes and Ornaments of Speech, which are occasionally expanded into an allegory. As with many peoples of lively imagination, but who have had no literature, the Malagasy are, as a rule, ready and fluent speakers, and many of them have considerable oratorical powers. The native language is pleasant and musical in its sounds, full of vowels and liquids, and free from all harsh and guttural utterances; and the mental habits of the people induce a great amount of illustration in their ordinary speech, which is full of proverbs and similes. In their more formal and public addresses these are also found in abundance, as well as allegories, fables, and figures derived largely from natural objects.

Here is one of the first examples, which is entitled,

The Desolate (one) forsaken by Friends.

I (am) a straggling piece of peel from the young shoots of the plantain tree; but when I still had possessions, while I still was in happy circumstances, then I was loved by both father's and mother's relations. When I spake, they were shamefaced; when I admonished, they submitted; so that I was to father's relatives their protection [1] and glory, and to mother's relatives the wide-sheltering sunshade; and was to them (as) the calf born in the summer,[2] both amusement and wealth, of whom they said: This one is the great *voàra* (a species of *ficus*), ornament of the field; this the great house, adornment of the town; this is protection, this is glory, this is splendour, this is boasting; this will preserve the memory of the dead, for (he is as) wide-spreading grass in the deserted village, and succeeding his fathers. Yes, they thought me a memorial stone set up, and I was (received) both with shoutings and acclamation.[3]

Nevertheless I am (but) a straggling piece of peel from the shoots of the plantain tree; and now I am left spent and desolate and having nothing, and hated by father's family, and cast off by mother's relations; and considered by them but a stone on which things are dried in the sun, and, when the day becomes cloudy, kicked away. Yes, O people, O good folks, for while I admonish you I also reproach myself, for I am both reproached and openly ashamed. Wherefore, hark ye, take good care of property; for when property is gone, gone is adornment; and the lean ox is not licked by its fellows, and the desolate person is not loved. So do not waste the rice, for those whose planting-rice is gone, and who have to enter into the fellow-wife's house, are in sad case. Do not trample on my cloth, for I cannot arrange the cotton to weave another, and it is ill having rags to wear in the winter.

It will be observed how large a number of figures there is in these few sentences; some of the allusions are explained in foot-notes, but other points are somewhat obscure to those unacquainted with the habits and customs of the Malagasy.

Many of the shorter of these "flowers of oratory" have the

---

[1] The word thus translated means, literally, a post set up as a protection to taboo a house or piece of ground.

[2] That is, in the rainy season, when there is plenty of fresh pasture.

[3] Memorial stones are largely used in the central provinces, and consist of massive monoliths erected with immense labour and expense.

sententious forms of the proverbs; and others take the shape of a conversation between imaginary persons, whose names often afford a key to the sentiments they express. The language readily lends itself to such coinage of names; some one of half a dozen different prefixes being joined to words or short sentences immediately turns them into proper names, each appropriate for the speakers, whether male or female, old or young, &c.

Very frequent allusions are made to fidelity to friendship, which is a strongly marked feature of the Malagasy character, as shown by the practice of brotherhood-by-blood covenants. Here is an example, entitled,

Mutual Love.

Let us two, O friend, never separate upon the high mountain, nor part upon the lofty rock, nor leave each other on the wide-spreading plain. For, alas! that this narrow valley should part such loving ones as we are; for thou wilt advance and go home, and I shall return to remain, for if thou, the traveller, shouldst not be sad, much less should I, the one left. I am a child left by its companions, and playing with dust[1] all alone; but still should I not be utterly weak and given up to folly, if I blamed my friend for going home?

Some of the pieces remind us of the English nursery rhymes of the type of the "old woman who could not get home to get her husband's supper ready;" as is the following:—

The Bird who could find no Place to lay her Eggs.

I (sought to) lay, says a bird, upon High-tree.[2] The high tree was blown by the wind; the wind was stopped by the hill; the hill was burrowed by the rat; the rat was food for the dog; the dog was controlled by the man; the man was conquered by the spear; the spear was conquered by the rock; the rock was overflowed by the water; the water was crossed by little "red-eye" (a small bird).

Several of the pieces in this section of the book refer to

---

[1] The common amusement of native children, equivalent to the "mud pies" of English children.
[2] Here personified by the addition of the personal prefix *Ra-*, and the word for tree meaning strictly "the lofty one."

divorce, and to the attempts often made to bring back to the husband a wife who had been put away. This facility is one of the least pleasing features of Malagasy society ; the power of divorce being usually in the husband's hands, and being often exercised for most trivial reasons, and effected in an absurdly easy fashion. It will be seen, however, in the following piece, that the woman was sometimes quite equal to her husband in power of repartee, and could speak with stinging sarcasm of his fickle conduct and heartlessness :—

Sending home a divorced Wife.

Where away, O pair of bluebirds ? are you going east, or going west ? If to the west, I will bind you hand and foot to tell to *Ràbarimàso* that for a whole year and throughout seven months thy friend has not bathed in warm water, but tears longing for thee have been his bath. Therefore say : May you live, says *Ratsàrahòbitsìmbahofàty*[1] [that is, the husband], for thou art not forgotten by him, though the distance be great and though the streams be in flood. And when *Rafàraèlanàndefèrana* [Mrs. Long-enduring], heard that, she said : Upon my word, I am astonished at thee, Andrìamatòa [a term of respect to an elderly man or eldest son] : when you married me, you thought the road was not big enough for me, but when you divorced me, you considered me a mere nothing ; when you asked for me, you spread out like the broad roof of the house, but when you put me away, you folded up like its gable. So enough of that, Andrìamatòa, &c.

And so she proceeds to pile up figure upon figure to illustrate his ill-treatment of her ; telling him :

Perhaps you think me a poor little locust left by its companions, which can be caught by any one having a hand. . . . A protection (she tells him) can be found from the rain by sewing together the mat umbrella, but it is *love* that is spent, and *love* that is scattered, and *love* that has removed, and the cut ends of the threads are not to be joined together.[2]

To all this the husband rejoins :

Unfortunate that I am, Rafàra, wife beloved, I sent unfit persons ; to

---

[1] There is some significance in this long name, but it is not quite clear to me from its literal meaning.   [2] Referring to the threads used in weaving cloth.

get you home were they sent, nevertheless to keep us separate is what they have accomplished ; so come home then, Rafàra, for our children are sad, the house is desolate, the rice-fields are turned into a marsh, &c.

Whether these efforts were successful is left to conjecture; one may hope that after such moving appeals the injured and indignant wife came back to her family ; especially since they are followed by this additional address by the husband to the people at large to help him out of his difficulty :—

Second speech of Ratsàrahòby.

Help me, good folks, for the fowl I had all but caught has flown off into the long grass, and the bird I had almost obtained for rearing has been carried off by the flood, and the bull I should have obtained for fighting has escaped to the top of the high mountain. So help me, good people, and say thus to Rafàra : I will be humble in spirit without obstinacy, and will agree to what you have done ; for if thou art as the storm destroying the rice, let me be the tree trunk plucked up. And if thou art as hail destroying the rice, let me be the wide field on which it is scattered. And if thou art as the thunderbolt falling to the earth, let me be the rock on which it dances. And if thou art as the whirlwind blinding the eyes, let me be the lake, substitute for eyes. Because gone is my obstinacy, for gentleness only remains, for there is no support of life, since Rafàra is the support of life ; so send me home Rafàra, lest I become a fool.

In Malagasy philosophy, as in that of all nations, there occurs frequent mention of life and its shortness ; and in the absence of any certainty as to a future life, a sentiment somewhat parallel to the old heathen saying, " Let us eat and drink, for to-morrow we die." For example :—

Take your fill of Pleasure while you live.

O ye prosperous people, O ye well to do folks, take your fill of pleasure while you live ; for when dead and come to the "stone with the little mouth" [the native tombs, among the Hova, are made of large undressed slabs of blue granite, in one of which a small entrance is cut], it is not to return the same day, but to stop there to sleep ;[1] it is not to visit only, but

---

[1] Here is a play upon native words (*mòdi-màndry*) which are used alike for sleeping away from home for a night, and also for dying.

to remain. The covering stone[1] is what presses down over one, the red earth is above the breast, a temporary roof and tent walls surround one ;[2] no turning round, no rising up.

Another piece speaks of

Things here on Earth not enduring;

and after referring to the different leaves, fruit, and flowers of various trees, proceeds to moralise thus :

Thou dost not perhaps remember the sayings of the ancestors : Consider, O young folks, your stay here on the earth, for the trees grow only, but are not joined together, for if they were they would reach the skies. But it is not thus, for they have their time of springing and of growing, and of being cut down. And just so with men : to them come prosperous days, and days of misfortune ; they have their days of youth, and of old age, and of death ; but those who die happy and in heaven follow Impòina[3] and Radàma,[3] they are the fortunate ones.

A characteristic feature in native ideas is shown by another piece, which enforces the doctrine that " It is better to die than to suffer affliction."

Many of the compositions in this section of the book are in praise of wisdom and denunciation, of folly ; in fact, perhaps no people are more ready to give and receive good advice than are the Malagasy. It is universally recognised as the privilege of all to give admonition to others, even to those highest in rank, if it is administered in the form of advice or *ànatra*.

There are a great many references to animals in these admonitions ; almost every bird known to the Malagasy is used as a simile, and its habits are described with great accuracy ; so that a complete collection of all the references to the animal life of Madagascar found in the proverbs and fables would throw no little light upon the fauna of the island.

---

[1] The four stones forming the sides of the Hova tombs are covered in by one huge slab, called the *ràngolàhy*.

[2] Referring to the native customs at a funeral, and in making a new tomb.

[3] Hova sovereigns : the first of whom, also called Andrìanampòinimèrina, died in 1810, the second in 1828.

Here is a curious piece in the form of a dialogue, exhorting those in sorrow not to hide it from their friends:—

The Bereaved one questioned and attempting to hide (Sorrow).
Who is that person before thee?
I know not, for I did not overtake him.
Who is yonder person behind thee?
I know not, for he did not overtake me.
Why then are you so erect?
I am not erect, but chanced to rise.
Why then do you sob so?
I am not sobbing, but merely yawning.
Why are you as if beside yourself?
I am not beside myself, but am thinking.
Why are you as if weeping?
I am not weeping, but have got dust in my eye.
Why are you sighing?
I am not sighing, but have a cold.
Why are you woebegone?
I do not wish to appear woebegone, but my child is dead!
Then she bursts into a flood of tears and makes all the people sorry.[1]
Consider well! do not hide your calamity.

A fatalistic sentiment appears in the following, entitled:—

Dying is not to be avoided.

The guinea-fowl when flying departs not from the wood, nor, when hiding, from the earth, and the *Fanòro*[2] shrub dies on the ground. All the hairs of the head cannot bind death, and tears cannot hold him; therefore give up the dead, for the earth is the forsaking place of the beloved ones, the dwelling of the living, the home when dead.

Here is a bit of "tall talk," in which the powers of nature are invoked to help against an enemy. It should be noted that all the natural objects mentioned are personified by adding to them the personal prefix *Ra-*, which can hardly be paralleled in English by our prefixes Mr. or Mrs., &c., without a somewhat comic effect, which is quite absent in the Malagasy.

[1] When a death occurs in any house, the relatives and friends assemble in large numbers to condole with the family, to *mitsàpa alàhèlo, i.e.*, "to touch sorrow."
[2] *Gomphocarpus fruticosus*, R. Br.

The Far-reaching Power of the Imagination.

The sun is indeed my father, the moon is my mother, the stars are but my subjects ; Bètsimitàtatra [the great rice-plain west of Antanànarìvo] is my rice-plot, the meteors are my guns, and the thunderbolts are my cannon, with which I will fire at those who hate me.

Here is another example of the same habit of boasting of one's own power, in the form of a dialogue between two men :—

Each Boasting.

Says Rafàralàhy [*i.e.*, last male, or youngest son] : " Art thou Andrianàivo, who art child of Namèhana : rising up, eating the *àviàvy*[1] (fruit), and when stooping, eating *amòntana*[1] (fruit) ; at evening playing with citrons, and in the morning bowling lemons ? " " Just so."

Then says Andrianàivo [middle male] : " Art thou Rafàralàhy, who art child of Iarivo : when poor, having money sought for by creditors ; riding on horseback yet not calumniated, and carried in a palanquin, yet not abused ? " " Just so."

A careful study of these Malagasy sayings, together with the native proverbs, throws considerable light upon the notions of the people as regards morals. Many of them contain much good counsel as to the avoidance of various vices and follies, together with rebukes of the loose native habits with regard to marriage ; for example, there is one against forsaking one's wife to marry a richer one ! Then we have warnings against bad company, gluttony, dishonesty, and prodigality, and very many against lying and liars. The good and the evil man are compared, patience under misfortune is commended, and we are cautioned against trusting in appearances in the following allusion to the habits of the crocodile, the most feared of all the animals inhabiting Madagascar :—

The Slow-going one is to be Feared.

A red male crocodile going down the Ikòpa with the stream, its sly advance unheard, its movements unobserved, lying still in the pools with-

---

[1] These are both fine trees, very common in the central parts of Madagascar ; they are species of *Ficus*, both bearing edible, though not very palatable, fruit.

out diving, and lying in the water without paddling. So then, say I, good folks, perhaps the old fellow [lit., "your senior"] is dead and therefore does not show up, or is somehow prevented and so does not return.

But the people say : Thou art indeed childish and dost not perhaps consider that the crocodile, when he lies in the deep pools and does not dive, there is the warm place where he sleeps ; and when he lies still in the water, not moving a foot, that there is the place where he obtains his food. So let that teach you that the old fellow is not dead by any means, but has still an eye to business.

This reference to the crocodile is but one out of scores of passages noticing the habits of animals in these pieces, and which reveal, as already remarked, most accurate knowledge of their habits. In one of them the eels in the Lake Itàsy are represented as in council, expressing their disappointment that a stone breakwater, made to prevent a too great rush of water out of the lake, has not proved a place for their greater enjoyment, but where they may more easily be caught. In another piece the different cries and habits of various birds are compared, and the unfitness of all for carrying a message, one, the *Vòrondrèo* (*Leptosoma discolor*, a peculiar species of roller), which has a loud distinct cry ; while as to others, *Fítatra* (a species of warbler, the *Pranticola sybilla*) would be always looking for food ; the *Sòy* (a species of *Nectarinia*) would be too melancholy ; and the *Fódy* (the cardinal-bird, *Foudia madagascariensis*), which goes in flocks, would always be flying off with its companions.

This observation of bird life is also illustrated in a short piece which enforces the familiar English household maxim that

Everything has its Place.

The whitebird (a species of egret [*Ardea bubulcus*], which feeds on the flies and parasites of cattle) does not leave the oxen, the sandpiper does not forsake the ford, the hawk does not depart from the tree, the valley is the dwelling of the mosquito, the mountain is the home of the mist, the water holes are the lair of the crocodile. And the sovereign is the depositary (lit., "resting-place") of the law, and the people the depositary of good sense.

Equally numerous are the allusions to the various trees and plants and their qualities, and the way in which they illustrate human weaknesses and follies.

Love of children is a marked feature in these native sayings. They are called "the fat (that is, the best) of one's life" (*mènaky ny aina*), and are said to be "loved like one's self," &c. Equally distinct is the love of home and of one's native place: "Yonder road," says one piece, "is dreary and difficult, twisting about here and there, but for all that it is the way leading to the door of the house of father and mother."

Still more fully and pathetically is this warm family affection expressed in the following lament of a captive taken in war, with which we may conclude this division of the subject :—

Oh that I could see Father and Mother!

Where away yonder, O bird, art thou speeding away by night? Hast thou lost in the game, or art thou fined, that thou thus hastest away?

Neither in gaming have I lost, nor a fine do I dread; but the road to be travelled I sweep over, and in the place of enjoyment do I rest.

Ah, just so, O bird; would that I also were a bird and could fly, that I might go yonder to the top of the high tree to look over and see father and mother, lest they should be dead, lest they should be ill; long have we been separated; for *we* are held in bondage by the people, and *they* are persecuted with gun and spear. We are slaves here in Imèrina (the central province and home of the dominant Hova tribe); manure is our friend, the spade is our brother by blood, and the basket is our companion,[1] Our necks wait for the wooden collar, our backs await the irons, and our feet the fetters. And father and mother sigh out their lives at Vòhibè; so salutation (lit., "may they live") until we meet again, for long has been our separation.

Most of the principal towns and villages in Imèrina are noted for some circumstance or other, either in their natural position, or their productions, or the disposition of the people, as clever, covetous, or brave, &c. This is sometimes expressed in stinging proverbs, which are quoted by their neighbours with great gusto,

---

[1] Alluding to the constant work in the rice-fields done by the slaves, in digging, carrying manure in baskets, &c.

and are heard with equal chagrin by the unfortunate objects of these satirical *bon-mots*. Thus the people of Ambòhipèno are held up to scorn in the saying, "The arums of Ambòhipèno : they had rather let them rot than give one to a neighbour."

The sixth section of *Specimens of Malagasy Folk-lore* consists of a short series of seven Speeches, under the heading of *Haingom-pitenénan' ny Ntaolo ràha nifanànatra izy*, that is, "Ornaments of Speech among the Ancients, when they mutually admonished." Although in Mr. Dahle's selection these follow the native songs, they would seem to be more properly placed next to the first division of the book, *Haintény làvalàva*, or "Oratorical Flourishes," as they partake somewhat of the character of these; and we shall therefore consider them in this place. There is some little difference in the style of these pieces, and in that of the *Haintény làvalàva ;* and as they afford good illustrations of some features in native oratory and its profusion of figures, two or three of them may be translated in full, although some of the allusions are very obscure.

A Plea for Friendship.[1]

1. As regards ourselves and not other people ; for we are people born of one mother and people of one origin ; one root, one stock, brethren following the footprints of the cattle—not broken, even if torn ; a hundred measures of rice, mixed in the storehouse, houses built north and south (of each other),[2] right and left hand, eyes and nose, rice in two measures, yet born of one person only.

2. Therefore let us love one another, for those far off cannot be called ; for the distant fire, as they say, one cannot warm at ; and a hundred measures of rice cannot be carried (by one).

3. There is none overtaken by another [that is helped by strangers] ; for if we call for other people's relatives, they say, it is night, but if we call our own relatives, then it is broad day,[3] for look, even the name of Such-

---

[1] On the ground of relationship ; lit., "a plaiting of friendship."

[2] The old Hova houses were always built with their length running north and south, the front of the house facing the west, the lee-side.

[3] Referring to the strong and universally admitted claims for help in various circumstances that relationship involves.

an-one is become "Not-overtaken-by-another" (or "Not-indebted-to-strangers").

4. Therefore as for thee, O Senior like to a father, thou art an *ambòra* tree for holding fast, and the thick forest for hiding, and the hoof for feasting, and the sun and moon, and the sky to cover over, and the earth for treading upon.

5. Thou art the breast joining on to the wings, and palm of the hand joining to the forefinger, and knee joining the muscles.

6. Thou art the sole *vòamàintilàny* (seed) remaining, and the tree, sapling of the forest, and the bird substitute for meat, and thou art Chief of the place, and Such-an-one still living (amongst us).

Thanksgiving Speech.

Pleasing, friends; swallowed (*i.e.*, acceptable), friends; sweet, friends; great and cannot be swallowed are ye. Sweet indeed is honey, but there are dregs; savoury (lit., sweet) indeed is salt, but it is like a stone; sweet indeed the sugar-cane, but it is like wood; but the good done by you is incomparable. Nevertheless, friends, be of good cheer, for the good you have done will not be pleasing (only) on the day of doing it, like the feet of the cattle treading the rice ground,[1] but will be pleasing taken home to sleep on, for it shall be rewarded when awaking; for that is water bathed in to remove grease, and fat anointing to cause to shine, and cloth to wear to keep off shame. For money is soon spent, and other things come to an end, but friendship, that is enduring.

Another speech is an admonition to companions who shirk their share of government (unpaid) service :—

Short is our word, Sirs, a speech of the old, and if long, yet height without bulk, and if too short, then rolled about; so let it be like the trench for sweet potatoes made by Ikarijovòla, and the germs (fig. topic) extracted.

With regard to yourself, Such-an-one; the people (lit., "the under the day") go upon the Queen's service, but thou hidest away in secret, and dost not go to do thy share, but only just now putfest in an appearance. So that here now thou actest like the little butterfly by the water : able to close up its wings, able to expand them; thou dost like the water-fowl : black when diving, black when emerging; for if thou dost like the little

---

[1] Cattle are employed to trample over the softened mud of the rice fields before planting.

crab in the hole: grasped by the hand and yet not got, sprinkled with water, and not coming out—then we detest that, Sir! And now if it appears that what is under the eye is not seen, or is under the tongue and is not chewed, or near the nose and not smelt, or looked at and not known —then we utterly detest that, Sir! So, although your feet even may go, and although your knees even may skulk along, and although your chin may touch the ground, we will not let you off unless you perform the service for the honour of the sovereign.

Here is another piece, the subject of which is

Do not use Evil Speech.

1. It is not well that men should make a hammer with two heads: both speaking good and speaking evil. For it is an evil thing, friends, to act like the tongue of the ox, licking carefully the hump and licking also the feet; able to enter into the nostrils, able to enter also the mouth.

2. Take heed to the mouth, friends, for the mouth is a compartment (or room), the mouth is just like a piece of cloth—tearing this way, and tearing that way; the mouth is like Alakaosy (the unlucky month), and if one does not butt another, one butts one's self. For the good (speaking) mouth is, they say, as a meal; but the evil mouth is, they say, a thing cleaving to one.

The evil mouth is just like the loin-cloth, binding its only owner. For there is no one guilty in body, they say, but they who are guilty in mouth are guilty. For the unguarded mouth, they say, is cause of calamity, and those who are free of speech, they say, reveal secrets; so that what is done by the mouth, they say, endangers the neck.

3. Take heed, friends, to the mouth, and do what is right, for that only brings lasting good. For if one does good when young, they say, they have something to take to old age, yea, even to take with them in death. For that has given rise to the popular saying, "Do good that you be not forgotten, even when you have mouldered away." For the good done, they say, is a memorial (lit., "a set-up stone"), and the good done is good packed up for a journey.

It will be noticed in this speech what a frequent repetition there is of the word *hòno*, "they say," or "it is said"; apparently guarding a speaker from personal responsibility for much of his counsel, and sheltering him under the authority of others. This is quite characteristic of the native mind, which shrinks from very direct assertion or accusation, and always prefers an indirect mode of statement.

The symbols and figures which it will have been seen in the preceding pages to be a marked characteristic of Malagasy speech are not, however, confined to words, but are sometimes extended to actions. Every reader of the Old Testament scriptures is aware of the frequent use made of such methods of teaching by the Hebrew prophets, as seen in the Book of Ezekiel (iii. 1-3; iv.; vii. 23; xxiv. 1-4; xxxvii. 15-17), and in 1 Kings xxii. 11.

In Malagasy history there are some interesting examples of a similar employment of symbolic acts, especially before the general use of writing had made written letters common. Towards the close of the last century, Andrìanimpòina, King of Imèrina, had reduced under his authority a great part of the interior of the island, and, confident of his own power, sent a messenger to the principal chief of the southern central province, Bètsilèo, telling him that he was "his son" (a common Malagasy expression implying that one person is subordinate to another), and requiring him to come and acknowledge his father. The Bètsilèo chief, however, replied that he was no son of the Hova king, but that they were brothers, each possessing his own territory. The Hova returned for answer, "I have a large cloth (to cover me), but thou hast a small one; so that if you are far from me you are cold; for I am the island to which all the little ones resort, therefore come to me, thy father, for thou art my son." When the Bètsilèo chief received this message he measured a piece of wood between his extended arms (the *réfy* or standard measure of the Malagasy, between the tips of the fingers when the arms are stretched apart to the utmost), and sent it to the king, with the words, "This wood is my measure; bid Andrìanimpòina equal it; if he can span it, then I am his son, and not his brother." Upon Andrìanimpòina trying it he was unable to reach it, for the Bètsilèo chief was long in the arms. But the Hova king would not give up his point, and replied, "My measurement of the wood is of no consequence, for kingship does not consist in length of arms; thou art little, therefore my son; I am great, therefore thy father." (*Cf.* 2 Kings xvi. 7.)

Still the southern chief was unwilling to submit, and sent a particular kind of native cloth ornamented with beads, with a request that an ox should be cut up upon it, as another sign whether he was to acknowledge the Hova king as his superior or not. This test also turned out to his own advantage; but at length Andrìanimpòina would have no further trifling. He sent back the cloth with a piece cut off one end of it, and a spear-hole through the middle, as a significant warning of his intentions unless immediate submission was made. The lesson was not lost upon the weaker chief; he returned a humble answer, begging that he might not be killed, saying, "While it is to-day, all day let me eat of the tender (food) of the earth, for Andrìanimpòina is lord of the kingdom."

Something of a similar kind of symbolic act is related of Queen Rànavàlona I. When she came to the throne in 1828 there was a little boy not many months old at that time, of the true seed royal, and descended from the line of the ancient kings. The queen then announced that she had made this boy her adopted son, and that he should be her successor; even if she should have children of her own, his right to the throne should remain good. Afterwards she had a son of her own, whom she named Rakòton-dRadàma; many thought that her own son would succeed her, but the declaration in favour of the other was never rescinded, and hence arose much animosity between the two princes. When the queen became old and feeble, the subject of the succession came up, and she settled it in a singular way, substantially as follows:—She held a meeting of her officers, judges, and heads of the people, with great solemnity, within the palace, when she announced her intention of making a valuable present to each of the two princes. Two fine vases or covered vessels were placed on the table, and the two young men were called in; the elder was first directed to choose which he would have. He did so, and on opening the vase it was found to contain some beautiful gems and valuable ornaments. The younger, her own son, then opened his vase, and found it contained only a handful of earth. The queen then addressed the assembly, saying that the elder prince was to be advanced to high honour and riches in the land; but, as the land could not be divided, the younger prince, who had received from God the handful of earth, should be her successor. (He eventually became king under the name of Radàma II., but only reigned about eighteen months.)

SECTION II.: RIDDLES AND CONUNDRUMS.—The second division of Mr. Dahle's book consists of about three hundred Malagasy proverbs, here called "Shorter clever Speeches resembling Proverbs"; but, as this branch of native wisdom and observation really requires a separate paper in order to do it justice, we shall not here give extracts from this part of the book. Besides which, it will be necessary to take illustrations from larger collections than this supplementary one from the work we are chiefly using as a text-book.

The third and fourth sections of the book comprise a small collection of Malagasy riddles and conundrums, *Fampànonònana* and *Safìdy*, the latter meaning "choosings," two somewhat similar things being offered for choice in enigmatical language. Such playing upon words is a favourite amusement of the people; and, as some of them show considerable shrewdness a few examples may be given, all of them beginning with the question, *Inona àry izàny?* ("What then is this?").

1. At night they come without being fetched, and by day they are lost without being stolen?

The stars; for, according to the common belief, they go completely away from their places by day.

2. Cut down, and yet not withering?

Hair, when cut off.

3. Six legs and two feet (lit., "soles")?

Money scales, which have always three strings (legs) for each pan, which is called in native idiom its "tongue," but in the riddle is compared to a foot.

4. Lying on the same pillow, but not on the same bed?

The rafters of a roof, which lean on the same ridge-piece (or pillow), but rest (that is, the opposite sides) on different wall-plates (or beds).

5. Coarse rofia cloth outside and white robe inside?

The manioc root, which has a brown skin, but very white floury substance, here contrasted with the ordinary native habit of wearing coarse and often dirty clothing below, and a fine white cloth or *làmba* over all.

6. If boiled, never cooked; but if roasted, ready directly?

Hair.

7. Cannot be carried, but can easily be removed?

The public road; for, until quite recently, there have been no rights of way in Madagascar, and any one can divert a path as he may please.

8. Fetch the dead on which to place the living?

Ashes and fire, alluding to the common native practice of fetching a live coal or two in a handful of ashes.

9. Standing erect he gazes on heaven (lit., "the Creator"); stooping down he gazes on the oxen's footprints?

Rice, which while growing stands erect, but when ripe bends downwards.

10. Its mother says, Let us spread out our hands, but its children say, Let us double up our fists?

The full-grown fern and the young fern shoots, alluding to the rounded knobs at the heads of the latter, compared with the outspread fronds of the plant when full grown.

11. The foot above the leg?

The leaves of the horìrika, an edible arum, whose broad leaf is compared to a foot and its stalk to a leg.

12. Cut, and yet no wound seen?

A shadow and *water*.

13. The mother says, Let us stand up, but the children say, Let us lie across?

A ladder and its rungs; the latter are called "children of the ladder" (*zàna-tòhatra*).

14. Has a mouth to eat with, but has no stomach to retain food?

A pair of scissors. A cutting edge is called in native idiom its "tongue" (*léla*).

15. God's little bag, whose stitching is invisible?

An egg.

16. Living on dainties, yet never fat?

A lampstand, which is continually fed with fat.

ORATORY, SYMBOLIC ACTIONS, AND CONUNDRUMS. 211

17. Earth under the person, the person under dry grass, dry grass under water, and water again surrounded by earth?

A water-carrier and the waterpot he (or she) carries, together with a ring of dry grass used as a pad for the waterpot, the water carried, and the earthen *sìny* or pot enclosing the water.

18. When the little one comes the great one takes off its hat?

The great store waterpot in a house, from which the straw cover or hat is removed when water is drawn with a *horn or tin ladle*.

19. Dead before it begins to bluster?

A drum, referring to the bullock's skin of which it is made.

20. Many shields, many spears, yet cannot protect wife and children?

The lemon tree, alluding to the spines on the branches and the round fruits.

In the appendix to the book three specimens of conundrum games are given, the custom being for the proposer to mention first a number of things from a dozen to thirty, calling upon the rest of the party to guess what they are when he has done. In the first of these a number of insects, birds, and household objects are mentioned by some more or less vague description of them, such as: Adornment of the sovereign? *The people.* Horns (*i.e.*, protection) of the people? *Guns.* Top-knot of the town? *A big house.* Two-thirds of his sense gone before he gets arms and legs? *A tadpole*, when it changes to a frog; &c.

In the second game all the different parts of an ox are described in an enigmatical way, thus: God's pavement? *Its teeth.* Two lakes at the foot of a tree? *Its eyes.* Continually fighting but never separating? *Its lips.* Blanket worn day and night and can't be torn? *Its skin;* &c.

In the third game occur the following: Fragrance of the forest? *Ginger.* Fat of the trees? *Honey.* The lofty place, a safe refuge from the flood? *Antanànarìvo.* The lofty place good for sheltering? *Ambòhimànga.*[1] Rising up and not questioned? *The roof-posts of a house:* for a native, when rising up from the mat, would invariably be asked, *Ho aiza moa hianao?* ("Where are you going?").

[1] Because of the woods which clothe the slopes of the hill.

CHAPTER XI.

MALAGASY SONGS, POETRY, CHILDREN'S GAMES, AND MYTHICAL CREATURES.

Songs to the Sovereign—Dirges—Sihànaka laments—Ballad of Benàndro—Friendship — Children's games — Rasarìndra — Sòamìditra — Sakòda—"Leper" game—"Star-killing"—New Year's games—Counting games—Marvellous creatures —*Songòmby—Fanàny*, or Seven-headed Serpent —*Tòkandia*, or "Single-foot"—*Kinòly—Dòna* or *Pìly* (serpent)—*Làlomèna* (Hippopotamus ?)—*Angalàpona—Sioua*.

SECTION I.: SONGS.—Next in order in this collection of folk-lore we find a number of native songs or *Hìran' ny Ntaolo* ("Songs of the Ancients"). The Malagasy people are very fond of singing and of music, and have a very correct ear for harmony. They like singing in parts, and when they hear a new tune will often improvise a tenor, alto, or bass accompaniment. The native tunes are somewhat plaintive, and are often accompanied with the regular clapping of hands and the twanging of a rude guitar or other instrument. On moonlight nights the children and young people will stay out of doors until the small hours of the morning, singing the native songs, in which they take immense delight. It will be seen from the following specimens that although these songs are not rhymed or metrical, they have nevertheless a certain rhythmical "swing" or flow, and a parallelism of structure, and are arranged in somewhat regular form as regards couplets and stanzas.

Several of these songs are in praise of the sovereign, and were chiefly composed in honour of the persecuting Queen Rànavàlona I., who reigned from 1828 to 1861. In heathen times, that is, until the accession of Queen Rànavàlona II., in 1868, it was customary to salute the sovereign as the "God seen by the eye," the visible divinity (*Andrìamànitra hìta màso*). Here is one of these laudatory effusions addressed to the former queens :—

> 1. Salutation, Rabòdonàndrianimpòina ![1]
>   Suns (there are) not two ;
>   Suns but one only (namely),
>   Rabòdonàndrianimpòina !
>
> 2. Going to Imànga,[2] she's no stranger ;
>   Coming to Iarìvo,[2] sovereign of the land.
>
> 3. A shield of beaten gold ;
>   Rising up (she is) light of the heaven ;
>   Stooping down, lamp of the earth.

Another song is in more regular form, consisting of six stanzas of five lines each :—

> 1. Rabòdonàndrianimpòina.
>   South of Ambàtonafàndrana,[3]
>   North of Ambòhimitsìmbina,
>   West of Imàndroséza,
>   East of Ambòhijànahàry.
>
> 2. May you live, Rabodo,
>   And Rambòasalàma-Razàka,[4]
>   And Rakòto (son of) Radàma ;[5]
>   And the whole (royal) family,
>   Not to be counted up.

Some of these songs are wordy and full of repetitions, especially in the choruses, which are very much in what we should call, in English, the "tra-la-la" style ; but several are composed in a grave and serious strain, some enforcing the

---

[1] This was the official and semi-sacred name of the queen.

[2] Shortened forms of Ambòhimànga and Antanànarìvo, the ancient and present capitals.

[3] This and the three following words are the names of the northern, southern, eastern, and western portions of the capital city, the royal palaces being in the centre, and on the summit of the long rocky ridge on and around which the city is built.

[4] The queen's nephew, and heir to the throne until the birth of her son ; see p. 207.

[5] Her son, afterwards king as Radàma II. (1861–1863) ; see p. 208.

honour due to parents, others expounding the nature of true friendship. In one of these latter the hearers are cautioned not to make "mist friendship," which soon dissolves; nor "stone friendship," which cannot be joined again if broken; but to form "iron friendships," which can be welded again if severed; or "silk friendship," which can be twisted in again; not "tobacco friendship," liked but not swallowed; nor "door friendship," liked indeed, but pushed to and fro; and so on.

As in the proverbs and oratorical pieces, so also in some of these songs, the different places in the central province are referred to, in some cases with a punning on their names, to the effect that although they may be *called* So-and-so, those only who act in accordance with the name have truly such-and-such qualities. Thus:—

> A place-name is Tsianòlondròa (lit., "Not-for-two-people");
> Yet it's not the place is (really) Tsianòlondròa,
> But 'tis the wife who is "not-for-two people."

> A place-name is Ambòhipòtsy (White-village);
> Yet it's not the place is (really) Ambòhipòtsy,
> But those who hate uncleanness *are* white.

> A place-name is Ambòhibelòma (Village-of-farewell);
> Yet it's not the place is (really) Ambòhibelòma,
> But it's those who go home who say, Farewell.

Among these Malagasy songs are some called *sàsy*, which are employed as dirges for the dead. An example given by Mr. Dahle consists of five different strains, the first of which is in three stanzas; of these the second may be given as a specimen:—

E, malahelo ô! e malahelo ô!	Ah, sorrowful O! ah, sorrowful O!
Tomany alina!	Weeping by night!
E, malahelo ô ny vadiny etoana!	Ah, sorrowful O! is here his wife!
Tomany alina!	Weeping by night!
E, malahelo ô ny zanany etoana!	Ah, sorrowful O! are here his children!
Tomany alina!	Weeping by night!
E, malahelo ô ny havany etoana!	Ah, sorrowful O! are here his relatives!
Tomany alina!	Weeping by night!
E, malahelo ô ny ankiziny etoana!	Ah, sorrowful O! are here his slaves!
Malahelo izy rehetra!	Sorrowful are they all!

The following description of the burial customs and chants of the Sihànaka tribe is translated from the account given by an intelligent young Hova evangelist who lived among them for three years (1867-1870):—

"Their customs when watching a corpse are as follows: A number of women, both young and old, sit in the house containing the corpse, and the chief mourners weep, but the rest sing and beat drums. There is no cessation in the funeral customs and singing day or night until the burial, although that sometimes does not take place for a week, in the case of wealthy people. The dirges sung on these occasions are distressing and strange to hear, and show plainly their ignorance of the future state and of what is beyond the grave; for the dead are termed 'lost' (vèry), lost as people who are left by their companions, and do not see the way to go home again; and death they look upon as the messenger of some hard-hearted power, who drives hard bargains which cannot be altered, and puts one in extreme peril (lit., 'in the grip of a crocodile'), where no entreaties prevail. The dead they call 'the gentle (or pleasant) person;' and they will not allow his wife and children and all his relatives to think of anything but their bereavement, and the evil they have to expect from the want of the protection they had from the dead; for now 'the pillar of the house on which they leaned is broken, and the house which sheltered them is pulled down and the town they lived in is destroyed, and the strong one they followed is overcome.' And after that they declare that the living are in trouble, and seem to agree that it had been better not to have been born.

"While they are yet singing in the manner just described, a man goes round the house and sings a dirge in a melancholy tone, upon hearing which those in the house stop suddenly and are perfectly still. Then the one outside the house proceeds rapidly with his chant, as follows :—

> O gone away! O gone away, oh!
> Is the gentle one, O the gentle one, oh!

> Ah, farewell, ah, farewell, oh!
> Farewell, oh! farewell to his house!
> Farewell, oh! farewell to his friends!
> Farewell, oh! farewell to his wife!
> Farewell, oh! farewell to his children!

Then those within doors answer, 'Haié!' as if to say, Amen.

"Then they inquire and reply as follows, those outside asking, and the others in the house answering:—

> What is that sound of rushing feet?
> The cattle.
> What is that rattling chinking sound?
> The money.
> What is making such a noise?
> The people—

referring to the property of the deceased. Then the one outside chants again:—

> O! distressed and sad are the many!
> O! the plantation is overgrown with weeds!
> O! scattered are the calves!
> O! silent are the fields!
> O! weeping are the children!

Then those in the house answer again, 'Haié!'

"Then the one outside the house again sings:—

> O gone away, gone away, is the gentle one!
> Farewell, oh! farewell," &c., &c.

The longest piece in Mr. Dahle's collection of songs is a kind of ballad, in forty-four stanzas of three lines each. It relates the fortunes of an only son called Bènàndro, who would go off to the wars, notwithstanding the entreaties of his father and mother. Of course he at last overcomes their opposition, and goes away with a confidential slave, but soon comes to grief, for he is taken ill, dies on the road, and the slave has, according to native custom, to bring back his bones to his disconsolate parents, who are ready to die with sorrow at their loss. Although full of repetitions it has a swinging, almost rhythmical, flow, very like some of the old English ballads, as will be seen by a few specimen verses :—

    1. Bènàndro a darling son,
       Bènàndro a darling son,
       Bènàndro a dearly loved one.

    2. Then rose, say I, Bènàndro O !
       Besought his mother O !
       Besought his father O !

    3. O pray do let me go,
       O pray do let me go ;
       For gone are all the young men, O !

    12. Then answered back his father, O !
        Then spake to him his mother,
        "Stay here, O piece of my life.

    13. The road you go is difficult,
        Diseases dire will cut you off,
        Stay here, do thou stay here.

    14. The insects too are numerous,
        The fever too is dangerous,
        Stay here, O piece of my life."

However, he goes away under the charge of Tsàramainty ("The Good Black"), who is charged to nurse him if ill, to feed him when hungry, to be, in fact, in the place of his father and mother. But falling ill he remembers with sorrow his self-willedness, gives directions to Tsàramainty to take his "eight bones," that is, the principal bones of the four limbs, to his parents. Their grief at hearing of his death is pathetically described :—

       Gone indeed is Bènàndro O !
       Gone, and will return no more ?
       Take me to thee, Bènàndro O !

       I grieve for thee, Bènàndro O !
       I long for thee, Bènàndro O !
       Take me with thee, Bènàndro O !

Here is one of those moral exhortations in which the Hova Malagasy delight :—

       Exhortation to Friendship.

  1. Let the living love each other ; for the others (the dead) cannot attain it ; for the others are gone home.

2. Let the living love each other; for the dead are not companions; for the dead belong to the dead, the living belong to the living; for the dead cannot be hoped for, but the living can be hoped for.

3. Let the living love each other; for the kind-hearted attain (life's) end; people love what touches the heart; and remorse does not come before (the deed), but after; and it is you (O men) who shall be full of remorse, who, angry, give up your heart (to vengeance); but for us, we suffer no remorse; when angry, we can be pacified, for vengeance which gets the mastery becomes a parent of much guilt.

4. Let the living love each other; and do not build two houses too distant; for the distant (neighbour) cannot be called in, but the near will be preferred, and the many (together) are happy; for ants consume a small store.

5. Let the living love each other; do like the locusts: when fat, they fly off together.

SECTION II.: CHILDREN'S GAMES.—The next division of our text-book treats of Children's Games, "*Lalaon' ny Ankizy*," and as these are not without interest as illustrations of national habits and ideas, a few extracts may be given. There is a short introduction, evidently from a native source, describing the way in which Malagasy children play:—Two or three joining together go to fetch their companions, the parents saying, "Go and play, for here are your friends calling you, for it is bright moonlight" (lit., "moonlight (is) the day"). And so they all go on to other houses until a number are assembled, and they choose some spacious piece of ground. All having come together, they find out who of their companions are absent, two or three, or more, who are lazy and won't come, and these they make fun of, singing out, "Those who won't play because all their thoughts are about eating, friends of the iron cooking-pot; take care you don't choke with a little bit of skin." Those indoors hearing this, answer, "That's all very fine; you see our fat fowls, and so say, 'Come and play.'" (These children who don't play are often still killing fowls or geese, or cooking their share, the gizzards and livers, and feet and heads.) So when they go out, either that evening or on the following day, they are saluted with shouts of "Stuffed with gravy, Ikalovy! Stuffed with gravy, Ikalovy!" and also, "Keep by yourselves like lepers, O!"

The first play on the list is called *Rasarìndra*, the meaning of which word is not very clear, but the game seems very like the common game of English children called "Fox and Geese."

Rasarìndra.

They all stand in a row, every one with his or her[1] *làmba* (the outer cloth) tightly girded round the waist, the tallest in front, and the younger and weaker behind them, each taking hold of the tightly-bound dress of the one in front. Then one who is biggest is chosen to catch the rest, and this one is called "the robber." And another of the big ones is chosen to be "children's mother," to take care of the little ones. As soon as all are arranged, the "robber" calls out, "Where is Such-an-one for us?" mentioning first those who are hindmost. Calling out thus she comes near to the mother, who answers, "We won't give up Such-an-one." Then touching the biggest one, she says, "Where is the children's mother for us?" Then they all shout out, "We won't give up children's mother." Then the catcher calls out again, "Where then is our little lamb?" So the youngest at the end of the line answers "Meh" (imitating the bleat of a lamb). Then the catcher replies, "Here's our little lamb," and does her best to catch the youngest and last of the row. Having caught this one, she then tries to catch those next in the line, one after another, until they are all caught, the children's mother meanwhile protecting them all in her power.

Then follow descriptions of two games somewhat resembling what is known in England as "Oranges and Lemons," and ending with "Here comes a light to light you to bed; here comes a chopper to chop off the last man's head." They are called

Sòamìditra (lit., "Good entering") *No.* 1.

Two of the tallest in the party stand up, and face each

[1] These games are chiefly practised by girls, or by girls and very young boys.

other, leaving a space between them for a gateway; and clapping their hands together they sing :—

> Sòamiditra é, miditra é, é miditra é!
> Good entering O, entering O, entering O!

Then the lesser ones form a line and take fast hold of each other, and stooping down, sing out :—

Valala manjoko à;	Locusts stooping O!
Kitraotrao!	Fight, fight!
Valala mandry à;	Locusts lying down O!
Mandriaria!	Lie down, down!

Aud so they go on, entering the gateway formed by the two tall ones, and when the least come up to them then these two turn round also.

Sòamìditra No. 2.

The second variation of the above game has more singing in it; but the children arrange themselves in the same way, the two tallest ones and the rest singing alternately as follows :—

Manasa, relahy, manasa e?	We bid (you), friends, we bid you?
Tsy ho any, relahy, tsy ho any e!	We won't go there, friends, we won't go there!
Nahoana, relahy, nahoana e?	Why not then, friends, why not?
Tsy ho vary, relahy, tsy ho vary e!	Not for rice, friends, not for rice!
Ho vary, relahy, ho vary e!	For rice, friends, for rice!
Tsy ho hena, relahy, tsy ho hena é!	Not for meat, friends, not for meat!
Ho hena, relahy, ho hena é!	For meat, friends, for meat!
Tsy ho akoho, relahy, tsy ho akoho é!	Not for fowls, friends, not for fowls!
Ho akoho, relahy, ho akoho e!	For fowls, friends, for fowls!

And so they go on, mentioning other kinds of food, and then all the different fruits. When this is finished, the little ones go forward to enter, making at the same time a loud noise and singing :—

> Varavaran' Andriambolamena,
> Ka intelo miditra toy ny akanjo,
> Mpandrafitra arivo toy ny fantanana.

> Doorway of Golden Prince,
> Entering three times like the dress,
> Carpenters a thousand like the weaving staff.[1]

Another "variant" of this song is given by my friend, the Rev. J. Richardson, Principal of the L.M.S. Normal School at Antanànarìvo, who has done much for the musical progress of the Malagasy by instructing them in the Tonic Sol-fa system, and has also written numerous excellent hymns as well as some capital school songs. As he also supplies the Sol-fa notation of the tune, I venture to extract a paragraph or two from a paper of his on "Malagasy Tònon-kìra (songs) and Hymnology" in the *Antanànarìvo Annual*, No. II., 1876, p. 24. He says, "The only one (song, that is) where an approach to rhythm can be found is a little children's play song. The children join hands, and the first two take up the strain, saying,

> We bid you come, we bid you.

Then they are answered by the whole body,

> We'll not go there, we'll not go.

The leaders again sing out,

> And why (not come), and why (not)?

The whole body then reply again,

> It's neither rice nor *saonjo* (an edible arum.[2])

The leaders cry out, and lift up their arms with hands joined as in a country dance,

> It's the Cardinal-bird's house.

To which the whole troop of children cry out as they pass under,

> It's a red house.

---

[1] This is the literal translation, but the allusions are obscure.
[2] *Colocasia antiquorum.*

These two last strains are repeated until all have passed under. I append music and words in the original:—

KEY F OR E.				D.C.
	:s	s :—.s :m	r :—.r :d	d :— :—	s :—
The leaders:	Man-	a - sa re-	la - hy, man-	as'	é
The rest:	Tsy ho	a - ny re-	la - hy, tsy ho	any	é
The leaders:	Na-	hoa - na re-	la - hy, na-	hoan'	é
The rest:	Tsy ho	va - ry re-	la - hy, tsy	saonjo	é

	s	d
The leaders: Tranon-drafody la-	hy
The rest: Trano me-	na

This little thing is very popular among the youngsters, and they spend hours upon hours over it. It is the most correct as to rhythm that I can find in the *Tònon-kira*, although I have a pretty large collection in my possession."

The two next plays described are called *Sakòda*, a word whose meaning is not at all clear. The first of these is played thus: the children sit in two opposite rows; one side calls out, singing to the other, and is answered as follows :—

Rafara e, Rafara !	Rafàra O, Rafàra ![1]
Ahoana e, ahoana ?	What is it then, what is it ?
Nankaiza e ivadin-driako ?	Where has your husband gone ?
Lasa e nandranto.	He's gone away a-trading.
Rahy maty e, atao ahoana ?	Should he be dead, what then ?
Fonosin-dravin-tatamo.	Wrap him in leaves of water-lily.
Ravin-tatamo tsy mahafono azy,	Water-lily leaves won't wrap him,
Fa lamba mena no mahafono azy.	But a red làmba[2] will wrap him.

Then they change the song and sing :

Very vakana aho, rizavavy !	I've lost my beads, lasses !
Vakana inona, rizavavy ?	What sort of beads, lasses ?
Jijikely, rizavavy.	Little beads, lasses.
Hombaina mitady va, rizavavy ?	Shall we go with you to seek them, lasses ?
Kilalaoko omeko andriako,	My toys I'll give my lady,
Kilalaoko omeko andriako !	My toys I'll give my lady !

---

[1] A common name for a girl, a contraction of Rafàravàvy, the "last female," or youngest girl, in a family.

[2] Among the Hovas and some other tribes the dead are always wrapped tightly in a number of red cloths or *làmba*.

And when that is finished they all rise and leap about like frogs, at the same time slapping their chests; and those who are tired first and stop are considered as beaten.

The *Sakòda* No. 2 is much the same kind of game, but with different words.

Another game is called *Dian-tràndraka*,[1] *i.e.*, "Hedgehog-steps," and is played by all the party arranging themselves in rows, those behind taking hold of those in front, all singing and bending down in imitation of the movements of the animal which gives its name to the play.

Another game, resembling our English children's play of "Tig" and "Touching wood," is called *Kibòkabòka* (*bòka* is the Malagasy word for a leper); it is played thus:—

The children all take fast hold of hands and form a large ring, and put one of the number to stand in the middle of the circle. Then they go round and from side to side, singing,

> Those who touch this one are lepers;
> Those who touch this one are lepers.

And those who touch the one in the centre they call *bòka* (a leper) and place in the middle as well, not stopping the game until every one has been touched. And when that is finished, every one bows down to the ground and says: "Listen, O grandfather beneath the earth, for I am no leper, for the lepers at Naméhana[2] only *are* lepers." Then they spit, saying "Poà."[3]

In the second form of this game the children assemble in some numbers, and one of them hides a small stone, concealing it inside the palm of the hand, putting it opposite one or other of his fingers. He then bids his companions choose, and when one guesses right the finger where the little stone is, that one is called *bòka*, and they all rush away to save themselves upon

---

[1] The *Tràndraka* is a small animal allied to the hedgehogs, belonging to the family Centetidæ, of the order Insectivora.

[2] This is one of the old towns in Imèrina, where those afflicted with this disease live separate from other people.

[3] It is a common practice with the Malagasy to spit if they smell anything offensive. See *Folk-Lore Record*, vol. ii. p. 37.

some stone. But when they come down on the ground they are chased by the one called *bòka*, and if he touches any one then his leprosy removes to the one touched. And so they go on until all have had their turn. At the end they all spit, and say "Poà, for it is not I who am a leper."

Another game is called *Mifàmpibàby*, *i.e.*, "Carrying each other on the back," the little ones being carried by the big ones round the house, with the following ditty :—

> Carry me on your back, O big one !
> Where shall I carry you, eh ?
> Carry me to follow a clod, oh ?
> What sort of clod is that, eh ?
> The Tàkatra's[1] nest, I mean, oh !
> That Tàkatra whose mate is dead, eh ?
> Take me home, O big one.

"Star-killing" (*Mamòno kìntana*) is the name of another children's play, also a favourite one on moonlight nights. A number of them sitting together get a little sheep's dung ; and then, looking at the stars, they choose one of the brightest, and say, "We'll kill (or put out) that one." Then one of them who has a good voice sings the following, the rest taking up the strain :—

> Rubbed with sheep's dung,
> Tomato seed, gourd seed ;
> Cucumbers full of flattery,
> Flattered by that deceiver,
> Shall he die whose fate is evil ? &c. &c.

A somewhat more elaborate game is called *Pètapètaka Inènibè* (*pètaka* means "adhering to," "sticking to," and *Inènibè* is "granny"). A number of children being gathered together they all choose one about whom they say, "Dead is Granny Mrs. Moon-dead-by-day-but-living-by-night" (or "Extinguished-by-day-but-lighted-by-night,"*Ravòlanamàti-àndro-ka-vèlon'àlina*). This one they place in the middle and cover her up with a

---

[1] The *Tàkatra* (*Scopus umbretta*) is a stork which builds a very large and conspicuous nest in the trees, carrying up a great quantity of dry grass and sticks, &c.

quantity of clothes. Then they all pretend to weep, and sing out:

> Oh granny O! oh granny!
> Desolate, desolate, say I, O!
> Your grandchildren young locusts passing.
> And so wake up, wake up, say I, O!
> For miserable are the many children;
> And so come back, come back, say I, O!
> For starving are the many little ones!

Then they call out for some time, telling the calamity which has befallen them. Then they keep quite still for a little while, which they call the night for sleeping, and for the old lady to appear to them all in their dreams (literally, for "pressing," or "squeezing," a word used to express the supposed inspiration of people by the Vazìmba[1] or by the spirit of their ancestors). During this time the one they call the dead old lady pretends to inspire (or appear in dreams to) them all, and calls out softly:

> Oh little children, O!
> Oh little children, O!
> Cross over all of you,
> For on return of this
> Sunday will be here.
> And I shall rise up then.

After a little pause they all speak, saying: "Granny pressed me (or appeared to me) that she'll be alive" (again). Waiting a little longer still, they say, "The time's come." Then granny gets up, and they pat her with their hands, saying:

> Pétapétaka Inénibé,
> Pétapétaka Inénibé.

Then they all rejoice very much, dancing and beating their

[1] These are believed to be the inhabitants of the central provinces of Madagascar, and unacquainted with the use of iron; and are said to have been driven westward by a Hova king, named Andriamanélo. See Chapter II. p. 26, *ante*. A remnant of this tribe is said to be still existing in the western part of Madagascar. Their tombs are regarded with superstitious dread, and they are supposed to appear to people in their dreams. They are mostly malevolent spirits, according to the popular belief.

breasts, and singing and making a loud humming noise, with these words :

> Kodònga Rambìta,[1]
> Kodòngo-dàhy ;
> Kodònga Rambìta,
> Kodòngo-dàhy !

The annual festival of the *Fandròana* or Bathing, at the new year, is a time of great rejoicing among the Malagasy, or, more strictly speaking, among the Hova in the central provinces. On the day when bullocks are killed, the children in Antanànarìvo assemble in great numbers in Imàhamàsina, a large plain below the city to the west, and at Isòanieràna, to the south-west. They all put on clean lambas and dresses, wearing earrings and necklaces, and some being carried in palanquins. They carry with them fruit of different kinds, and small plates, bottles, glasses, and baskets, and go along singing until they come to the places just mentioned. Arrived at Imàhamàsina each party places the fruit on the plates, and fills the glasses with water ; one division then calls out :

> May we enter, ladies ?

The others reply :

> Pray walk in, ladies.
> Certainly, ladies.
> We bring you a little feast.
> May you live long, ladies, in good health ;
> Yes, may God bless us all, ladies ;

and so on, imitating the formal and polite speeches of their elders when paying visits. Then having eaten the fruit they sing and dance, during the afternoon singing a number of songs, whose titles only are given. The children in the country places have a somewhat different custom, for they take meat with them to feast upon.

Before concluding this part of the subject, another children's

---

[1] Many of the words in these games are really untranslatable, as they have no equivalent in English.

amusement may be mentioned, although it is by no means confined to children, viz., songs and ditties intended to help in learning to count. Mr. Richardson, in the second number of the *Publications of the Malagasy Folk-lore Society*, gives ten specimens of these productions, one of them being a song of ten verses of four lines each, but most having only ten lines, and some only four. In some of these ditties there is a punning on the form of the different words for the numbers up to ten, some word of similar sound being brought in to help the memory. This is much the same as if we, to help to remember the number "one," brought in the word "won" in connection with it; or with "four," "before"; or with "eight," "abate," &c. Here is a specimen verse or two:—

1. E, Andrian*isa* ! e Andrian*isa* !
Aza man*isa* ny efa tsy nety e !
E, homba anao aho re !
E, ry izy aroy e !

1. O Mister One ! O Mister One !
Do not count (lit., "do one") the unwilling, O !
O, I'll go along with you !
O, he's yonder there !

6. E, Andrian*enina* ! e Andrian*enina* !
Aza man*enina* [1] alohan'ny, olona e !
E, homba anao aho re !
E, ry izy aroy e !

6. O Mister Six ! O Mister Six !
Do not regret before people O !
O, I'll go along with you !
O, he's yonder there !

8. E, Andriam*balo*, e Andriam*balo* !
Mi*valo* [2] fanahy tsy haditra e !
E, homba anao aho re !
E, ry izy aroy e !

8. O Mister Eight ! O Mister Eight !
Begging pardon, will not be obstinate, O !
O, I'll go along with you !
O, he's yonder there !

In the following the numbers are simply applied to different objects:—

Isa ny amontana,	One the *amòntana* (tree).
Roa ny aviavy,	Two the *àviàvy* (trees).
Telo fangady,	Three spades.
Efa-drofia,	Four *rofia* (palms).
Dimy emboka,	Five gums.

---

[1] Playing on the similarity of sound between the words *énina*, six, and *manénina*, to regret. The words are shown by italics.

[2] A play on the words *bàlo* = *vàlo*, eight, and *mivàlo*, to abjectly beg pardon; on account of these similarities in sound to unpleasant ideas, both six and eight are considered unlucky numbers. See *Folk-Lore Record*, vol. ii. p. 38.

SONGS, POETRY, AND MYTHICAL CREATURES. 229

Eni-mangamanga,   Six blues.
Fito paraky,   Seven tobacco (plants).
Valo tanantanana,   Eight castor-oil (shrubs).
Sivy rongony,   Nine hemp (plants).
Folo fanolehana !   Ten twistings !

In another, words are chosen in each of the ten lines that contain the words for the numbers from one to ten; they are mostly names of plants, grasses, &c. :—

H*is*atra (the peel of rushes).
Ts*ind*roa*d*roatra (a grass, *Sporobolus indicus*, R.Br.).
T*clo*rirana (*Cyperus* sp.).
E*fa*nina (?)
D*ingad*ingana (a shrub, *Psiadia dodonæ æfolia*, St.).
Vo*nine*nina (a herb, *Epallage deutata*, D.C.)
F*ita*tra (a bird, sp. of Warbler, *Pratincola sybilla*, L.)
Kim*balombalo*ntandroka (the core of a horn).
S*iva*na (Eng. a sieve).
Tsi*polopolo*tra ! (the seeds of *Bidens* sp.).

Some seem merely nonsense rhymes; and others carry on the last syllables of one line to the first of the next :—

Aingisa,   Voa manisa,
Aingoa,   Voa manapily,
Talonga,   Pily maka,
'Ndrafanga,   Maka ity,
Diminga,   Ity koa,
Aiminga,   Tabarasily,
Tsitonga,   Sily kely,
Valonga,   Tangorom-bola,
Tsivaza,   Hazon-dandy,
Aigò !   Tsy folo va izao ò ?   (Isn't that ten ?)

Roa an-jaza ;   Two for the child ;
Telo am-behivavy ;   Three for the woman ;
Efatra an-dehilahy ;   Four for the man ;
Raika tsy tia be !   One's not liked much !

SECTION III.: MARVELLOUS CREATURES, OR BOGEY STORIES.—The Malagasy, like most uncivilised peoples, are fond of the marvellous, and many are the wonderful stories told of strange creatures and unearthly appearances some of them have seen. Several of the extraordinary creatures are described in Mr. Dahle's book, and I shall therefore give a translation of what is said about each of them, only omitting a few sentences which are merely wordy repetitions. In a note to the heading of *Sàmpon-jàvatra Sàsany Màhagàga,* or "Sundry Marvellous Stories," it is said that these stories come from the Bètsilèo district, the southern-central province of Madagascar. It will be seen that some of the strange creatures here described are not animals, but have some connection with humanity: the *kinòly* being a grisly reappearance of men after death; the *angalàpona* being a kind of water-sprite; while the *siona* is a diminutive elf of pilfering propensities.

1. *The Songòmby.*[1]—The *Songòmby*, they say, is an animal as big as an ox and fleet of foot, and is said to eat men. In former times (not very long ago) the people in the south thought the horse[2] was a *Songòmby* come from abroad. The way it is caught, they say, is thus: A child is fastened at the entrance of the *Songòmby's* den, so that it cries, and a net is spread at the entrance, whereupon the creature comes and is snared. Near our town (says the author of this account) is a hole in the rock where the people think there is a *Songòmby*. When it sees any one it attacks them fiercely, but the female, it is said, does not fight much, but only encourages the male, so that they always go together. It once happened, they say, that a certain man was going about by night, and met with the *Songòmby*. He fought most bravely all night, and, being a very strong man, was not hurt. Another story about it is that a naughty child was put by its father and mother outside the house, and would have been devoured by one of these creatures had it not been quickly rescued. And another day, the tale goes, a child was punished in the same way, the parents calling out, "Here's your share, Mr. Songòmby!" Then the beast really came up, where-

---

[1] The two words apparently composing this name mean respectively as follows: *sònga,* "having the upper lip turned upward, uncovered," and *òmby,* an ox. *Songòmby* means, figuratively, "lion-hearted."

[2] The horse is of quite modern introduction into Madagascar; it is called, by a corruption of the French word, *sòavàly* = *cheval.*

upon the child cried out, "Oh, here he really is!" But the parents replied, "Well, let him eat you," thinking it was only the child's deception. After a little while they opened the door, and lo! the child had gone. So the parents and the villagers made a great stir, and took torches to seek it, and lo! there was child's blood dropped on the road all the way to the beast's den. Many other stories are also told, which the people think confirm the truth of the existence of this creature.

2. *The Fanàny with Seven Heads.*—This creature, they say, is something which comes from man, for there are certain people whose intestines turn into *Fanàny;* but sometimes it does not come from their intestines, but from their corpse as a whole when it becomes corrupt. On this account it is said to be a frequent custom in certain districts in the south for the people to take the intestines of their dead relatives and place them in a river or small pool, so that they may turn into a *Fanàny*. But the people who change into this creature, they say, are of royal (or noble) descent. So that because of this belief they kill oxen when they see a large creature they believe to be a *Fanàny*, and give it blood and rum to drink and ox-hump to eat. When it first appears they say it ascends into the town where it was produced, that is, where the person from whom it came formerly lived, and there the people of the place ask it, "Art thou Such-an-one?" And if the name they mention was really its own, it nods its head; but if it does not correspond, it shakes its head. They then go on mentioning the names of all the famous deceased nobles in the surrounding district until the creature acknowledges one of them as its own; and as soon as this is arrived at, they kill oxen as just described.

The animal is similar in appearance to the water-snake and the *Mànditra* (another snake). It is a fierce creature, and has seven heads; and when it has grown full size, each of its heads has a horn growing on it. There was a certain man named Ralàko, who conversed with me (says the narrator of this), and this he says he saw: The *Fanàny* fought with a bull during the night, and each fought hard. And during the conflict the *Fanàny* did not bite with its mouth, but fought with its seven horns; each of these was successively broken, until at last it was killed by the bull. Just before death it drew itself up and swelled out to the size of a mountain, so that all the villages in the neighbourhood could not be inhabited on account of the effluvium. It was a man from Imàmo (the western part of Imèrina, the central province) who told me this, and it was there, he said, that it happened.

There is also another story about the *Fanàny* as follows: When it becomes big, they say it encircles a mountain (Itritrìva[1] is said to be one of such mountains); and when its head and tail meet and there is anything to spare besides what goes round the mountain, the creature eats it; and when that is done, some say that it sticks its tail into the earth and mounts up to the sky; but others say that it goes into some great piece of water sufficient for its size. It remained in the lake of Itritrìva, they say, but when it became too big for the lake it removed to Andràikìba (a lake west of Antsìrabè, in the same neighbourhood), and there it remains up to the present time.

I have seen the animal called the *Fanàny* (says the native narrator), but I have not seen either its seven heads or any appearance of them; and on asking the people the reason of this, they replied that it was yet too young. The size of the creature they pointed out to me was about that of an adult *mànditra*, or somewhat less.

3. *The Tòkantòngotra or Tòkandìa* ("Single-foot" or "Single-step").—This is a large white animal (but smaller than the *Songòmby*), and, as its name implies, its feet are not cloven, and it does *not* mean that the animal has a single leg in front and a single one behind, as several European writers have described. It is an exceedingly swift animal, so that no other creature has a chance of escaping it. It eats men, and goes about at night

---

[1] This is the name of an extinct volcano in the Northern Bètsilèo country. The crater is occupied by a lake of profound depth. See Chap. V.

like the *Songòmby*. There are people who say they have seen it, but few compared with those who testify to the existence of the *Songòmby*.[1]

4. *The Kinòly.*—This creature is said to be human. When any one dies who turns into a *Kinòly*, he is buried by the relatives, until the intestines and the skin of the stomach all decay; and when that is the case, they open up the tomb so that the *Kinòly* may go out; so it goes out. Their eyes are red and their nails long, but they are no longer like the living; yet the whole body, except the portions already mentioned, is like that of a human being. They are said to be constantly thieving; and when any one leaves out cooked rice or other food, they take it. Sometimes they also steal rice in the husk, but it is said they can hardly carry any burden; and a story is told of some one who saw two *Kinòly* stealing rice, and hid himself to observe their procedure. They filled with rice some vessel they carried, and the male one carried the burden, putting it on his shoulder; but as soon as it rested there, he cried, "I'm killed; O my shoulder!" Then said the female, "There's no carrying it; where is it? I'll carry it." Then she carried it on her head (that is their custom when both husband and wife die); but as soon as it was placed there, she called out, "I'm killed; O my head!" Another story is told of a person suddenly meeting a *Kinòly* one day, and, seeing the redness of its eyes and the length of its nails, said, "How is it your eyes are so red?" It replied, "God passed by them." Then he asked again, "How is it your nails are so long?" It replied, "That I may tear out your liver" (or inside), upon which it tore the man. In the Bètsilèo province people say that there are *Kinòly* up to the present time, and this not long ago, but quite recently. Among the inhabitants there are many who believe in the reappearance of these bowelless people; but they think it is a cause of lamentation, both to the person himself and also to his relations, to become a *Kinòly*.

[1] It is commonly said that those who even see the *Tòkandìa* are immediately struck dead or senseless.

5. *The Dóna or Pìly.*[1]—This animal is one of the fiercest of creatures; it is big and long, and its skin is striped, so that makers of *làmba* take it as a pattern for striped cloths. During the day it is quite gentle, so that even an infant can play with it and take no harm, but when night comes on there is hardly any other creature so fierce. They say it bellows like a bull. If any animal or man meets it at night, it encircles him at the loins and compresses him so tightly that in a very short time the object attacked is dead. It has the power of making its body big or little, something like indiarubber. It is very crafty, so that when it meets with a serpent (*Mènarària*), which is a creeping creature like itself, it appears to be afraid, and makes its body small. Then comes the serpent and twines round it, and then raises its tail to strike the *Dóna* (for the tail of the *Mènarària* is barbed, they say, like a spear, and it kills its victims by this means). Then the *Dóna* swells its body suddenly, so that the *Mènarària* is broken, as if cut with a knife. Such is its power that it is said to be able to force its way out of its hole, although opposed by the strength of the strongest man stopping it up with a cloth stuffed in at the entrance. Whistling, it appears, makes the *Dóna* angry, although in the daytime it is usually tame.

6. *The Làlomèna or Làlimèna.*—This animal is like the ox, but lives in the water. It has two horns, and they are very red, and it is said to be amongst the strongest of the animals which live in the water. It is difficult to say exactly what its appearance and qualities are, for there is much of the fabulous mixed

---

[1] *Pily* is the name of a serpent. This account is, I think, hardly correctly put under the heading of superstitious beliefs; except in two or three points, it is rather a piece of natural history observation, for there is no question at all about the existence in the western and warmer parts of Madagascar of one or more species of boa. These examples of the widely-spread tropical pythons belong to a peculiar genus, *Sanzinia*; hanging from the branches of the trees, these serpents are said to pounce suddenly on their victims, and, enveloping them in their folds, speedily squeeze them to death. They are even said to kill oxen, and occasionally man, but doubtless a good deal of superstition is mixed up with the native accounts of them.

up with the accounts of it. It seems possible that this word retains traditions of the Madagascar species of Hippopotamus, an animal whose sub-fossil bones have been found in the alluvial deposits of Antsìrabè in the Vàkinankàratra district, south of Imèrina, as well as on the south-west coast, and which possibly was still living when the island was first peopled. These remains are said to be called those of the *Làlomèna* by the people there.

7. *The Angalàpona.*—This creature is among things which are related to man, they say, although it is not so large as a human being. Its abode is said to be in the water, but yet it is not wetted by it, for they say there is a cave within the water into which water does not enter, and there the *Angalàpona* lives. The door by which it goes out and in turns in the water, and so is the road by which it passes to and fro, but yet it is not at all wet, although traversing water in this way. As regards its size, it is a little larger than a young child. Its hair is very long, so that when it stands upright it almost reaches the ground. It is considered by the people to be the director of divination and (fortunate) day foretelling, &c., so that the diviners call upon it when working the oracle with the words, "Arise, for thou hast come from Long-hair," &c.

There are two persons still living who say that they have certainly seen it; their names are Rènisòaràhanóro and Rainitsimanàhy. The former (a woman) chanced to be in the uninhabited country, and was called by a name, a name which is pleasing to the *Angalàpona*. (For names such as Rasòa[1] and the like are pleasing to this creature, so that it fetches such as bear these names.) So the *Angalàpona* came and took her towards its den, passing through the water, but neither it nor the woman was wetted at all. But when they came to the cave, she would not go forward, but remained at the side of the door; neither would she eat food, disliking the things eaten by the

---

[1] This is a very common female name among the Malagasy, both in this short form and also in combination with other words. *Ra* is the personal prefix, *sòa* is "good, pleasant agreeable."

Angalàpona, such as raw eels and cray-fish and the like. And so because she would remain always at the doorway, her clothes became covered with water-plants. So the *Angalàpona* and his wife considered together what they should do with her, and they agreed to send her back home. This they did after giving her (power to work) divination. And now she is applied to by the people for that purpose.

And Rainitsimanàhy's account is that he was in the uninhabited region, and at the time when every one is fast asleep an *Angalàpona* came and desired him to be its husband. But as he would not agree to this, it followed him about perpetually.

Many of the people say that they have seen this creature, especially those who are afflicted with a disease called *jìla*.

8. *The Siona*.—The creature so called has also something human about it, but it is different both from the *Kinòly* and the *Angalàpona*. It is said to live away from men, and when any one goes through the uninhabited country and does not take care of his rice, or chopper, these are taken by the *Siona*, they say, and conveyed to its abode. When the woodmen go to sleep, and leave a fire still burning (for their custom is to place a big log on the hearth before sleeping, so that they may be kept warm), then this creature comes and warms itself. Its food is a root called *Avóko* (*Vigna angivensis*, Baker) and other substances. All over its body it is covered with lichen growing upon it, so that when it lies down on a rock it is not distinguishable, although seen close to the place. When any people are ill and out of their mind, their friends are afraid lest they shall become a *Siona*; and very lately it was reported that some people narrowly escaped this fate, from which they were only saved by the strenuous efforts of their friends.

CHAPTER XII.

MALAGASY FOLK-TALES AND FABLES.

Bonìa—Crocodile and Dog—Three Sisters and Itrìmobé—The Members of the Body—The Little Bird—Rapéto—The Lost Son of God—The Five Fingers—The Earth and the Skies—The Birds choosing a King—The Lizards—Hawk and Hen—Vazimba—Chameleon and Lizard—Serpent and Frog—The Rice and Sugar-cane—Two Rogues—Wild Hog and Rat.

WE now come to the last division of the subjects treated of in our text-book (Rev. L. Dahle's *Malagasy Folk-lore*), that of Folk-tales and Fables—or, as they are called in Malagasy, *Angàno* or *Arìra ; i.e.,* fables, tales, and legends. These occupy nearly two-thirds of Mr. Dahle's book (294 pp.), and include eighty-four separate pieces, some occupying only a single paragraph, while others extend to a considerable length. The longest story, that of Bonìa, occupies forty-seven pages ; another, twenty-three pages ; another, thirteen pages, and so on, down to a page or two. About twenty of these stories are fables chiefly referring to animals ; several relate passages in the adventures of two Malagasy rogues, whose fuller history had previously been published in a separate form ; some partake of the character of nursery rhymes ; some are mythic, professing to explain the origin of man and nature ; and several are giant stories, in which a monster called Itrìmobé is a prominent actor.

In various numbers of the *Folk-lore Journal* for 1883 and 1884 I gave translations of thirty-eight of these compositions, and those who are interested in such studies will there find a good variety of them. Here, however, we can only include a specimen or two of each class of folk-tale, but probably these will indicate sufficiently clearly the character of the whole.

The most favourite, as well as the longest Malagasy folk-tale, is that of *Bonìa*, or, as the name is given in some variants of the story, Andrìan-àri-saina-bonìa-màso-bonìa-manòro (!) Of this tale Mr. Richardson says: "It could, with a little 'padding' and the additions contained in our various renderings, be lengthened out into a good-sized three-volume novel, so many are the incidents and *dramatis personæ ;* while the most concise form of it (18 pp.) is that published in the first number of the [Malagasy] *Folk-lore Society's Publications*, and obtained by the writer [Mr. R.] from a teacher in the London Missionary Society's Normal School. Its length and wealth of incident certainly establish its claim for a first place in all notices of the Malagasy tales." Several of the following stories are translated from *Folk-lore and Folk-tales of Madagascar.*

The Crocodile and the Dog.

Once upon a time a crocodile and a dog chanced to meet suddenly on the road. Then said the crocodile, "Where are you from, my younger brother?" "Just hereabouts, my elder brother," said the dog. Upon that the dog also asked the crocodile, "Where are you from, elder brother?" "I've just come from such a place, younger brother," said he.

And said the dog, "What do you think about my proposal? do you agree or not?" "What proposal is that, younger brother?" "Let us strike up a friendship together," said the dog. "Yes, all right," said the crocodile; "if a little fellow like you knows what is right, much more a senior like myself. Come along then, young friend." "Agreed," said the dog. So the two struck up a firm friendship, and went on talking thus: "Whoever proves false," said the crocodile, "shall be scouted." "Agreed," said the dog.

Some little time afterwards the crocodile said, "Come, let me give you a meal, young friend." So he supplied the dog with food, and when he had eaten his fill, the dog said, "Come, carry me over, old friend." So the crocodile carried him; but half-way across, he stopped and sank down into the water. Upon that the dog struggled a little, but presently got across; and as soon as he landed the crocodile emerged from the water. So the dog said, "You've broken the agreement, old fellow." "Why, wasn't I there below you all the same? For I want you to be able to swim." Nevertheless if the dog had not been able to swim, he would have been drowned.

Then said the dog in his turn, "Come now, old fellow, do you go yonder with me to-morrow." "But where is the place of meeting, young friend?" "Yonder, at such-a-place," said the dog. "Agreed," replied the crocodile. On the morrow accordingly the dog took him some distance towards ground covered with the trailing tendrils of gourds. But it was to pay him out for what he had done. So the dog said, "I will give you a signal, old fellow; when I bark, then run off, for people are coming." The crocodile, be it said, had brought his wife and family with him. And when they all arrived the dog set food before them, but before the meal was half-way through he began to bark. So off they all ran, but some of the young ones were entangled in the trailing tendrils of the gourds and killed.

So when they got to the water, the crocodile said, "What kind of a dog are you? What's the meaning of this, fellow?" "There's no retribution, but the past returns,"[1] said the dog. The crocodile rejoined, "If my descendants and heirs do not destroy dogs from henceforth, then let me have no heirs to inherit!" And this was the origin of the enmity between dogs and crocodiles.

The Three Sisters and Itrìmobé.

There was once a certain couple who were very rich, and they had three children, all daughters. And of these children of theirs, the youngest, Ifàravàvy ("last female"), was the prettiest.

---

[1] A native proverb: "*Ny tody tsy misy, fa ny atao miverina.*"

One day Ifàra had a dream, and told it to her sisters; said she, "I have had a dream, lasses, and I dreamt that the son of the sun came from heaven to take a wife from among us, and it was I whom he took, for you two he left behind."

Then the two sisters were very angry about it, and said, "It is true enough that she is prettier than we are, and if a prince or noble should seek a wife, he would choose her, and not care for us; so let us consider what to do. Come, let us take her out to play, and find out from people which of us they consider the best looking." So they called Ifàra, and said, "Come, Ifàra, let us go and play."

So they went away all dressed in their best, and soon met an old woman. "Granny," said they, "which of us three sisters is the prettiest?" "Ràmatoà (the eldest) is good looking, Ràivo (the middle one) is good looking, but Ifàra is better looking than either." "Oh, dear," said they, "there's no doubt Ifàra is prettier than we are." So they took off Ifàra's *làmba* (the outer native dress, a large oblong piece of cloth).

Presently they met an old man. "Grandfather," they said, "who is the prettiest of us three sisters?" "Ràmatoà is good looking, Ràivo is good looking, but Ifàra is better looking than either." "Dear me! although deprived of her *làmba*, she is still prettier than we are." So they stripped her of her underclothing.

Then they met with Itrìmobé. (This was an immense monster, half human and half beast, a man-eating creature, and with a frightfully sharp tail.) "Oh, dear, if here isn't Itrìmobé! "Who is the prettiest of us three sisters?" But with a snarl he answered just as the old woman and old man had answered.

So the sisters were beside themselves with anger because Ifàra was prettier than they were, and they said, "If we were to kill Ifàra, perhaps father and mother would hear of it and kill us, so let us go and get some of Itrìmobé's vegetables, so that he may eat her." So the sisters said to her, "Come, Ifàra, let us see who can find the nicest vegetables." "Come along then," she said, "let us take some of those yonder" (meaning those of

Itrìmobé). "Shall we get the ripe or the young ones?" said Ifàra. "Get those just sprouting," said they. Then they went to get them, but the two sisters took the full-grown ones. So when the three showed theirs to each other Ifàra's were the worst. "Oh, dear!" cried she, "why yours are the full-grown, you've cheated me." "It's yourself, girl, who would take the unripe," said the two; "go along and fetch some full-grown ones."

So Ifàra went off to get them; but while she was gathering them she was caught by Itrìmobé. "I've got you, my lass," said he, "for you are taking my vegetables; I'll eat you, my lass." Then Ifàra cried, "I am sorry, Itrìmobé, but take me for your wife." "Come along, then," said he (but it was that he might take her home to be fattened, and after that eat her).

The sisters were exceedingly glad at this, and went away to tell their father and mother, saying, "Ifàra stole Itrìmobé's vegetables, so he has eaten her." Then the old people wept profusely for sorrow. So Itrìmobé fed up Ifàra at his house, and would not let her go out of doors, but covered her with mats, while he went into the country hunting things to fatten her, so that Ifàra became very fat, and the time approached for Itrìmobé to devour her.

But one day, when Itrìmobé happened to have gone abroad hunting, a little mouse wearing plantain fibre cloth jumped by Ifàra's side and said, "Give me a little white rice, Ifàra, and I'll give you advice." "What advice can you give me?" said Ifàra. "Well, then, let Itrìmobé devour you to-morrow." "But what is the advice you can give me?" said Ifàra, "for I'll give you the rice." So she gave some white rice to the little mouse clothed in cloth of plantain fibre; and it said to her, "Be off with you, and take an egg, a broom, a small cane, and a smooth round stone, and escape southwards."

So Ifàra took the things and set off; but she put a plantain-tree stem instead of herself in her bed, and locked up the house. Presently Itrìmobé came home from the fields bringing, with him a spear for killing Ifàra, and a cooking-pot; so he knocked at the door, but no one opened. Said he, "Dear me, Ifàra's got so fat she can't move." So he broke open the door, and coming up to the bed thrust his spear through the mat, so that it stuck fast in the plantain-tree stem. Then he said, "Oh dear, Ifàra's so fat the spear sticks fast into her." So he stuck it in again and licked the spear. "Why," said he, "Ifàra must be fat, for her blood has no taste!" But when he had opened the mat to take her for cooking, lo and behold, the plantain-tree stem! "Oho! the worthless wench has run off!" said he.

Then he snuffed the air to the east, but there was nothing there; he snuffed to the north, nothing there; he snuffed to the west, nothing there; he snuffed to the south, "Ah, there she is!" Off he sets, runs after her with all speed, and at last overtakes her; "I've got you, Ifàra!" So Ifàra threw down her broom, saying, "By my sacred father and mother, let this become a dense thicket which Itrìmobé cannot pass through." Then a very dense thicket grew up. But Itrìmobé took his tail and cut away perseveringly at the thicket until it was all cleared off. "I've got you now, Ifàra!"

Then Ifàra put down her egg, saying, "By my sacred father and mother, let this egg become a great pool of water." Then a great pool appeared. But Itrìmobé began to drink up the water and kept pouring it into the river. At last the water was dried up. "I've got you now, Ifàra!"

Then Ifàra put down her small cane, saying, "By my sacred father and mother, let this cane become a dense forest." Then a dense impassable forest grew up. But Itrìmobé with his tail hewed down the forest, and kept at work until the whole was felled. "I've got you now, Ifàra!"

Then Ifàra put down her smooth round stone, and said, "By my sacred father and mother, let this become an inaccessible precipice which Itrìmobé cannot climb. So it became an immense precipice. Then Itrìmobé cut away with his tail incessantly, but at last his tail became so blunt he could do nothing more. He attempted to climb, but was unable. Then he called out, "Pull me up, Ifàra, for I won't harm you." But Ifàra replied, "I won't take hold of you until you have stuck your spear in the ground." So Itrìmobé stuck the spear in the ground, and Ifàra threw him a rope, which he laid hold of. But when he was nearly up he said, "I've got you, Ifàra, my lass!" Then Ifàra let him fall, and he was impaled on his spear and was killed.[1]

So Ifàra was there upon the rock; and she wept and was sad at heart for her father and mother. Then came a crow, and when Ifàra saw it she sang to it as follows:

> "O yonder crow, O yonder crow!
> Take me to father's well,
> And I will smooth thy tail!"

"And you say I eat unripe earth-nuts, and am I going to carry you there? Stay where you are," said the crow.

Then came a hawk, to whom she said:

> "O yonder hawk, O yonder hawk!
> Take me to father's well,
> And I will smooth thy tail!"

"And you say I am the eater of dead rats, and am I going to carry you there?"

After that a "Réo" bird (*Leptosomus discolor*) came, repeating its cry, "Reo, reo, reo," which, when Ifàra saw, she called to thus:

> "O yonder *Réo*, O yonder *Réo*!
> Take me to father's well,
> And I will smooth thy tail!"

"Reo, reo, reo," said the bird, "come, let me carry you, my lass, for I feel for the sorrowful." So the bird took her away and placed her on a tree just above the well of her father and mother.

Soon there came a little slave girl of theirs to draw water;

---

[1] Malagasy spears have a small blade at the foot, by which they are stuck in the ground when encamping, &c., so that the large blade stands upright.

she washed her face, and seeing a reflection in the water, cried out, " My word ! to have a pretty face like mine, and yet carry a waterpot on my head ! " But it was the reflection of Ifàra's face she saw in the water and took it for her own. So she broke the waterpot in pieces. Then Ifàra called out from the tree, " Father and mother are at expense to buy waterpots, and you break them ! " So the slave-girl, whose name was Itrétrikandévo, looked all about her and said, " Wherever was that person speaking ? " So she went off home.

On the morrow she came again to fetch water, and washing her face again, saw a reflection in the water, and breaking the waterpot said, " A handsome face like mine, indeed, and have to carry water on my head ! " But it was Ifàra's face she saw there. And again Ifàra spoke from up the tree, " Father spends money buying, and you break." And again Itrétrikandévo looked about her, saying, " Whoever was that speaking ? "

So she ran off to the village, saying to her master and mistress, " There was somebody speaking yonder at the well, but I could not see who it was, yet the voice was like Ifàra's ! " So the pair went off to see, and when they got there Ifàra came down, and all three wept for joy. Then Ifàra told them how her sisters had deceived her so that she might be seized by Itrimobé. So they disowned the two daughters and kept Ifàra as their child.

The Dispute for Seniority among the Members of the Body.

Once upon a time, it is said, the Ear, the Eye, the Mouth, the Hand, the Foot, and the Belly disputed together about seniority, and in this manner went the dispute :—

Said the Ear, " I am the eldest of all, because it is I who hear all things whatsoever."

And when the Eye heard that, he answered, " It isn't you who are the eldest, but I ; for although you, Ear, may even hear, if it wasn't for me, the Eye, seeing, then you would see nothing of the way you ought to tread."

And when the Mouth heard that, he was angry, and said, "You fellows here are talking nonsense, and disputing as to who shall be the head; while neither of you is the eldest, but it is I myself; for although you, Ear, may hear, and you, Eye, even may see, if it was not for me, Mouth, speaking, you would remain silent as stone or wood."

And when the Hand heard that he was startled, and said, "Why, you ought to be ashamed of yourselves for talking such rubbish, and each of you saying, 'It is I who am eldest.' Why don't you think a little before you speak? For although you all may be here, ear and eye and mouth, if it wasn't for me, the hand, which takes hold and works, what could you all accomplish? So let every one be still, for there is no one of you eldest, for I, the hand, alone am the eldest."

And when the Foot heard that, he burst out laughing, and said, "What a set of fools! just look at the shadow first before you peer into the glass. People like you, indeed, quarrelling about seniority! For what are you but maize hung up, so that although you, Eye, may see, and although you, Mouth, may speak, and although you, Hand, may take hold, if it wasn't for me, the foot, to go and carry you, what would you be better than the bottom of the basket, to sit still without any other business than to be friends with the ashes?[1] Don't dispute any more about seniority, for none of you is worthy to be senior. For it is I, the foot, only who am senior."

And the Belly, when he heard all that, said, "How is it these fellows have a mouth that is never tired, and lips above and below, and are not torn to pieces like a rag?

"This Ear, forsooth, making himself to be senior! The dog has ears just as much as you, and hears the abuse and evil words spoken by others; but its belly does not know rest, and is happy to bear the abuse of others.

"And you, Eye, making yourself to be senior! Every living thing sees the darkness and the light; but the belly

[1] Alluding to the ashes carried in baskets as manure for the rice-fields.

does not observe, for the eye looks upon the good and the evil.

"And you, Mouth, also, making yourself to be senior! The pig, too, has a mouth the same as you, but its belly is happy in doing evil, and devours that which it had vomited.

"And you, Hand, also making yourself to be senior! The crab has hands just as much as you, but its belly has no thought, so its hands can do nothing of themselves, either separately or altogether.

"And as for you, Foot, making yourself to be senior! You see that the ox has feet just as much as you, but its belly is foolish, and so it is made a treader of rice-fields and a breaker up of clods.[1] So this is what I declare to you: Don't dispute any more about seniority, for it is I alone who am the eldest, because it is I, the belly, who am thinker and observer, and receptacle for the food which is to strengthen you all."

So they all humbled themselves to be juniors, and the belly only was agreed to as the eldest; and they gathered together there all the emotions expressed in such phrases as "My heart is troubled," "My liver is troubled," "My bowels are troubled," "My belly is troubled," &c.

The meaning of this amusing fable will be clearer if it is remembered that the Malagasy use the word for belly (*kibo*) in a very wide sense, as including heart, bowels, liver, womb, stomach, &c.; and that in these organs they (like Orientals generally) place the seat of the emotions and feelings, and the intelligence also. The similarity of the main idea of the fable to that of Æsop's "The Belly and the Members," is obvious, an idea which is probably found in almost every nation, as is also seen in its very full use as an illustration by St. Paul in 1 Cor. xii. 12-25. It will be noticed that seniority is equivalent among the Malagasy to headship or lordship.

[1] Oxen are driven about on the soft mud of the rice-fields, over which water has been allowed to flow, after they have been dug up by the spade.

The Little Bird and he who ate it.

Once upon a time there was a young bird of the species called *antsàly*, and it was stoned by a certain man; so the bird cried out thus:—

> "Throws stones indeed, does this man, O,
> Throws stones at the little *antsàly*, O!
> Throws stones O!"

So the man still went on throwing; and, the bird's foot being struck, it fell to the ground and was caught by the man. And when he had got it, it began to sing thus:

> "Obtained indeed has this man, O,
> Obtained the little *antsàly*, O!
> Obtained O!"

Then the man took the bird home. And when he had come to his wife the bird spake again thus:

> "Obtained indeed has this man, O,
> Obtained the little *antsàly*, O!
> Obtained O!"

So the man's wife was astonished, and said, "Dear me, why this bird speaks! Whatever you may think, it's an unlucky business; for I never in all my life saw such a thing as this." But the man said, "If you won't eat it, I'll eat it by myself." So he killed the bird and cut it up, and said to his child, "Take hold, child, for it bothers me." But the mother interposed, saying, "If you're my child don't you take hold of it, for it's unlucky." So the child would not take hold, for it was afraid of its mother. Then the bird called out again:—

> "Will cut up indeed, will this man,
> Will cut up the little *antsàly*!
> Will cut up!"

Then the wife said again, "Dear me, are you really bold enough to do that? A bird speaking! and you dare cook it?" But the man did not answer and went on by himself, and presently really began to cut. So the bird called out again:

> "Is cooking indeed, is this man,
> Is cooking the little *antsàly!*
> Is cooking!"

And after a little while the bird was cooked and the man ate; but the people in the house would not eat, for they were afraid. Then the bird called out again:

> "Is eating indeed, is this man,
> Is eating the little *antsàly!*
> Is eating!"

And after the man had eaten he sat down north of the hearth,[1] and his wife sat south of it, and the children east of it. And after a little time the man's stomach began to swell, and the bird also called out again in his stomach thus:

> "Is full indeed, is this man,
> Is full of the little *antsàly!*
> Is full!"

Then his wife spoke again to him, "Now you see what you've got! for you were admonished and wouldn't take warning." But the man could not answer, but wept, and his tears flowed apace. And then, wonderful to relate, the bird's parents out in the field called out:

> "Gone where is the little *antsàly?*
> Gone where is the little *antsàly?*
> Gone where?"

And their child there in the man's stomach answered thus:

> "Here indeed I am, father,
> Here indeed I am, mother,
> Here!"

---

[1] Hova houses are always built north and south, and north of the hearth, which is an open fireplace of earth and stones, is the place of honour in the house.

So the parent birds heard it and came near ; and coming west of the compound called out thus:

> "Gone where is the little *antsàly* ?
> Gone where is the little *antsàly* ?
> Gone where ? "

So the bird answered again :

> "Here indeed I am, father,
> Here indeed I am, mother,
> Here ! "

And when the pair heard that, they came into the house and also said, " Was it you (pl.) who ate our child ? " Then the children in the house answered, " It was daddy who ate it." So the birds spoke again, " Why was it that thou atest our child ? " But the man answered nothing, but wept profusely. Then the birds tore up the man's belly with their claws and got their child ; and then the three went home into the woods, but the man who would not be warned by wife and children died.

Rapéto.

The stories which people relate of this Rapéto are exceedingly puzzling ; still, we may safely say that they are fabulous.

The town where he lived, they say, is Ambòhidrapéto, west of Antanànarivo.[1] And the fables related of him are these—

1. They say he was so tall as to touch the skies. And although it was at Ambòhidrapéto that he ate rice, the rice he cooked would be in the forest to the east [that is, twenty miles away].

2. They say he went to amuse himself at Ambòhitràrahàba,[2] and it was only one step from there to Ambòhidrapéto. [The places are about six miles apart.]

3. Those rocks, with hollows like human feet in them, on the

---

[1] Ambòhidrapéto, that is, "Town-of-Rapéto," is a small town on a low hill about three miles west of the capital.

[2] This is a large village about three miles north of the capital.

roadside near Ambòhitràrahàba are, they say, the impressions of his legs and feet and knees, by which he showed his strength.[1]

4. They say he fetched the moon as a plaything for his children; but he was struck by a meteorolite, and so was killed.

The Lost Son of God (a Nature-myth).

(This piece was obtained from Fisàkana.)

The following is a fable related by the people of old times when they met together and talked :—

The son of God, they say, came down here upon earth, and Rakòriàho and Ravào were his nurses. And this son of God, 'tis said, was lost, and neither he or his nurses could be found. And all things of whatever kind sought for him; whether the stones which were below the earth, or the trees which covered the earth, or the people which dwelt upon the earth, or the water or the beasts. So that everything, whether living creatures or things without life, sought him diligently, for the son of God was lost. Still, among them all not one found him. And so they sent to inquire of God. And when the messengers arrived God said, " Let everything stay in the place where it went." So the stones went seeking below the earth; and as for the trees, the half part stuck fast in the ground, and so became fixed there by the word of God, "Stand still"; and that, they say, caused some stones to be below the earth; and the trees to have their roots in the ground, and their branches standing above, so that if the roots and the branches separate they die. And the people also spread abroad, seeking northward and westward and southward, and lastly eastwards. (That, they say, is why prayer is made towards the east.[2]) And that is why people are spread abroad in various countries.

---

[1] There are certain rocks with some curious hollows in them in the place described. They have probably been produced by rain-water and the unequal hardness of portions of the surface.

[2] The sacred portion of a Hova house is the north-east corner, the *zòrofiraràzana*, or " corner of invocation " (from the root *ràry*, a chant).

And God said also, "Let not your mouths cease to utter the word 'Rakòriàho'" (and that is said to be the origin of the salutation of strangers, *Akory hianao?*); and its meaning is as if one said, "Is Rakòriàho there?" And the dog is the protector of Ravào; then said God, "Let not Ravào be absent from your mouth." And that is why the dogs say "Vovo,"[1] and the meaning of that is as if they said, "Is Ravào there?"

And the son of God was said to have been lost in the water. So God said to the waters, "Ye are not allowed to rest day or night, until Rakòriàho and Ravào are found." And that, they say, is what keeps the waters moving day and night, for they are still seeking Rakòriàho and Ravào, who were the nurses of the son of God

The Cause of the Separation of the Five Fingers.[2]

Each of the fingers, it is said, had their own thoughts, and after this fashion:—

The little finger said, "I am so hungry."

The next to it answered, "If you're hungry go and steal, that you may be satisfied."

Then said the next also, "Bring plenty, for we shall want some."

And said the forefinger (in Malagasy "the pointer," *fanòndro*), "These fellows turn their back on (or give bad advice) to the little one; if one steals won't he be punished?"

But the thumb said, "I do not understand these fellows' talk, so I'll separate, for I'm big, since you are plotting mischief."

And that, they say, was the reason of the fingers separating into five, and the thumb opposing the rest. And the two middle fingers have no special name,[3] because they had bad

---

[1] An onomatopoetic word in the Hova language for barking.

[2] The second and third fingers have no name in Malagasy, while the thumb, forefinger, and little finger have each a name of their own.

[3] Literally, the five "branches"; the fingers, including the thumb, being called *ràntsan-tànana*, "branches of the hand."

thoughts, and they have no particular business to do, and no work they are skilful to perform.

The Earth proposing to fight with the Skies.

The people in former days, it is said, when they wanted to pass away the time told a story as follows:—" Once upon a time the earth rose up and mounted aloft in order to fight the sky. So all parts of the earth agreed to set off at the same time, and the rocks, they say, were to be the cannon balls to fire at the sky. And early morning was the time fixed to go up. But it is said that the plains and the valleys crept slowly and sluggishly, and it was full day before they ate their breakfast, and so they lagged behind ; and that is the reason of the inequality of the valleys and the plains and the mountains, for they did not all keep step together. And so the heavens and the earth did not mingle, because all the earth did not mount up at the same time.

The Birds agreeing to make a King.

Once upon a time all the birds on the earth agreed together to choose one who should be their king and leader, but the Owl did not come, because it happened that his mate was sitting just then. So all the birds agreed that whoever saw the Owl and did not beat him should also be an outcast and be treated as an enemy.

For this reason the Owl does not go about by day, but goes by night ; for if any birds see him they all strive together to beat him.

And the big Hawk also sought to be king, and appointed himself, but the others did not agree to it, so he went away from them all at enmity with them. And whatever bird this Hawk sees he swoops down upon, because he is their enemy ; and the rest chose one who should be their king. So they chose the *Railòvy* (a Shrike, *Dicrurus forficatus*), because of his good position, and long top-knot, and variety of note.

And that is said to be why people consider the *Raìlòvy* to be king of the birds.

The Sìtry and the Antsiàntsy.

(These are two small species of Lizard.)

These creatures are both small animals, yet many people pay them honour. They say that when a certain person called Rasòavòlovolòina has a child born, the *Sìtry* went off to visit her, but was stoned and killed.

Then came the *Antsiàntsy*, and was also stoned by Rasòa and killed.

And when Rasòa went out to feel the sun's warmth, then came also the *Tàkatrà*[1] (the tufted umber) and the *Sìtry* and the *Antsiàntsy* went to the door of Rasòa's house.

And when evening came on, then the whole of the animals came and mourned at the door and devoured the child of Rasòa, and every one of them, it is said, lamented. And on account of that, Rasòavòlovolòina took an oath (or invoked a curse), saying: "If any of my descendants should kill a *Sìtry* or an *Antsiàntsy* they must wrap up its corpse in silk."[2]

There are still many people who believe this story, and dare not kill either of the lizards; and should they accidentally kill them, they wrap the corpse in a silk cloth. "Those who kill them," say some folks, "will die young."

The Hawk and the Hen.

A Hawk, they say, had a son born to her, and a Hen came to nurse her. And after the Hawk had been nursed a week she went to take exercise, and gave her son to the Hen to nurse. But when it was broad day and the hawk did not come, the Hen grew angry and killed the young one.

So when the Hawk came home and saw its young one dead,

[1] Many native superstitions have collected about the bird. Vide *Antanànarìvo Annual*, Vol. IV., 1891, p. 295.
[2] Malagasy corpses are wrapped in red silk *làmbas*.

it was enraged and beat the Hen, but the Hen held its ground, for they were equal in strength.

After some time, not seeing what to do, the Hawk invoked a curse, saying: "Whoever would be my true offspring must kill the young of this Hen, because she killed my young one."

And that is said to be the reason why the hawk eats chickens, but not hens.

The Vazìmba.

The Vazìmba, it is said, lived in this part of the island [that is, in Imèrina, the central province of Madagascar] in former times; and as to their appearance they are said to have been small people with little heads; and it is reported that they still exist on the western coast. (See Chap. II., p. 26.)

One day a Vazìmba went to play by the water and took the animal called "the seven-headed *Fanàny*" (see p. 231); and when the snake called *Tòmpondràno* (that is, "lord of the water") passed by, the Vazìmba sent him with this message, "Go," said he, "speak thus to father and mother, 'This is the word of thy son, Ravazìmba: I have gone under the water and send you my farewells; therefore offer the blood of some living creature, and its feet, and hair or feathers, and the fat, for if you do thus you shall be blessed.'" So the snake went, they say.

This is the reason some give for calling certain snakes *Tòmpondràno*. They believe that the Vazìmba gave them power, and hardly any one will kill these creatures; and should any one dare kill one they will wrap it up in silk."[1]

And some time after that the Vazìmba sent the Kingfisher to his father and mother with this message, "Salutation to father and mother, and say to them: 'Thus saith Ravazìmba, send me fowls and sheep.'" And when the Kingfisher had thus spoken he returned to Vazìmba again, who said to him, "Because you were diligent and wise I will give you honour;

---

[1] Following the same custom as when people are buried, corpses being wrapped in red silk *làmbas*.

I will put a crown on your head, and clothe you with purple by day and night; when you lay eggs I will nurse you; and if any one kills you, them will I kill while young." And that is why the Kingfisher is so beautiful, and makes its hole for a nest by the water. Therefore up to the present time many people dare not kill or eat the Kingfisher. Many believe this, and honour the little bird so called.

Here in Imèrina many people used to supplicate of the Vazìmba thus: "If thou wilt prosper me," or, "If I recover from this disease," or "If my child, or my wife bears a child," &c., &c., "then I will anoint thee [meaning the ancient graves called Vazìmba graves] with fat and will reverence thee, and then I will sacrifice sheep and fowls in thine honour."

The Chameleon and the Lizard.

These two creatures, it is said, are children of sisters born of one mother,[1] and one day they happened to be sitting together at the foot of a tree. The Lizard began the conversation thus: "A pleasant thing it is to live, good friend." The Chameleon replied, "Living is pleasant enough, but life is full of danger." The Lizard was astonished to hear that, and said, "You, fellow, think so because you're so thin and have bulging eyes." The Chameleon replied, "And you, fellow, imagine so because you're ugly and dirty-brown coloured, that's why."

And thus the two abused one another until Raòlombélona (Mr. Human-being) came up, and they were each startled. The Lizard slunk into his hole, and the Chameleon climbed up the tree, and it is said they were never friends afterwards.

The Serpent and the Frog.

Once upon a time the Serpent called *Mànditra* [a species of boa] swallowed a Frog, and the Frog began to revile the Serpent

---

[1] Sisters' children are considered by the Malagasy as almost the same as children of the same mother; they could no more intermarry than can brothers and sisters, while the marriage of brothers' children is quite common.

thus: "What a speckled appearance, and a blunt head, and goggle eyes! What's become of your feet and hands?" So the Serpent answered, "My feet are worn off in pursuing you frogs; and my eyes stand out because dim with looking after you; and my skin is speckled because I'm full of your precious father!"

So the Frog was angry and cursed the Serpent; and that is why it is hotly pursued by the serpents.

The Rice and the Sugar-cane.

The Sugar-cane, they say, came to the Rice, to seek friendship with it, and spake thus to it: "I say, O Sir Rice, come, let us be relatives and friends together, and share together the difficult and the bitter, making no difference, for we have one origin, for each is the produce of the ground; besides that, alike are the things befalling and the things obtained; equal while living, similar in death. Why look, our names even are almost alike, there's but a slight difference between *vàry* (rice) and *fàry* (sugar-cane); so let us strike up a firm friendship."

The Rice, however, it is said, answered thus: "Your words are true enough when you relate and particularise our origin, for we certainly are both the produce of the ground, equal while living, and similar in death. But still, here's something which prevents us agreeing, so it's no use, for it's a thing we can't agree about; so let there not be that friendship, and do not you blame us. For it's an exceedingly bad thing to agree without thought; for those who go along with fishermen, they say, stink of fish; those who make friends with vagabonds are themselves vagrants; and those who make friends with workers are workers themselves. And so you see, my good fellow, the reason of our declining friendship with you is *your changing in the end;* and that is why we can't join together. For you see that *we* have not that changing, whatever may befall *us*. You see that we are damped to become rotten, and when we have become so, we are soon put in the ground; but after a little time we are still rice all the same. And when we have become green on the earth again, then we are uprooted and stuck in the ground, where there is much water; yet we do not change, but still remain rice. And after growing again until we are ripe, we are then reaped with the knife; yet we do not change, but still remain rice. And after stopping a little while more, we are then beaten on the stone; yet we do not change, but still remain rice. And not only so, but we are buried in the rice pit; we do not change, but still remain rice. And also, we are drawn out thence, and dried in the sun; and when dry we are pounded in the mortar and our skin stripped from us, yet we do not change, but still remain rice. And not only so, but we are put into the cooking pot and covered with water, and heated with a fierce fire; and unless well boiled and thoroughly soft, we are not removed from it. And when removed we are chewed, and when masticated are swallowed. And in all these calamities which overtake and befall us we do not change, but still remain rice. And the land where we are not found is called famine-stricken, and the country where we are not found is called desolate.

"But as for you sugar-canes, on the other hand, you are cut down and chopped up, and stuck about in the ground; and then you do not change at all, but are still sugar-cane. And after you have grown and become tall, you are cut down with the knife; and still you do not change, but are still sugar-cane. And afterwards you are chewed into fibres with the teeth and crushed in the mill, but yet that does not change you, for you are still sugar-cane.

"But that is not all, for you are steeped in a great pot; and after a little while you are put into a boiling pot and heated intensely by the fire a long time, and after you thicken, they stop. And upon that you change, and take another name, that is, *sugar.*

"And when you have been sent back to the boiler again, then you no longer are a substance in a lump any more, but become steam and distilled drops, and go out along a bamboo or a brass pipe, and emerging thence, you become *rum*, making wise men fools, and are no longer sugar-cane. So that we cannot be friends with you sugar-cane," said the Rice.

Ikòtofétsy and Imàhakà.[1]

One day, it is said, Ikòtofétsy and Imàhakà displayed an idol, but it was only a piece of manioc-root which they had covered with scarlet cloth.[2] And the day was very cloudy, and just as if heavy rain was coming on; the wind also blew very hard. So they called the people together, and bade them assemble in an open space; and then they brought out the idol, but it did not move[3] (because it was only manioc-root). So Ikòtofétsy and Imàhakà said, "Since we brought out the god, and you did not bring tribute to him, he will not show you his glory, and is angry; therefore there will be heavy rains to-day, and the waters will be flooded." (At the same time they knew well that rain would fall plentifully, and the streams be all flooded.) Accordingly, the rain soon fell heavily on that day, and the waters were indeed all flooded; and the people were all exceedingly astonished, and feared greatly.

Then Ikòtofétsy and Imàhakà procured a serpent (called *Mànditra*), and wrapped it up in scarlet cloth as they had done with the piece of manioc-root, and placed it in a basket. And the two fellows spoke thus to the people: "This is the word of our god: he was angry yesterday, but we besought him, and so the heavy rain ceased; so now look, for he will

[1] This is one of a number of short stories which are very popular with the Malagasy, giving the adventures and various tricks of two clever rogues. The most complete collection of these was published at Antanànarivo some years ago. The meaning of Ikòtofétsy is the "cunning lad"; that of Imàhakà is not quite so clear, it perhaps means "the light-fingered one," or one able to carry off by theft.

[2] Malagasy idols were of no great size, and were usually covered with red cloth.

[3] It was believed that the idols had power to make their bearers move or stop, according to the will of the idol.

appear to-day, therefore let us all dance, and every one bring an offering." So they brought the serpent in the basket, and set it down on the ground, and it struggled violently, because it was a living creature. So the people were all confounded and filled with fear, and every one danced a long time. Then they each paid a little money as an offering, and the two men, it is said, collected on that day money to the amount of ten thousand pieces. So they put back the serpent into the basket again. And then they said to the people, "Should any of you be ill, come here to us, and bring money to the value of a halfpenny and twopence, and a red cock, as an offering. Besides which, if you will forget the god, you will die young."

And so, it is said, numbers of people worshipped that manioc-root, and the two men became very rich. And after that also many of the people fetched [what they supposed to be] pieces of the idol, but it was only pieces of wood which Ikòtofétsy and Imàhakà gave them.

Rasòalàvavòlo.

Under water, it is said, is the home of Rasòalàvavòlo, and she is beautiful, and has very long hair, and that is why she is called Rasòalàvavòlo (*làva vòlo* is "long-haired"). Some say she is a Vazìmba,[1] but others say that she belongs to one of the conquered royal families. Both stories, however, are equally untrue, since the whole account is a fiction.

They say, nevertheless, that a woman named Rasòavòlovolòina went to visit her, and to ask for a child,[2] and offered two silver rings, and had given to her two round smooth stones, which, they say, became two male children. When the two brothers grew up they went to visit Rasòalàvavòlo under the

---

[1] One of the supposed aboriginal inhabitants of the central provinces of Madagascar, see *ante*, p. 26.

[2] This is what native women very often do, visiting some of the numerous sacred stones and presenting small offerings, in the hope that they may bear children.

water, and offered her a string of coral beads, but she happened to be asleep when the brothers came, and so did not talk with them (lit., "blew water on them") and they were the ancestors of all the people who have lived since that time here in Madagascar.

And there are still many who believe this fable, and who come to the story-tellers to beg for children, but it is only a piece of fiction.

The Wild-hog and the Rat.

Once upon a time, 'tis said, a Wild-hog and a Rat chanced to meet, and the Rat saluted the other, saying, " How do you do, say I ? " So the Wild-hog replied, " Oh, I'm tolerably well, but how are you, young friend ? " " Oh, I'm very well," said the Rat, saying at the same time, " Come, my elder brother, let us have a game." The Wild-hog replied, " Well, all right, young friend ; but what sort of a game shall we have ? " " Let us collect dry grass, and when we have got plenty, let us cover ourselves with it and set it on fire. Said the Wild-hog, " Oh, that's a good idea, but perhaps you would not dare do it ? " " Oh, I'll venture it, but if I should shirk it, I'll never eat food again ; and you also, if you daren't venture it, then you must not eat from this time forth," said the Rat. " Agreed," replied the Wild-hog. So they pledged each other to keep their word.

Then said the Wild-hog, " Now you shall go in first, and I'll go afterwards." Very well," said the Rat, pushing himself into the midst of the fuel ; but he burrowed rapidly into the ground, and hid himself in the hole. Presently the Wild-hog called out, " Shall I light it now ? " " Yes," said the Rat. So the Wild-hog set fire to the heap, but it did not hurt the Rat, as he was safe in the hole. So as soon as it was all burnt up, out he came unhurt, and strutting about and looking very big, he shouted out, " What do you say to that ? How's that ? " adding, " Come, you must go too, Mr. Wild-hog."

"Entered, the Wild-hog, ah!
Pushed in, the Wild-hog, ah!
Is taken in, the Wild-hog, ah!
Is snugly hid, the Wild-hog, ah!
Is covered up, the Wild-hog, ah!
Is choked, the Wild-hog, ah!
Sleeps, the Wild-hog, ah!
　　The Wild-hog, ah!
Breathes hard, the Wild-hog, ah!
Endures, the Wild-hog, ah!"

So he set fire to the dry grass, and soon it was in a blaze; but alas for the poor Wild-hog, who struggled and turned about, for his back was scorched; so he cried out, "Help me, Mr. Rat, I am burnt; help me, younger brother, for I'm scorching; help me, my friend, or I'm consumed; help me, you wretch, or I'm killed."

But the Rat gave him no help for all that, for he was splitting with laughter, but he danced about, and shouted out thus:—

"Burn away, fire!
Go along, fire!
Consume him, O fire!
Blaze away, fire!
Die, Mr. Worn-out!
Die, you old wretch!
Die, old Spade-mouth!
Die, old Fetch-what-you-see!
Die, old Short-loin-cloth;
Die, old Snout-grubber!
　　How do you like it?
　　How are you now?
Soon you are done for,
Soon you squeal out,
Soon you are shrivelled,
Soon you are doubled up,
Soon you won't move."

But after a little the Wild-hog made a desperate effort and got out from among the fire, but his skin and his fore and hind feet were terribly burnt, although he was still alive. So the Rat said, "It was all a joke of mine, but go and bathe in the water." So the Wild-hog went and did so, but as soon as he had bathed he was dead.

CHAPTER XIII.

DIVINATION AMONG THE MALAGASY, TOGETHER WITH NATIVE IDEAS AS TO FATE AND DESTINY.

The *Sikìdy*—Subject investigated by Mr. Dahle—Little organised idolatry among the Malagasy—Diviners—Divination and fate—Invocation of the *Sikìdy*—Sixteen figures of the *Sikìdy*—Sixteen columns of the *Sikìdy*—Erecting the *Sikìdy*—Working of the *Sikìdy*—Identical figures—Unique figures—Combined figures—Miscellaneous *Sikìdy*—Gun charms—Trade charms—Medicinal charms—Fortunate places and days—*Ati-pàko*—Fate as told by zodiac and moon—Lucky and unlucky days—House divination—Fate as told by the planets—Days of the week—Decreasing influence of the *Sikìdy*.

FOR more than two centuries past it has been well known to those Europeans who have resided for any length of time in Madagascar, that a somewhat elaborate system of divination, called *Sikìdy* or *Sikìly*, is practised by almost all the various tribes inhabiting the island. Within the last five or six years the subject has been investigated in a most complete manner by the Rev. Lars Dahle, and I propose to give in this chapter a summary of the information Mr. Dahle has obtained, omitting many of the minuter points of philology. Mr. Dahle has brought to his researches a very accurate knowledge of Arabic, as well as of the Semitic languages generally, and hence he has thrown a flood of light upon what had previously been hopelessly obscure.

Mr. Dahle thus describes the native beliefs in the efficacy of divination :—" If you want to look into the future, to detect secret enemies or dangers, to find out what is to be your lot of good or evil, the *sikìdy* is the means of doing it. And the best of it is that it does not, like the Fates or Parces of old, mercilessly leave you to your destiny, but kindly undertakes *to avert the dreaded evils*. If you are sick, the *mpisikìdy* or diviner does not at all—like many of our modern doctors—treat you 'tentatively,' which really means leaving you and nature to settle the matter between yourselves as best you can; neither are they shallow-minded enough to treat the case merely 'symptomatically.' As diligent men, they set to work immediately, and, as truly scientific doctors, they first try to find out the cause of the evil, and then the means of removing it. And if they can give you no other benefit in a desperate case, they will at least cheer up your spirits with a good assurance, generally terminating in a very emphatic phrase, to the effect that 'if you die, you shall be buried on the top of their head.' And even if your spirit has actually left you, they do not give you up in despair, as I shall have occasion to point out subsequently.

"I am, however, reluctantly forced to admit that I am not able entirely to exculpate my friends from the accusation that there is a slight tinge of medical heresy about them, inasmuch as their old system of *fàditra* (*i.e.*, expiatory offerings or *piacula*) seems to rest upon the homœopathic principle, *Similia similibus curantur ;* for the *fàditra* (*i.e.*, the thing the diviner ordered to be thrown away to prevent or avert an evil) was generally something that in name, shape, or number, &c., was similar to the evil in question. For example, if the *sikìdy* brought out *màty ròa* ("two deaths"), two locusts should be killed and thrown away, to prevent the death of two men; if it brought out *maràry* ('sick'), a piece of the tree called *Hàzo maràry* ('sick tree') should be made a *fàditra*," and so on.

"The people had a remarkable trust in their diviners and their art; this appears even in the names by which they called them. In Imèrina and Bètsilèo (the two most important central provinces of the island), it was quite common to style them simply *Ny màsina* ('The sacred ones'), a term which, however, did not so much imply sanctity as strength and superhuman power. In the outlying provinces—especially in the south and west—they are generally called *ambiàsa* or *ombiàsy*, as they were also called among the Antanòsy at Fort Dauphin as early as the time of Flacourt, and this term is the Arabic *ambia*, 'prophet.'

"The word *sikìdy* (probably from the Arabic *sichr*, 'charm, incantation') has been generally translated 'divination,' but it has a somewhat wider sense, as it includes both the investigation of what is secret, and the art of finding out the remedy for it, if it proves to be of such a nature that such a remedy is required; but the second depends on the first. There are three kinds of *sikìdy* which are employed almost exclusively in finding out what is secret; while the other kinds have more to do with remedying the evils. The first class, however, forms *sikìdy par excellence*, manipulated according to a rather intricate system; the second class depends upon it, and seems to be of a somewhat more arbitrary character."

Before proceeding further, a word or two must be said as to the Malagasy notions of *vìntana* or fate, as the practice of the *sikìdy* largely depends on these beliefs. The word *vìntana* Mr. Dahle believes to be an obsolete collateral form of the Malagasy word *kìntana*, "a star" (Malayan *bìntang*), and, in its restricted meaning, denotes the destiny of a man as depending on the times as declared by the stars at the time of birth, and also the fitness (or the reverse) of certain times for certain actions (*e.g.*, for a burial). The first of these was the *vìntana* proper; the second was more accurately styled *San-àndro* (literally, "the hours of the day," from the Arabic *sa'a*, "hour," but also used in a wider sense of "any moment." As might be inferred from its name (if the above explanation of it be correct), the *vìntana* in its turn rests upon astrology. The different days of the month, and the months throughout the year, are each supposed to be connected with different constellations. Mr. Dahle has shown that the native names of the months are all Arabic in origin, and are the names of the twelve

Signs of the Zodiac, while the names for the separate days of the months are the twenty-eight "Moon-stations" on which the Malagasy (originally Arabic) chronology and astrology depend. In the *san-àndro* an important part is played by the "Seven Planets" of the ancients, that is, including the sun and moon, not excluding the earth, and of course also the more distant planets, which were then not known at all. The astrologers had, however, a good deal to do outside the domain of astrology and fate, for they had not only to find out, and, if necessary, counteract the influences of nature, but also those of bad spirits and bad men, as well as of the evil eye.

I. THE AWAKENING OF THE SIKÌDY.—The *sikìdy* was generally manipulated with beans or certain seeds, especially those of the *fàno* tree, a species of acacia.[1] When the *mpisikìdy* had placed a heap of these seeds or beans before him and was about to begin, he inaugurated his proceedings with a solemn invocation, calling upon God to awaken nature and men, that these might awaken the *sikìdy* to tell the truth. The following is the formula used :—

"Awake, O God, to awaken the sun! Awake, O sun, to awaken the cock! Awake, O cock, to awaken mankind! Awake, O mankind, to awaken the *sikìdy*—not to tell lies, not to deceive, not to play tricks, not to talk nonsense, not to agree to anything indiscriminately ; but to search into the secret, to look into what is beyond the hills and on the other side of the forest, to see what no human eye can see.

"Wake up, for thou art from the long-haired Silàmo (Moslem Arabs), from the high mountains, from Rabòrobòaka and others" (here follow nine long names). "Awake! for we have not got thee for nothing, thou art dear and expensive. We have hired thee in exchange for a fat cow with a large hump, and for money on which there was no dust. Awake! for thou art the trust of the sovereign and the judgment of the people. If thou art a *sikìdy* that can tell, that can see, and does

[1] *Piptadenia chrysostachys*.

not only speak of the noise of the people, the hen killed by its owner, the cattle slaughtered in the market, the dust clinging to the feet (*i.e.*, self-evident things), awake here on the mat!

"But if thou art a *sikìdy* that does not see, a *sikìdy* that agrees to everything indiscriminately, and makes the dead living and the living dead, then do not arise here on the mat."

It is evident that the *sikìdy* was looked upon as the special means used by God for making known His will to men; and it is at the same time characteristic enough that it was thought necessary to "awaken" God (*cf.* 1 Kings xviii. 27). In the long list of persons through whom the people are said to have got the *sikìdy* are the Silàmo (from "Islam"), chiefly Arabs, who are also called *Karàny*, "readers," *i.e.*, those who read the Koràn. Several other Arabic words occur in this invocation, as well as in the whole terminology connected with the *sikìdy*, as will be noticed further on. Most of the names given above, in the list of "authorities" from whom the Malagasy are said to have received the practice of divination, are rather obscure. Among them is that of the "Vazìmba," who are supposed to be the aboriginal inhabitants of the island before the arrival of its present Malayo-Polynesian and Melanesian colonists. They may be mentioned either because the diviners were anxious to have the *sikìdy* connected with everything that was mysterious and pointed back to the mythical days of old; or, possibly, because the Vazìmba were really the people who first received the *sikìdy* from the Arabs, and that the other tribes in their turn got it from the Vazìmba.

It may be added that individual *mpisikìdy* of any repute seem each to have had their own form of invocation, or at least made considerable variations in the wording of it, although its general bearing seems to have been very much the same.

II. THE SIXTEEN FIGURES OF THE SIKÌDY.— Having finished his invocation, the diviner began to work the *sikìdy* (lit., "to raise it up"), taking beans or *fàno* seeds, and arranging them on a mat on the floor according to rules to be presently

DIVINATION AMONG THE MALAGASY.   267

explained. These beans or seeds must be represented by dots. They were as follows :—

		Hova Names.					Sàkalàva.	Arabs of E. Africa.
1.	⁞⁞	Jamà (or Zomà)	...	...	...	...	Asombòla	Asombòla
2.	⁞⁞	Alàhizàny	...	...	...	...	Alizàha	Alàhòty
3.	⁞⁞	Asòralàhy	...	...	...	...	Asòralàhy	Alasàdy
4.	⁞⁞	Votsìra (= Vontsìra)		...	...	...	Karìja	Tabàta horòjy
5.	⁞	Taraiky	...	...	...	...	Taraiky	Asàratàny
6.	⁞⁞	Sàka	...	...	...	...	Alakaosy	Tàbadahila
7.	⁞⁞	Asòravàvy	...	...	...	...	Adabàra	Afaoro
8.	⁞⁞	Alikìsy	...	...	...	...	Alikìsy	Alijàdy
9.	⁞⁞	Aditsimà (Aditsimay)		...	...	...	Alatsimay	Alizaoza
10.	⁞⁞	Kìzo	...	...	...	...	Alakaràbo	Alakaràbo
11.	⁞⁞	Adikasàjy	...	...	...	...	Bétsivòngo	Adizòny
12.	⁞⁞	Vànda mitsàngana (= Mikarija)		...	...	Adàlo	Alàhamàly
13.	⁞⁞	Vànda miòndrika (= Mòlahidy)		...	...	Alahòtsy	Alakaosy
14.	⁞⁞	Alokòla	...	...	...	...	Alikòla	Adàlo (?)
15.	⁞⁞	Alaimòra	...	...	...	...	Alìhimòra	Alìhimòra
16.	⁞⁞	Adibijàdy	...	...	...	...	Alabiàvo	Bihiàva

The names in the first row are those in use in the interior; the order seems immaterial, but that here followed seems most systematic, commencing with the fullest form (⁞⁞), and taking away one bean (or dot) for each figure until only four (⁞) are left, and then adding one again to each, by which proceeding we get the first eight figures. The next eight are formed by placing twos and ones in various combinations. The theory of the whole is evidently that not more than eight beans can be used in any figure, and that all of the figures must contain four in length (or height), while there may be two or one in breadth. The names in the second and third columns were obtained from an Arab trader, and are, several of them at least, easily recognisable as the Arabic names for several of the months, but for many centuries naturalised among the Malagasy; and these, as already mentioned, are the Arabic names for the Signs of the Zodiac, while others seem to be those of the Moon-stations. Mr. Dahle has minutely examined the list of Hova names, some of which are Malagasy, but obscure in meaning, while most of them appear to be of Arabic origin, and several are also evidently derived from astrology; among others, the constellations Virgo, Aries, Aquarius, Sagittarius, Pisces, and Capricornus seem to be denoted.

III. THE SIXTEEN COLUMNS OF THE SIKÌDY (lit., "The Sixteen Mothers of Sikìdy").—To the sixteen figures, or various combinations of the beans or seeds by ones and twos in the *sikìdy*, correspond the sixteen columns (called by Mr. Dahle "rubrics"), places, or rows, in which they are arranged in working the oracle; one figure being placed in each column, not, however, that all the figures must necessarily occur. The same figure may occur more than once, and some of the sixteen figures may not occur at all in the sixteen columns, as that is purely a matter of chance. If the columns are arranged in the manner usual in the practice of *sikìdy*, we get the combination of squares given on the next page.

It will be seen at a glance, however, that we have got more than sixteen names here, although the rows or columns are really not more than twelve, corresponding probably to the twelve Signs of the Zodiac. If a skilful diviner is asked for *Ny sikìdy 16 rèny*, he will only enumerate the names given in the first (top) row (*Talé—Vòhitra*), the four to the right of it (*Zatòvo—Fàhavàlo*), and the eight below (*Tràno—Fàhasìvy*), giving us the sixteen complete. The others seem to be considered as accessory and of secondary importance. Some of them are simply repetitions, with this difference, that they refer to things in *another* person's house, not in that of the inquirer for whom the *sikìdy* operation in question is undertaken. Others are placed to the left side of the lower square, and others at the six corners.

Mr. Dahle proceeds to investigate each of the thirty-four words shown in the diagram; and points out that while the majority of them are Malagasy, about four or five are evidently Arabic. The Malagasy words are those in ordinary everyday use, as those for wealth, relations, village, youth, woman, enemy, house, road, inquirer, God, diviner, wild-cat, dog, sheep, goat, fowl, much bloodshed, &c. Of the four or five derived from the

Arabic, the first word, *Talé*, apparently meaning "investigator" or "explorer," always represents in the *sikìdy* the person or thing concerning whom (or which) the inquiry is made.

In reading or examining the columns, the first four (*Talé—Vòhitra*) and the eight below (*Tràno—Fàhasìvy*) are read from above downwards. The eight to the right (*Zatòvo—Firìariàvana*) are read from right to left. The four to the left

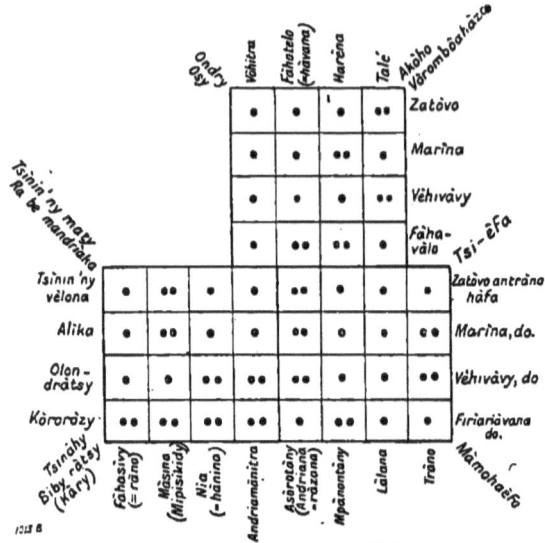

Arrangement of Columns in the *Sikìdy* Divination.
ARRANGEMENT OF COLUMNS IN THE SIKÌDY DIVINATION.

(*Kororòsy—Tsìnin' ny vélona*) are read from left to right, while the names at the corners are read diagonally.

IV. THE ERECTING OF THE SIKÌDY (*i.e.*, the placing of the figures in the columns).—So far, we have only seen the machinery, so to speak, with which the divination is worked; now let us try to understand how the diviner proceeded in order to gain the information desired in the great variety of inquiries made of him. In the diagram here given, all the columns are filled with figures, just as a veritable *mpisikìdy* would do, except that dots are used instead of beans or seeds. The rules for "erecting the *sikìdy*" will now be given.

1. The first four columns (*Talé—Vòhitra*) are filled with figures in the following manner. From the heap of beans before him the *mpisikìdy* takes a handful at random, and from this handful he takes out two and two until he has either two or one left. If two are left, he puts two beans, if one, one bean, into the first or upper square of *Talé*. In the same manner he fills the remaining three, *Harèna*, *Fàhatèlo*, and *Vòhitra*, square by square, from above downwards.

2. When these four columns—one of which represents the person or thing regarding whom or which the *sikìdy* is made—are filled in the manner described, the remaining eight are filled by a combination of these first four, or of others that have already been filled by a combination of these. This is done in such a manner that two figures are chosen and compared square by square from above downwards. If this combination gives an *odd* number (*i.e.*, if one of the two combined squares has one bean, and the other two), only one bean is put in the corresponding square of the new figure to be formed; but if it gives an *even* number (*i.e.*, if the two combined squares both contain one bean, or both two beans), two beans are put into the new figure.

3. These combinations are subjected to the following rules:—

> (a) *Talé* and *Harèna* (*i.e.*, a combination of the two in the manner described), form *Làlana*.
> (b) *Fàhatèlo* and *Vòhitra* form *Asòrotàny*.
> (c) *Làlana* and *Asòrotàny* form *Mpànontàny*.
> (d) *Zatòvo* and *Marìna* form *Nìa*.
> (e) *Vèhivàvy* and *Fàhavàlo* form *Fàhasìvy*.
> (f) *Nìa* and *Fàhasìvy* form *Màsina*.
> (g) *Màsina* and *Mpànontàny* form *Andriamànitra*.
> (h) *Andriamànitra* and *Talé* form *Tràno*.

A glance at the diagram here given will show that all the eight figures below have actually been formed according to these rules. If we, for instance, compare *Talé* and *Harèna*, from which *Làlana* is to be formed, we get dissimilar numbers all the way, as all the pairs of squares have one and two, and consequently *Làlana* gets only one bean in all its squares. Exactly the same procedure—*mutatis mutandis*—takes place in the filling in of the remaining seven columns below.

V. THE WORKING OF THE SIKÌDY.—When the *sikìdy* is "erected" or arranged in the manner just described, the question arises: What is to be done with it? How to work it so as to get an answer to your questions, a medicine for your sickness, or a charm against the evils of which you may be apprehensive, &c.?

Let it be remarked at the outset, that the *sikìdy* properly deals with *questions* put to it. To answer these is its proper function. But if you ask what is the root of an evil, or the means of removing or averting it, &c., the answer will of course point out to you the cure of your evils as well, and so far, appear as *ars medica*. There are, however, kinds of *sikìdy* in which no question is put, but the remedy for the evil is prescribed at once. But as these are rather different from the ordinary *sikìdy*-process, they will be noticed in a separate section. What concerns us now is, the *ordinary sikìdy*, the business of which is to give answers to our questions.

The first thing to be done, after having "erected the *sikìdy*," is to see what figure we have got in the column named *Andrìamànitra* (God); for, out of the sixteen figures, only half of them (Nos. 1, 3, 5, 7, 9, 12, 13, 14) are considered to "agree" with *Andrìamànitra*. These are called the "Nobles" or "Kings" of the *sikìdy*, whereas the remaining eight are called its "Slaves." If any of these latter figures happen to get into the said column, the *sikìdy* becomes invalid, and the whole has to be broken up and commenced anew; for the *sikìdy* has not done proper honour to God in putting a slave in His column, and cannot be expected to tell the truth in His name.

This point, however, being successfully arranged, the next business is to choose one of the *four* first columns (*Talé—Vòhitra*) to represent the question, or, rather, the person or thing it refers to. As *Talé* is to represent everything that cannot be put under the headings "property," "relations," or "village," the choice cannot be very puzzling; but this being settled, the proceedings branch out into the following parts, which Mr. Dahle terms: (A) The *Sikìdy* of Identical Figures; (B) The *Sikìdy* of Different Figures; and (C) The *Sikìdy* of Combined Figures.

A. *The Sikìdy of Identical Figures.*—Having settled which of the four first columns is to represent the question, the next thing is to examine which of the sixteen figures happens to be in the column representing it. This being found, we go on examining all the other figures except the others of the first four (for these have nothing to do with the answer), that is to say, those on the right side, those on the left, and those on the two corners to the left.

If we, thus examining them, find that any of them is like the one representing the inquiry, this may or may not settle the question, or, in other words, give us the answer. This depends on the nature (name) of the column in which it is found. This Mr. Dahle illustrates thus: "If I expect a ship, and am going to inquire about its coming by means of the *sikìdy*, the column *Harèna* (or property) will of course represent it. If in this column I find, for instance, the figure *Jamà* (⁞), and on further examination find the same figure in the column *Tràno* (house), this gives me no answer, as there is no natural connection between the two conceptions. If, on the contrary, I find the same figure in the column called *Làlana* (road), then of course I know that the ship is at any rate *on the way*. I have then got an answer to the chief question; but there may still be good reasons for a sharp look-out, for there may be difficulties in its way. Suppose that I also find the same figure in the column named *Fàhavàlo* (enemy), my mind will immediately be filled with gloomy apprehensions of *pirates !* Not a bit more cheerful will be my prospects if I find the same figure under *Ra bé mandrìaka* (much bloodshed). But what a consolation, on the other hand, if the same figure reappears in the column *Nìa* (food); for then I must certainly be a blockhead if I do not understand that, although the ship may have a long voyage, there is no scarcity of food on board; and so on. It is easy enough to see that a man with much practice and a good deal of imagination could produce much 'information' in this manner; and I suppose that in a good many cases the *mpisikìdy* were able to find an answer already in this first act of their proceedings, even if the means of finding it might seem scanty enough to ordinary mortals."

But there is much more still that may be done; for, besides the answers available from the fact of the identity of the figure representing the question with one or more of those in the other columns, it is of great importance to find out whether any two or more of the other figures are alike, and in how many columns the same figure occurs in a *sikìdy*. The detailed particulars given by Mr. Dahle on the point may be put, for the sake of brevity, into a tabular form :—

Columns with same Figures.		Native Word for Combination.	Meaning.
1. *Fàhasìvy* and	*Màsina*	= *Tsi-ròngatra*	= does not move or agitate.
2. ,, ,,	*Nìa*	= *Màti-ròa*	= two deaths; this is, two will die, but two locusts may be thrown away as a *fàditra* or *piaculum*.
3. *Fàhatèlo* ,,	*Harèna*	= *Vahòaka*	= a crowd of people.
4. *Tràuo* ,,	*Mpànontàny*	= *Tsìndrilàsy*	= enemy approaching.
5. ,, ,,	*Làlana*	= *Sàmpona*	= hindrances expected.
6. *Andro* ,,	*Asòrotàny*	= *Làhi-àntitra*	= old man; that is, the sick will recover, and reach old age.
7. *Fàhasìvy* ,,	*Asòrotàny*	= *Ravòakòny*	= a mouthful thrown out (?).
8. *Vòhitrà* ,,	*Fàhatèlo*	= *Fotòan-tsi-mihàtra*	= the fixed time will not be kept.
9. *Làlana* ,,	*Nìa*	= *Fèhi-tsi-ròso*	= the troops will not advance.

The following five possibilities refer to somewhat different cases, thus :—

10. If the figure *Alokòla* (∷) occurs three times in different columns, three stones are to be thrown away as a *fàditra* to avert evil.
11. If *Vànda mitsàngana* (⁝) occurs three times, the feathers of a white hen are to be a *fàditra*.
12. If *Alaimòra* (⁝) occurs twice, it means that the son of a mighty man is likely to be a mighty man too.
13. If *Sàka* (⁝) occurs in *Tràno* and *Vontsìra* (⁞) in *Talé*, or *Alaimòra* (⁝) in *Tràno*, and *Adibijàdy* (⁝) in *Talé*, the case will follow the analogy of the one preceding it ; *e.g.*, if my child, who was formerly ill, was cured, this one will be cured ; if it died, this one will die too.
14. If a *sikìdy* happens to contain eight *Vontsìra* (⁞) they are called "the eight healthy men," and are considered an excellent remedy against disease, as will be shown later on.

It is evident that many of these "meanings" can be construed into answers to questions, although the general tendency of many of them seems to be rather to point out the *fàditra* to be used against the evil. But it might happen that the figures were all unlike one another, at any rate that those which were like the one in the column representing the question were so incongruous with it that even the inventive imagination and the greatest acuteness, sharpened by long practice, would prove unequal to the task of construing it into a reasonable answer to the question. In such cases the *mpisikìdy* was obliged to have recourse to other operations, viz., the *Sikìdy tòkana* and the *Lòfin-tsikìdy*, of which the first one is comparatively simple, while the latter one was very complicated. Each of these will now be briefly explained.

B. *The Sikìdy of Unique Figures.*—If it happens that any of the twelve principal columns (*Talé—Vòhitra* and *Tràno—Fàhasìvy*) gets a figure which does not occur in any of the other columns, this is called *Sikìdy tòkana*, "a *sikìdy* that stands alone" ; and consequently there are twelve possible kinds of this species of *sikìdy*. Often many of the columns may happen to have unique figures ; in the diagram, for instance, *Màsina*, *Asòrotàny*, *Tràno*, and *Talé* have each one occurring in no other column. But it would be remarkable (although it is possible) if all the twelve columns got figures, so that all the rules for *sikìdy tòkana* became applicable in the same *sikìdy*.

The twelve columns are enumerated in a certain order by the diviners. First comes *Andrìamànitra* (God), then the four at the top of the diagram, and finally the seven remaining ones below. In all the twelve classes of *sikìdy tòkana* the meaning depends on which of the sixteen figures it is that occurs as unique in the column in question. In many cases only a few of them have any special meaning attached to them, as will appear from the following rules regarding each class :—

1. *Unique Figures in the Column Andrìamànitra.*—As only eight of the figures can be placed in this column without making the whole *sikìdy* invalid, as previously mentioned, we only get eight varieties :—

> (*a*) If figure 9 occurs, it denotes that a thing can be done seven times without any hindrance.
>
> (*b*) If figure 7, you must throw away a cooking-pot full of rice, and are likely to get rich.
>
> (*c*) If figure 3, which is here called *Màhatsàngana*, is taken (*i.e.*, the beans composing it) and applied to a reed (*vòlotsàngana*) of the same length as the man for whom the *sikìdy* is worked, and this is thrown away, it will bring good luck.
>
> (*d*) If figure 14, it is an excellent charm against gun-shot (*òdibàsy*).
>
> (*e*) If figure 13, the beans composing it are taken and mixed with a herb called *tàmbinòana ;* the sick person licks this six times, and it is then put on the top of his head.
>
> (*f*) If figure 12 (here called *Hèloka*, guilt), the six beans of the figure are placed on as many rice-husks, which are then thrown away as a *fàditra*.
>
> (*g*) If figure 1, a tree called *àndrarèzina* (a species of *Trema*) is to be the *fàditra*.
>
> (*h*) If figure 5, a white hen and a tree called *fòtsinanahàry* (" white one of the Creator ") are to be the *fàditra*.

2. *Unique Figures in Talé.*—This is the only column in which *all* the figures have a special meaning ; but as they are much in

the same style as those already given under *Andrìamànitra*, it would be tedious to give them in detail. Mr. Dahle observes here: "I do not intend the reader to practise the *sikìdy* (this secret I shall of course keep for my own use!), but only wish to give him an idea as to what it is."

3. *Unique Figures in the other Columns.*—In the other fourteen columns the number of figures having special meanings varies from one to fourteen out of the sixteen possibilities; but space and time do not allow any further details, especially as their general character is shown by the examples given under *Andrìamànitra*. Most of them simply suggest an answer to a question, frequently also giving a remedy against the evil intimated by the answer. As a specimen, however, it may be mentioned that when the figure *Sàka* occurs in the column *Tràno*, it is considered as an excellent remedy for sterility if the five beans of the figure are mixed with milk, which is then to be put into fourteen fragments of pumpkin shell, and given to fourteen children, who are then to put some rice into a pot, from which the sterile woman eats it. Many of the rules in this kind of *sikìdy* refer to sterility, sickness, or death.

Under this section of *Unique Figures*, Mr. Dahle describes two other kinds of *sikìdy* which are closely connected with the preceding ones, and called respectively (1) "*Sikìdy mutually corresponding*," and (2) "*Sikìdy providing a substitutory sacrifice.*"

It would, however, be tedious to go further into detail on this part of the subject; but it may be remarked that in the original papers minute particulars are given of these various forms of *sikìdy* and of the ways of working them.

The same may be said of (C.) *The Sikìdy of Combined Figures*, which shows how further combinations of the figures in various columns are obtained by the observance of strict rules in each case; as many as eighty-one new columns contributing materials for as many new answers to questions. This *sikìdy*, says Mr. Dahle, reminds him of the Danish proverb:

"Deceit is a science, said the Devil, when he gave lectures at Kièl."

VI. MISCELLANEOUS SIKÌDY.—In all the varieties of *sikìdy* hitherto dealt with, the chief object in view has been to get an *answer to questions*, while it has been only a secondary and subordinate object to find out the *remedies against evils*, that is, if the answer informed us that some evil might be apprehended. But now we come to some *sikìdy* practices, the chief object of which was to *remedy the evils*, or to procure a *prophylactic* against them. In other forms of this miscellaneous *sikìdy* the object aimed at was to find *times* and *directions* when and where something was to be found, or was to take place.

Rules are then given for the obtaining by means of the *sikìdy* of charms for various purposes, especially (1) charms against gun-shot; (2) trade charms; (3) love charms; (4) general charms; (5) charms against vomiting; (6) charms against dislike to food; (7) charms against food having a ghost in it; (8) and charms for bringing back a semi-departed spirit.

I. *Andron-tàny* (lit., "days of the land," but in the sense of the different quarters or directions of the compass, as expressed by the place in the house assigned to each day). What is really meant by this somewhat indefinite heading is, the art of finding out in what direction you are to seek for a thing that is lost, stolen, or strayed, &c. And this is denoted by the *sikìdy* bringing out a certain figure in a certain column, showing that the thing wanted was to be looked for in a certain direction. For in the old native houses, which are always built with the length running north and south, and the single door and window on the west side, the names of the twelve months are given to twelve points of the compass, four at the corners and two on each side. For instance, if the *sikìdy* brought out a figure which pointed to the south-east, the diviner did not call it so, but said it pointed to Asòrotàny, *i.e.*, the constellation Cancer and also the name of a Malagasy month, which, in the arrangement just mentioned, has its place assigned to it at the south-eastern corner of the house.

J. *Andro fòtsy* (lit., "white days," *i.e.*, the days on which something expected or sought for was to happen). "Suppose," says Mr. Dahle, "I have lost a slave. It is of the utmost importance to me to know on what day I shall find him; for then I do not trouble myself about searching for him before the day is come. Consequently I go to the diviner. He knows that certain combinations in certain columns denote the different days of the week; and if, for instance, these columns prove to be *Harèna* and *Fàhasìvy*, then he knows that what he asks about will occur on Wednesday (*Alarobìa*). And so with the other days of the week."

The Bètsimisàraka have, besides the systematic kind of *sikìdy* already described (*Sikìdy alànana*), at least six other kinds. These are said to be much simpler than the ordinary kind of divination; one, for instance, has only two columns or rows; another kind can hardly be properly called *sikìdy* at all. The procedure is simply the following: You take an indefinite number of grass stalks, and you then take out two and two until you have only one or two left. But you must have settled in your own mind at the outset whether one left shall mean good luck, and two bad luck, or *vice versâ*.

Another kind of *sikìdy*, the *Ati-pàko*, is thus described: "A mode of recovering stolen property without detecting the thief; all the servants or *employés* are required to bring something, as a small bundle of grass, &c., and to put it into a general heap. This affords an opportunity to the thief of secretly returning the thing stolen."

VII. We now come to the last division of our subject, viz., that of VÌNTANA and SAN-ÀNDRO, or, as Mr. Dahle thinks this section might be termed, (1) *Zodiacal and Lunary Vìntana*, and (2) *Planetary Vìntana*.

A. What, then, is *vìntana?* If a man was ill, people often said, "Perhaps the *vìntana* of his son is too strong for him, or he has become subject to some misfortune," so they said, "*Vìntany izàny angàha*" ("Perhaps that is his *vìntana*"). Or perhaps he was perpetually unsuccessful in business, and they said, "*Olona ràtsy vìntana izàny*" ("That man must have a bad *vìntana*"). Even immorality (*e.g.*, an unmarried woman becoming pregnant) was excused by the remark, "*Vìntany hiàny angàha izàny*" ("Perhaps that is her *vìntana*"), meaning that there was no helping it.

Vìntana seems like the *fatum* of the Greeks and Romans, an invisible power that made itself felt always and everywhere. The destiny of a man (his *vìntana*) depends on what day he was born (partly also on what time of the day), or, rather, on what constellation of the Zodiac governed the day of his birth. It was therefore incumbent upon the *mpamìntana* (those who dealt with the *vìntana*), or the *mpanàndro* (day-makers or declarers), who were also diviners, to inquire about the day or time of the day of a child's birth in order to make out its *vìntana*, *i.e.*, under what constellation it had been born, and what influence this would have on its destiny.

As the names of the constellations of the Zodiac also became the names of the months, and of the days of the month (at least in the interior provinces), it is not clear what influence was attributed to the moon; but that it was not considered to be without some influence appears from the following facts:—
(*a*) Although the days of the months had seemingly borrowed their names from the constellations of the Zodiac, they really represented the 28 "Moon-stations" of the Arabs. In Flacourt's time (230 years ago) these were still retained on the south-east coast,[1] but in the interior of Madagascar they have been superseded by a somewhat simplified nomenclature, that is, by simply calling them first and second, or first, second, and third (or equivalent names), as the case may be, of each month,

---

[1] Here, for example, are the three Moon-stations in Alàhamàdy: (1) As-sharatàni, (2) Al-butàina, (3) Az-zuràyya, or names of the first three days in every month.

Alàhamàdy, Adaoro, and the rest.[1] (*b*) The Malagasy year was a lunar one (345 days). And (*c*) both the sun and the moon take their place as governors of the days of the week.

Besides the division of the year into months, the Malagasy have from time immemorial known a hebdomadal unit, the week, the days of which have Arabic names. These days were thought to be under the special influence of the "Seven Planets" (*i.e.*, what were by the ancients so called, viz., the Sun, the Moon, Mars, Mercury, Jupiter, Venus, Saturn), as will be noticed presently under *San-àndro*.

"It is easy to see," says Mr. Dahle, "that the whole life of a Malagasy would be thought to be under the influence of these heavenly bodies, and consequently at the mercy of those who are supposed to understand these often very intricate affairs. People are generally under the spell of those who know their destiny beforehand (while they do not know it themselves), who have the power of remedying the evils of it, and are able to tell them both *what* they ought to do, and *when* they should do it. When we remember the great influence that astrologers had over emperors, kings, and princes during the Middle Ages, and even far into the seventeenth century, we can easily understand what powers they must have had (and still have) in a country like Madagascar."

[1] The following are the Malagasy month-names, with their Arabic derivations and equivalent Zodiac signs :—

Malagasy.	Arabic.	Zodiac Signs.
1. Alàhamàdy	Al-hamalu	= *Aries.*
2. Adaoro	Atz-tzauru	= *Taurus.*
3. Adizaoza	Al-dsehauza'u	= *Gemini.*
4. Asòrotàny	As-saratanu	= *Cancer.*
5. Alàhasàty	Al-asadu	= *Leo major.*
6. Asombòla	As-sunbulu	= *Spica* in *Virgo*, which constellation it represents here.
7. Adimizàna	Al-mizana	= *Libra.*
8. Alakaràbo	Al-aqrabu	= *Scorpio.*
9. Alakaosy	Al-qausu	= *Sagittarius* and *arcus.*
10. Adijàdy	Al-dsehadiu	= *Capricornus.*
11. Adàlo	Ad-dalvu	= *Aquarius.*
12. Alohòtsy	Al-hutu	= *Pisces.*

With regard to lucky and unlucky days, the following remarks may be made :—

1. Although the different months were thought to have their peculiar character (according to the constellations they were named from) and their special *piacula* and offerings, &c., it does not appear that one month was considered more unlucky than another. The difference in this respect was a difference between the different *days* of the month ; which, it must be remembered, were named after the month-names also, eight having two, and four three, days respectively allotted to each, as 1st, 2nd, and 3rd of Alàhamàdy; 1st and 2nd of Adaoro ; and so on, but each of the twenty-eight being also called by the names of the *Manazil-ul-kamari*, or moon-stations.

2. The characters of the days evidently did not depend so much on from what month-name it took, as on what moon-station it represented. Therefore we often find two successive days with the same name common to both, of which one was considered good, the other bad ; *e.g.*, the 1st and 2nd of Asòrotàny were good, and were, and are still, favourite days for *fàmadìhana* (the ceremony of removing corpses from an old family grave to a new one) ; but the third day was considered bad.

3. Some days were considered absolutely bad ; *e.g.*, the 3rd of Asòrotàny, the 2nd of Asombòla, the 2nd of Alakaosy, and the 1st of Adijàdy ; others were absolutely good, *e.g.*, the three days called Alàhamàdy, and the 2nd of Alakaràbo ; others again were considered indifferent, *e.g.*, the 1st and 2nd of Alàhasàty.

4. Some days again were not considered good in general, but still good enough for special purposes ; *e.g.*, the 1st of Alakaràbo was excellent for a house-warming ; the 2nd of Adijàdy was good for marking out the ground for a new town ; and the 3rd of Adimizàna was a lucky day to be born on, but a bad day for business.

5. Some days had a special peculiarity of their own ; *e.g.*, children born on the 2nd of Adàlo generally became dumb! so they said.

6. Even the bad days were generally so only in the sense of having too strong a *vìntana*. This was especially the reason why children born on these days were considered a very doubtful gift. Hence the infanticide in former times in the central provinces of Madagascar, and still practised in most parts of the country where Christianity has not yet been taught. Sometimes, however, the diviner managed to remedy the evil in one way or another; and occasionally nothing more was required than to give the child a name which intimated that the child would *not* do any harm, notwithstanding its strong *vìntana*. Hence such names as Itsimanòsika,[1] Itsimandràtra,[2] Itsimanìho,[3] Itsimanòlaka,[4] &c., all expressing in a general way that the child would be harmless. Those born on the 2nd of Adàlo were often called Itsimaròfy ("One who is not ill"), to avert the danger of dumbness.

Not only were the twenty-eight days of the month called after the month-names (and also after the moon-stations), but, as already mentioned, a Hova house of the old style had also its sides and corners named after the same fashion, beginning with the first month-name, Alàhamàdy, at the north-eastern corner, that is, the *sacred* part of the house, where the family charm was placed, and where prayers and invocations were offered. The inmates, on *each day*, had to take particular care not to go to the corner or side assigned to that particular day, or, at all events, not to place a sick person there, for, by so doing, they would provoke the spirit of that region.

Mr. Dahle says that the *vìntana* is really the key to the whole system of idolatry in Madagascar, and to everything connected with it, at least so far as it got any real hold on the people; while the *sikìdy* practice is also closely mixed up with it, although many points still need further investigation.

B. The last division of the subject, that of *San-àndro* or *Planetary Vìntana*, must be discussed very briefly. The word

[1] One who does not push. [2] One who does not hurt.
[3] One who does not elbow. [4] One who does not weaken.

san-àndro, in its use among the Malagasy, means the peculiarities or character of the days of the week as depending on the Seven Planets, considered as governors of these days. The following is a list of the days of the Malagasy week, together with their respective *san-àndro* names, and their special numbers and characters :—

English Name.	Malagasy Name.	San-àndro Name.	Arabic Origin.	Meaning.	Character.	Number.
Sunday	Alahàdy [1]	Samòsy	Shams	Sun	good	1
Monday	Alàtsinainy	Alakamàry	Al-gamar	Moon	bad	5
Tuesday	Talàta	Mariky	Marrik	Mars	good	2
Wednesday	Alarobìa	Motarita	Utarit	Mercury	good	6
Thursday	Alakamisy	Mosataro	Mushtari	Jupiter	bad	3
Friday	Zomà	Zohàra	Zahro	Venus	bad	7
Saturday	Asabòtsy	Johady	Zahal	Saturn	neutral	4

The fourth column of the above list gives the Arabic names of the Seven Planets, from which the *san-àndro* names of the week-days were clearly derived.

Any one who has the slightest knowledge of Latin will see immediately that what were in Malagasy the extraordinary day-names, only used in *san-àndro*, were in Latin the ordinary day-names (*Dies Solis, Lunæ, Martis*, &c.) ; and their retention in part amongst modern European nations, with changes, as among ourselves, for Teutonic god-names, for some days, is well known. The explanation of this rather curious fact, no doubt, is that the astrology of Babylonia spread both to Arabia and from thence to Madagascar, and also to Europe ; and that, according to this astrology, the planets in question, and the gods identified with them, held the sway over the days of the week ; and it depended on the supposed nature of each planet whether the day under its sway should be considered a lucky or an unlucky one. *Why* such differences were supposed to result

[1] Mr. Dahle had previously shown (in *Antanànarìvo Annual*, Vol. I., pp. 205, 206) that these native names for the days of the week are of purely Arabic origin, the first five names being simply numerals from one to five, the first four being cardinals used as ordinals, and the fifth an ordinal (" One day," " Two day," &c.) ; the sixth is from *Dschuma*, " Congregation Day," the Sabbath of the Mohammedans ; while the seventh is simply the Hebrew " Sabbath," slightly altered in spelling and termination.

from the different planets it is difficult to say; but the notion of lucky and unlucky days has been tenaciously held by the common people in the different countries of Europe, and still retains its hold in many places.

It will be observed that the last column of the above list gives a certain number connected with each day-name, and that these do not follow the order in which the days occur in the week, except in the case of the first. These numbers have, however, great importance in the practical part of *san-àndro*, as will be seen.

1. *The San-àndro of the Dead, or Direct San-àndro.*—This had reference, apparently, exclusively to burials; if a corpse was to be buried, it would probably be done on a "good" day (Sunday, Tuesday, or Wednesday); but the proceedings depended greatly on the *numbers* characteristic of the *san-àndro* of that day. If, for instance, it was on Wednesday, the special number of which is 6, they had to stop six times with the bier on the way to the grave, throw down a stone at each stopping-place, and carry the corpse six times round the grave before they buried it. And so, *mutatis mutandis*, with the other days, according to their special numbers.

2. *The San-àndro of the Living, or the San-àndro which was counted "Backwards."*—This appears to have had reference only to sacrifices; in offering these, the invocations made by the priest referred, not to the *san-àndro* of the day the offering was made, but to that of "the day before yesterday," in other words, two days backward. Offerings could only be brought on the three "good" days; but the *sikìdy* could be performed on any day.

3. *The Character of the Seven Days of the Week in relation to Evils and the Foretelling of Evils.*—The following rules were given to Mr. Dahle by his native "professor";—

  1. *Sunday* was the proper day for everything *white*: white-haired people, white stones, &c.
  2. *Monday*: the day for everything *green* and blackish: grass, forests, greenish birds, people with blackish skin, &c.

3. *Tuesday:* the day of people who have many *scars* and are marked from small-pox.
4. *Wednesday:* the day of *women* and everything *female*
5. *Thursday:* the day of *slaves.*
6. *Friday:* the day of *nobles* and everything *red* (red or scarlet clothes, &c.), characteristic of the higher nobility.
7. *Saturday:* the day of young people and everything *young.*

So if a man suffering from some evil came to a diviner on a Sunday, he would be told that his complaint had been caused by some white stone ; or by drinking milk, in which there were some ghosts, or that he had been bewitched by some white-haired woman ; or, at any rate, that he was in danger of some such mishap, and had better look out carefully. If he came on Thursday, his trouble was almost sure to be attributed to some slave or he was warned to beware of his slaves, lest they should murder or bewitch him. And so on, for the other days, according to the nature of the day.

4. *Foretelling of the Tàsik' àndro, i.e.,* the day on which one may be in special danger of getting ill through the influence of the *vìntana.*—This division of the *san-àndro* was a peculiar compound of *vìntana* and *sikìdy* subjected to certain rules, by which, beginning with Tuesday, different columns in the *sikìdy* point to the different days of the week ; *e.g.*, if a combination of the two columns *Tràno* and *Làlana* in the *sikìdy* erected gives a figure which is like *Talé* (which represents the man in question), he is in danger of being taken ill on Tuesday. If the figures in *Làlana* and *Mpànontàny* are like *Talé*, Wednesday is the unlucky day for him ; and so on with other combinations.

As Mr. Dahle says, the *sikìdy* and *vìntana* were once the most tremendous powers in Madagascar; let us thank God that their spell is broken, and their influence passing away.

CHAPTER XIV.

FUNERAL CEREMONIES AMONG THE MALAGASY.[1]

Two great divisions of the people—Idea of impurity in connection with death—A revolting custom—Funeral feasts—*Tankàrana*—Their carved coffins—Analogies to those of Philippine Islanders—Bètsimisàraka—Rànomèna—Tambahòaka, Taimòro, and Tanòsy—The *Fanàno*—Tandròy and Màhafàly—Sàkalàva—The Zómba or sacred house—Vazimba—Béhisotra and Tàndròna — Sihànaka — Bezànozàno — Tanàla — Vorimo — Ikòngo — Hova — Bètsilèo—Bàra—Funeral of Radàma I.—Enormous wealth put in tomb—Silver coffin.

FUNERAL rites and ceremonies are not the same among all the different races inhabiting Madagascar. Regarded from this point of view, the Malagasy may be divided into two groups: first, those whose cemeteries are hidden in the depths of the forests, or in the midst of rocks, in solitary places, which are held in great awe;[2] and secondly, those who inter their relatives by the roadside, and often in the midst of their dwellings.[3]

The majority of these place the dead in the hollowed-out trunk of a tree, which they cover with a lid in the shape of a pent, or rounded roof; the Hova, however, simply wrap the corpse in *làmba*, more or less numerous according to the wealth of the family; and it appears that the Bàra content

---

[1] Translated from an article by M. A. Grandidier in the *Revue d'Ethnographie*. Paris, 1886, pp. 213-232.

[2] These are, the Bètsimisàraka and other tribes on the east (with the exception of the Tambahòaka, the Taimòro and the Tanòsy, who have a considerable Arab admixture), and the Tandròy, the Màhafàly, the Sàkalàva, the Tankàrana, and the Bàra.

[3] These are the Sihànaka, the Taimòro, the Tambahòaka, the Tanòsy, and especially the Hova and the Bètsilèo.

TAISAKA CHIEFS.

themselves with placing the corpse perfectly naked upon the ground. Besides this, however, the Malagasy always immediately proceed with the toilet of the deceased, the nearest relatives of the same sex washing the corpse, dressing its hair and wrapping it in new cloths.

The two principal eastern tribes, the Bètsimisàraka and the Tanàla, as well as the Tankàrana, the Tankoàla, and certain tribes of the Bàra, do not bury the coffin; they place it either simply on the ground, or on a little framework surrounded by a palisade and covered with a pent roof, or in a fissure of rock; but all the others, that is to say, the greater part of the inhabitants of the island, place it in the ground and cover it with a heap of stones of rectangular shape. The head of the corpse is turned towards the east,[1] and they enclose in the tomb various articles, such as earthen vessels, pots of incense, cloths, &c.

All the Malagasy hold the notion of impurity in connection with a corpse. No funeral procession can pass near a sovereign, or even near to his dwelling or the sacred stones; those who have followed it are obliged to purify themselves, and in those districts where the tombs are placed far from dwellings, every person found in a cemetery is considered as a sorcerer and is punished with death. It is further worthy of notice that the Malagasy have a great fear of, but also a profound respect for, the dead. They think it of the first importance that they should be buried in the ancestral cemetery or tomb; and not only the Hova, but the greater portion, if not all, of the native tribes often bring from great distances the bones of their relatives so that they may be deposited in their native soil. When they cannot recover the body of a deceased relative, they inter in its stead his pillow and sleeping mat, and in any case they erect a funeral monument in commemoration of the departed, con-

---

[1] I have, however, been told that the Sihànaka turn the head of the coffin towards the north, and the Hova place in their graves the corpses of grandparents at right angles to those of their descendants.

sisting of a slab of stone, a timber post or other structure. A vow to the dead, to the *lólo*, as the coast people term them, is sacred.

There is a custom, as repugnant as it is extraordinary, which is prevalent almost everywhere except among the Hova, by which the corpse is not interred immediately after death; the relatives wait until the body is decomposed, and often collect the putrid liquid which flows out, setting it aside. It is needless to say that in such circumstances the "waking" of the corpse is far from agreeable, and it is only by drinking neat rum, by burning incense and suet and even hides, that the parents and friends are able to bear the nauseous odours which poison the air. During all this time many of the native tribes offer food and drink to the corpse. This custom is essentially Malagasy, for it is not practised by the Hova, who are of Malay origin, nor by the families of the chiefs of the east coast tribes, who are descended from Arabs or Europeans; it seems to have for its object to prevent interring with the bones the corruptible matter which causes decomposition of the flesh, and which they consider impure.

Funerals are also all over Madagascar accompanied by real feasts, at least in all families who are rich or in easy circumstances. They kill oxen, often in considerable numbers, they drink rum to excess, they eat plenty of rice and meat, they fire off muskets, the whole being interspersed with doleful songs and weeping. The relatives never eat the flesh of the oxen killed on the occasion of the death of one of their own family. Mourning is always marked, either by unbraided and dishevelled hair, or at the decease of sovereigns, by the head being shaved, coarse and dirty garments only being worn, the people neither washing nor combing their hair, nor allowing themselves to look in a mirror, should they happen to possess one.

Such are, in brief, the principal funeral customs of the Malagasy. We shall now proceed to point out, in the briefest possible manner, the differences which exist between the usages of the different tribes, beginning with those of the north and the east. It is nevertheless well to remark that among certain of them, especially those whose Christianity has commenced to exert its happy influence, these old customs are beginning to disappear.

The Tankàrana.—The Tankàrana are accustomed to wrap the dead either in an ox-hide, or in split bamboos, or in rabannas (*rofia* cloth), which they tie round with cords of *rofia* fibre, and leave them exposed for a long time under a shed, where they do not cease to burn various resins in little clay vessels. Beginning on the third day, they frequently tighten the cords, until there is hardly anything left but the bones, which they afterwards place in a hollowed tree trunk, generally of rather small dimensions. This coffin, closed with a lid formed like a roof, is then carried to a solitary spot, usually an uninhabited island, where it is put in a hollow of the rocks, or simply on the ground; a supply of provisions is placed near the deceased. The coffins are renewed when they become decayed from age. The following description has been given of one of these coffins, which was sent to the Natural History Museum, in Paris, in 1886, by a (French) naval officer, M. P. Germinet, commander of the *Romanche*, and which comes from the little rocky islet called Nòsy Lòapàsana, whose name signifies "hollowed out by tombs."[1]

This coffin, cut out of a tree trunk, measures 5 feet long by $8\frac{1}{4}$ in. broad; the cavity which has been hollowed out of it is 4 feet long by 5 in. to 6 in. wide. At the place for the head, two recesses increase the width to $6\frac{1}{2}$ inches. The lid, in form like a roof, is 5 ft. $4\frac{1}{2}$ in. long by 9 in. broad; it is ornamented by a zigzag pattern cut in relief, which follows the edges, the ridge, and the hips (so to speak) of the roof-like cover; also by a transverse strip of herring-bone ornament at about the middle

[1] This islet is situated at the head of Diego Suarez Bay; the maps show it under the name of Ile du Sépulchre.

of the length and meeting at the ridge, and with four small circles with cross lines cut in them. The lid fits into a rebate formed all round the hollow of the coffin, and which forms a projection of a little more than ¾ inch. The general form of the coffin is in all respects similar to that of the wooden sarcophagi which M. Alfred Marche has discovered in the burial caves of Marinduque and of other small islands near Luzon in the Philippine Archipelago.

Inside the coffin, the skeleton, which is that of a young person of twelve or fourteen years of age, is very nearly in exact position, the head being seen at one end, and at the other the bones of the legs and feet. The rest of the body, evidently compressed transversely and mouldering in its wrappings, shows some of the bones more or less displaced in the midst of the remains of *rofia* and other cloths, which are still tightly bound by *rofia* cords. At the foot of the corpse are three small vessels of baked clay mounted on a stand, which must have served for the burning of perfumes during the ceremonies preceding the interment.[1]

[1] It is not without interest to notice here that this example, buried in a coffin resembling the ancient sarcophagi used by certain tribes of the Philippines, presents the exact characteristics of cranium common to the Indonesians. M. Hamy, who has taken the principal measurements, has stated, indeed, that the cranium is very plainly brachycephalic (diam. ant. post, 168 millim., d. transv. max., 143 ; ind. ceph., 85·1).

This exaggerated brachycephalic character cannot, in his opinion, be attributed, except in a very small degree, to the age of the example, the cephalic index never rising, among the young negroes of Africa, above 78. This brachycephalism is, besides, in harmony with the existence of a large occipito-parietal plate, such as one meets so frequently in crania from the Indian Archipelago. The vertical diameter is, at the same time, sensibly inferior to the transverse, a circumstance which is not usual among true negroes.

Here are, in addition, the principal measurements given by M. Hamy as to the cranium from the tomb at Nòsy Lòapàsana : Circ. horiz. 496 millim. ; diam. ant. post. 168 ; d. transv. max. 143 ; d. basil. brcgm. 138 ; ind. ceph. 85·1 ; 82·1 ; 96·5 ; front min. 110 millim. ; max. 120 ; biorb. ext. 102 ; bizygom. 124 ; height of face, 76 ; breadth of orbit, 37 ; height 36 ; length of nose, 46 ; breadth, 26.

Three adult skulls, collected at the same time and at the same place by M. Germinet, give the following means of the respective dimensions : Circ. horiz. 504 mm. ; diam. ant. post, 176 ; d. transv. max. 141 ; d. basil. brcgm. 136 ; ind. ceph. 80·1 ; 77·2 ; 96·4 ; front. min. 100 ; max. 118 ; biorb. ext. 108 ; bizyg. 132 height of face, 90 ; orbit, breadth, 39 ; height, 36 ; nose, length, 54 ; breadth, 27.

BETSIMISÀRAKA CEMETERY.

Among the chiefs of the Tankàrana, the ceremonial is somewhat different. The corpse is exposed on a stage of bamboo hurdles, sheltered by a roof, and covered over with aromatic herbs and hot sand, which the attendants constantly renew until complete mummification is effected. It is at length deposited in a coffin which is anointed with a mixture of grease, rum, and salt. The putrid liquid which exudes during the operation just described is received in vessels placed under the stage, and the slaves of the deceased chief anoint their bodies with it from time to time.

The Bètsimisàraka.—The Bètsimisàraka keep their dead in their houses for a long time, and the products of decomposition are received in a vessel to be buried at a distance, in a place where the relatives erect a stone, to which they afterwards come frequently to offer prayers. A lamp burns night and day at the head of the corpse, and during all the time of its being exposed to view, the widow ought no more to leave the funeral couch than she would do if her husband were still living. The coffins, which are formed of a hollowed-out tree trunk with a roof-shaped lid, are placed in a dense wood,[1] and laid on the ground in regular order at a little distance one from the other, as shown opposite. At the head they generally place various articles which belonged to the deceased, especially a bottle of rum, a very natural offering in a country where drunkenness is a universal vice. Certain families, however, place their coffins higher up, on a little stage, and construct a shed to protect them from the rain and the sun; in these cases every corpse has its separate house. Others place the corpse in the hollowed-out trunk of a tree, resembling a barrel, of which both ends are closed by circular pieces of wood.

The customs followed at the decease of a chief are altogether different, for the interment follows immediately and

---

[1] In some places, Anonibè, for instance, the coffins (which are exactly the shape of large dog-kennels, except that the two sides of the roof do not project) are placed, sometimes thirty or forty together, under the trees by the sea-side.

by night, without any notice being given to the people of the event; the news of the misfortune which has happened to the tribe is not, in fact, announced until much later. It is well to remark here that the Bètsimisàraka chiefs are of foreign extraction.

The Rànomèna.—Among the Rànomèna, who at present inhabit the district between Fànantàra and Màrohìta, and are descended from the inhabitants of that part of the east coast where, in ancient times, Arabs landed under the leadership of Raminìa, it is customary to place the corpses on the roadside. A hole is formed to receive the liquids coming from the decomposition of the body, and the place is marked by means of a piece of rock, to which the children of the deceased come to offer their prayers. The cemeteries are relegated to the depths of the woods, and no one goes there except at the time of interment.

The Tàmbahòaka, Taimòro and Tanòsy.—The Ròandrìana, or chiefs of the Tàmbahòaka, the Taimòro and the Tanòsy, who are of Arab origin, are interred at night, one or two days after death. During the lying-in-state, which takes place in the same chamber in which the person died, reddish-brown *làmba* or cloths are hung up, and a lamp is kept burning at the head of the corpse until it is removed for burial; and, on the first day, food is placed at the side of the bed or bier. The relatives fasten to the arms of the deceased small strips of paper covered with cabalistic signs and Arabic words. During all this time the news of the event is kept secret outside the royal village, and it is only after a month has elapsed that a white flag is hoisted at the summit of the house where the corpse has lain, informing the people generally of the fact. After this the funeral ceremonies are performed with great pomp. White is the colour for mourning in (many parts of) Madagascar, as in the far East.

The tombs of these Ròandrìana, which are called *lònaka*, exactly the same word as that applied to the royal residences, are formed, among the Tanòsy, of two slabs of stone, one at the head, the other, not so high as the first, at the foot of the tomb. A circular palisading surrounds each tomb, and this is kept in repair by the family of the Zàfindrasàra, who alone are allowed to enter it. The bodies of the chiefs are not placed in a coffin, but simply wrapped in a *làmba*. In former times the Taimòro chiefs were interred in a house situated in the village, but this custom has been abandoned.

The commonalty, the *vòhitra* or free people, are interred in a coffin which is either on the very edge of the roads (in Antaimòro), or in the midst of the woods (in Antanòsy). The tombs, which the people call *amònoka*, consist of a trench lined inside with stones and closed by a slab of stone placed on the ground, with a white flag floating from a pole; and these are not regarded with the same dread as they are among the other coast peoples. Funerals take place, as in the case of the chiefs, very shortly after death. When a woman has become disgraced among her family through violating some of the requirements of caste, she is placed at the feet of her relatives, transversely, instead of by their side, according to the usual custom. The men are placed on the bier on the right side, the women on the left side, but the head is always turned towards the east. The general belief is that the liquids produced by the dissolution of the body give birth, at least in the case of the chiefs, to a colossal sea-serpent, which they term *Fanànina* or *Fanàno*.[1]

[1] There seems a remarkable parallel to this Malagasy belief in the transmigration of the souls of chiefs into some animal in the practice of the Samoans, as thus described by the Rev. Dr. Turner: "*The unburied* occasioned great concern.... Nor were the Samoans, like the ancient Romans, satisfied with a mere *tumulus inanis* at which to observe the usual solemnities; they thought it was possible to obtain the soul of the departed in some tangible transmigrated form. On the beach, near where a person had been drowned, and whose body was supposed to have become a porpoise, or on the battlefield, where another fell, might have been seen, sitting in silence, a group of five or six, and one a few yards before them with a sheet of native cloth spread out on the ground in front of him. Addressing some god of the family, he said, 'Oh, be kind to us; let us obtain without difficulty the spirit of the young man!' The first thing that happened to light upon the sheet was supposed to be the spirit. If nothing came, it was supposed that the spirit had some ill-will to the person praying.

The Tanòsy who, not being willing to accept the Hova yoke, quitted the neighbourhood of Fort Dauphin and went to settle in the upper regions of the Onilàhy or St. Augustine river (S.W.), are still accustomed to bring their dead to the land where they formerly lived. Having waited until the bones have become divested of the flesh, they follow the custom of the Sàkalàva and Màhafàly tribes, and place the coffins under a heap of stones arranged in an oblong form. Some families erect near the villages, in remembrance of their dead, wooden posts or pillars bearing on the top a human figure, or one of a bird, roughly carved, and on the different sides patterns more or less regular, and figures of animals, such as oxen, birds, and especially crocodiles.[1] A scrap of white cloth flutters from the end of this post, to which are also fastened the skulls and horns of the oxen killed at the time of the funeral.

The Tandròy and Màhafàly.—The Tandròy and the Màha fàly wrap the dead in several *làmba*, and carry them to the cemetery on the day following the decease in a kind of hand-barrow or bed formed of a framework of wood with strips of leather interwoven. The corpse, laid upon the ground, is covered over with earth, and over it is constructed an oblong heap of stones. The rich people have coffins.

The Sàkalàva.—The Sàkalàva bring the dead out of their house immediately after decease, and place them, wrapped in many *làmba* (*even*, not *odd*, in number), upon a stage about six feet high called *tàlatàla*, the head being turned towards the

That person after a time retired, and another stepped forward, addressed some other god, and waited the result. By and by something came ; grasshopper, butterfly, ant, or whatever else it might be, it was carefully wrapped up, taken to the family, the friends assembled, and the bundle was buried with all ceremony, as if it contained the real spirit of the departed" (*Samoa a Hundred Years Ago and Long Before*, p. 150).—J. S.

[1] One may compare the figure of the cover of a coffin from Marinduque (Philippine Islands), by which it appears that, in the further East, as in Madagascar, crocodiles are carved on funeral memorials. This coffin lid, as well as the two coffins which are previously described, form part of the collections brought by M. Alfred Marche to the Museum of Ethnography at the Trocadero (Paris).

east, and a piece of cloth being thrown over the corpse, on which are placed articles which must be deposited in the bier. A fire is lighted under the foot of the corpse, and incense is burnt to overcome the effluvia. The women keep at the north-east side of the stage, and the men at the south and south-east. It is customary for the friends of the deceased to bring small presents on these occasions. On their arrival the women squat down opposite the family, which is gloomily silent; then, without speaking, they begin to weep and sob, and all the females present join them in this manifestation of their sorrow. Silence prevails after some minutes until the arrival of a fresh party of visitors. These *tàlatàla* are afterwards destroyed, and the pieces are thrown into water in an uninhabited place. The corpse is carried to the burial-place upon a *kibàny*, or kind of bier or hand-barrow, and is then put, lying on its back, in a coffin formed of the hollowed-out trunk of a tree, which is supported on four feet cut out of the wood, and the bottom of which is pierced with an opening so as to allow the putrid matter to flow away. This coffin is completely covered with another tree trunk, which is a little larger and also hollowed out. The coffin is laid in a trench with various objects belonging to the deceased, such as bowls, plates, boxes, &c., and is covered up with earth. An oblong-shaped heap of stones, of which the length runs east and west, shows the place occupied by the tomb. At the head a small piece of white cloth is fastened to a pole like a flag. There are some families, especially that of the Vòroniòka, who do not inter their dead in a coffin; they simply wrap them in a large mat and cover them up with stones. The house of the deceased is abandoned and allowed to go to ruin; no person dares to touch it under any pretence whatever; and any one who, even without knowing it, should happen to use for any purpose the materials of such a house, would be liable to severe punishment, sometimes even to death itself.

Just before death the Sàkalàva are accustomed to make public confession before their family of the crimes and principal il deeds which they have committed during their life.

In order to offer their prayers to the *lolo* (spirits) of their relatives, the Sàkalàva do not go to the burial-place, which they hold in great dread, but to the deceased's house, which has been allowed to fall into ruin.

For princes, the ceremonies are altogether different. The corpse, enclosed in an ox-hide, remains exposed for two months, either in an encampment made for the purpose, under a tent, where incense is burnt night and day, or, in the case of a king, in the midst of a forest, under the care of a particular family. Then it is carried, with great ceremony and festivities, to a royal cemetery, which, in the south-west, is called *Mahàbo* (lit., "that which elevates"), and in the north-west *Zòmbavòla* (lit., "silver shrine"). But previously, if the body is that of a deceased king, the royal relics or *jìny* [1] are brought out ; these consist of one of the vertebræ of the neck, a nail, and a lock of hair, and which, placed in the hollow of a molar tooth of a crocodile,[2] are kept with religious care by his successor, together with those of the ancient kings, in a special house, which is held to be sacred.

The name which the kings bear during their life may no longer be pronounced after their death; another is substituted for it, often of immoderate length, for it always commences with the word *Andrìana* (lord) and finishes with the word *arìvo* (thousand), with one or several other words placed between them. Thus Ràboky, who reigned at Bàly, at no very long time past, is never named by his old subjects as other than Andrìanàhatàntiarìvo, or "The lord who can bear a thousand calamities"; Tsimanòmpo, the last Bàra king of the district of Isàntsa, is now mentioned only under his surname of Andrìantòmponarìvo, or

[1] This word *jìny* is really the Arabic word *djinu*, which signifies, as is well known, a demon or invisible spirit, having supernatural power.

[2] The tooth of the crocodile intended to receive the *jìny* must be taken from a living animal ; they choose one of the largest size, and bind it firmly with strong cords ; then they insert between its jaws, at the desired place, a burning potato, and after a quarter of an hour, the coveted tooth can easily be extracted. The animal is then set free.

"The lord who is master of a thousand." When a king bears a name having the meaning of something in common use, or approaching that of some word in the vernacular, this word must no longer be pronounced by any of the inhabitants of the country. Thus, after the death of Vinàny, king of Mènabé, whose name recalls a very commonly used word all over Madagascar, *vilàny*, which means a cooking-pot, the Antimèna no longer calls this indispensable article of household use by any other name than by one made for the occasion, viz., *fiketràhana* (lit., "the boiling utensil"). Any one allowing himself to pronounce the former name of a deceased king would be considered as a sorcerer and punished as such, that is to say, by being put to death.

The Vazìmba.—The Vazìmba, who inhabit Mènabé on the banks of the Mànambòlo, seem to be the last relics of the aborigines of the island; their funeral rites therefore possess a very special interest.

After having washed the corpse and clothed it in its finest garments, they place it in a squatting posture upon a *kibàny* (a bed or couch), as if it were still living; and the relatives or friends attend it night and day, talking to it, putting into its hand a spoon, full of rice or any other kind of food, &c. Formerly the liquids produced by the decomposition of the flesh were taken to a special place, which was sprinkled with the blood of an ox in order to nourish the *fanànina* or snake, which they believe to be produced from these putrid liquids. Since the conquest of the country by the Sàkalàva king Làhifòtsy, these customs have been to some extent abandoned, and as soon as the effluvium becomes too offensive, the corpse is buried. But, at the end of about a year, they take it out of the ground and wash the bones, which are placed in a new coffin, and are then buried for good and all.

The Béhìsotra and Tandròna or Tànkoàla.[1]—The two tribes

---

[1] Béhìsotra is probably a mistake for Bèmihìsatra. The Tandrona live in the north-central part of the island in the neighbourhood of Màndritsàra, where they

who inhabit the north-west coast between Pàsandàva Bay and the Bay of Bèmbatòka have the same funeral customs as the Tankàrana. So we learn from a letter recently written by M. Vian, a naval surgeon, who was in the Bay of Màhajàmba, and had the opportunity of visiting one of their cemeteries, which is a natural cave, in which he found several coffins about 4 feet long by 1 foot 2 inches wide. It is certain that the Sàkalàva chiefs who have settled in the north-west and the north of Madagascar have not exerted on the habits of the inhabitants of that part of the island (Ankoàla and Ankàrana) so great an influence as they have in the west (Fiherènana, Mènabé and Ambòngo).

The Sihànaka.—The Sihànaka take secretly away, far from their villages, those who are ill, and of whose recovery they are hopeless, and place them in a solitary spot, where no one goes but the person appointed to attend them. After death, the corpse is brought into the house, where it lies in state for a certain time, according to the wealth of the deceased and the number of oxen killed. After these ceremonies, the house is abandoned, and the corpse is interred. The family erect to the memory of the deceased a tall pole forked at the summit, like a pair of ox-horns. This is called *jìro*, and is placed on the side of a road near the place of interment.

The Bezànozàno.—The burial monuments of the Bezànozàno are composed of a single stone or slab erected at the head and to the east of the trench where the coffin is deposited, and of other stones, to which are fixed, on stakes, the skulls of the oxen killed during the funeral ceremonies. Sometimes tin boxes or mats which belonged to the deceased are also placed on these stones.

The Tanàla.[1]—The free Tanàla, called also Hova, do not inter

first settled after leaving their original Sàkalàva home in Mènabé. Both the Bèmihisatra and the Tandròna are merely branches or sub-tribes of the Sàkalàva, the Tandròna having a certain amount of African blood in them. Another important branch of the Sàkalàva in this part of the island is the Bèmazàva.—J. S.

[1] The word Tanàla is merely a descriptive term, there being no one tribe

their dead until they have lain in state for a month or so. For three days they leave the corpse uncovered, but after this they wrap it in red cloths (*làmba*) and place it in a coffin, which they do not carry to the cemetery until the completion of the month. The liquid products of decomposition flow upon the earthen floor of the house and are simply covered over with earth. During all the time of the lying-in-state, the surviving partner (husband or wife) sleeps in the house as if his or her spouse was still living. The custom obtains also among the Bètsimisàraka, the Tanòsy, and other tribes. The coffin is deposited in a solitary place in the forest, and is surrounded by a palisade of tree trunks which hide its cover.

The *Andrìana* or chiefs, whose ancestors are of foreign (Arab) extraction, are, on the contrary, interred on the very day of their death. The coffin, with a lid in the shape of a roof, and on which is fixed a pair of horns, is carried into the dense forest and placed under a kind of shed. An image, suspended in a corner of the house where the death took place, receives for six weeks all the signs of grief and marks of regret from the people, after which it is thrown into the nearest river with great ceremony. The royal cemetery is visited from time to time in order to renew the coffins when they fall into decay, and also to change the *làmba* in which the bones are enveloped.

The Vorìmo.—The Vorìmo, who live at some distance from the sea between the rivers Mangóro and Màhasóra, keep the dead in their houses for two or three weeks, and with all their weeping, they feast, eating and drinking to excess. The corpse, wrapped in a number of *làmba* and mats, is then taken to the tomb, which is situated in a solitary place in the forest, and is composed of a little enclosure of stones, in a rectangular form, of which the interior is entirely filled with earth.

In order to offer prayers to their departed relatives, the

known by that name. It signifies forest-dwellers, and includes several different tribes. The inhabitants of the south-east-central parts of Madagascar are doubtless meant here, as these are often specially though erroneously referred to by Europeans as the Tanàla.—J. S.

Vorìmo, like the Tanàla, prepare near their villages a kind of altar, formed of three or four large stones, on which they place their offerings of rice and other things.

Where a family has been unable to recover the corpse of one of its members, or cannot bring it to its ancestral home, they erect to its memory a slab or pillar of stone, which is called *Tsàngambàto*, (lit., "standing stone"). They also place upright stones at the spots where, during the funeral ceremonies, the corpse had been temporarily deposited.

The Ikòngo.[1]—The Ikòngo do not erect any tombs; they inter their dead in the forest, and are content with marking the place by the help of a notch cut in the nearest tree. Their funerals are unaccompanied with cries or weeping.

The Hova.—The graves of the Hova differ in a very marked way from those of which we have spoken. They are, in fact, family caves or vaults, large subterranean chambers, placed east and west, of which the soil forms the base, and whose sides consist of large slabs of stone, closed over at the top by an enormous one. They are entered by a doorway cut out of the stone wall on the west side of the tomb. The corpses are deposited, wrapped up in *làmba* and mats, some upon the ground, and others upon stone shelves which are fixed horizontally all round (or rather on the three sides of) the mortuary chamber. Those of the head of the family and of his wife are placed along the wall opposite the entrance, *i.e.*, on the east side ; while those of his family are laid on the sides to the north and south. Over the cave, the top of which is always raised a little above the surface of the ground, there is a structure, almost square in shape, formed of four walls of stones laid without mortar, the interior of which is filled with earth, while the top is often covered with small pieces of quartz, which are sometimes fetched from a distance.

---

[1] *Ikòngo* is really only the name of a mountain. The inhabitants living in its neighbourhood are called Sándrabè (?), and are merely a sub-tribe of what Europeans call the Tanàla.—J. S.

The building of their tombs is considered by the Hova as a very important undertaking. All the relatives, friends, and slaves are called together and leave all their other occupations. It is indeed no easy matter to bring, often from a considerable distance, the five enormous slabs which are to form the walls and roof of the vault. In order to detach these from the bed of rock, they commence by choosing a mass of granite or gneiss (this stone being found extensively throughout the central parts of the island), which naturally divides into layers of a few inches in thickness.[1] Here they mark out the shape and dimensions of the slabs required by means of straight lines of dried cow-dung, which are set on fire. When the outline of the slab is thoroughly heated, cold water is dashed over it, producing a crack all along the lines; there is then nothing further to do but to raise the stone by means of levers, and to drag it to the place where the tomb is to be constructed; this is the longest and most difficult part of the whole business, for it may be several hundred, sometimes several thousand, yards over which these heavy stones have to be dragged, across hills and valleys. This work is an occasion of feasting and rejoicing, during which many oxen are killed, and other expenses incurred in feeding those who assist. The Hova tombs are always erected in such a position as to attract attention; sometimes they are even placed opposite the house of the head of the family.

Besides the tombs properly so called, throughout the whole province of Imèrina there are to be seen pillars or slabs of stone erected in memory of deceased relatives, and which are called *Tsàngambàto* (lit., "standing stone") or *Fàhatsiaròvana* (lit., "that which makes remembered").

The Hova do not keep the dead in their houses as long as most of the other Malagasy, and they do not usually place

[1] This has frequently been stated, but it is incorrect. The slabs are mostly taken from rock masses which show no divisional planes whatsoever, and often run directly across the grain (foliation) of the rock; the splitting is due simply to contraction when cold water is thrown upon them after heating.—J. S.

them in coffins; they wrap them in reddish-brown *làmba*, often in considerable numbers; and they carry them to the tomb on a *fàrafàra*, or kind of bier. In former times they placed upon the tomb or all round it—as is still the practice of the Bètsilèo, the Bezànozàno, the Sihànaka and other tribes—the skulls of the oxen killed at the time of funerals; but this custom is now abandoned.

On returning from a funeral, the relatives who have led the mourning wash themselves and purify the clothes they wore by steeping a silver coin in some water over which they have invoked the blessing of God by prayers. At the end of the meal which terminates the funeral ceremonies, all those who have taken part receive also the *àfana*, or sprinkling with this same holy water.

The mourning observances are rather strict. The nearest relatives allow their hair to be dishevelled. The women wear no jacket (*akànjo*) or skirt, wrapping themselves only in the *làmba*. The men go without hats and let their beards grow; they wash only the tips of their fingers, and their clothing must be soiled and dirty. Dancing and singing are forbidden. At the close of the mourning the relatives take part in a meal, at which is observed the *àfana*, or purification of all concerned, by the sprinkling upon them of the water consecrated to God.

The mourning ceremonies are much more severe at the decease of the sovereign. All the people, both male and female, must shave their heads, with the exception of the heir to the crown and a few favoured individuals. Throughout an entire year no one can sleep upon a bed or sit upon a chair; they must sleep and sit upon the ground. All mirrors must be turned with their face towards the wall, for it is not allowed during all the time of mourning for any one to look at themselves in a glass. All labour, except necessary agriculture, is stopped.

From time to time the Hova families practise a ceremony which they call *mamàdika* (lit., " turning over "), and which consists in going to their tombs to turn the corpses on one side, so that they may not be fatigued by remaining too long in one position. This ceremony is usually observed during the year following the death of one of the members of the family. This is a time of feasting and rejoicing; all the relatives are invited, and, dressed in their best clothing, with music going before the procession, repair to the family tomb in order to visit their dead relations, whom they turn round, as above described, and wrap up in new *làmba*. One day I saw passing, with violins and drums, a procession which was moving the bones of a Hova woman of rank from the tomb of her last husband but one into that of her last husband, where she would finally rest. Throughout several years she had been made to visit these two tombs alternately, keeping company with each of her deceased spouses for several months; they were now bringing her from the tomb of her first husband, because the wife who had replaced her in the affections of the deceased had died and required her place.

Many of these customs, although practised until the last few years, are completely disappearing under the influence of civilisation and Christianity.

The Bètsilèo.—The Bètsilèo bury their dead in subterranean caves, which are not, like those of the Hova, lined with stone, but are simply excavated in the ground at a depth which is often considerable, and to which access is gained by a long trench, which they are obliged to open at each interment, and which is filled up again afterwards. The corpses are placed upon mats spread on the ground, and are covered with a simple piece of cloth. Rich people have coffins with lids in the shape of a roof, and covered with coloured stuffs.

The exterior monument is not always placed exactly above the grave, and varies somewhat in character. Sometimes, as in Imèrina, it is formed of four walls from four to eight yards in length, and about four and a half to five feet high, but it differs in this point: the interior is not filled with earth, and on the banks of the Matsìatra a tree—*hàsina* or *fàno* (species of *Dracœna* and *Piptadenia* respectively), or some other kind—is planted in the middle. Between the rivers Manía and Matsìatra these funeral monuments are surrounded and surmounted by a number of wooden posts more or less ornamented with patterns cut in relief, and joined together with transverse bars also carved; the corner posts are terminated by an ornament in the form of a vase. In other cases, the memorial is a simple pillar of dressed granite, measuring from eighteen inches to two feet square, and from six to nine feet high, and carrying on its top a band of iron, bristling with points, to which are affixed the skulls and horns of cattle; or it is surrounded at the angles with carved wooden posts, fixed together with transverse pieces of wood. In some cases it is reduced to a single post, ornamented with carving, and surmounted by the usual vase-shaped finial, and with a wooden stage, to which are fixed the bleached skulls from the oxen killed at the funeral ceremonies.

Some families do not place their dead in the ground; they deposit them in natural grottos, or in caves hollowed out by hand, on the perpendicular faces of certain mountains, places to which no access can be gained except by very lofty scaffolding.

The *Andrìana* or nobles among the Bètsilèo are not interred for some time after their death. About the third day, when the body is already swollen, it is rolled upon planks so as to thoroughly soften the flesh; and on the following day the relatives fasten it tightly to the central post of the house with thongs cut from the hides of the oxen killed for the funeral ceremonies, and then make a large incision in each heel. Large earthen pots are then placed under the feet to receive the putrid liquid which escapes from the decomposition of the body. These pots are examined with the greatest care, for the corpse cannot be removed from the house, and no one can work in the fields, until a certain small worm or maggot has made its appearance in one of the vessels. They wait sometimes for two and even three months before being able to proceed with the interment. The vessel is shut up in the grave together with the body, and they arrange a long bamboo, one end of which is plunged into the liquid, the other being flush with the surface of the ground, in order that the maggot, after its transformation into a serpent or *fanàno*, may be able to come out of the tomb and go and visit its relatives; for the Bètsilèo believe that the soul of the departed reappears under the form of a reptile. Formerly it was not in the case of the nobles only that these repulsive ceremonies were observed, but now they are entirely confined to them.

The Bàra.—It appears that the Bàra lay their dead entirely naked upon the ground and cover them over with stones; their tombs are not more than from a foot to eighteen inches in height. Certain families, among others those who inhabit the Isàlo chain of mountains, also place them quite naked, either in caverns, or among rocks, with the skulls of the oxen killed during the funeral ceremonies; for a third part, and often even a half, of the oxen belonging to the deceased are killed on these occasions. The Rev. J. Richardson found in the western part of the Bàra country posts of eight or nine feet high, and bearing at their summits rude female figures of the natural size, which were probably placed as memorials of persons who had died at a distant place.

Such are the principal funeral customs of the Malagasy. We can see from the sum of the facts I have brought together that there is a close resemblance between the burial customs of the Malagasy and those of the Indonesians, which afford one more proof, if any were necessary, of the emigration into Madagascar of some of the peoples of the extreme East.

Funeral Ceremonies at the Burial of a Hova King (Radàma I.)

The foregoing paper, translated by permission from an article by Mons. A. Grandidier, may, I think, be appropriately concluded by the following account, written by an eye-witness, of the remarkable ceremonial employed at the burial of a Hova sovereign during the early part of the present century:—

On Sunday, the third day after the announcement of the death of Radàma (August 4, 1828), there was a large *kabàry*, or national assembly, held in a fine open space in the city, on the west side of the hill on which Antanànarìvo stands. In this space were assembled from 25,000 to 30,000 persons, seated in groups according to the districts to which they belonged.

At the close of this *kabàry* it was proclaimed that, according to the custom of the country, as a token of mourning, every person in the kingdom of every age must shave or cut off closely the hair of their heads, and whosoever should be found with their heads unshaved, after three days from the proclamation, should be liable to be put to death. Also, that no person whatsoever should do any kind of work (except those who should be employed in preparing the royal tomb, coffin, &c.); no one should presume to sleep upon a bed, but on the floor only, during the time of mourning. No woman, however high her rank, the queen only excepted, should wear her *làmba* or cloth above her shoulders, but must, during the same period, go always with her shoulders, chest, and head uncovered.

During the interval between this Sunday and the 12th instant, the mournfully silent appearance of the city, though tens of thousands of persons were constantly crowding through the streets—some dragging huge pieces of granite or beams of timber, or carrying red earth in baskets on their heads, for the construction of the tomb; others, and those chiefly females, going with naked heads and shoulders, to the palace to mourn, or else returning from that place after staying there as mourners perhaps twelve hours, was exceedingly impressive. The air of deep melancholy on the countenances of all, and the audible moanings of the multitudes who filled the courts of the palace and the adjoining streets, quite affected us, and produced the conviction that the grief was real and deep for one whom they regarded as their benefactor and friend, and as the best king that Madagascar had ever known. The wives of the principal chiefs from the neighbouring districts were carried to and from the place of mourning, each on the back of a stout man, just in the manner boys at school are accustomed to carry one another: the lady having her person, from the waist to the feet, covered with her white *làmba*, or cloth.

On Sunday, the 11th, her Majesty sent to us to say that we might be present the day after, to assist at the funeral ceremonies; and that General Brady would, at eight a.m., receive us[1] at his house and conduct us to the palace. Accordingly, at eight on the 12th we attended, when General Brady and Prince Correllere conducted us through the crowded streets of mourners, through the guards of soldiers, and through the still more crowded courts of the palace, which were thronged chiefly by women and girls, couched down, or prostrate in many instances, making audible lamentations.

There are several courts, with one or more palaces in each, separated from each other by high wooden railings; and the whole of the courts and palaces are surrounded by a heavy railing of great height, twenty-five feet, including a dwarf stone wall on which the wooden railing is fixed. The whole extent of this railing was covered with white cloth, as were also the oldest and most sacred of the palaces. The favourite palace of Radàma, in which he died, and where in fact the body then lay, is called the Silver Palace; it is a square building, of two floors, and two handsome verandahs running round it. This palace is named the Silver Palace on account of its being ornamented, from the ground to the roof, by the profusion of large flat-headed silver nails and plates of the same metal. The roof of this palace (as indeed of all the principal houses), a very high-pitched roof, is so high, that from the top of the wall

---

[1] George Bennet, Esq., one of a deputation from the London Missionary Society, and then completing here in Madagascar their visitation of the various stations occupied by the Society in different parts of the world.—J. S.

to the ridge is as great a distance as from the foundation to the top of the wall supporting the roof. We found it covered from the roof to the ground with hangings of rich satins, velvets, silks, their native costly silk *làmbas*, &c., and all the vast roof was covered with the finest English scarlet broadcloth.

In front of this palace had been erected a most splendid pavilion, surrounded by highly-decorated pillars, which were wrapped round with various coloured silks, satins, &c. The pavilion was ten feet square, raised on pillars also richly ornamented. A platform of wood was thrown over upon the pillars, and above this platform hung, supported by one transverse pole, an immense canopy or pall of the richest gold brocade, with stripes of blue satin and scarlet cloth, the whole bordered by a broad gold lace and finished by a deep gold fringe. All the arrangements were in good taste, and formed together a most brilliant spectacle.

We had nearly reached the Silver Palace when we were stopped, it being announced that the corpse was at that moment about to be brought out to be conveyed to the more sacred White Palace previous to its being entombed. We immediately saw about sixteen or twenty females brought out of the apartment where the corpse lay, each lady on the back of her stout bearer, weeping and lamenting aloud; these were the queens and princesses of the royal family, and formed the first part of the procession from one to the other palace; our place was appointed immediately after the queens, but it was with difficulty we could get along, many females having thrown themselves on the path which was to have been kept open. The mourners had done this that the corpse might pass over them, and we in fact were many times under the necessity of treading upon their prostrate persons. The corpse was carried into the White Palace that it might, in this more sacred place, be stripped of its old clothes and clothed with new, and also that it might be placed in a wooden coffin. In this palace we were honoured with a station not far from the corpse, which was being fanned by about sixteen or twenty young ladies, daughters of principal chiefs.

At eight, on the morning of Tuesday, we were again at the palace, and were conducted by General Brady and Prince Correllere through the crowds of mourners, indeed over some of them, as well as over ten fine favourite bulls of the late king; these lay directly in our path, and we could not help treading on them. The paths were all covered with blue or white cloth of the country. The corpse had been transferred at the close of the day before to a huge coffin or chest, of their heaviest and most valuable wood. The coffin was then carried from this White Palace back to the Silver Palace in solemn procession, the queens, &c., following next the coffin, and we succeeded them; some of the Europeans had accepted the honour of assisting to carry the coffin, which was a tremendous weight judging from appearance. I declined the honour, charging myself with the care of our missionary ladies.

On again reaching the Silver Palace the coffin was not taken in, but raised upon the wooden platform over the pavilion, over which the splendid pall or canopy of gold was drawn, which concealed it entirely from view. In this pavilion, under the platform (which was raised about seven feet), upon mats placed on the ground, the royal females seated or threw themselves in seeming agonies of woe, which continued through the day; and at sunset, when the entombment was taking place, their lamentations were distressing in the extreme. All the day great multitudes had been employed in preparing the tomb, which was in the court and not far from the pavilion. This tomb, at which tens of thousands had been incessantly working ever since the announcement of the king's death—either in fetching earth or granite stones or timber, or else in cutting or fitting the stones, timber, &c.—consisted of a huge mound of a square figure, built up of clods and earth, surrounded or faced by masses of granite, brought and cut and built up by the people.

The height of this mound was upwards of twenty feet;

about sixty feet square at the base, gradually decreasing as it rose, until at the top it was about twenty feet square. The actual tomb, or place to receive the coffin and the treasures destined to accompany the corpse, was a square well or recess, in the upper part of this mound or pyramid, about ten feet cube, built of granite and afterwards being lined, floored, and ceiled with their most valuable timbers.

At the foot of this mound had been standing most of the day the large and massy *silver coffin*, destined to receive the royal corpse. This coffin was about eight feet long, three feet and a half deep, and the same in width; it was formed of silver plates strongly riveted together with nails of the same metal; all made from Spanish dollars: *twelve thousand dollars* were employed in its construction. About six in the evening this coffin was by the multitude heaved up one of the steep sides of the mound to the top and placed in the tomb or chamber. Immense quantities of treasures of various kinds were deposited in or about the coffin, belonging to his late Majesty, consisting especially of such things as during his life he most prized. *Ten thousand hard dollars* were laid in the silver coffin for him to lie upon; and either inside, or chiefly outside the coffin, were placed or cast all his rich habiliments, especially military. There were eighty suits of very costly British uniforms, hats and feathers; a golden helmet, gorgets, epaulettes, sashes, gold spurs, very valuable swords, daggers, spears (two of gold), beautiful pistols, muskets, fowling-pieces, watches, rings, brooches, and trinkets; his whole superb sideboard of silver plate, and large and splendid solid gold cup, with many others presented to him by the King of England; great quantities of costly silks, satins, fine clothes, very valuable silk *làmbas* of Madagascar, &c.

We were fatigued and pained by the sight of such quantities of precious things consigned to a tomb. As ten of his fine favourite bulls had been slaughtered yesterday, so six of his finest horses were speared to-day and lay in the courtyard near the tomb, and to-morrow six more are to be killed. When to all these extravagant expenses are added the twenty thousand oxen, worth here five Spanish dollars each (which have been given to the people and used by them for food during the preparation for and at the funeral), the missionaries conjecture that the expense of the funeral cannot be less than *sixty thousand pounds sterling*. All agree that though these people are singularly extravagant in the expenses they incur at their funerals, yet there never was a royal funeral so expensive as this, for no sovereign in this country ever possessed one-fifth of his riches.

The silver coffin having been placed in the tomb, the corpse in the wooden one was conveyed by weeping numbers from the top of the platform over the pavilion to the top of the pyramid and placed beside the chamber. Here the wooden coffin was broken up, and the corpse exposed to those near. At this time the royal female mourners, who had been all day uttering their moans in the pavilion, now crawled up the side of the pyramid to take a last view of the remains. They were most of them obliged to be forced away; their lamentations were now very loud and truly distressing to hear. The expressions used by them in lamentation were some of them translated for us; the following was chiefly the substance:—"Why did you go away and leave me here? Oh! come again and fetch me to you!" The body was transferred from the coffin of wood to that of silver. Those who were engaged in this service seemed to suffer from the effluvia, though many were constantly employed sprinkling eau-de-cologne. When the transfer had taken place the wooden coffin was thrown piecemeal into the tomb.

During the whole of this day, while the chamber in the tomb was being prepared, the King's two bands of music, with drums and fifes, &c., were in the court and played almost unceasingly, relieving each other by turns. The tunes were such as Radàma most delighted in—many of the peculiar and favourite airs of England, Scotland and Ireland, with waltzes, marches, &c.

During intervals cannon and musketry were fired outside of the courts of the palace, and answered by musketry from the numerous soldiers inside of the courts.

On the whole, while this funeral of Radàma was the most extravagant, it was the most splendid and orderly thing that could be conceived amongst such an uncivilised people.

[Extracted from *Voyages and Travels Round the World*, by the Rev. Daniel Tyerman and George Bennet, Esq. London, 1840, 2nd ed., pp. 284–286.]

MALAGASY LOOM AND WEAVING A LAMBA.

CHAPTER XV.

DECORATIVE CARVING ON WOOD, ESPECIALLY ON THE BURIAL MEMORIALS OF THE BÈTSILÈO MALAGASY; TOGETHER WITH NOTES ON THE HANDICRAFTS OF THE MALAGASY AND NATIVE PRODUCTS.

Absence of artistic feeling among the Hova—The Bètsilèo—Carved memorial posts—Various forms of tombs—Character of the carving—*Vàtolàhy* or memorial stones—Graves at great depths—Carving in houses—Collection of rubbings—General style of ornamentation—Symbolic meaning ?—Malagasy handicrafts—Spinning and weaving—Different kinds of cloth—Straw-work —Bark-cloth—Metal-work—Pottery—Building—Canoes and boats—Cultivated products of country—Exports.

TO those who have paid attention to the indigenous art developed amongst the uncivilised races of mankind, and are acquainted with the elaborate and varied ornamentation used by the Malayan, the Polynesian, and the Melanesian tribes, there is something very surprising in the almost total absence of ornamental art amongst the Hova and some of the other peoples inhabiting Madagascar. If we look at any illustrated book describing the inhabitants of the Pacific Islands, or, still better, if we carefully study the ethnological galleries of our British Museum, or the Pitt-Rivers collection at Oxford, we shall find that every group, and sometimes every solitary island, has each its particular style of ornament, special to itself, and easily distinguishable from that of other groups or islands. Their canoes and paddles, clubs and spears, houses and beds, dishes and spoons, pipes and snuff-boxes, gourds and bowls, are all ornamented, sometimes most elaborately and beautifully ; and this decoration extends to their own persons, in the practice of tattooing, and in the patterns woven into the cloth or matting of their dresses, or stamped upon the bark cloth they procure from various trees. But we see hardly anything of all this in Imèrina, the central province of Madagascar. It is true that many of the large stone tombs built of late years have some architectural pretensions, and decorative carving is employed on them, but the details are mostly copied from drawings of European buildings, and cannot be properly considered as examples of indigenous art.[1] I was therefore much interested during a journey to the south of Madagascar, made in the year 1876, to discover that amongst the Bètsilèo there is a decided and special style of ornament, which is used in their houses, their tombs, and many of their household utensils, as spoons, gourds, dishes, &c.; and that a kind of tattooing is very common amongst them, in which some of the same ornamental details are also introduced. It should perhaps here be noted that this tribe of Malagasy occupy the southern central highlands of Madagascar. They are darker in colour than the Hova, and although physically bigger and stronger, were conquered by them in the early part of the present century. They are variously estimated as numbering from six hundred thousand to a million

---

[1] The only examples I can recall of anything distinctively characteristic of the Hova Malagasy as regards decoration are a slight ornamentation of the long gable timbers or "horns," and also in the dormer windows, of the old-fashioned native houses, which sometimes have a chevron or "dog-tooth," or small semicircular ornament cut on their lower edge ; also the conventionalised square flower and leaf pattern, used on their finer silk cloths or *làmbas;* and, perhaps, some of the patterns in the straw-work of their fine mats and baskets. In the interior ornamentation of some of the royal houses at Antanànarivo there seemed to me to be a certain distinct style prevalent. This is chiefly seen in the painted decorations of the upper parts of the walls, and sometimes of the ceilings, which, both in the colouring and large bold style of the patterns, always reminded me somewhat of Assyrian ornament, as shown in the decoration of the palaces at Persepolis. There is very little that is decorative in Hova pottery, but a special kind of vessel made for cooking the beef at the New Year's festival is rather elegant in shape, much resembling some of the Anglo-Saxon pottery. These vessels are circular and somewhat flattened, and are frequently ornamented with a series of lines and zigzags, very closely resembling those on the early fictile productions of the Germanic races.

and a half. Probably they are really somewhere between these two estimates, *i.e.*, somewhat over a million in number. I had occasionally heard from missionaries who had lived in or visited the Bètsilèo country that there was a good deal of decorative carving in this southern province; but no one, so far as I am aware, has yet described at all adequately the character of this ornament, or the different varieties of tombs and burial memorials seen in the Bètsilèo province; and although my observations were only those made on a rapid journey through the country, on my way to the south-east coast, and on a subsequent journey to Fianàrantsòa, the capital of the province, they may perhaps have some interest as a slight contribution towards a fuller knowledge of the subject, and may, perhaps, lead those who are resident in the province to give it that thorough investigation which it deserves.

I first noticed something new in the tombs in the tract of country between Isándrandàhy and Ambòsitra. Within two or three hours' journey from the latter place I observed that the upright stones placed near graves were not the rough undressed blocks or slabs common in Imèrina, but were finely dressed and squared, and ornamented with carving. (In Imèrina, I may here remark, the Hova tombs consist of a vault made of large undressed slabs of blue granite rock, with stone shelves, upon which the dead are laid, tightly wrapped up in a number of native cloth *làmbas*, the outer ones of silk. The door is of stone, with pivot hinges, above and below, fitting into sockets; and the whole structure is usually finished with a square erection of dressed stonework, in two or three stages, often with a kind of headstone, on which, since the introduction of letters, is frequently cut the name and titles of the head of the family. When the corpse of a person of rank and position cannot be obtained for burial in the family tomb, as occasionally happens in war, a rough undressed slab of stone is erected as a burial memorial. These are often ten or twelve feet high, and are termed *vàtolàhy*, which means literally "male-stone"; and

I have sometimes thought that this word, and the shape of the stone, may indicate some ancient connection with phallus worship.

On one of the days of my stay at Ambòsitra, I walked to the top of the rising ground on the western slope of which the town is principally built. Here there was an old *Amòntana*[1] tree, and memorials to some of the early kings of the Bètsilèo. The chief of these was a piece of timber seven or eight inches square and about ten feet high, having pieces of wood projecting from a little below the top, so as to form a kind of stage. Each face of the timber was elaborately carved with different patterns arranged in squares. Some of these were concentric circles, a large one in the centre, with smaller ones filling up the angles; others had a circle with a number of little bosses in them; others had a kind of leaf ornament; and in others parallel lines were arranged in different directions. The narrow spaces dividing these squares from each other, had in some cases an ornament like the Norman chevron or zigzag, and in others, something similar to the Greek wave-like scroll. The whole erection with its ornamentation bore a strong resemblance to the old runic stones, or the memorial crosses in Ireland and parts of the Scottish Highlands. The north face of this memorial post was quite sharp and fresh, but the others were worn by the weather, and the carving was filled up with lichens. I was greatly interested with this carving, as being almost the first specimen I had seen of indigenous Malagasy art; and I greatly regretted having no appliances with me for taking a "rubbing" or a "squeeze." Not very far from this memorial there were some others, consisting of two pairs of posts, each with a lintel, like a gateway, except that the opening was filled up by a large flat upright stone. These posts were carved much in the same style as the single one just described, but were not so massive, and were more weathered. The tops of the posts were carved into a shape somewhat resembling a vase.

[1] *Ficus Baroni*, Baker.

I then remembered that, two or three days before, we had passed a newly set-up memorial stone carved in three large squares, with much the same kind of ornament as these posts had in wood.

I now regret still more not having obtained some sketch of this group of burial memorials, because, on visiting Ambòsitra again twelve years subsequently, I found that the whole had been utterly swept away. The Hova governor had appropriated the site for his official residence and courtyard, and the picturesque tombs of the old Bètsilèo chiefs and the fine trees had been destroyed to make way for a great brick building, raw and commonplace, whose erection had been a heavy tax upon the unpaid service of the people.

On our journey from Ambòsitra to Fianàrantsòa, at about two hours' distance from the former place, we passed a tomb by the roadside with a carved wooden post similar to those at Ambòsitra. I got down from the palanquin and examined it; some of the carving was similar to what I had already seen, but there were other graceful forms which were new, and some of the compartments were like the English Union-Jack. But it was on the following day, when passing over the elevated line of road between Zomà Nandihĭzana and Ambòhinàmboàrina, that I was most astonished and interested by the profusion with which the carved memorials were scattered along the roadside, as well as in all directions over the tract of country visible on either hand. Leaving an elevated valley—if one can so describe it—a long, nearly level hollow on high ground, with hills on either side not a mile apart, and gently curving round to the south-west—we came out at last to an uninterrupted view, and in sight of a rounded green hill, about a quarter of a mile to the west of the road. This place is called Ikangára, and has a few houses and a little church on the top. But between it and the road there was a large number of tombs and memorial posts, so my companion and I went to inspect them. They were well worth a visit, as in a small space there were grouped together many different kinds of monuments, with wood carving in great variety. Within a short distance were some forty or fifty tombs, and on examining them there appeared to be the following kinds :—

(1) The largest tombs—there were two of them—were of small flat stones, built in a square of some twenty to twenty-five feet, and about five feet high. But around them was a railing of carved posts and rails, those at each corner with the vase-shaped top already described; these were connected by a transverse rail, and this again was supported on each of the four sides by upright posts which finished under the rail. All the upright timbers were carved in patterns like those seen at Ambòsitra and on the road the previous day.

(2) Another kind of tomb was formed by a square structure of small flat stones, four or five feet high, and perhaps a dozen feet square; but on the top was a square enclosure of four carved posts with the vase-shaped heads, connected by lintels, and with an intermediate upright. This structure was about four feet square, by seven or eight feet high, and in the centre was a single carved post.

(3) A third kind of monument was a massive block of granite, from eight to ten feet high, and from eighteen inches to two feet square, with carved posts at the four corners and touching them. On the top these were connected by carved cross pieces, and upon these the skulls of the bullocks killed at the funeral of the person the monument commemorated were placed. Many of these horned skulls remained in their places.

(4) Another kind of memorial was a massive square post of wood, about twenty feet high and fifteen inches square, carved on all four sides from top to bottom. There were four or five of these enormous posts here. In one case there was a pair of them, as if to form a kind of gateway; two or three were split nearly all down their length by the action of the sun and weather.

(5) Still another kind was an oblong block of dressed

granite, with an iron hooping round the top, in which were fixed a dozen or more pairs of slender *iron* horns. There were two of this kind of monument at this place, and we afterwards saw others on the road.

(6) Besides the foregoing there were numerous specimens of the smaller carved post such as we had already seen at Ambòsitra, with the vase-shaped head and a small open staging near the top, on which were fixed upright sharp-pointed pieces of wood. These were for placing the ox skulls upon.

It may be here noted that the humped and long-horned ox being the largest animal known in Madagascar, this animal, especially the bull, is very often used in native proverbs, royal speeches, songs, and circumcision observances, as a symbol of power and authority, while the horn is frequently employed as an emblem of strength, much indeed as it was employed by the Hebrews and other Asiatics. Among the Sihànaka people lofty round poles are erected near their tombs, and at the top of these a forked branch of a tree is fixed, carved into a close resemblance of a pair of horns. And in the Tanàla, or forest region, the extremities of the gable timbers of the houses are fashioned into the form of horns. Among the Hova these are simply crossed and slightly ornamented, small wooden figures of birds being often affixed to them, but they are still called "house horns," or *tàndro-tràno*. In royal proclamations the soldiers are styled "horns of the kingdom." There are many interesting customs among the Malagasy, showing that the ox has retained the semi-sacred character it bears among many nations; in some tribes only the chiefs are allowed to kill the animal, evidently because the chief or king is also the high-priest of the tribe; while among other Malagasy peoples the ox is only killed at certain seasons which have some religious significance. The native kings are saluted as *òmbelàhy*, or "bulls"; and the same expression frequently occurs in forms of benediction at the circumcision and other festivities.

To return, however, to the interesting group of tombs at

Ikangàra. Many of these memorials were sorely weathered and defaced, and others were falling, or had fallen, and were rotting away. But there was a great variety of pattern, many of them being well worth preserving and copying.

On the roadside, before we turned from the main path to look at Ikangàra, were a number of the more simple tombs, of a kind that seem peculiar to the Bètsilèo. They consist of a plain square, almost a cube, of thin undressed stones laid very evenly. In some instances these had upright slabs at the corners and centres of the sides, so that they were not unlike Hova tombs, but the majority were of small stones only, laid horizontally. From the number of handsome tombs and memorials near this little town, we judged that it must have been an important place in former days. We stayed some considerable time examining this ancient cemetery, and then proceeded on our way southwards.

Our road lay along the top of a long ridge, with a valley on the west and an extensive plain on the east, with numerous hills, and old fortifications on their tops. Over the plain were dotted small villages and numberless green *vàla*, or homesteads of the Bètsilèo, enclosed in a circular and impenetrable fence of thorny mimosa or *Tsiàfakòmby*, i.e., "impassable by cattle" (*Cæsalpinia sepiaria*, Roxb.). About a quarter of an hour after leaving Ikangàra, we came to an old fortification running along the crest of the ridge, and called Ianjànonakèly; a low stone rampart extended for a hundred yards or more along the hill, and there were many tombs. Indeed we were struck by the number of tombs and carved monuments on the roadside all the way to Ambòhinàmboàrina. The most common form is the plain square tomb of thin, small, undressed stones, and the upright *vàtolàhy*, or block of granite, from eighteen inches to two feet square, and eight to ten feet high. While the *tsàngambàto* in Imèrina are all of rough undressed slabs of blue rock, these in Bètsilèo are of fine-grained, hard white granite, in massive blocks, and dressed to a beautifully smooth face. They are often in couples, and in one instance there were two stones, with an elaborately carved post between them. But the combinations of the different kinds of memorial were very numerous; there was something new every few yards; and all over the plain, near every little cluster of houses, we could see these white memorial stones.

South of the Matslatra river, and nearer Fianàrantsòa, I noticed that there were very few of the upright square memorial stones compared with what we saw the previous day, and that there were no carved wood pillars at all. All the tombs, which hereabouts were very numerous, were the plain square or cube of undressed flat stones. The majority of these, I was surprised to find, were hollow, many having trees—*Hàsina, Fàno*, and others—growing out of the middle, which has a circular opening, and overshadowing the whole tomb, a sight never seen in Imèrina. From this it was clear that the chamber in which the corpses are deposited does not project at all above the ground, as it does in Hova tombs; and I afterwards ascertained that this chamber is excavated at considerable depth beneath the square pile of stones, which is therefore not a grave, but only marks the place of one far below the surface. I noticed also that there was in most cases a long low mound of earth extending from one side of the tomb to a distance of from thirty or forty to eighty feet and upwards. This, it appears, marks the line of a long tunnelled passage gradually descending from the surface to the deeply sunk burial chamber. Mr. Richardson says that some of the Bètsilèo tombs are "as much as sixty feet deep, and are approached by a gradually descending passage opening some forty or fifty feet distant from the burial chamber. The tombs of the rich are sometimes 15 or 16 feet square, and are quite on the surface of the ground; and the four walls and roof are formed of five immense stone slabs, which are brought from great distances, and involve almost incredible labour. I measured one slab of granite, which was more than 18 feet long, 10 feet wide, and nearly 3 feet thick in some parts. I was once in a tomb 18 feet long, 14 feet wide, and 10 feet high, formed of five stones, in one of which, to the west, had been cut an opening, and a rude stone door, working in stone sockets, had been fixed there. The finest memorial stone I saw was almost circular, and was 4 feet in diameter, and about 20 feet high above the ground. Sometimes these stones are covered with carved oxen and birds. The most honourable superstructure is a solid mass of masonry erected over the stone tombs just described. These are square in shape, and about 6 feet high. A cornice is worked round the top, and on this are laid the skulls of all the oxen killed at the funeral regularly arranged. I have seen one, now rapidly falling into decay, on which were no less than 500 such skulls! The most symmetrical I ever saw was a new tomb, on which, in the outer square, were arranged 108 skulls of oxen in most regular order, every other skull being that of an ox whose horns had grown downwards. There were also two other squares of skulls arranged behind this one. It was a strange sight to see so many skulls of oxen with the horns, arranged thus, and bleaching in the sun."

All through the country south of the so-called "desert," or uninhabited region, near Ivòtovòrona, we were struck by the tattooing on the chest, neck, and arms of many of the people. In some cases the men had figures of oxen, and in others an ornament like a floriated Greek cross; while the women had a kind of tattooed collar, which looked like deep lace-work or vandyking on the neck and chest. But I have never seen tattooing on the faces of the people.

I regretted that, our journey being made chiefly for the purpose of seeing districts further south than Bètsilèo, we were unable to visit some of the larger old Bètsilèo towns, such as Ifànjakàna, Nàndihìzana, Ikálamavòny, and others, where I was told there is a great deal of the peculiar carving to be seen not only in the tombs, but also in the dwelling houses and furniture. We did, however, see two specimens of this native art as used in building: first, just before entering the Tanàla country, and again, immediately on leaving the forest on our return home. The first example was at a village of forty houses called Iválokiánja, about two hours south-east of Imáhazóny. Here we went into one of the houses in the village for our lunch; it was the largest house there, but was not so large as our tent (11 feet square), and the walls were only 5 feet 6 inches high. The door was a small square aperture, 1 foot 10 inches wide by 2 feet 4 inches high, and its threshold 2 feet 9 inches from the ground. Close to it, at the end of the house, was another door or window, and opposite were two small openings about a foot and a half square. The hearth was opposite the door, and the bed-place in what is the window corner in Hova houses. In this house was the first example I had seen of decorative carving in Malagasy houses; the external faces of the main post supporting the roof being carved with a simple but effective ornament of squares and diagonals. There was also other ornamentation much resembling the English Union Jack. The gables were filled in with a neat platted work of split bamboo. The majority of the houses in this and most of the Bètsilèo villages are only about 10 or 11 feet long by 8 or 9 feet wide, and the walls from 3 to 5 feet high. A stranger seeing many of these native houses for the first time would say that they had no doors, and only very small windows, for the doors are so small and high up that entering such a house is a gymnastic feat requiring considerable agility, and more amusing to an onlooker than pleasant to the performer. All ideas of dignity must be laid aside.

The other example we saw of carving used for house ornamentation was at a small cluster of half a dozen houses called Ifandríana, some three hours before reaching Isàndrańdàhy on the way from Ambòhimànga in the Tanàla. The three centre posts of the timber house, in which we stayed, were all covered with carving of much the same character as that used in the memorial posts already described, but it was not quite so well executed. The nearly square window shutters had each a circular ornament carved upon them, much like the conventional representations of the sun, with rays, proceeding from a centre, thirteen in number. During a more recent visit to the Bètsilèo province, I had opportunities of seeing some other interiors; and in these not only were the three posts of the house and the windows carved, but also the woodwork enclosing the fixed bedstead—quite a little room of itself—as well as other timberwork about the building. In a paper contributed by Mr. Shaw to the *Antanànarivo Annual* for 1878, he remarks:—" The most distinctive indigenous art of the Bètsilèo is the carving, which is noticed by every one travelling in any part of the province. There is an endless variety of patterns, though a great number are formed by combinations of three or four simple designs, that appear, in some form or other, on nearly every house-post or door, which are highly ornamented."

One of the most perfect examples of the carved memorial post we saw the same day, in the morning, at the picturesquely situated village of Ivòhitrámbo. This place is perched like an eagle's nest on the summit of a lofty cone of rock, on the edge of the interior plateau, and overlooking the great forest, the country of the Tanàla tribes, above which it towers about 2,500 feet. This memorial was close to the village, and was very perfect, the carving very sharp, and the stage near the top, consisting of several pieces of wood crossing one another, in good preservation, with about thirty ox skulls and horns still in their places.

It may be added that in many cases figures of oxen and men are carved in some of the panels or compartments of these memorial posts, but the ornament is chiefly conventional. The Bètsilèo name for these memorial pillars is *tèza* or *tèzan-kàzo*; the root *tèza* means "durability, anything firmly fixed," and also, "fixed upright."

In his little book entitled *Madagascar of To-day*, Mr. Shaw says, " Perhaps the most elaborately carved post I saw during my residence of eight years in the Bètsilèo was at a small village about a day's journey north-west of Fianàrantsòa. This was the central post of a high house belonging to one of the chiefs. It was twenty feet high and carved from top to bottom. Each of the four surfaces, about eighteen inches broad, was divided into sections by cross-cuts forming squares with the edge of the post. In each of these were different designs formed according to the individual tastes of the many men who were probably impressed into the service of the chief to perform the work. Some consisted of radiating triangles, whose apices met in the central point; some were filled with pairs of circles touching each other at the circumference; others were concentric circles, and the corners of the squares filled with smaller curves springing from the outermost circle; other squares were filled with zigzag lines running parallel to each other, or running diagonally across the square, while others were rough imitations of birds, bullocks, crocodiles, &c."

Before leaving the subject of Bètsilèo art it may be added that gourds, fifes, tobacco boxes (a piece of finely polished reed or bamboo), and other articles are often very tastefully ornamented with patterns incised on the smooth yellow surface, the lines being then filled in with black. These patterns consist of lines, zigzags, scrolls, and diaper grounds, often very artistically arranged.

As already remarked, my visit to the Bètsilèo in 1876 was too short and hasty to allow of a thorough examination of these interesting examples of indigenous art. And not thinking of meeting with such specimens of carving, I had not prepared myself beforehand with any appliances for taking drawings or copying them in any way. But an article in the *Antanànarivo Annual* for 1876, which I have largely reproduced in this chapter, did, to some extent, have the effect I desired in drawing the attention of some of my brother missionaries to the subject, and especially in inducing Mr. Shaw to make a number of rubbings of the more characteristic specimens of the ornament employed. Still, these by no means convey a proper idea of the rich effect of many of these sculptured memorials, for hardly anything but photography and the autotype process could adequately reproduce the many varieties of elaborate carving that are to be found ; but still, much might be done by careful measurements and sketches and enlarged photographs. Many of the finest specimens of carving in the memorial posts and tombs are being fast obliterated by the action of the weather, and if not secured within a few years, the patterns carved upon them will soon be past recovery. Indeed, when passing by Ikangàra seven years ago, I found the interesting group of burial memorials already described fast disappearing. Some of those I had seen in 1876 were quite gone, either rotted away by the rain and damp, or fallen to the ground and half buried in *débris*, and the whole presenting a much less striking appearance than during my first visit twelve years previously. (Of course these remarks apply chiefly to those carvings which are out of doors ; those in houses have a much greater chance of preservation, but even here the desire to have larger and more modern fashioned dwellings, especially of sun-dried brick, will probably cause the destruction of many of these old-fashioned adornments.) Besides this, it is very probable that the incoming of ideas and fashions from foreigners will eventually lead to the discontinuance of this primitive style both of memorial and of ornament, although I have more recently found that such carvings are still executed, and such memorial posts still set up by the people. Still, as examples of indigenous art, it is very desirable that they should be copied as soon as possible, and perhaps it might be practicable to secure a few examples of the best carved pieces of wood themselves, and have them carefully deposited in some place of safety for reference and preservation. Apart from their intrinsic interest, these carvings may prove of value in showing links of connection between the Bètsilèo and some of the Malayan and Oceanic peoples, and thus aid us in understanding more clearly the race affinities of the people of Madagascar. Mr. Shaw observes, "It is a significant fact that the simple designs [of the Bètsilèo carvings] are almost identical with the same species of ornamentation in Polynesia. On a carved hatchet-handle from Mangaia (Hervey Islands) in my possession are some patterns precisely like those on the spoon-handles manufactured by the untutored Bètsilèo. The wooden and horn spoons and wooden bowls for rice are also remarkably well carved, of good shape, beautifully smooth, and gracefully ornamented."

I have been unable to ascertain whether there are any traditions among the Bètsilèo as to the origin of this peculiar style of ornamentation, or whether the different patterns employed have any religious or symbolic meaning.[1] Not having resided in the province, I have had no opportunity of making any inquiries of this sort, although many questions now suggest themselves as interesting. I hope that my brother missionaries stationed among the people will try and ascertain something more on these points.

It will be understood that even Mr. Shaw's collection, valuable as it is, cannot give an adequate idea of the size of some of these memorial posts, many of which, as already mentioned, are twenty feet high, and eighteen inches square in section, while those he exhibited, in two of the rubbings, are only about four feet high. It would indeed be a rather formidable task to take a complete copy of these largest memorials, and would require many appliances and assistances, as well as an amount of time such as missionaries can rarely give to pursuits outside their more immediate and special work. I trust, however, that my descriptions will give some clear idea of these productions of the Bètsilèo, and will show the decided love of ornament which they manifest in their peculiar style of wood carving.

[1] In the discussion that followed the reading of this paper, one of the members expressed a strong opinion that these ornaments must have had originally some religious signification. He also pointed out the fact (which I had not myself noticed) that in all the circles the rays were thirteen in number, therefore probably bearing some meaning. Miss Buckland remarked that many of the patterns closely resembled those on articles from the Nicobar Islands.

MALAGASY HANDICRAFTS.

This chapter seems an appropriate place for saying something further about other manual arts practised by the people of Madagascar. I proceed therefore to describe briefly their chief handicrafts, and it must be remembered that these are strictly *manu*factures in the original and literal sense of the word made by *hand*, and not by machinery, steam-engines and power looms being still unknown to the Malagasy.

Spinning and Weaving.—Most of the Malagasy races are expert in the various arts in which dexterity of hand is requisite —manufactures, strictly so called—and their long, tapering fingers look as if formed for skilled work. In the processes connected with spinning and weaving, the Malagasy show no small amount of skill. They make a variety of cloths, both coarse and fine, of silk, cotton, and hemp, and from the fibres of the *rofia* palm leaf, the aloe, and the banana. With rude spindles of wood and bone, twirled by the hand, they spin the thread; and then, with very simple looms, they weave the yarn thus prepared. But the weaving is regular and firm, and the fabrics produced are excellent in quality.

The coarser cloths from the fibre of the *rofia* palm not only form the usual clothing of the poorer classes and the slaves, but they also constitute a considerable portion of the exports from the eastern side of the island. Many thousands of them, under the name of *rabànnas*, are sent to Mauritius and Réunion, where they are used for a variety of purposes. The fibre is prepared from the fine pinnate leaves of the *rofia* palm; these are stripped of the cuticle above and below, leaving a glossy, straw-coloured material, which is divided into threads of various breadths, as may be desired, by a sort of iron comb. The straw-tinted ground is varied by an endless variety of longitudinal stripes, the dyes for which are procured from coloured earth and vegetable substances. Very fine and strong cloths are also made from this fibre; some of these have the woof of cotton, obtained by unravelling English or American calico.

A very favourite cloth, called *àrindràno*, is made with a white ground of fine twilled cotton, with narrow stripes of black and coloured threads, and broad borders of black twilled silk, in which is a central pattern of colour. These form the *làmba*, or outer native dress, which is folded gracefully, something in the fashion of the ancient Roman *toga*, one corner being thrown over the shoulder. European cottons are also largely used by the Hovas and the east coast tribes, a piece the size of a good-sized sheet or tablecloth forming a very good *làmba*. These often have borders of coloured silk sewn on to the ends of the stuff.

But the skill and taste of the Malagasy, as regards weaving, are shown most in the handsome silk *làmbas*, which are woven by the Hova women. These are of considerable variety of pattern and colouring (within certain conventional limits), often very rich and elegant in their effect, and with a peculiar kind of square leaf or flower introduced into the stripes, and various combinations of small diamond-shaped patterns. These silk *làmbas* form a considerable portion of the wealth of every Malagasy family, as they are worth from twenty to fifty dollars each. They are only worn on special occasions, such as the New Year's festival, and at marriages, &c. Dark-red silk *làmbas* are used as the outer wrapping of a corpse among the Hovas, no coffin being employed for burial, but a great number of cloths instead. This dark-red *làmba* also forms a sort of official dress for the judges and head-men of the districts; and in many of them fine metal beads are woven into the stuff, so as to form a variety of ornamental patterns across the ends of the *làmba*. Almost all Hova women, from the Queen down to the slave, can spin and weave; in some tribes, a girl is called *zaza-ampéla*, *i.e.*, "spindle child," a close analogy to our English word "spinster."

Straw-work.—But besides spinning and weaving, the dexterity of the Malagasy women is seen hardly less in their straw-plaiting. From the great variety of grasses, as well as from the tough outer peel of the *zozòro* (*papyrus*) rush, they plait many kinds of baskets, large and small, coarse and fine, plain and coloured, and also mats of various degrees of fineness. Among the Hovas these are used for flooring, and lining walls and partitions, but among the Bètsilèo and south-eastern tribes, mats are the chief articles of clothing. Broad-brimmed straw hats of excellent quality are made by the Hovas, and this is their general head-dress. A considerable variety of straw caps and head-coverings are made and worn by the other tribes, some being peculiar to particular districts. The straw mats used for clothing are sewn into a kind of sack, which is kept in its place by a girdle of bark cloth. Some tribes are especially skilful in this manufacture. The Sihànaka and Bètsilèo make mats of a great length, a number of these forming part of the yearly tribute they pay to the Central Government. The Hovas also are very ingenious in making minute square baskets of straw, some of them not larger than $\frac{3}{4}$-inch cube, in which the plait, with beautiful patterns, is as fine as the finest weaving.

Bark Cloth.—The bark cloth just mentioned, as used for girdles, is made by the people of the south-east coast and the forest tribes; but in this branch of handicraft the Malagasy cannot compete with the delicate fabrics prepared from the bark of trees by many of the Polynesian races. The bark cloth of the Taimòro, Tanàla, and other tribes, is a coarse reddish-brown material, of little strength, except in the direction of the fibre ; but its use, as well as the non-employment of skins for clothing, is one of the many links of connection between the Malagasy and the Malayo-Polynesian peoples, and serves (among many other peculiarities) to mark them off distinctly from the African tribes, who make such large use of the skins of animals as articles of dress.

Metal Work.—In metal work, the Malagasy also show great skill in execution and ingenuity in design. In gold and silver work the native smiths make most fine and delicate chains, and they can produce copies of any article of jewellery with wonderful exactness. Their iron work (which is all wrought, not cast) is of excellent quality, and they can also turn out brass and copper work of good finish. In the Memorial Churches erected at the capital (1864-1874), the ornamental iron work—finials, railings, floriated hinges, &c.—were all executed by native workmen. Among the Hovas, the smelting and working of iron seems to have been known from a remote antiquity; and they employ the same double-piston bellows which are used in the Malayan Peninsula and Islands. There seems to be no trace of a stone age when iron was not known to the Hovas; although, according to tradition, the aboriginal tribe, called Vazimba, whom they displaced in the central province, were ignorant of the use of metal, and used spears made of burnt clay, and of the tough wiry bark of certain palms.

Pottery.—In fictile art, the Malagasy are not so advanced as are many peoples who, in most other things, are their inferiors. Perhaps, however, this arises from the large use made by many of the tribes of vegetable substances and leaves for plates and dishes and waterpots, so that the necessity for articles of pottery has not been felt; and also from the absence in the maritime plains of suitable clays. Amongst the peoples who live in and near the forests, wooden dishes are largely manufactured; and the forest and coast dwellers also use the leaves of the pandanus, the banana, and the travellers'-tree for holding food and liquid; while the jointed and chambered bamboo supplies them with vessels for drawing and storing water. Dishes of finely-woven straw or rush are also employed. But, in the central provinces, where vegetable materials are more scarce, and where clay is abundant, pottery is manufactured, and water vessels of various kinds are produced, as well as rude dishes, plates, and cooking pots. A special kind of vessel, made for cooking the beef at the New Year's festival, is elegant in shape—much like some of the Anglo-Saxon pottery now and then found in ancient "barrows," both in ornament and outline. Some of the water jars are of fine quality, and deep red in colour, like Samian ware.

The horns of the fine humped cattle are manufactured into a variety of articles, especially spoons, dishes, and plates. Almost every tribe has some special pattern of wooden spoon peculiar to it, some of which are very elegant and beautifully finished. They are often ornamented with various devices burnt in on the handles.

Building.—In the building art, the Malagasy, as a whole, have made but little advance beyond constructing the small and simple dwellings required by a semi-civilised people. Except in the central provinces, the houses are constructed almost entirely of vegetable materials, and without any metal fastenings, all being tied together with tough, fibrous plants.

Canoes and Boats.—Water-carriage is largely made use of on the rivers and coast lagoons. The native canoe is made of the hollowed-out trunk of a tree, chiefly the *varòngy* (*Calophyllum inophyllum*), and some of the canoes are forty feet long, with about three feet beam. On the south-east coast, a native boat, called *sáry*, is used. This is a built boat of planks, but no iron is used in its construction, everything being tied together by the wire-like fibre of the *anìvona* palm, while the holes are plugged by tree-nails of hard wood. The seams are caulked with strips of bamboo, and loops of the same material form rowlocks for the larger oars. The seats pass right through the sides, and thus stiffen the whole, and bind it together, for there are no ribs or framework. These boats rise up at the stem and stern, and will carry fifty people, or a large quantity of goods. They are used for going out to the shipping through the heavy surf, where no canoe could possibly venture. These ingeniously made boats have evidently been in use for a considerable period, as they are referred to by some of the earliest French books on Madagascar, written from 150 to 200 years ago. On the west coast outriggers are adopted, and canoes fitted with these and with sails venture out to sea in a very fearless way. The natives along that portion of the island are bold navigators, and until the early portion of this century, they were accustomed to make an annual piratical expedition to the Còmoro Islands, in which hundreds of canoes, carrying thousands of men, were employed. Most of these must, therefore, have been boats of considerable size and seaworthy properties.

Products and Exports.—Besides rice, a number of roots and vegetables are also cultivated by the Malagasy, the manioc root or cassava forming a considerable portion of their food, as well as yams, sweet-potatoes, beans, millet, Indian-corn, &c. The sugar-cane is also cultivated, and in the warmer districts grows to a great size. A coarse sugar is made, but, except in the neighbourhood of the capital, the cane is chiefly used for the manufacture of a spirit called *tòaka.* Coffee, spices, ginger, chillies, tobacco, indigo, hemp, and cotton are also grown, but not in large quantities. There is a considerable variety of fruit, many kinds being indigenous, as the banana and plantain, pine-apple, loquat, grape, citron, lemon, mulberry, raspberry, &c., and others introduced by Europeans, as the peach, mango, pomegranate, guava, and fig.

It is, however, the opinion of some who are well qualified to judge of the matter, that the fertility of the soil of Madagascar as a whole has been overrated, and that it does not present as good a field as many tropical counties for European settlers. But bearing this in mind, there still is reason to believe that in many parts of the island the soil is capable of supplying many of the most valuable products of the tropical zone. Rice, sugar, coffee, and spices, silk, cotton and hemp, indigo and tobacco, might all be produced in practically unlimited quantities. At present, however, rice, sugar, vanilla, and coffee are the only articles out of this list which are grown for exportation. The cultivation of coffee is yearly increasing, and numerous small plantations have been formed along the shores of the east coast rivers by Creole traders. For several years past large quantities of gum-copal and indiarubber have also been exported, but owing to the reckless manner in which the trees supplying the latter have been cut down, it is feared that the whole trade will come to an end before long unless some steps are taken to remedy the evil. In the southern part of the island, a lichen, called *orseille*, which is valuable for dyeing, is collected in considerable quantities. Ebony and numerous hard and beautiful woods resembling teak, rosewood, and mahogany, are found in the forests, and are used for cabinet work, and in building, and also in making the parquetry flooring in the best class of houses.

The most important item of export at present is cattle. The colonies of Mauritius and Bourbon derive their entire supply of beef from the fine humped oxen which are shipped by thousands from the eastern ports. In later times, however, the trade is leaving somewhat the eastern side of the island, the ships fetching the cattle from the north-west coast, owing to their greater cheapness in the Sàkalàva country. A considerable trade has also sprung up between the south-west ports and Natal. Hides are sent down in large quantities from the interior, being dried and salted for exportation. The valuable woods found in the forests now also form an important article of trade.

CHAPTER XVI.

ODD AND CURIOUS EXPERIENCES OF LIFE IN MADAGASCAR.

The comic element everywhere present—First experiences—Native dress—Borrowed garments—Christmas Day exhibitions—Interruptions at divine service—A nation of bald-heads—Native houses and their inmates—Receptions by Hova Governors—Native feasts—Queer articles of food—First attempts at speaking Malagasy—"Try a relative"—Transformations of English names—Biblical names—Odd names—English mistakes—The "southern" side of his moustache—Funeral presents—Church decoration—Offertory boxes—Deacons' duties.

THIS world of ours would be but a dull place to live in if there was no room in it for humour and fun, and if we could not sometimes indulge in a good hearty laugh. But happily there is no spot on its surface where the elements of the comic and ridiculous are not present; and Madagascar certainly forms no exception to the general rule. We hope, therefore, no one will be shocked at hearing that even in missionary experiences there is occasionally a decided element of the amusing, the odd, and the absurd; anyhow, during several years' residence in this island most people come across a few curious experiences, and hear of a good many more; and if all these could be remembered and noted down, they would afford ample materials for more than one paper. This, however, is now an impossibility, but perhaps I may be able to recall enough to serve to while away a leisure half-hour; and some of these reminiscences may perchance throw a side-light or two upon certain phases of native character and habits.

One's first landing in Madagascar—especially if one has had

no previous experience of a semi-civilised country—must, I think, strike most people as having some very comic aspects: the only partially clothed appearance of so many of the "natives"; the often absurd mixture of European and other dress; and the odd gibberish, as it seems to us, of an unknown language—all these tend to excite one's amusement. I vividly remember my first ride in a *filanjàna* at Tamatave, and how I was in fits of laughter all the way from my lodging to the Battery; the being carried in that fashion by men struck me then—I can hardly now understand why—as irresistibly comic. At that time—more than thirty years ago—gentlemen very often travelled from the coast to the capital in the long basket-like *filanjàna* which is never used now, nor has been for a long time past, except by ladies and children. In one of these contrivances I came up myself in October, 1863; but I suspect few gentlemen would now care to run the gauntlet of the amusement and "chaff" they would excite by riding through Antanànarìvo in a similar conveyance. Yet even in 1873, the late Rev. Dr. Mullens also travelled up to Imèrina in a lady's *filanjàna*; but it struck him at the time as rather ridiculous, for he said how it reminded him of one of Leech's pictures in *Punch*, of a London exquisite driving a very small basket carriage, and being saluted by a street *gamin* with the words, "Oh, Bill, here's a cove a-drivin' hisself home from the wash."

I referred just now to the oddness of native dress, especially when only portions of European costume are used. One sees some absurd enough sights now and then, even at the present time, in Antanànarìvo, but these are nothing compared with the ridiculous combinations which often met one's view a few years ago. To see a company of native officers come up from the parade ground in all their variety of dress was a very mirth-provoking spectacle. If a hundred or two of men had been fitted out from an extensive old-clothes' shop, with the object of making every one different from every one else, it could hardly

[*Photograph by* Dr. Fenn.
A HOVA OFFICER, MALAGASY ARMY.

have produced a greater variety or have had a more *bizarre* effect than was actually the case. All sorts of cast-off uniforms; every kind and shape of hat, from the smartest to the shabbiest (the "shocking bad" not excepted); every imaginable civilian dress, policeman's, fireman's, &c.—all might be seen, and in the queerest combinations, often finished off by the commonest of green and red woollen comforters. The sharp observation of a friend of mine (of the Society of Friends) even detected in an Andohàlo crowd the low-crowned "broad brims" once belonging to some good East Anglian Quaker farmers, and pronounced that they must certainly have often figured in the sedate proceedings of "an Essex Quarterly Meeting." One of the richest points in these exhibitions was the extreme self-consciousness of the wearers of these wonderful suits, and their evident pride in their personal appearance, together with the serene conviction that they were cutting a great dash.[1]

In the earlier years of the residence of those of us who have lived here longest we can remember what curious notions our native friends and our house servants had about borrowing (with and without our leave) our clothes. Requests from the former to borrow one's best "go-to-meeting" suit to wear at weddings, either their own or that of some relative, or on other festive occasions, used to be very frequent; and it took a good many refusals and a good deal of persistence before they could be got to understand that such loans were *not* congenial to our feelings. Our servants, however, did not always take the trouble to ask leave, but would borrow coat, trousers, or shirt; and we occasionally had the pleasure of discovering portions of our own dress on the back of cook or house boy, as we sat at church, or on the way home. With new servants it was a

[1] It must, however, be said that a great improvement has taken place during the last few years in all these particulars, largely through the efforts of the English officers who have been engaged in training the Malagasy army. Most of the native officers are now dressed in neat and appropriate uniforms, and very many have a thoroughly soldierly bearing; while the simple white uniform of the rank and file has replaced the cross-belts and loin-cloth which formed the sole dress of the common soldiers not many years ago.

common thing to borrow a tablecloth as a *làmba;* and more than once the mistress of the house has been horrified, as her attention has wandered a little from the eloquence of the preacher, to recognise the familiar pattern of her best diaper table-linen enfolding the form of one of her domestics sitting not far from her. It is well known, too, that some of our washerwomen have made quite a business of letting out shirts, trousers, &c., as well as various articles of female dress, belonging to their English clients, to native customers for Sunday wear, and so adding to the legitimate profits of their business. In such cases also, we have occasionally had the gratification of seeing at church how well our own garments have fitted native wearers of the same.

In our congregations of a few years ago there was a primitive simplicity about dress which would rather astonish us nowadays. I well remember being amused by this one Sunday at the old Ambàtonakànga chapel. In the middle of the sermon a little boy of three or four years old, and perfectly naked, came to the door and looked about to find his mother among the people closely crowded together on the matted floor of the building. Presently she noticed the little urchin, and taking his tiny *làmba* which lay beside her, she rolled it up into a ball and tossed it to him over the heads of her neighbours. The child quietly unfolded it and, wrapping it about him with all the dignity of a grown-up person, gravely marched to his place, without any one, I think, but myself taking any notice of the incident. On special occasions, however, our congregations used to turn out in gorgeous array, the ladies in silks and satins and wonderful head-dresses, and the men in black coats and pantaloons and "chimney-pot" hats; so that it was for some little time quite impossible to recognise one's most intimate acquaintance in their unaccustomed "get-up." Christmas Days were the chief of these high festivals; and I well remember how, on my first Christmas Day in Antanànarivo, I was utterly "taken aback" on entering the dark and dingy old chapel at Ambàtonakànga to find such a transformation scene; for instead of the clean white *làmbas*, which did somewhat brighten up the place on ordinary occasions, my native friends seemed to be darker than ever in their dark cloth clothes, and utterly (and comically) uncomfortable in their unusual finery. A little before my arrival here European dress was much more commonly worn by the well-to-do Malagasy than was the case after the decease of Radàma II., and the ladies' crinolines were, at more than one of our chapels, slipped off at the door and hung up on a nail outside in charge of one of the deacons. There were few raised seats in those days, and it was difficult to make the steel hoops, &c., lie comfortably or gracefully while their wearer was squatting on the floor. Then, of course, there was a considerable wriggling and contriving to get into them again, as the congregation dispersed, as I have witnessed on more than one occasion. Another curious sight as people left church used to be the taking off of smart pairs of boots, which gradually became too irksome to feet unaccustomed to such restraint, and were carried by their owners either in their hand or suspended to a stick over their shoulder. The wearer having sacrificed his (or her) feelings to genteel appearances during service-time, would again rejoice in freedom from conventionalities on the walk home.

Native churches certainly deserve credit for reverence and general propriety of behaviour during divine service. In some newly formed congregations, however, curiosity occasionally gets the better of the proprieties; thus my friend the Rev. J. Pearse was once interrupted in the middle of an earnest discourse by a woman who was determined to know whether he would not sell her a smart green sunshade he happened to have with him, and how much he wanted for it. And it was not without considerable effort and coaxing that the good lady was at length induced to defer her inquiries to a later period of the proceedings. During a tour to the south-east coast in 1876, I was preaching one Sunday afternoon in the centre of a village on the banks of the river Màtitànana, and was a little confused, when about half through my address, by the old chief of the place coming forward to give me a fowl — which clucked and struggled most noisily in the process—and also a bottle of rum, which was handed up in full view of the audience. It was a little difficult to resume the thread of the discourse. This, however, be it remembered, was in a heathen village.

I was speaking just now of clothing—and of the occasional want of it—among the Malagasy. There are, however—but perhaps it would now be more correct to say there *were*—occasions happening now and then when even the natural covering of the body, the hair of the head, was not to be seen. At the decease of a Malagasy sovereign, one of the customs which have been enforced up to the death of Queen Rasohèrina (in 1868) was, that every person, high and low, rich and poor, male and female (with a few exceptions in the case of the very highest personages in the kingdom), must shave the head. As may be supposed, the effect of this was most curious; one's most familiar native friends seemed totally altered and unrecognisable, for no hat or other head covering could be used. One of my brother missionaries wrote to me: "On Friday morning (April 3, 1868) the people presented a very strange spectacle. They looked as if they had been suddenly transformed into Hindoos; we found a nation of bald-heads, some of them quite glossy. It was amusing to meet our friends, as in many cases we did not recognise them until they spoke to us. A man walked up into the town with me in the morning, and from his familiarity I conclude he was a man I had known very well; but I did not find out who he was, and have not been able to recall his identity since. The strangest part of the business was that the clipping was all done at once, for on Friday morning the entire country round Antanànarìvo was was clean clipped, except some score or so of privileged Malagasy and the Europeans." At the decease of the late

Queen Rànavàlona II., however, this custom was not enforced; probably it will not be again revived.

Native houses are not as a rule at all desirable places to stay in. In the central provinces of Madagascar they are certainly dirtier and more uncomfortable than on the coast or in the forest regions, where the entirely vegetable materials employed —bamboo, traveller's-tree, or palm leaves and bark—and the greater dimensions, make the houses there very passable as temporary resting-places. But the clay or wooden houses of the Hova, Bètsilèo, and other interior tribes are almost always dirty and infested with vermin; and "A Night with the Fleas," or with the rats, or the mosquitoes, or the pigs, or the poultry, or all of them put together, is one of the common experiences of Madagascar travelling. Fleas of extraordinary agility seem able to mount to the highest stretcher bedsteads it is convenient to use, and make night one long-continued attempt to ignore their ubiquitous presence. Rats descend from the roof and perform marvellous acrobatic feats over rafters and cords, playfully running races over one's person and even one's face, with a loud squeaking and squabbling which rouses us up with a start in the few intervals of unconsciousness allowed by the lesser plagues. Mosquitoes often come in with a hum like a small swarm of bees, and unless one is provided with netting, make all attempts at sleep futile; and even if the net has been carefully tucked around one, two or three stragglers often get in and make the net a very questionable benefit, as effectually keeping *in* some of the tormentors as it keeps *out* their companions. Pigs being often domiciled in the house, resent their exclusion on the night of your stay, and break through the slight barriers you put up against their entrance with a grunting defiance of your intrusion into their domains; or if they do not get *into* the house, they will persist in settling down *under* it, as the floors are often raised above the ground. An equal maintenance of vested interests is shown by the fowls, who will *not* understand that you have engaged the apartments for your exclusive use, and again and again will manage to get in to their accustomed corner, raising a terrible dust as you attempt to dislodge them. For, besides the dirt on the floors, and the blackened mats on the walls, old houses are also liberally provided with strings of soot hanging from the rafters, or from the rough upper story often formed in the roof. Such ornaments are considered by the Malagasy as an honourable distinction, a sort of certificate of an old and long-established family. But they are rather inconvenient in case of a sudden gust of wind, or a heavy shower of rain, or in ejecting a persistent hen and chickens, as just mentioned. A plentiful sprinkling of soot-flakes on bedding and clothes, on tablecloth and provisions, is, of course, the result of any of these incidents in your stay in many a native house.

In going about most parts of Madagascar we come now and then to some more important places, military stations and centres of districts, where Hova governors are stationed. These officials are usually very kind and hospitable, but it is sometimes very amusing to see the state and ceremony they keep up. The military force under their command is often very limited, and frequently it is impossible to get together any but a very small proportion of even the few soldiers they have at their disposal. But as soon as they hear of your approach (for it is considered courteous to send on word in advance), some of the subordinate officers are drawn up to receive you, together with as many soldiers as they can muster (often more officers than rank and file, *e.g.*, four officers and two soldiers). As soon as you make your appearance, a great many words of command are shouted out, all in English, or at least as near an approach to that language as they can manage; the Queen is saluted, then the Prime Minister, then the governor at the place, and then the second in command, together with the playing of any music they have available and the beating of drums; and not until then is it etiquette for your own presence to be recognised and for you to be welcomed. Coming into the *ròva* or government house, the governor gives you a hearty shake of the hand and, as soon as you are seated, commences a long and formal list of inquiries, which runs somewhat as follows: "Since you, our friends and relatives, have arrived, we ask you: How is Ranavàlomanjàka, Sovereign of the land? How is Rainilaiàrivòny, Prime Minister and Commander-in-Chief? How is So-and-so, Secretary of State?[1] How is the kingdom of Ambòhimànga and Antanànarìvo? How are the cannon? How are the guns? How are the Christians?" &c., &c. (Often the queries are much more numerous, including any governor higher in rank than the questioner whom we may have recently seen; and I remember that in going round the Antsihànaka province, a little two-pounder brass cannon at Ampàrafàravòla was carefully inquired after. All these inquiries must be severally and gravely replied to, including assurances of the well-being of the cannon and the guns (muskets).

Native feasts are often amusing occasions, sometimes being very lengthy and occasionally very noisy. I shall not soon forget one at Ankàrana (in the Taimòro country) given in my honour. The dinner there was, I think, the longest, and certainly *was* the noisiest entertainment at which I have ever assisted. It consisted of the following courses:—1st, curry; 2nd, goose; 3rd, roast pork: 4th, pigeons and waterfowl; 5th, fowl cutlets and poached eggs; 6th, beef sausages; 7th, boiled tongue; 8th, sardines; 9th, pigs' trotters; 10th, fried bananas; 11th, pancakes; 12th, boiled manioc; 13th, dried bananas; and last, when I thought everything must have been served, came hunches of roast beef. By taking a constantly diminishing quantity of each dish I managed to appear to do some justice to them all. The healths of the Queen, "our friends the two Foreigners," then those of the Prime Minister and chief officers of State were all drunk twice over, all followed by musical (and drum) honours. As already remarked, it was a very noisy occasion, for there was a big drum just outside in the verandah, as well as two small

[1] Other chief officers of Government are occasionally mentioned.

ones, with clarionets and fiddles, and these were in full play almost all the time. Then the room was filled by a crowd of inferior officers and servants, and the shouting of everybody to everybody else, from the governor downwards, was deafening. It was a relief when the two hours' proceedings came at last to a conclusion.

A good deal might be said about the queer articles of food occasionally used by the Malagasy. Locusts, divested of their wings and legs and dried in the sun, are very largely eaten and may be seen in heaps in almost every market. Besides these, certain kinds of moths are also used for food, as well as the chrysalides of various insects, different species of beetle, and even some sorts of spiders! I must confess, however, that my information as to these delicacies is all second-hand! I could never bring myself to try these *bonnes bouches*, so much esteemed by my native friends.

A very fruitful source of amusement (to those who have had a longer knowledge of the language) is the unavoidable ignorance of Malagasy on the part of new-comers and the absurd mistakes arising therefrom. I fear that very often we say some shocking things in preaching and public speaking during the earlier years of our residence in the country; that we say innumerable ridiculous things goes without saying; and were it not that the Malagasy have not (at least so I think) a very quick sense of the ludicrous, and are also very tolerant to the mistakes foreigners make, our congregations must certainly during our early attempts be often convulsed with laughter. Very seldom, however, do we see anything of the kind; and I often think that old European residents see a vast deal more that is absurd in the attempts of newer arrivals than do the Malagasy themselves. A venerable missionary, deservedly honoured especially in connection with the re-establishment of the L,M.S. Mission in Madagascar, used every Sunday to thank God that He had given us another Day of Judgment! using the word *fitsaràna* (judgment) for *fitsahàrana* (rest). On another occasion he, quite innocently, used over and over again in a sermon a word which, as he pronounced it, meant something extremely offensive; at last even the Malagasy could stand it no longer, and the women began to go out; the preacher could not understand this and repeated the word with redoubled emphasis, adding, "*Aza mivoaka, ry sakaiza*" ("Don't go out, friends") which they, all the more, *would* continue doing. Another brother informed his audience that God was the "midwife of all living things," using the word *mampivèlona* (*vèlona*, living), which is only used in that sense, instead of *mamèlona*, which means to support, nourish, or keep alive; the two prefixes having come to express two very different ideas. Those who were present at a Congregational Union Meeting a few years ago still remember with amusement how an earnest brother jumped up, and in a stentorian voice shouted out, "*Solìka sy rano: tsy azo ampifangaroharoina izy roroa*" (*i.e.*, "Oil and water: they cannot be mixed"), but by his putting the accent in *sòlika* in the wrong place he produced a most comical impression. But such anecdotes could be given almost to any extent, and similar mistakes need not be further dwelt upon.

It is well known to all who have studied Malagasy that for a long time the "relative" form of the verb is one of the most puzzling features of the language. Several years ago, when the facilities for learning Malagasy were far less than they are now, some of us were much amused by the announcement made by a more recently arrived brother one Sunday morning, that he was "going to try a 'relative' to-day." It was evidently still a very unfamiliar form to him. Another brother, after being much bothered and perplexed by the intricacies of this "*pons asinorum*" of the language, decided upon a short and easy road out of the difficulty; he determined to stick to the active and passive forms and to ignore the annoying "relative" altogether!

Another frequent source of queer mistakes is the difficulty, to Malagasy tongues, of pronouncing our English names. These are often so altered both in writing them and in speaking them that they become utterly unrecognisable by the uninitiated. Who, for instance, could detect under the form *Mìsitèritòrinèrina* the simple English name "Mr. Thorne"? or in the word *Itsàridisaonina*, the name of "Richardson"? The names "Briggs" and "Jukes" and "Sims" are less altered in their Malagasy forms, "*Biringitra*," "*Jòkitra*," and "*Sìmpitra*," but are still funny enough. Our distinctive titles of respect, Mr., Mrs., and Miss, are very difficult for the Malagasy to distinguish; and so "Miss Craven" becomes "Misitera Giravy"; and "Craven," "Graham," and "Graves" can hardly be recognised as having any difference; while "Wilson" and "Wills" are continually confounded together. I well remember how annoyed my wife was, during our early time of residence at Ambòhimànga, by the native pastor inquiring for me as "James." He had heard my wife address me thus, and therefore concluded that it was the proper way for *him* to speak of me. The Malagasy have no exact equivalent for our Mr., Mrs., &c., for their name-prefixes Ra- and Andrian- are inseparable parts of their proper names. Official names also suffer curious transformations; thus "bishop" becomes "*besòpy*" (lit., "much soup") and "*besòmpy*," while in Bètsilèo it figures as "*besòfina*" (lit., "great eared"!). Strangely too, not only are Episcopalian clergymen all styled "*besopy*," but their adherents also are distinguished from other Christians by the same name; each and all are "bishops." In the same way, also, students at the College are called "*kolèjy*," and scholars are called "*sekòly*"; they are themselves colleges and schools! The French Resident soon became known in the country districts as *rèsiandànitra*, which, literally translated, would mean "conquered in heaven"! The name of the famous prime minister of Prussia, Prince Bismarck, has actually become a Malagasy word as an equivalent for cunning, craft, in the form of *bizy*: "*manao bizy*" is "to act craftily." This phrase originated in the time of the Franco-Prussian war, when the fame of Bismarck first reached this country.

While speaking of words introduced by Europeans into the Malagasy language, a word or two may be said about other proper names, chiefly Scriptural ones, which have become thoroughly naturalised here. Many of these have taken curious forms, and this chiefly arises from the fact that *oral* instruction came first, some time indeed before these Bible names had to be printed. It would appear as if the first missionaries, in conversing with the Malagasy about the Saviour of the world, had very naturally spoken of Him by the same name, pronounced in the same way, as that which they and all English-speaking peoples use. They apparently did not consider what would be the most correct form of this sacred name, as well as of other names, that is, the nearest representation of their Greek originals. And so the English form "Jesus Christ" came to be "*Jesosy Kraisty*" in Malagasy, a tolerably close reproduction of our pronunciation of it; while "*Jeso Kristo*" (or "*Ieso Kristo*" would no doubt have been more correct. In the Revised New Testament, "*Kristy*" has been substituted for *Kraisty*, but the older pronunciation holds its own. In some of the books formerly issued by the Jesuit Mission, the French pronunciation of the Redeemer's name was phonetically reproduced thus, "*Jeso-Kry*"! but in their later publications the spelling of the sacred name has been approximated to that employed in Protestant books. Other curious words which have now become naturalised in Malagasy are Jews (*not* "Jew"), written "*Jiosy*" and pronounced exactly like "juice"; and Gentiles (*not* "Gentile"), written "*Jentilisa*"; so that the Malagasy speak of *one* Jews, and of *one* Gentiles!

Many English names have become naturalised among the Malagasy, especially the names of some of the missionaries resident among them. Thus we find Rajaonsona (Mr. Johnson), Raoilisona (Mr. Wilson), and Rasoelina (Mr. Sewell). On one occasion a missionary was conducting service at a country chapel, and at the close was requested to baptise an infant. On asking the name of the child, he was startled and not a little confused by the parents giving *his own name* (Christian and surname included) as the one he was to give to the young neophyte. One of the oddest names I have heard of is Radèboka, which I am assured was taken from the title of the "day-book" which the parents had seen in the Hospital! Another odd name is Ramosèjaofèra, in which we have, first the native name prefix *Ra*, then the French "*monsieur*," altered to *mosè*, and finally the native name *Jaofera*. An absurd mistake arising from ignorance of Malagasy is perpetuated on the title-page of a Malagasy vocabulary published in England some years ago, but prepared by three young native officers, one of whom has been for several years past governor of Tamatave. The English editor apparently intended to describe it as "a *book* (Mal. *boky*) written by Rabezàndrina" and his companions; instead of which it reads, "*Boka no anarany Rabezandrina*," &c., &c., which is literally, "Lepers are the names of Rabezandrina," &c. The three authors were long known to some of us as "the three lepers."

But it is not the Malagasy only who make absurd mistakes about names unfamiliar to them. It is known to many in England who have friends in Madagascar that the name by which we missionaries and other foreigners are designated by the natives here is "Vazàha." But a worthy minister in England, who had got hold of the term, slightly mistook its exact meaning; and, supposing it to be the name of a division of the Malagasy people, he gravely informed his hearers at a public meeting that "the Vazàha are a tribe in Madagascar who are still but imperfectly acquainted with the Gospel!" Many native customs strike us as very odd, and doubtless not less so do many of our customs appear to the Malagasy. Thus they are accustomed to employ the points of the compass in speaking of the positions of things in the house, where we should say, "to the left" or "to the right," or "in front of you" or "behind you." One of my brother missionaries was once dining with a native friend, and while eating some rice, a portion happened to adhere to his moustache. His host politely called his attention to the circumstance, and on my friend wiping the wrong side, his entertainer cried, "No, no! it's on the *southern* side of your moustache!" It sometimes takes a little time for our Malagasy friends to understand *our* ways. Thus I remember that when living at Ambòhimànga we were visited one day by an old friend who happened to be then staying at the ancient capital. After a little conversation my wife brought out a good-sized plum-cake, and cutting a slice or two offered it to him. To her great astonishment he quietly took—not a slice—but, the whole of the cake! and commenced eating it. But finding himself, after a little time, rather embarrassed by its quantity, and that it was a good deal more than he could then comfortably manage, he gradually stowed it away in his pockets, remarking that his children would like it. We altered our way of handing cake to native friends from that date.

The native custom of giving and expecting bits of money on all imaginable occasions seems very odd to Europeans. At births and marriages, at deaths and funerals, when ill or when getting better, at the New Year, when building a house or when constructing a tomb, when going on a journey or on returning from one, in times of joy or in times of sorrow—at each and all of them these wretched little bits of cut-money are expected from visitors. It is true that at funerals a return is made in the shape of presents of beef; and the solemnities of death and mourning are mixed up with the—to us—very incongruous elements of the slaughter-house and the butcher's-shop. But if one leaves before the oxen are killed, a present of poultry instead of beef is made; and I have more than once come home from a funeral, or, at least, from the preliminary "lying-in-state," with a goose or a duck dangling from the poles of my palanquin.

Some curious things are seen by those who travel much about Madagascar in the way of church decoration. (I am here, it should be said, speaking almost exclusively of buildings erected, by congregations in connection, at least nominally, with the L.M.S.) When it is remembered that these number more than 1,200, and are scattered over a very wide extent of country, some missionaries having as many as seventy, eighty, or ninety of these under their nominal charge, it will be clear that to only a very small proportion of them can he give any personal attention or advice as to their construction or adornment. As it is, it is only in the case of the villages nearest to his station, and here and there at important centres, that an English missionary can do much to guide and advise country church builders. The majority of village churches are therefore entirely the product of native skill, and their decoration the outcome of native taste. In many cases, especially in some of the districts nearest to Antanànarìvo, the village churches are models of what such places should be; and with their glass windows, their neatly coloured interiors, and well-made platform pulpits—sometimes elaborate structures of massive stonework—they do credit to the simple country people who have built them. But it cannot be truthfully said that the majority of Madagascar village churches are of this kind. By far the greater number of them are rough structures of clay walls with sun-dried brick gables and thatched roofs; and their only furniture a raised platform of earth or brick, with a rough table serving both for pulpit and for the Communion, a clumsy form or two for the singers, a few dirty mats on the floor, some lesson-sheets on the walls, and perhaps a blackboard for every-day school use. There is certainly no fear at present of the majority of our congregations being led astray by æstheticism in religious buildings or worship.

But frequently there are at the same time some attempts at decoration, and these are often very incongruous and occasionally highly comical (though doubtless unintentionally so). In a little church away north, and otherwise very neatly finished, is a band of ornament round the walls which is exactly like the figures on an ace-of-clubs card, and has probably been copied from this. In other places figures of officers and soldiers marching and even fighting are prominent; in others are seen sportsmen firing at impossibly big birds perched on trees; in others again (as in the former Antsàhamànitra church at Ambòhimànga) a large tree is conspicuous behind the pulpit, bearing tremendous pumpkin-like fruits. (In this same church, however, there were also some very tasteful groups of flowers painted on the keystones of the window arches.) In the church at Vòhipéno (Matitanana) I remember that the front of the pulpit was decorated in the following way: part of the space was occupied by a picture of a European ship with two masts; the other part had a church with a tall tower and spire; over these was the legend, "*Hoy izay tompony ity trano ity : Matahora*" ("Says the lord of this house: Fear"); and there were also four birds and a coloured border. Figures of clocks are frequently seen, and also those of a spear and shield, whether with any reference to "the shield of faith" and other Christian armour, I cannot say. It is worthy of note that no example of symbolism or sacred monograms or emblems has ever come under my notice, although passages of Scripture are now not unfrequently painted on the walls of village churches. Trees with fruit and flowers, often showing some taste, are seen in many places; and in one or two places a very effective decoration has been formed by painted sprays of leaves or flowers scattered over the wall, giving the effect of a simple diaper or wall-paper pattern.

During a tour I took in 1874 round the Antsihànaka province with Dr. Mullens and Mr. Pillans, we were much amused by the variety of the receptacles used at the doors of the village churches for the weekly offerings of the congregations. In one district old sardine tins were the favourite article employed; further on we found that Morton's jam tins were most in vogue; while in yet another district old tin flasks formerly filled with gunpowder were in greatest request for the purpose.

In certain Malagasy village churches—not very many, we should hope—some very curious additions to the ordinary furniture have been seen by occasional visitors. The wish of the late Queen that her subjects should worship the true God was in many places interpreted by petty officials as giving them authority to force the attendance of the people, and to punish them if they were negligent. The command, "Compel them to come in," was, in fact, often very literally carried out. Travelling down to the Bètsilèo province on one occasion, Dr. Davidson, while stopping for his mid-day meal at a country chapel, noticed a good-sized stone near the door, the object of which much exercised his mind. On inquiring the use of this stone, he was told that if the people were negligent of the "means of grace" and did not attend service regularly, they were seized and obliged to carry the stone to the top of a neighbouring hill and down again, to punish them for their sins and remind them to be more diligent in future. Another kind of penance used to be enforced at Tsiafàhy: people who were irregular in attendance at chapel were obliged to creep on their hands and knees round the *fàhitra* or ox-fattening pen in the village, as a punishment for inattention to their religious duties. At a country chapel in the Friends' District, Mr. H. E. Clark saw, on one occasion, a deacon sitting at the door with a handful of small pebbles. When this official noticed any one in the congregation asleep, or inattentive, or irreverent, he threw a pebble at the offender to rouse him up, or as a gentle reminder to be more careful.[1]

Much that is amusing might be noted with regard to native preaching: odd illustrations, strange misapprehensions and misapplications of Scripture, curious answers to questions about Biblical subjects, &c.; but enough has, I hope, here been said to justify my remark at the commencement of this paper, that the monotony of our daily routine is frequently enlivened by curious and comic occurrences, and that, together with the more serious duties of our work, there is often "a decided element of the amusing, the odd, and the absurd" in our life in Madagascar.

[1] It need hardly be said that all true missionaries utterly repudiate and denounce all such ways of promoting Christianity.

TRAVELLERS' TREES, LOWER FOREST, MADAGASCAR.

CHAPTER XVII.

*THE FAUNA AND FLORA OF MADAGASCAR IN CON-
NECTION WITH THE PHYSICAL GEOGRAPHY OF THE
ISLAND, WITH NOTICES OF THE EXTINCT FORMS OF
ANIMAL LIFE OF THE COUNTRY.*

General characteristics of mammalian fauna—Remarkable difference to that of Africa—An ancient island—Wallace's "Island Life"—Oriental and Australian affinities—Vegetable productions—Botanising in Madagascar—Three-fourths of flora endemic in the island—Three different regions described by Mr. Baron—Floral beauty—Orchids—The Eastern Region—The Central Region—The Western Region—Extinct forms of animal life—Grandidier's discoveries—Geology—Huge lemuroid—Link between apes and lemurs—Small hippopotamus—The Æpyornis—Crocodiles—Enormous terrestrial lizard—Primæval Madagascar.

SECTION I.: GENERAL CHARACTERISTICS OF THE MALAGASY MAMMALIAN FAUNA.

BEFORE describing the Malagasy animals, something must be said about the peculiarities of the fauna of the island taken as a whole.

A large extent of country in Madagascar is covered with forest, a belt of which, broad in some places and narrow in others, is believed to surround the island in an almost unbroken line; while there is, in addition to this, a considerable tract of country, less densely wooded, occupying much of the western and southern plains. Here, then, there appears to be a congenial habitat for a vast number of living creatures—birds, reptiles, and arboreal mammals—in the thousands of square miles of woods, which cover not only a great portion of the warmer coast region, but also the eastern slopes of the elevated interior highlands.

From these circumstances, as well as from the variety of other physical conditions prevailing in the country—mountains and open downs, cool interior highlands and sultry tropical plains, fertile river valleys and (in the south-west) arid deserts—it might be supposed that Madagascar, situated, as it is, almost entirely within the tropics, would be abundantly filled with animal life. But it is not so, at least, not nearly to such an extent as one would expect, and a stranger crossing the forests for the first time is always struck with their general stillness and the apparent scarcity of animal life along the route. The fauna of the country does, it is true, include some most interesting and exceptional forms of life, but it is almost as remarkable for what is omitted in it as for what it contains. Not only so, but from the position of the island with regard to Africa—being separated from it by a sea only 230 miles wide at its narrowest part, a distance further reduced by a bank of soundings to only 160 miles—one would also suppose that the fauna of the island would largely resemble that of the continent. But it is remarkably different: whole families of the larger mammalia are entirely absent; there are no representatives of the larger felines, no lions, leopards, or hyænas; none of the ungulate order, except a single species of river-hog, sole relative here of the hippopotamus,[1] no rhinoceros or buffalo; and there is no zebra, quagga, or giraffe, or any of the numerous families of antelope which scour the African plains. There is no elephant browsing in the wooded regions of Madagascar, and, stranger still, there are no apes or monkeys living in its trees. The few horses and asses existing in the island are of recent introduction by Europeans; even the humped cattle, which exist in immense herds, are not indigenous, but have been brought at a somewhat

---

[1] There was, however, formerly a small species of Madagascar hippopotamus, apparently only recently extinct, for its bones are found in a sub-fossil state, will be noticed more fully further on.

remote period from Africa; and the hairy fat-tailed sheep and the goats, as well as the swine and dogs found in Madagascar, are all of foreign introduction.

But notwithstanding all that, the zoological sub-region, of which Madagascar is the largest and most important portion, is pronounced by every naturalist who has studied it to be one of the most remarkable districts on the globe, bearing, says Mr. Alfred R. Wallace, "a similar relation to Africa as the Antilles to Tropical America, or New Zealand to Australia, but possessing a much richer fauna than either of these, and in some respects a more remarkable one even than New Zealand.[1] The Madagascar fauna is very deficient in many of the orders and families of the mammalia, only six out of the eleven orders being represented,[2] but some of these, especially the Lemuroida among the Quadrumana, the Viverridæ among the Carnivora, and the Centetidæ among the Insectivora, are well represented in genera and species.

No less than forty distinct families of land mammals are represented in Africa, only eleven of which occur in Madagascar, which also possesses four families peculiar to itself.[3]

---

[1] The whole surface of the globe is divided by Mr. Wallace into six zoological "regions," in each of which broad and clearly marked distinctions are shown to exist in the animal life as compared with that of the other great divisions. Each of these regions is again divided into "sub-regions," Madagascar and the neighbouring islands forming the "Malagasy Sub-region" of the "Ethiopian Region," the latter being a zoological division which includes Africa south of the Tropic of Cancer, together with its islands, excepting the Cape De Verde group. The following diagram shows the geographical position of each region, and, to a considerable extent, their relation to each other:—

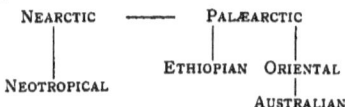

[2] These are, Primates, Cheiroptera, Insectivora, Carnivora, Ungulata, and Rodentia.

[3] Cheiromydæ (one genus and one species, the Aye-aye); Indrisidæ (three genera and ten species and varieties); Lemuridæ (six genera and twenty-eight species and varieties); and Cryptoproctidæ (one genus and one species, the *Fósa*).

The following is a list of all the genera of mammalia as yet known to inhabit the island, together with the number of species belonging to each, these latter, including well-marked varieties, now amounting to 107:—

PRIMATES.	Species and Varieties.		Species and Varieties.		Species and Varieties.
Sub-order Lemuroida.		Miniopterus	2	Oryzorictes	5
Propithecus	8	Emballonura	1	Centetes	1
Avahis	1	Triænops	2	Hemicentetes	3
Indris	1	Taphozous	1	Echinops	1
Lemur	15	Nyctinomus	6	Ericulus	2
Hapalemur	2	Rhinopoma	1	RODENTIA.	
Lepidolemur	4	Myzopoda	1	Eliurus	1
Phaner	1	CARNIVORA.		Hypogeomys	1
Mirza	1	Fossa	1	Nesomys	3
Cheirogaleus	5	Viverricula	1	Brachytarsomys	1
Cheiromys	1	Cryptoprocta	1	Hallomys	1
CHEIROPTERA.		Felis	1	Schoenomys	2
Pteropus	2	Galidia	5	Pseudomyoxodon	1
Cynonycteris	1	Eupleres	1	Brachyuromys	2
Phyllorhyna	1	INSECTIVORA.		UNGULATA.	
Vesperus	1	Sorex	2	Potamochoerus	1
Vesperugo	3	Microgale	5		
Scotophilus	2	Geogale	1	Hippopotamus (*sub-fossil*)	
Vespertilio	1				

We have here a total of 46 genera and 107 species and varieties of mammals, many of the genera being peculiar to Madagascar. All the species are peculiar, except, perhaps, some of the wandering bats.

The assemblage of animals above noted is remarkable, and seems to indicate a very ancient connection with the southern portion of Africa before the apes and all its present ungulates and felines had entered it, no doubt from the north. The presence of nearly a hundred species of mammals is a certain proof in itself that the island has once formed part of, or has been very closely connected with, a continent; and yet the character of these animals is altogether different from the assemblage now found in Africa or in any other existing continent. A very slight acquaintance with the present fauna of Africa would at first sight prevent us from thinking that

Madagascar could ever have been united with it; and yet, as the tigers, the bears, the tapirs, the deer, and the numerous squirrels of Asia are equally absent, there seems no possibility of its having ever been united with that continent. Let us then see to what groups the mammalia of Madagascar belong, and where their probable allies must be looked for.

It will be seen from the tabular list already given that the most prominent feature of the Madagascar mammalian fauna is the lemurian, the ten genera and thirty-nine species and varieties which are here represented forming about four-fifths of the whole mammalian population of the island. The lemurs, which are the most lowly organised of the Quadrumana, and probably also the most ancient animals of that order, are still found scattered over a very wide area, but they are nowhere so abundant as in Madagascar, having doubtless been elsewhere largely exterminated in the struggle for existence by the later developed monkeys and apes. Straggling and disconnected examples are, however, found, ranging from West Africa, where there are two endemic forms, to Southern India, Ceylon, and Malaysia. The Lemuroida of these regions seem to hold their own by their nocturnal and arboreal habits, being mostly found in dense forests. The African forms of lemur seem not more closely allied to those of Madagascar than are the Asiatic forms, so that it appears probable that all these animals are but the remains of a once widely-spread and much more numerous group. This is confirmed by the fact that lemurian animals once inhabited North America and Europe, and possibly the whole northern hemisphere, as their remains have been found in Eocene deposits of the Jura and of South-west France, and in the Upper Eocene of Paris.

The twenty-five species of Bats need not detain us at this point, as they are all, as might be supposed from their powers of flight, more or less nearly allied to forms found in other parts of the world.

We then come to the Carnivora, which are represented by a

peculiar jaguar-like animal, the Cryptoprocta, which forms in itself a distinct family and has no near allies in any other part of the globe, and by nine civets, belonging to genera peculiar to this country. "Here we first meet with some decided indications of an African origin, for the civet family is more abundant in this continent than in Asia, and some of the Madagascar genera seem to be decidedly allied to African groups." Although now almost confined to the Ethiopian and Oriental regions, the civets were abundant in Europe during the Miocene period.

Coming to the next order, the Insectivora, we find them represented in Madagascar by two families, one of which—the shrews—is found over all the continents, but the other—the Centetidæ—is all but confined to this island, none being found anywhere else on the globe except one genus in the West Indies, in Cuba and Hayti, "thus," says Mr. Wallace, "adding still further to our embarrassment in seeking for the original home of the Madagascar fauna." This group, however, is, like the Lemuroida, of high geological antiquity, and is found in numerous peculiar forms in various parts of the world, but in no equally limited area are so many distinct types found as in Madagascar.

The Madagascar Rodents consist only of five rats and mice of endemic genera, one of which is said to be allied to an American genus; but it is probable that in this order other species will still be discovered.

As regards the last order, the Ungulata, this is represented in Madagascar by but one living species, a river-hog allied to an African species, and by an extinct form of hippopotamus. But, from the semi-aquatic habits of these animals and their powers of swimming, it appears probable that their presence in the island is explained by a former more close connection with the neighbouring continent.[1]

---

[1] For the substance, and in many sentences the wording, of the three preceding pages, I am indebted to those valuable works of Mr. Wallace, *The Geographical Distribution of Animals*, chap. xi., vol. i., and *Island Life*, chap. xix.

For a full discussion of the difficult problem of the derivation of this very particular fauna, I would refer the reader to Mr. Wallace's interesting work *Island Life*, chap. xix. I can only here indicate in a very brief fashion the principal points which now appear pretty well established from a consideration of all the available facts. If we bear in mind the special and isolated character of many of the Madagascar birds, as well as the Asiatic affinities of some ; the peculiarities of the mammalian fauna, as just detailed ; the Oriental and American relationships of many of the reptiles ; and the Oriental, Australian, and even South American affinities of some of the insects ; and if to these facts we add the geological character of the island, and the now well-known conditions as regards the depths of the surrounding ocean, the following deductions may be fairly drawn :—

Madagascar is a very ancient island geologically considered, and many of the animals now found here are very antique forms, survivals of a once much more widely extended fauna, which in early times was spread over the continents, but has in them become nearly or quite extinct through the introduction of other forms of animal better fitted to survive in the struggle for existence. In this great island, however, cut off from the fiercer competition of continental life, many of these earlier types, *e.g.*, the Lemurs and the Centetidæ, have held their own, and so Madagascar has become, to a certain extent, a kind of museum of ancient forms of life to be seen nowhere else on the globe. There can be no doubt that Madagascar had anciently a much closer connection with Africa than exists at present, and that from that continent most of its present fauna was derived, before, however, Southern Africa had received from the Euro-Asiatic continent most of its present characteristic animals. At the time when Madagascar was thus more closely connected with the continent, Southern Africa was probably a large continental island, like Australia, separated from its northern portion by a shallow sea, now represented by the Sahara and the

Arabian deserts. About the same time also it is probable that numerous groups of islands, now represented only by still slowly sinking banks and atolls in the Northern Indian Ocean, brought Madagascar into much closer connection with South-eastern Asia, and so some of the Oriental and Australian affinities of its fauna are perhaps accounted for. And as for the likeness of some of its forms of life (*e.g.*, the Centetidæ among Insectivora, the Urania among butterflies, and some of the serpents and tortoises among reptiles) to the living creatures of still more distant countries, these are no doubt only remnants of a fauna once spread over all the intervening regions, but now found only in such widely separated islands as Cuba and Madagascar.

It will be evident, therefore, that although the mammalian fauna of Madagascar consists, except in the case of some of the lemurs, chiefly of small and inconspicuous animals, many of these creatures are of exceptional interest to the zoologist, and throw no small light upon earlier conditions of life upon the earth.

Having thus sketched the leading characteristics of the Madagascar Fauna, I proceed to give a brief outline of the Flora of the island, for the main facts of which I am indebted to a paper of my friend, the Rev. R. Baron, F.L.S., contributed in November, 1888, to the *Journal of the Linnean Society —Botany*.[1]

SECTION II.: THE FLORA OF MADAGASCAR.

The vegetable productions of the island are now tolerably well known to science, since the country has been explored by European botanists in many different directions. Its highest mountains have been ascended, its lakes and marshes crossed, and its encircling forests have been penetrated in a number of places; and large collections of plants have been made at various times,

[1] *The Flora of Madagascar*, with map showing Botanical "Regions."

which have been described in the scientific journals of England, France, Germany, and Holland. By far the largest number of these have been collected and sent to England by Mr. Baron, who is at present the chief authority on the flora of Madagascar.

In 1889 the number of plants from Madagascar which had been named and described was about 4,100, and these have since been increased to probably over 4,300. The south-western portion of Madagascar, and the lowlands of its southern part generally, are at present the least known as regards the botany, but every year sees some addition made to our knowledge of the island, and the blanks on the map are being rapidly filled up.

Mr. Baron graphically describes his experiences in botanical collecting :—

"Botanising in Madagascar, as those who have travelled in wild and uncivilised regions in other parts of the world will easily believe, is a totally different experience from botanising in England. Your collecting materials are carried by a native, who may be honest or not, in which latter case the drying paper will begin gradually and mysteriously to disappear, and the leather straps with which the presses are tightened will, one by one, be quietly appropriated. For a Malagasy bearer has a special weakness for leather straps, they being largely used for belts, so that both for the sake of your own comfort and the honesty of the men, the sooner you dispense with them the better. As for the dried plants themselves, they are secure from all pilfering; for of what possible use or value they can be, it puzzles the natives to conceive. You might leave your collection in a village for a whole month, and you would find on your return that it was still intact. If, after the day's journey, you sit down in a hut to change the sheets of paper containing the specimens, the villagers will be sure to come in, and, standing round in a circle, gaze at you in mute astonishment, turning over the plants so well known to them. After a few minutes' silent gaze, there will perhaps be a sudden outburst of amused laughter, or it may be a little whispering, which, if it were audible, would be something to this effect: 'Whatever in the world is the man doing?' or, 'What strange creatures the white men are!' Some of the people doubtless think that you are a kind of sorcerer. For these dried plants, whatever can you do with them? you cannot eat them; you cannot make them into broth; you cannot plant them, for they are dead; you cannot form them into bouquets or wreaths, for they are brown and withered. Is it surprising, then, if some of the natives think that you are dabbling in the black art, and that your plants, in the form of some strange and mysterious decoction, are to supply, it may be, a potent rain-medicine, or a love-philter, or a disease-preventing physic? For among the natives themselves there are many herbal quacks, who, for a consideration, are able not only to prescribe for the cure, and even prevention, of disease, but also to furnish charms against fire or tempest, locusts or lightning, leprosy or lunacy, ghosts, crocodiles, or witches. The explanation which I have most frequently heard given, however, by the more intelligent of the natives as to the use of the dried plants, is that the leaves are intended to be employed for patterns in weaving.

"It is not, then, the natives that you have to fear in regard to your collections of plants, it is the weather—it is those heavy showers that, unless protected with extreme care by waterproof coverings, succeed in soaking your specimens and your drying paper, so that you have occasionally to spend half the night in some dirty hovel in doing what you can, by the aid of a large fire, to save your collection from destruction."

A large extent of country in Madagascar is covered with primeval forest. These woods are most extensive on the eastern side of the island, where they clothe the hills and the eastern slopes of the edge of the upper table-land, where the principal water-parting of the country, running north and south, is found. It is believed that the whole island is encircled by a belt of forest, but this statement still requires confirmation, although there is no doubt that there are extensive forests also on the western side. The eastern forest attains its greatest breadth in the north-east of Madagascar, a little north of the Bay of Antongil, where it is from 40 to 60 miles broad. Further south, however, it is much narrower, probably not averaging more than 25 miles in breadth. It has been calculated that in the whole island there is an area of 30,000 miles of forest-covered country, or about one-eighth part of the total area. Besides dense forests, there is a large extent of country on the coast plains covered with scattered patches of wood and brush, so it will be easily seen how large a field there is in Madagascar for botanical research.

This large extent of wooded country is, however, being diminished every year by the wholesale destruction of the forest in burning it for rice-planting, and it is grievous to see how recklessly it is cut down and destroyed for this and other more trivial reasons. The large concessions of forest land to European companies for timber-cutting and plantations also tend in the same direction, and unless some plan of forest conservation is soon effected, the beautiful woods, with most of their flora and fauna, will eventually disappear.

Mr. Baron believes that the great bulk of the Madagascar plants have been already gathered, and so there are now sufficient data to enable a few general conclusions to be drawn as to the character and distribution of the flora. I will again quote from his paper to give these conclusions :—

"The following figures will show at a glance the number of Natural Orders and genera of flowering plants represented in Madagascar as compared with those known throughout the world, according to Bentham and Hooker's *Genera Plantarum*:—

Total known in the World : Orders, 200 ; Genera, 7,569.
,, ,, Madagascar : ,, 144 ; ,, 970.

The number of genera here given comprises those only that

are indigenous to the island. If we include the numerous plants that have at one time or other been introduced, the total number of the genera would be probably raised to about 1,050.

"Of the 4,100 indigenous plants at present known in Madagascar, about 3,000 (or three-fourths of the flora), are, remarkable to say, endemic. Even of the Gramineæ and Cyperaceæ about two-fifths of the plants in each order are peculiar to the island. There is but one natural order confined to Madagascar, the Chlænaceæ, with twenty-four species, which, however, Dr. Baillon places under Ternstrœmiaceæ. Of ferns more than a third are endemic, and of orchids as much as five-sixths, facts which in themselves are sufficient to give a very marked individuality to the character of the flora.

"Of the 4,100 known plants, there are:—

Dicotyledons	3,492
Monocotyledons	248
Acotyledons [1]	360
	4,100

"The following list shows the number of species in the Orders most largely represented, and their percentage of the total flora (*i.e.*, of the 4,100 plants mentioned above):—

	No.	Per cent.
Leguminosæ	346	8·4
Filices	318	7·8
Compositæ	281	6·9
Euphorbiaceæ	228	5·6
Orchideæ	170	4·1
Cyperaceæ	160	3·9
Rubiaceæ	147	3·6
Acanthaceæ	131	3·2
Gramineæ	130	3·2

"The Palms and Asclepiads are as yet imperfectly known. Of the former only eighteen are described, although the island

---

[1] "This includes only the Filices, Equisetaceæ, Lycopodiaceæ, and Selaginellaceæ. The remaining Acotyledonous Orders are as yet very imperfectly known. Of Mosses about 250 have been described, and of Rhizophoreæ 5."

undoubtedly possesses a large number. Many Asclepiadaceous plants have been collected, but the majority of them are still lying unnamed in various European herbaria. The number of endemic genera now reaches about 148."[1]

Many interesting particulars are given by Mr. Baron as to these endemic genera, but these must be omitted in this place, with one exception. *Leptolæna pauciflora*, belonging to the endemic order Chlænaceæ, is, says Mr. Baron, "a hard-wooded tree, from the trunk and branches of which, at a certain season of the year, there is a ceaseless dropping of water, sufficient indeed to keep the ground quite damp. This is caused by a number of hemipterous insects crowding together in a slimy liquid. May this afford an explanation of the similar well-known phenomenon exhibited by the *Tamai-caspi*, or Rain-tree, of the Eastern Peruvian Andes?"

As regards the distribution of the vegetable life of Madagascar, Mr. Baron sees sufficient reason to divide the island into three Regions, and he gives a number of figures and comparisons to justify his conclusions. Roughly speaking, these three Regions, which he calls Eastern, Central, and Western respectively, correspond closely to the (1) eastern side of the island, east of the crest of the mountain range which forms the main water-parting of the country ; (2) the central portion, including the upper table-land, consisting chiefly of gneiss and other crystalline rocks ; and (3) the western side of the island including the extensive coast plains, comparatively level, on the west and south-west.

The great bulk of the plants common to the three Regions are widely-spread tropical species, while few plants reach right

[1] "A few other endemic genera have been described since this paper was written, and require to be added to the list given above. They are : *Santalina* (1) under Rubiaceæ, *Mcnabca* (1) in Asclepiadeæ, *Pcricstcs* (1) and *Camarotea* (1) in Acanthaceæ, and *Leucosalpa* (1) in Scrophulariaceæ. It may also be added that since the publication of the above about 160 new plants (including 31 species of *Croton*) have been described from Madagascar, bringing the total number of species known in the island (excluding the mosses and some other of the lower cryptogams) up to 4,260."

over the island from east to west. Among these few is the *Rofia* palm (*Raphia ruffia*); while a fern (*Gleichenia dichotona*) is perhaps the commonest and most widely-spread specimen in the whole island.

An examination of the list of plants found in the three Regions shows a wide difference between the floras of the Central Region and of the two others to the east and west; and this is not to be wondered at when it is remembered that the Central Region has a great elevation above the sea (from 3,000 to nearly 9,000 feet). But it is not so easy to account for the great difference between the floras of the Eastern and Western Regions, seeing that they have the same position, as regards latitude, and do not differ much in height above the sea (although the western side of the island is decidedly hotter). Mr. Baron gives a very simple reason for this, pointing out that the elevated central region of the island, running north and south, is no doubt of very great antiquity, reaching possibly from the Palæozoic era, and has therefore always formed a barrier (except at the south) between the floras of the Eastern and Western Regions. "The floras therefore, even if they were formerly similar, which is doubtful, have had abundance of time to become differentiated in character; and if they were originally different, they have been kept, by the existence of the mountain barrier, distinct to the present day."

As regards floral beauty in Madagascar, all who have travelled much in the island will agree with the statements of Dr. A. R. Wallace in his *Malay Archipelago* and *Tropical Nature*, that, contrary to the common opinion, tropical countries and tropical forests are not rich in flowers, although they are unrivalled for luxuriance of foliage. Madagascar is no exception to this rule, for it possesses comparatively few plants having beautiful flowers. There is nothing to compare with an English meadow, with its clover and its buttercups and daisies, or with a field of poppies, or with the effects produced by gorse and broom and heather. Nor are there many flowering trees in the forests, and any one expecting to see great numbers of beautiful flowers there will be disappointed. There are, it is true, a considerable number of handsome flowers, both on the open downs and in the woods, but they do not occur, with some few exceptions, in large masses, so as to strike the eye, or to produce a distinct effect in the landscape.[1] One of the most conspicuous flowers in the upper forest in the month of November is that of a liana (*Strongylodon Craveniæ*), which has a stem about as thick as a one-inch rope, and spikes of creamy-yellow flowers set pretty closely on the main stem. These spikes are from 10 to 16 inches in length, each containing from 40 to 60 large flowers growing closely together, so that they are very conspicuous in the forest, forming immense festoons of flowers, mounting to the tops of the highest trees, crossing from one tree to another, and shining almost golden in colour in the brilliant sunshine.

The Orchids are a prominent feature in the woods near the east coast, especially several species of *Angræcum ;* of these *A. superbum* is the most plentiful, while *A. sesquipedale*, with its long spur and large pure white flowers, is also very conspicuous. In the interior of the island there are several striking ground orchids; one yellow, another brilliant scarlet, and another blue in colour. Among trees and shrubs which have the most handsome flowers are species of *Rhodolæna, Impatiens, Ixora, Stephanotis, Poinciana, Astrapæa, Ipomæa, Kigelia, Combretum,* and others.

A few particulars may be added as to the special characteristics of each of the three botanical Regions.

The Eastern Region.—This is a comparatively narrow strip of country lying between the sea and the central highland, of the interior. It averages about 60 to 70 miles in breadth, and is about 900 miles long from north to south. It includes a littoral belt of grassy and wooded plains, with a series of lagoons stretching in an almost continuous line for 300 to 400 miles; then a tract of country with a wild confusion of rounded hills; and

---

[1] See, however, Chapter IV., p. 72.

thirdly, a series of two or three mountain ranges, running almost throughout the whole length of the island, and rising in the western range to a height of about 4,500 feet above the sea. Facing the Indian Ocean, and meeting the vapour-laden southeast winds, which blow for the greater part of the year, this eastern side of Madagascar is naturally the moistest portion of the island, and its vegetation is accordingly most abundant. A large proportion of its surface is covered with dense forest, and there are innumerable patches of wood and bush where there is no continuous forest.

The narrow littoral belt, with its attractive park-like scenery, has been made most familiar to English readers by descriptions of it in many books relating to Madagascar; since that portion of it which extends between Tamatave and Andovorànto is traversed by almost all travellers to the capital. Its soft green turf, its clumps of trees and shrubs, and its lake scenery, make this portion of the journey a very pleasant experience. Among the most striking features of the vegetation here are the tall fir-like *Casuarina*, or beef-wood tree, which grows in long lines mile after mile, near the shore ; several species of *Pandanus*, or screw-pine ; the Indian almond (*Terminalia Catappa*) ; the celebrated Tangèna shrub (*Tanghinia venenifera*), formerly used as an ordeal ; a species of fern-palm (*Cycas Thouarsii*), from which a kind of sago is obtained ; occasional plantations of cocoa-nut palm, which, however, is not indigenous to the island ; and many others, including some of the most beautiful flowering trees already mentioned. The Orchids have been referred to above ; and besides these, among other noteworthy plants, is a species of pitcher-plant (*Nepenthes*), with pitchers 4 or 5 inches long, and the curious and beautiful lace-leaf plant (*Ouvirandra fenestralis*), which is, however, found also in streams in the Central Region. Bordering the riversides and in marshes, a gigantic Arum (*Vìha*) from 12 to 15 feet in height, with a large white spathe more than a foot in length, grows by thousands, and is sure to attract attention.

RIVER SCENE IN FOREST, MADAGASCAR.

As one travels higher up the country, other trees and shrubs become prominent; among these is a most elegant species of bamboo, which, with its curving stems and light-green clusters of leaves, gives quite a character to the scenery; the celebrated Traveller's-tree (already described in Chapter I.); the Cardamom; the Rofia palm, with its enormously long leaves and feathery fronds; and many others.

With regard to the upper and forest-covered portion of the Eastern Region, Mr. Baron says that it is "remarkable for its great variety of plant forms, there being no single species, genus, or order of plants predominant over the rest, or which influences to any great degree the general physiognomy of the vegetation." For full particulars as to the most characteristic trees and plants the reader must be referred to Mr. Baron's paper; suffice it to say here that there are many kinds producing valuable and beautiful timber, some of which are becoming important commercially; others yield many useful products, as indiarubber, bark for dyes, gamboge, pepper, arrowroot, &c. As in most tropical forests, the numerous kinds of liana, from some not thicker than a stout thread to others as large as a ship's cable bind the trees together in an almost impenetrable tangle of cordage, through which it is most difficult to force a path.

The Central Region.—As already stated, this second botanical region occupies the elevated table-land of the interior of Madagascar. Taken as a whole, the greater part of this region consists of bare, dreary, and desolate moorlands, with little verdure, except in the hollows between the hills, and in those valleys and plains, mostly the beds of ancient lakes now dried up, where rice is cultivated by the people. Trees and shrubs are few, except where a few patches of forest still remain; and the moorlands and hills are covered with coarse, wiry, grey-brown grass. But for the usual bright skies and clear atmosphere, this part of Madagascar would be much more dreary and uninteresting than it really is. (For many aspects of this part of the country, see Chapter IV.) One peculiarity of this region is that its vegetation consists much more largely of herbs and small wiry plants than of trees and shrubs; in fact, about three-fourths of the plants belong to the former class. Another peculiarity of the flora here is, as might be expected, its more temperate character than that of either of the other two regions. Palms and other tropical forms are rare, while, on the other hand, Heaths, Gentians, and plants of the orders Umbelliferæ, Ranunculaceæ, and Crassulaceæ are plentiful, and such mountain forms as the Violet, the Geranium, and the Sundew, as well as the common bracken, the royal fern, and the male fern are found. Perhaps the most prominent trees in the Central Region are several species of *Ficus*, especially the *Amòntana*, with large glossy leaves, and the *Aviàvy*, which are frequently seen in the old towns and villages of the interior provinces, and also the *Nonòka*, the *Voàra*, and the *Adàbo*. Mr. Baron gives a list of sixty-three plants, only found on the slopes of the Ankàratra mass of mountains, all of which are endemic in Madagascar.

The Western Region.—This part of the island is much less known than those included in the other two regions. With the exception of two or three mountain ranges, which appear to run in a very straight course for several hundred miles, this region largely consists of extensive level or slightly undulating plains, covered with coarse grass and patches of forest, beside the encircling belt of wood not many miles from the shore line. The heat is much greater on the western side of the island than on the eastern side, while the rainfall is much less, especially in the south-west, where a small extent of country is almost a desert from the scanty amount of rain it receives. The vegetation here, therefore, is much less plentiful and luxuriant than on the eastern side of the island, and trees and shrubs are more restricted to the banks of rivers and streams.

The most common trees and shrubs here are species of *Ficus*, *Hibiscus*, *Eugenia*, and *Weinmannia*, and the Tamarind, which grows to a large size, as does also the Mango, while the

Rofia palm is found in large numbers. Three or four species of fan-palm (*Hyphæne* and *Bismarckia*) give a very distinct character to the scenery in many parts of the district. In the journal of a canoe voyage I made down the Bètsibòka river some years ago, I find the following reference to these trees: "Here the lovely fan-palms became very numerous. At times we passed close to the banks, a tangled mass of *bàraràta* (a graceful bamboo-like grass) bending down into the river, and the tall columns of the palms standing up from the very edge of the water, with their graceful crowns of green fans sharply defined against the blue of the sky. Surely of all the thousands of beautiful things in this beautiful world, palms are among the most lovely, and the fan-palm not the least in this glorious family of trees. It was a perpetual delight to the eyes to watch them as we swept rapidly by the banks with the strong current, as one after another they passed us by as in a panorama."

Another very noticeable tree is plentiful on the west coast, viz., the Baobab, which is remarkable for its enormous bulk of trunk and smooth light-brown bark. Many species of *Diospyros* are found in the forests, from some of which ebony is obtained. Along the west coast, and especially on the shores of the innumerable bays and inlets of the north-west, the Mangrove is found in immense numbers; while the most abundantly represented Order in the Western Region is the Leguminosæ, and next to that the Euphorbiaceæ.

A few words may be added as to the *Relationship of the Madagascar Flora*. Mr. J. G. Baker, of Kew, has shown that there is a close affinity between it and that of tropical Africa; this is probably more especially the case as regards the flora of the Western Region. And strange to say, there is also a slight amount of affinity between the flora of Madagascar and that of America. Further, an examination of this flora as a whole confirms what is shown also by the geology and the fauna of the island, namely, its great antiquity and its long isolation. "About three-fourths of the species and a sixth of its genera of plants are endemic; and it seems probable that Madagascar was joined to the African continent during some part or parts or the whole of the Miocene (including Oligocene) and early Pliocene periods," but was cut off from the mainland at least not subsequent to the later Pliocene period.

A large number of plants, trees, and shrubs have been introduced into Madagascar, including fruits, cereals, and vegetables; but although many of them have established themselves in the island and become naturalised, they can scarcely be incorporated in the native flora.

SECTION III.: EXTINCT FORMS OF ANIMAL LIFE IN MADAGASCAR.

Geology and Palæontology are very modern sciences in Madagascar, for except slight and fragmentary notices of fossils in 1821, 1854, and 1855, and the first discovery of the eggs of *Æpyornis* in 1851, hardly anything was known of the geology of the island or of its ancient forms of life until within the last thirty years. The travels and researches of M. Alfred Grandidier, however, from 1865 to 1870, gave the first accurate information as to the physical geography of the country, together with particulars as to the geology of various parts of it, and greatly added also to our knowledge of the fauna. And during the past twenty years a large number of facts have been obtained by various travellers, and collections of rock specimens and fossils have been made.

Although a very great deal yet remains to be done before it can be said that we have a fairly complete elementary acquaintance with Madagascar geology, especially in the central-western, south-western, and southern portions of the island, certain general conclusions appear pretty fairly established, and may be very briefly described. The central portion of the island (more, however, to the east of the true centre) consists of land elevated from 3,000 feet to between 8,000 and 9,000 feet above the sea, and extending for about 650 miles north and south, and about 180 miles at its greatest breadth from east to west. This portion of the island is very mountainous, in fact, there is here hardly any level land except in the valleys of the rivers, and in the dried-up beds of ancient lakes. The rocks of this interior region, as well as of the narrow belt of coast plains and hilly country between it and the sea to the east, consist of gneiss and other crystalline rocks, gneiss very largely predominating. Besides these ancient rocks there are also more modern ones, of various ages and of volcanic origin. The highest points in the island are the summits of the mass of Ankàratra, which is "the wreck of a huge but ancient subaerial volcano." Beside these and other ancient signs of subterranean action, there are many scores of volcanic cones, probably of much more recent origin, some of them possibly in activity during the earliest human occupation of the country. These extinct craters are distributed in two principal groups, one in Màndridràno, about forty-five miles E.N.E. of the summit of Ankàratra, and the other in the district of Bètàfo, at about the same distance to the southwest.

In the western half of the island sedimentary rocks appear to form the greater portion of the comparatively level country of which it is composed. These consist of sandstones, beds of clay and shale, and limestones, together with occasional deposits of lignite. The following is a list given by Mr. Baron of "the metamorphic and sedimentary strata of Madagascar, so far as they are at present known, referred to the European standard of geological chronology." But it must be remembered that this list refers chiefly to the north-west of the island, the central-western and south-western portions not having been yet examined by any competent geologist.[1]

[1] I am indebted for the main facts in the preceding paragraph to a paper by my friend and brother missionary, Rev. R. Baron, F.G.S., who is our chief authority on the geology and petrology of Madagascar. This paper, "Notes on the Geology of Madagascar," in *Quar. Journ. Geol. Soc.*, May, 1889, together with a later one in the same journal (Feb., 1895), "Geological Notes of a Journey

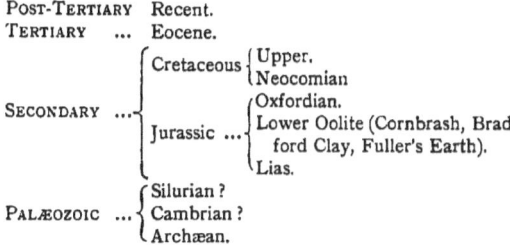

I now proceed to give a sketch of the most interesting forms of extinct animal life which have been discovered in Madagascar, most of them by very recent research.

Mammalia.—It has been for a long time known that the living fauna of the island is remarkably deficient in the most characteristic mammals of Africa, or indeed in any large quadrupeds, and that the lemurs and their allies are very numerous in species, and are the most prominent and typical forms of the Malagasy fauna. And as shown by the table at p. 356 of this chapter, bats, small species of carnivora, of insectivora, and of rodents, with one ungulate animal (a wild hog), compose the hundred and odd species of the living mammals of the country.

About three years ago Mr. J. T. Last, who has been collecting for some time for the Hon. Walter Rothschild, discovered a mammalian skull of strange aspect in a marsh at Ambòlisàtra, on the south-west coast of Madagascar. After an elaborate examination by Dr. C. J. Forsyth Major, this has been determined to belong to a large extinct Lemuroid animal. The skull is much longer in shape, as well as larger, than that of any of the living Lemuridæ, and the animal was probably nearly three times the size of any existing Lemur, approaching to the dimensions of the Anthropoid Apes. Dr. Major has accordingly formed a new family for this aberrant form of Lemuroid, which he has

in Madagascar," gives the fullest information yet obtainable as to Madagascar geology. They are illustrated by three geological maps.

named *Megaladapis madagascariensis* (fam. Megaladapidæ).[1] From its association with other vertebrate remains still to be noticed, Dr. Major believes that this Lemuroid skull belongs to a group of animals, part, if not all, of which have been seen by man at a relatively recent date.

Dr. Major has recently discovered other remains in Madagascar of an animal which appears to form a link between the apes and the lemurs, although partaking more of the character of the former than of the latter. No account, however, has yet been published of this discovery.

In the year 1868 the bones of a small species of hippopotamus were discovered by M. Grandidier on the south-west coast, and were described under the name of *H. Lemerlei*. Several years later the remains of other hippopotami were discovered at Antsìrabè, in the central portion of the island, by the Rev. T. A. Rosaas, and were described by M. G. A. Guldberg under the name of *H. madagascariensis*. And still more recently, remains of apparently a third species of this animal have been brought to light on the south-west coast, and this has been named *H. leptorhyncus*. These Madagascar hippopotami appear to have been about two-thirds the size of the African species, and are believed to have been contemporaneous with the earliest human inhabitants of the island.

In the same locality where the skull of the gigantic Lemuroid was found, Mr. Last has also discovered some bones of a species of swine (*Sus*), as well as of a river-hog (*Potamochœrus*), which may prove to be the same as the one now existing in Madagascar, and also numerous bones of a slender-legged form of zebu (*Bos*).

From these facts it appears that the paucity of large indigenous mammals which now characterises the fauna of Madagascar, was not always a marked feature of it; and doubtless fuller and more systematic research will bring to light remains of many other species.

[1] See *Trans. Roy. Soc.*, vol. 185, 1894, B. pp. 15-38, pl. 5-7.

Birds.—Forty-five years ago the scientific world was startled by the discovery in Madagascar of the eggs and bones of a gigantic bird, to which the name of *Æpyornis maximus* was given. The bones showed that this extinct creature was a struthious bird, apparently allied to the ostrich and the recently exterminated *Dinornis* of New Zealand, but with more massive feet and leg-bones. The eggs were, however, perhaps the most interesting relics of this ancient bird, for they largely exceed the size of any previously known egg, being $12\frac{1}{2}$ inches long by $9\frac{3}{8}$ inches broad, with a capacity of more than six of the largest known ostrich eggs.

During M. Grandidier's explorations in Madagascar, already referred to, he discovered other bones of *Æpyornis*, which were eventually described as belonging to two other species besides *Æ. maximus*, viz., *Æ. medius* and *Æ. modestus*. All these remains were, up to a recent date, known only from the coast regions, viz., south-east, south, and south-west. But in the excavations made by the Rev. T. A. Rosaas at Antsìrabè, which revealed the remains of *Hippopotamus* just referred to, bones of *Æpyornis* were also discovered, and among these were some of a fourth species, which was named *Æ. Hildebrandti*. More recently still, further excavations at Antsìrabè and in the south-west and west have brought a large quantity of other material to light, and from these MM. Milne-Edwards and Grandidier have been able to make a more complete study of the extinct birds of Madagascar, and to determine that they belong to many different species.[1] They say:—

"These various kinds of *Æpyornis* constitute a family, represented by very differing forms. At the present time at least a dozen can be distinguished, some of large size, others of moderate dimensions. The former had a height of about ten feet, while others hardly exceeded that of a bustard. Their anatomical characters justify their being arranged in two genera:

[1] "Observations sur les *Æpyornis* de Madagascar"; *Comptes rendus*, t. cxviii. January 15, 1894.

(1) that of *Æpyornis*, with large and massive legs; and (2) that of *Mullerornis*, with slenderer legs and feet, and which much resembled in their proportions the cassowary of New Guinea and the apteryx of New Zealand." The largest of the species of *Æpyornis* has been named *Æ. ingens*, and greatly exceeds in size *Æ. maximus*.

"The conditions under which the remains of these birds have been deposited seem to show that they frequented the margins of sheets of water, and that, if they did not swim there, they kept in the midst of the rushes bordering the lakes and the rivers. In fact, wherever they have been obtained, their bones are associated with those of small hippopotami, crocodiles, and tortoises, that is to say, with animals altogether aquatic in their habits. The *Æpyornis* must usually have lived in low-lying and frequently inundated plains; and there also they nested, as we may infer from the number of portions of the skeletons of very young birds which have been found there in abundance."

Besides the remains of the struthious birds just described, among the bones from Antsìrabè some portions which belonged to a large rail, nearly related to *Aphanapteryx*, have been recognised; as well as others of a species of wild-goose, but much larger than those of any kinds now inhabiting Madagascar. These remains again show the existence of extinct birds of aquatic habits, belonging to the same period as the *Æpyornis*, and living under similar conditions.

These large birds were certainly contemporaneous with Man, for there are to be seen, on some of their bones, some deep and very sharply distinct notches, which were made by cutting instruments, probably in removing the flesh. On the femur of a hippopotamus, of the same date, is also to be seen a hollow cut, going through the whole thickness of the bone and evidently produced by human hands.

These discoveries doubtless give promise of others still more important yet to be made, which will throw some light upon the early history of Madagascar, from the point of view of physical geography and zoology. It is impossible not to be struck with the analogies which the fauna of this island presents with that of New Zealand, where, at a recent period, there lived a large number of gigantic birds, the Dinornithidæ, represented by more than twenty species. These resemblances seem to indicate some former connection between these islands (as well as between the islands of the southern hemisphere generally), now separated by an immense extent of ocean; and this conclusion appears to agree with observations made with regard to the ancient fauna of the Madagascar group of islands.[1]

Reptiles.—It is well known to students of natural history that on small islands separated from each other by nearly half the circumference of the globe there still exist gigantic tortoises. These islands are the Galapagos, west of Ecuador in South America, and the island of Aldabra, north of Madagascar. On the mainland of the great African Island none of these great chelonians are now found living, but recent research has shown, as we might have supposed, that they formed part of the ancient fauna of the country. It is only owing to the fact of Aldabra being uninhabited by man that these huge defenceless creatures have maintained their existence in one of the outlying islands. The Aldabra tortoises have a carapace 5 ft. 6 in. long and 5 ft. 9 in. broad, and weigh about 800 lbs. The extinct tortoises of Madagascar appear to have been as large as the ones now living in Aldabra islet, and have been described as of two species, *Testudo abrupta* and *T. Grandidieri*.[2] As already mentioned, their skeletons, carapaces, and plastrons have been found associated with remains of *Æpyornis* and hippopotamus.

The rivers and lakes of Madagascar abound with crocodiles, and it is not therefore surprising that remains of this reptile have been found in the Quaternary deposits which have yielded

---

[1] The preceding paragraphs are translated from the paper of MM. Milne-Edwards and Grandidier already cited.
[2] See *Comptes-rendus*, vol. lxvii., 1868; vol. c., 1885.

so many relics of gigantic birds, pachyderms, and chelonians. M. Grandidier says: "The bones of crocodiles which I found belong to a different species from that which now inhabits the waters of Madagascar (*Crocodilus madagascariensis*); for while this latter is remarkable for the slenderness and length of its snout, and is allied to the common crocodile, the fossil species, to which we have given the name of *Crocodilus robustus*, has hardly any nearer neighbour than the convex-headed crocodile of India, or the black crocodile of Senegal. It is curious that this species, which I have found fossil on the west coast of Madagascar, now lives only in the great lake of Alaotra in Antsihànaka, its last refuge, where also it will not long remain, as this lake is filling up by degrees, and its extent diminishing every year. It was evidently a lacustrine crocodile, which was common in Madagascar when this island, extending far towards the east, and not having been yet overturned by the granitic eruption, was covered by enormous lakes; and here the hippopotami, whose remains I have discovered in such abundance, were found in large numbers."[1]

It will have been noticed that all the extinct animals which have been hitherto described belong to a very recent geological period, all of them probably having been living during the earliest human occupation of the island. But recent research has shown that in a very greatly more remote era, the Secondary or Mesozoic, pre-eminently the "Age of Reptiles," Madagascar, in common with other parts of the world, also had its huge saurians crawling over its surface, or swimming in its waters.

About three years ago Mr. Last obtained from some Jurassic deposits in the north-west of Madagascar, near the Bay of Narinda, vertebræ and portions of the limb-bones of an enormous terrestrial Lizard, as large, probably, says Dr. H. Woodward, as the *Atlantosaurus* of Marsh;[2] two genera, if not three, are

---

[1] See *Comptes-rendus*, vol. lxxv., 1872.

[2] *Atlantosaurus* was probably the most gigantic of all these huge lizards, being about eighty feet long, and having a height of thirty feet!

represented, one being like *Ornithopsis* or *Brontosaurus*.[1] In a paper by Mr. R. Lydekker, F.R.S., contributed to the *Quart. Journ. Zool. Soc.* (August, 1895), some of these bones have been described as belonging to "a Sauropodous Dinosaur," of the genus *Bothriospondylus*, and called by him *B. madagascariensis*. These remains belong to the Jurassic series of rocks.

In 1891 some fragments of the skull of a reptile were discovered by the Rev. R. Baron in a tenacious shelly limestone in the north-western part of the island. These have been determined by Mr. R. Bullen Newton, F.G.S., to belong to a reptile possesing crocodilian affinities, and from its narrow and elongate rostrum, "bearing a strong resemblance to the existing Gavial of the Ganges, though differing very widely from it in other and more important characters. It is not until we go much further in time that we find its congener among the Mesozoic crocodiles forming the family of the Teleosauridæ." Mr. Newton regards these remains as portions of a new form, and from them he founds a new species of the genus *Steneosaurus*, which he names *S. Baroni*. This genus has hitherto been known only in British and European areas, so that the discovery of this new species in a locality so far south as Madagascar is a matter of very high interest when considering its geographical distribution. From the few molluscan shells associated with the fossil, it appears to belong to the Lower Oolite age.

The above-mentioned mammals, birds, and reptiles (twenty-six or twenty-seven only in number) comprise all that is at present known of the ancient vertebrate forms of life in Madagascar. There are doubtless many others yet to be disentombed, and fresh discoveries are sure to be made on fuller investigation of the country. It may be confidently expected that the next few years will show a great increase in our knowledge of the palæontology of this great island, as well as of its geology, for the field is very wide, and both subjects have only been slightly touched as yet.

[1] *Brontosaurus* was about sixty feet in length.

A complete list of all the fossils from Madagascar known up to the present date is given by Mr. R. Bullen Newton in a paper in *Quar. Journ. Geol. Soc.* (February, 1895).[1] These, omitting the vertebrates already described, number 140, and belong to the Mollusca in Quaternary strata, to the Mollusca and Foraminifera in Tertiary (Eocene), to Mollusca, Echinodermata, Actinozoa, Foraminifera, and Plantæ in the Secondary (Cretaceous and Jurassic).

Let us try to sum up in a few sentences the results of recent research on the ancient animal life of the island.

It seems probable that Madagascar, when the first representatives of mankind occupied it, was a country much more fully covered by lakes and marshes than it is at present. In these waters, amid vast cane brakes and swamps of papyrus and sedge, wallowed and snorted herds of hippopotami; huge tortoises crawled over the low lands on their margins; tall ostrich-like birds, some over ten feet high, and others no larger than bustards, stalked over the marshy valleys; great rails hooted and croaked among the reeds, and clouds of large geese and other water-fowl flew screaming over its lakes; on the sandbanks crocodiles lay by scores basking in the sun; great ape-like lemurs climbed the trees and caught the birds; troops of river-hogs swam the streams and dug up roots among the woods; and herds of slender-legged zebu-oxen grazed on the open downs. These were the animals which the first wild men hunted with their palm-bark spears, and shot with their arrows tipped with burnt clay or stone.[2]

And as we look further back through long past geological ages, when the clays and sandstones of the oolite and the white masses of the chalk were being deposited in the coral-studded tropic seas and archipelagoes of Europe and other parts of the

[1] And reproduced in *Antanànarivo Annual*, xix., 1895.

[2] The Vazlmba, the supposed earliest inhabitants of the interior, are said not to have known the use of iron, but to have had spears made of the hard, wiry bark of the Anìvona palm, and to have employed arrow-heads made of burnt clay. No flint weapons have yet been discovered in Madagascar.

world, and when Madagascar was probably no island, but a peninsula of Eastern Africa, the mist opens for a moment, and we see vast reptile forms dimly through the haze: great slender-snouted Gavials in the streams and lakes, and huge Dinosaurs, sixty to eighty feet long, crawling over the wooded plains, and tearing down whole trees with their powerful arms.

Such are some glimpses of the Madagascar of the past which the study of its rocks and fossils already opens to the mental eye. We may confidently look for further light upon the dim and distant bygone ages as we learn more of the geology of the country. The thick curtain which at present shrouds the old-world time will be yet more fully lifted, and we shall probably, ere many more years have passed, be able to draw many more mental pictures of the extinct animal life of the great African island.

The Gresham Press
UNWIN BROTHERS,
WOKING AND LONDON.

www.ingramcontent.com/pod-product-compliance
Lightning Source LLC
Chambersburg PA
CBHW051736300426
44115CB00007B/592